Nelson's Handbook to the Isle of Wight: Its History, Topography, and Antiquities ; with Notes Upon Its Principal Seats, Churches, Manorial Houses, Legendary and Poetical Associations, Geology, and Picturesque Localities ; Especially Adapted to the Wants O

William Henry Davenport Adams

HAND-BOOK

TO

THE ISLE OF WIGHT.

"I have not only related what I saw of its present condition, but, so far as convenience might permit, have presented a brief view of the former estates and first antiquities of this people and country."—GEORGE SANDYS, A.D. 1615.

OSBORNE HOUSE.

[;

iT.

1873.

NELSONS' HAND-BOOK

TO

THE ISLE OF WIGHT;

ITS HISTORY, TOPOGRAPHY, AND ANTIQUITIES.

WITH NOTES UPON ITS PRINCIPAL SEATS, CHURCHES, MANORIAL HOUSES,
LEGENDARY AND POETICAL ASSOCIATIONS, GEOLOGY, AND
PICTURESQUE LOCALITIES.

ESPECIALLY ADAPTED TO THE WANTS OF THE TOURIST AND EXCURSIONIST.

BY

W. H. DAVENPORT ADAMS,

Author of " History and Antiquities of the Isle of Wight," " Records of Noble Lives," &c.

NEW AND REVISED EDITION.

LONDON:
T. NELSON AND SONS, PATERNOSTER ROW;
EDINBURGH; AND NEW YORK.
1873.

Inscribed by Permission

TO

ADMIRAL SIR AUGUSTUS W. J. CLIFFORD, BART., K.C.B.,

USHER OF THE BLACK ROD, ETC.,

(OF WESTFIELD, NEAR RYDE, ISLE OF WIGHT,)

BY

HIS OBLIGED AND FAITHFUL SERVANT,

THE AUTHOR.

PREFACE.

In the following pages the writer has endeavoured to observe a medium between the laborious amplification of the county history and the flimsy generalities of the common guide book. He has not touched upon the arid demesnes of parochial or manorial records ; nor has he usurped the functions of the genealogist, and crowded his pages with long dull pedigrees. But he has ventured more into statistical detail than is usual in books of this kind, and he has also given historical and biographical sketches with a greater fulness. He has sought to show something of the past as well as the present of the Isle of Wight; and not only to provide the tourist with a convenient manual, but the resident with a useful book of reference.

He would hope that he has laid down a plan which will be equally agreeable to both classes of readers. The tourist will find his *routes* marked out with the utmost accuracy of detail, and will know where to look and what to look for. The resident will find a mass of facts relative to his own parish, his own church, his own town, or his own village. Both will have before them a new and original history of the island,—embodying, it is believed, much novel information and valuable matter—an account of its antiquities, an alphabetical guide to its churches, and concise illustrations of its natural and geological curiosities. They will also have the opinions, upon points of scenery or historical associations, of the best authors who have written about the island, or, indeed, in any way alluded to it; for it has been the desire of the Editor to give the opinions of others rather than his own.

In the prosecution of his task he has consulted upwards of one hundred and thirty authorities, has burrowed among the manuscript treasures of the British Museum, and patiently recorded the results of his personal observation. He ventures, therefore, to hope that he puts forth, in the following pages, much that is new and interesting, and that they form a monograph on the island which will be received with indulgence both by the critics and the public.

W. H. D. A.

LONDON, 1862.

₊ The present Edition has been carefully revised, and much new matter inserted. The corrections, suggested by additional personal research, and communicated by obliging correspondents, will, it is hoped, leave few inaccuracies to be regretted. The Author, therefore, trusts that in its amended shape his little volume will continue to receive the public favour.

April, 1867.

CONTENTS.

PART I.

THE HISTORY OF THE ISLAND.

PART II.

A DESCRIPTION OF THE ISLE OF WIGHT.

PART III.

THE CHURCHES OF THE ISLAND, AND ITS WORTHIES.

PART IV.

THE TOURIST'S COMPANION.

Introduction.

1. Separated from the mainland by a narrow strait or channel, called the Solent, varying from five miles to three-quarters of a mile in breadth, lies the Isle of Wight. . . . .

> "Of all the southern isles who holds the highest place,
> And evermore hath been the great'st in Britain's grace."—DRAYTON.

Of "an irregular, rhomboidal form," its northern apex pointing almost directly to the mouth of the Southampton Water; in length, from east to west, about 22½ miles; in breadth, at its widest part, from Cowes to St. Catherine Point, upwards of 13 miles; it occupies an area of 136 square miles, or 98,320 statute acres (92,702, according to some authorities), and had a population, in 1861, of 55,362 souls.* The circumference of the island may be roughly estimated at 60 miles, though the voyage round it, must be calculated at 65.

2. To the north its shores are generally low and shelving; to the east, south, and south-west, they tower into formidable and precipitous cliffs, varying from 400 to 700 feet in height. A bold range of chalk hills, or *downs*, runs through the whole island, from east to west, like a gigantic backbone. From this striking chain branches off, about half way, another range of heights, which, running southward, terminates in the abrupt headland of St. Catherine Point; and here commences a *third* range, following the coast line as far as Shanklin, and the promontory of East End. The scenery of the eastern division of the island is generally of a diversified character—abrupt hills, deep shadowy vales, and broad green meadows succeeding each other in rapid and picturesque succession. In the western division the northern district is flat and monotonous, relieved only by the young firs of Parkhurst and the pleasant fields of Newtown; but the southern landscape and the extreme west are again distinguished by a delightful alternation of hill and valley.

3. The principal rivers, or rather streams, are the MEDINA (from the Latin *medius*, midmost, middle), which, dividing the island into two nearly equal

---

* Of 30,750 persons, aged twenty years and upwards, 2259 were engaged in professional occupations; 12,987 in domestic; 1540 in commercial; 4076 in agricultural; and 7654 in industrial. 2184 are set down in the census report as "non-productive."

divisions, known as the *East* and *West Medine*, rises at the base of St. Catherine's Hill, and after a course of three and twenty miles, broadens into a noble estuary between the towns of East and West Cowes; the EASTERN YAR, which rises near Niton, and flows into the sheltered lake called Brading Haven; and the WESTERN YAR, which forms the peninsula of Freshwater, rising at Freshwater Gate, within a few yards of the sea, and emptying itself into the Solent at Yarmouth. There are other streams—the Lukely, Newtown River, and Wootton River—but not of sufficient importance to claim special notice at our hands.

4. The most remarkable features of the littoral scenery are its abrupt, craggy, precipitous headlands, such as Bembridge Point, the Foreland, Dunnose, East End, Rocken End, St. Catherine Point, Atherfield Point, Brook Point, the Needles, and Headon Hill. These, indeed, are names with an ominous sound to the mariner, seldom a winter passing without flinging upon them the odium of additional disaster.

The *chines*,* or ravines formed by the action of running water upon yielding strata—from the Saxon *cinan*, to cleave (compare also the word *chink*)—are numerous upon the southern coast. The more notable are Shanklin, Luccombe, Blackgang, Ladder, Whale, Walpan, and Cowleaze Chines.

5. The *downs* or *dunes*,† conical hills of chalk, from whose summit may be obtained the most beautiful imaginable panoramas, are all of more than average height, and some, from their steep and precipitous character, are really noticeable. The tourist through the island will not fail to have his attention directed to Bembridge Down, Ashey Down, and the heights of Arreton, Shanklin, Bonchurch, Wroxall, Span, Week, St. Catherine, Brighstone, Buccombe, Montjoy, Lemerston, Mottistone, Chessell, Afton, and the Needles.

---

* The chines are "deep fissures which have been cut in the cliffs by the action of a streamlet falling over the summit. All of them have the same general features. There is a wide opening seaward which contracts inland with more or less rapidity, according to the hardness of the rock, the greater or less quantity of water which ordinarily falls over, or other circumstances. In some cases the ravine reaches for nearly a mile inland, and is lost at length in the ordinary bed of the brook; in others, it terminates abruptly in a waterfall. Although the stream must in every instance be regarded as the chief agent in cutting the chine, its enlargement is perhaps as much, or more owing to other influences. The action of the waves during great storms, when the sea is driven violently against the cliffs, has tended considerably to enlarge the opening of the chines, while the landslips, which continually occur after severe frosts, must have caused the steep slopes to fall in from time to time; but the deepening of the chines is always brought about by the stream, as may be observed in any of them where measures are not taken to prevent the constant wearing away of the rock."—*Knight.*

† "Two parallel chains of hills stretch in a direction east and west through the whole extent of the landscape. The northern range is of moderate height, and slopes towards the shore; the southern rises with a bolder sweep and to a much greater elevation, and exhibits the smooth and rounded aspect and undulated outline, which are so characteristic of the mountain masses of the white chalk as to indicate their geological character, even when seen from a considerable distance. The first line of hills consists of freshwater strata, which are superimposed on the eocene marine deposits. The southern range is the chain of chalk downs that traverses the island throughout its entire length, forming on the east the promontory of Culver Cliff; and on the west that of the Needles."—*Adapted from Mantell.*

6. The *geological features* of the island have been elaborately examined by Sir Henry Englefield, and more recently by Mantell, whose *Geological Excursions round the Isle of Wight* should be one of the tourist's inseparable companions. The northern division is formed by "the eocene strata deposited on the chalk when the latter was in a horizontal position."—*Mantell.* The southern division is "almost entirely composed of the different members of the cretaceous system. The white chalk forms a range of downs from the eastern to the western extremity, and is flanked on the south by the lower beds of this formation. These are succeeded by another group of chalk hills that expands into a broad and lofty promontory, in some parts between 800 and 900 feet high, crested by St Catherine's, Boniface, and Shanklin Downs. On the southern escarpment of this chain the inferior deposits of the cretaceous system re-appear, and fallen masses of these rocks form the irregular line of terraces which constitute the Undercliff. The downs on the southern coast are separated from those inland by an anticlinal axis which extends through this part of the island, and is produced by the upheaval of the firestone, gault, and greensand. The promontory of the Undercliff is flanked both on the east and west by extensive bays, which have been excavated in the clays and sands of the Wealden and inferior cretaceous deposits by the long-continued encroachments of the sea. The Wealden occupies an inconsiderable extent of surface; but in Sandown Bay on the east, and in Brixton, Brook, and Compton Bays on the west, the cliffs, which are formed of the upper clays and sands of this formation, are exposed to unremitting destruction from the action of the waves. The sea-shore is therefore strewn with the detritus of these fluviatile strata, and the shingle contains innumerable water-worn fragments of the bones of reptiles and other organic remains."— *Mantell.*

7. The botanist will find in this picturesque island—"which he who once sees never forgets, through whatever part of the wide world his future path may lead him" (*Sir Walter Scott*)—a greater wealth of floral beauty than in any other part of England. And the amenity of the climate is such, that even far into the winter bloom delicate plants which elsewhere have shrunk into decay—fuchsias, myrtles, and geraniums bearing the bleak winds without shelter or protection. The hedgerows, as the tourist observes with admiration, from May to September are literally alive with wild flowers. Every brake is rich in blossoms; every dell is prodigal of the daintiest odours and the most sparkling hues.

Within the limits we have prescribed to ourselves it is impossible to offer anything like a satisfactory catalogue of the *Flora* of the Isle of Wight; and the tourist will do well to provide himself with the elaborate and valuable *Flora Vectensis* of Dr. Bromfield, as edited by Dr. Bell Salter. Enough for us to note that along the sea-coast from Ryde to Sandown may be found the *Sea-side Rush, Drop-wort,* the *Smooth Sea-heath, Sea-holly, Yellow Cen-*

taury, *Sea Mat-grass,* and *Nottingham Catch-fly;* near the Culver Cliffs grow the *Portland Sponge* and *Orobanche (Broom-rape);* round Newport and Carisbrooke abound the *Arabis Hirsuta, Red-berried Briony, Autumnal Gentian, Grammitis Ceterach, Least Toad-flax,* and *Butcher's Broom;* the *Broad-leaved Helleborine* may be procured at Binstead; the *Orchides (Ophrys Apifera* and *Ophrys Muscifera)* decorate the downs of Ventnor, Bonchurch, and Shanklin; the *Bee-orchis* may also be gathered at Quarr and Binstead, and the *Fly-orchis* at Quarr and near Ryde.

For *ferns* the best localities are, the neighbourhood of Rookley, Freshwater, Alverstone, Thorley, Shanklin, Quarr, and Carisbrooke. The principal varieties are, the *Osmunda,* the *Bog-pimpernel* and *Bog-asphodel; Utricularia minor* (at Langbridge, near Newchurch); *Utricularia major* (at Freshwater marshes); *Trichomanes* (Carisbrooke and Quarr); the *Adder's Tongue* (Thorley and East End); and *Ruta muraria* (Freshwater, Afton, and Calbourne). The *Osmunda* and *Thelypteris,* and a variety of bog-plants, flourish at Credmore Wilderness, half a mile out of Rookley, on the Newport and Niton Road; the *Ceterach* will be found at Carisbrooke and Brading; the *Blechnum* at Alverstone; and the *Asplenium nigrum* is everywhere abundant.

At St. Lawrence grows the *Helleborus fœtidus;* the *Broad-leaved helleborine,* at Binstead and Bonchurch; the *Portland sponge,* on the Culver Cliffs; *Wood calamint,* near Apesdown; *Henbane,* in the neighbourhood of Bonchurch, and the Undercliff generally; *Purple stock (Mathiolo wiana),* on the chalk cliffs of Freshwater and Ventnor; the *Vicia sylvatica,* in Laccombe Wood; and *Arum Italicum,* at Steephill. *Wild flowers* are luxuriant in every lane and hollow; and, in their respective seasons, the *Primrose,* the *Snowdrop,* and the *Daffodil,* enamel the meads with beauty.

8. We have already alluded to the geniality of the climate, which renders the island a favourite resort for invalids. "From the variety," says an eminent physician, "which the Isle of Wight presents, in point of elevation, soil, and aspect, and from the configuration of its hills and shores, it possesses several peculiarities of climate and position that render it a highly favourable residence for invalids throughout the year." The Undercliff especially claims this honourable distinction: "It would be difficult to find in any northern country a district of equal extent and variety of surface—and, it may be added, of equal beauty in point of scenery—so completely screened from the cutting north-east winds of the spring on the one hand, and from the boisterous southerly gales of the autumn and winter on the other."—*Sir James Clark.*

9. The Isle of Wight is nominally under the control of a *Governor of the Island* (the Right Hon. Lord Viscount Eversley, G.C.B.), but for all general purposes it forms a portion of the county of Southampton or Hampshire. It

returns *one* member to Parliament, and its metropolis, Newport, returns *two*. It is divided into two Hundreds, or Liberties :—

(1.) The EAST MEDINE, containing 14 parishes : Arreton, Binstead, Bonchurch, Brading, Godshill, Newchurch, Niton, Shanklin, St. Helen's, St. Lawrence, Whippingham, Whitwell, Wootton, and Yaverland.

(2.) The WEST MEDINE, containing 16 parishes : Brighstone, Brook, Calbourne, Carisbrooke, Chale, Freshwater, Gatcombe, Kingston, Mottistone, Newport, Northwood, Shalfleet, Shorwell, St. Nicholas, Thorley, and Yarmouth.

The *principal Towns* are *Newport*, the capital, on the river Medine; *Ryde*, on the sea-shore, nearly opposite Portsmouth; *Ventnor*, on the south-eastern coast; *Yarmouth*; at the mouth of the Yar, opposite Hurst Castle; *East* and *West Cowes*, at the mouth of the Medine; *Brading*, at the head of Brading Haven; and *Sandown*, on the bay of the same name. *Cowes, Ryde*, and *Yarmouth*, are the ports of communication with the mainland.

10. The *Military Establishments* of the island are at *Parkhurst*, where there are capacious barracks capable of accommodating 3000 soldiers ; *Sandown, Yaverland*, and *Bembridge Forts*, strongly armed ; *Yarmouth ;* and the *New Defences* at *Sconce Point (Fort Albert), Fort Warden*, and *Freshwater (Fort Victoria)*, to which we shall more particularly allude in another part of our little work.

11. For *Ecclesiastical Purposes* the island is included in the see of Winchester, and is divided into two rural deaneries—one in the East and one in the West Medine. There is a *Public Grammar School* at Newport; and there are *Cemeteries* at Ryde, Binstead, Newport, Carisbrooke, Cowes, and Brading.

12. The *Population* of the Isle of Wight are chiefly occupied in agricultural pursuits, and the exports are confined to corn and cattle. There is a small manufactory of lace at Newport; and at Cowes, the Messrs. Ratsey's and Messrs. White's ship-building yards employ several hundred hands.

13. The *Antiquities* of the island, on which, in their proper places, we shall dwell at some length, are,—*Celtic*, consisting of barrows, earthworks, and a curious relic of the past called the Longstone; *Roman*, including the villa recently discovered at Carisbrooke; *Saxon*, barrows and architectural fragments; and *Norman*, including some portions of the ruins of Carisbrooke Castle and Quarr Abbey. There are two museums—at Ryde and Newport—devoted to the collection and preservation of memorials of the island history.

14. The *Churches* of the island may be arranged, with reference to their architectural characteristics, as under :—

Trans-Norman : Brading, Carisbrooke, Freshwater, Niton, Shalfleet (tower), Wootton, Yaverland. *Early English :* Arreton, Calbourne, Niton, Shalfleet, Whitwell, Wootton. *Decorated :* Brighstone, Mottistone, Shorwell. *Perpendicular :* Chale, Carisbrooke, Gatcombe, Godshill (towers), Shorwell.

2 ——— ——

yet
lli-

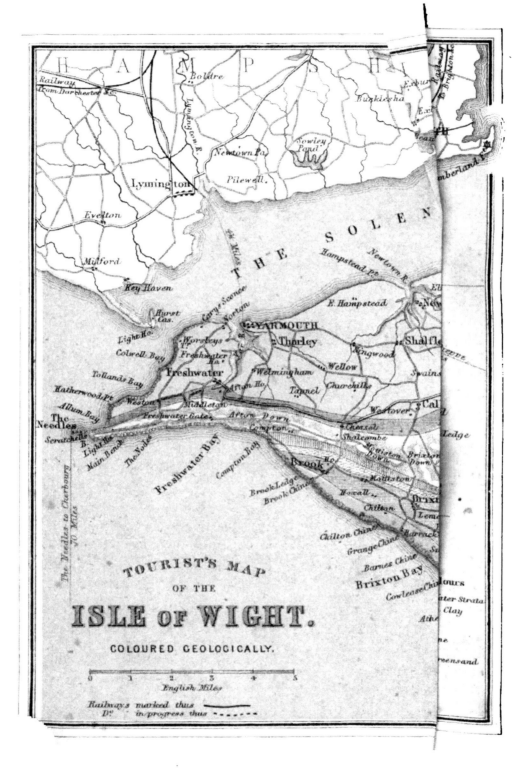

TOURIST'S MAP

OF THE

ISLE OF WIGHT.

COLOURED GEOLOGICALLY.

THE ISLE OF WIGHT.

PART I.—HISTORY OF THE ISLAND.

Dived in a hoard of tales that dealt with knights,
Half legend, half historic, counts and kings,
Who laid about them at their wills, and died,
And mixed with these, a lady.   TENNYSON.

SECTION I.—THE ISLE OF WIGHT DURING THE CELTIC PERIOD.

THE Isle of Wight having formerly been ignored by historical students, as offering little in its annals to interest the reason or amuse the fancy, its chronicles were usually restricted to the bare enumeration of names and dates, a few unmeaning generalizations, and some sonorous platitudes. But of late years there arose a suspicion that its history was not without its scenes of excitement and its picturesque illustrations of bygone days; and archæologists accordingly directed their studies to the elucidation of what was obscure, with the usual result of discovering much that was unexpected. And even in the narrow limits to which we are here confined, we think we shall bring forward enough of novel and important matter to convince the reader that the annals of the sea-girt Wight are well worthy the strict investigation they now receive; that they are fraught with suggestive scenes and romantic incidents, and adorned by names

which the world will not willingly let die.

The word *Wight* is generally accepted as a corruption of the Celtic *gwyth*, or "a channel;" its original name being *Ynys-wyth*, the "channel-island."—*Dr. Guest*. By Ptolemy it is referred to under the name of Ουικτηδις; and the Romans called it *Vecta*, *Vectis*, and *Vectesis*. The Saxons preserved, to a certain extent, the sound of the old Celtic appellation in their *Whitland* and *Wiht-ea*.

The aboriginal inhabitants of the Isle of Wight were, undoubtedly, a Celtic race; and there is some reason to suppose that they were by no means so barbarous as it has been the fashion to represent them. The Celtic antiquities still extant evidence their possession of some degree of artistic ingenuity and military skill; and we know not anything more deserving of attentive examination than the Celtic villages and earthworks which may yet be traced in the neighbourhood of Galli-

2

bury, Rowborough, and Newbarns. They have also left to the wondering investigation of a later age numerous *tumuli*, barrows, or sepulchral mounds, most of them containing specimens of their weapons and implements, their dress, and even their personal decorations. These barrows are found in great abundance on Chillerton, Brooke, Afton, and Mottistone Downs; on Brixton Down is a notable cairn; while on Shalcombe, Bembridge, Ashey, Wroxhall, St. Catharine, and Bowcombe Downs, are also many of these last resting-places of our remote ancestors.

The principal contents of these barrows —specimens of which are preserved in the Ryde and Newport Museums—are urns of baked clay, of different sizes and designs, and a bronze implement, not unlike the head of a chisel, called a *celt*.

There exists another memorial of the Celtic Period of the island history in the remarkable *Longstone*, near Mottistone, to which we shall hereafter direct the reader's attention.

According to Cæsar, the Belgæ, a Celtic tribe, invaded the southern coasts of England, subdued Hampshire, and colonized the Isle of Wight, which they named *Ictis*, about 85 years before the birth of Christ. This simple record of an important occurrence opens to the historian a wide field of speculation. For Diodorus Siculus, the Greek historian, also speaks of an island, named *Ictis*, whither the Britons conveyed the tin dug from the mines of Cornwall—as to a central depôt—until it could be removed to France, and afterwards dispersed over the Continent.

The Greek historian * also records that this tin was conveyed from the mainland in carts, "at low tide all being dry between it and the island," and from this passage, and from a reference immediately preceding it, to the promontory of Bolerium (the Land's End), it has been

B.C. 85.

conjectured that *St. Michael's Mount* is really the *Ictis* alluded to by Diodorus Siculus. But a recent writer * has attempted to demonstrate that the ancient Ictis is the modern Wight, and we offer a brief summary of his arguments for the consideration of the reader :—

I. It is true that *now*, at low water, no cart could cross from shore to shore; but then it is evident that great natural changes have taken place in the configuration of the northern coast of the island since the days of Diodorus Siculus; and it is well known that formerly between Anglesea and the mainland lay certain shallows, though now the Menai waters render it inaccessible to the pedestrian.

II. There is evidence in the local appellations that a great highway, or main road, once traversed the island from Gurnard Bay—through Rue Street, Gonneville and Carisbrooke—to Niton, where may even now be traced the remains of a large Celtic encampment. Close to Niton is Puckaster Cove, a natural harbour, well adapted to shelter the light craft of the Greek and Phœnician merchants who traded with the British for their valuable metal.

III. The Greek *Ictis* may evidently be traced in the Latin *Vectis*, and this similarity of sound may be accepted as no inconsiderable proof of the validity of our argument.

IV. And there is conclusive evidence that St. Michael's Mount could never have been the Ictis of the tin-merchants. because—in the Celtic era—*it was not an island, even at high water.* Florence of Worcester says, " It was originally enclosed, in a very thick wood, distant from the sea six miles," and its separation from the mainland only occurred, according to the Saxon Chronicle, in 1099.

For these reasons, then, we think it may finally be concluded that the Isle of Wight was the ancient Ictis, and the great depôt of the famous tin trade.

---

* See Diod. Sicul., v. 2.

* See Journ. Brit. Arch. Association.

SECTION II.—THE ISLE OF WIGHT UNDER THE ROMANS.

A.D. 43-45. " Vespasian was the first that brought the Isle of Wight to the subjection of the Romans, while he served as a private person under Claudius Cæsar."—*Speed.* Crossing from Gaul into the southern provinces of England, he fought there thirty battles, and reduced under the Roman power two powerful nations,—the Belgæ and the Damnorici,—captured twenty towns, and subdued the Isle of Wight.— *Suetonius.* Two hundred and forty years later (A.D. 296), Constantius, the Roman Emperor, who had been dispossessed of the British throne by the treachery of Carausius, and afterwards by the crimes of Allectus, got together a large fleet and army, and prepared to struggle with the latter for his lost crown. On nearing the British coast, we are told by the historian, " The mists so covered the whole surface of the ocean that the enemy's fleet, which was stationed off the Isle of Wight to surprise us, knew not of our proximity, and we passed through them in security, without hindrance or delay."

These passages are all, in the wide circle of Latin literature, which refer to the Isle of Wight; and its history for upwards of four centuries can only be pieced out, as it were, from the Roman memorials which time has suffered to survive. Enough remains, however, in Roman handiwork to attest the significance of Roman dominion. At Brighstone and at Clatterford have been discovered traces of Roman villas. At Bonchurch, within the memory of living men, the sea, encroaching on the cliff, has washed away the last vestiges of a Roman encampment. At Barnes there are numerous indications of a Roman pottery. Puckaster was once the site of a Roman stronghold, and off Puckaster, and in the Channel, was stationed, or cruised, the Roman fleet.—*Von Muller.* A recent and important discovery of a Roman villa of more than ordinary elegance has been made at Carisbrooke. " Many traces of Roman occupation are still to be seen in the neighbourhood of Ventnor. Wise men, indeed, tell us that the dark hair and brilliant eyes of the natives of this district are derived from a Roman ancestry."—*Rev. James White.* A great Roman road, there is reason to believe, once traversed the island from north to south, passing the principal Roman stronghold—originally a Celtic fortress—Carisbrooke, *Caer-broc,* the Fort upon the Stream. " There are, besides, many roads called *Streets,* which if not always planned by the Romans were adopted by them. These streets have, by their unusually large number in the island, the impress of extensive Roman residence. Thus, parts of the adopted British tin road from north to south are called Rue *Street,* North *Street,* Chillerton *Street,* and Chale *Street.* On the west there is Thorley Street and Street Place. On the east, Arreton Street, Bembridge Street, Haven Street, and Play Street; and again Elderton Street and Whippingham Street from north to south in the East Medina. There is some appearance of arrangement in the roads running from the north to the south, and of a reference to Carisbrooke Castle as a centre, in the streets from east to west."—*Rev. E. Kell.*

The ancient name of Newport, as shown in certain borough muniments, was *Meda* —apparently Roman, and indicating its position in the centre of the island. Grounds for believing that Newport, or Meda, was of Roman origin, and a town

---

* *Stread,* Celtic; *stratum,* Latin; *strc* Saxon.

of no inconsiderable importance, are briefly stated in the Appendix. The matter is one of great obscurity; but this, at least, is certain, that both there, and in other parts of the island, have been found vases, gems, rings, fibulæ, swords, coins, bracelets, and urns. The coins discovered in different quarters range over the whole period of the Roman occupation of Britain, and even descend to a later date. The Romans left England in A.D. 414 to 420; and at Shanklin, in 1833, were discovered coins of the emperors Arcadius and Honorius, the latter of whom did not reign until A.D. 424.

It is evident, then, that the Isle of Wight was regularly colonized by the Romans, who founded here a busy town, built important strongholds, and, charmed by the amenity of the climate and the beauty of the landscape—reminding them, perhaps, of their own fair Italy—built their summer villas in its fairest nooks.

> "The Roman saw its waters ebb and flow,
> Flush, and with quick and fiery sparkles glow;
> Primeval woods and dewy glades between.
> He saw the water-weed wave to and fro,
> Amid the lucid lapse, in glossy sheen;
> And owned a pensive power, a purity serene."
> *Edmund Peel.*

SECTION III.—THE SAXONS IN THE ISLE OF WIGHT.

Our brief *resumé* of the island annals now approaches a period when we shall have more reliable authority to guide us than the conjectures of enthusiastic archæologists.

Between the withdrawal of the last Roman legion from the shores of Britain and the coming of the Saxons, intervenes a period of clouds and shadows, wherein, so far as concerns the Isle of Wight, it is in vain we attempt to grope for aught authentic or satisfactory. The first record in the Saxon history of the island occurs in the year 530, when "Cerdic and Cynric (two Jutish war-chiefs) conquered the Isle of Wight, and slew many men at Wiht-garas-burh, or Carisbrooke."—*Anglo-Saxon Chronicle.* From the statements of other historians, it would seem that the islanders defended themselves with considerable courage, and all agree that their subjugation was not effected without great slaughter.

A.D. 530.

In 534, Cerdic, who founded the kingdom of the West Saxons, died, and Cynric, his son, succeeded to "the throne of spears." The Isle of Wight then passed into the hands of Cerdic's nephews, Stuf and Wihtgar, the latter of whom appears to have enjoyed the real sovereignty of the island, and to have founded a new city at Carisbrooke, or enlarged the old Celtic and Roman stronghold, and given it his name—Wihtgaraburh. He reigned ten years, died in 544, and was buried in the fortress which he had created.

Again we lose all trace of our island-kingdom for upwards of a century, and it is not until 661 that it once more reappears in the Saxon chronicles. Then, indeed, an important event is recorded: Wulfhere, king of Mercia (whose name is commemorated by several *Woolvertons* in the island), having defeated Cenwalt and the West Saxons, "passed through their province with a vast army, made war against the Isle of Wight, and conquered it. And by his agency, too, Ædelwald, king of the South Saxons, was first converted to the true faith. And in acknowledgment thereof, he gave to him, as he received him from the font, the Isle of Wight; and that he might convert it to the religion of Christ, he sent unto him Eoppa the priest, to preach it. Nevertheless he could not then convert it."

The cross and the sword, in the old days, were constant companions; and at length, in 686, the warrior succeeded in placing the priest—who blessed his arms and prayed for the success of the battle—in ecclesiastical superiority over the Wight. Ceadwalla, king of the West Saxons, aided by Mul his brother, "praiseworthy and gracious, terrible in power, and excellent in person, beloved by all, and of a wide-spread fame," subdued the island, and " caused it to be converted to the faith."—*Henry of Huntingdon.* This notable event is duly recorded by Bede, and in such simple language, that the reader will probably not be indisposed to have the old ecclesiast's own words placed before him :—

" After that Ceadwalla had conquered the kingdom of the Gevissi, he also subdued the Isle of Wight, which up to that time had been abandoned to idol-worship ; and he sought to exterminate the natives by a terrible slaughter, and in their place to establish his own followers. And he bound himself by a vow, although not then regenerated in Christ, that if he gained the island, a fourth part thereof, and of the spoil, he would dedicate to God. This vow he fulfilled by bestowing it, for God's service, upon Wilfrid the bishop, who was present with him. Now, the measurement of the said island, according to the English standard, being twelve hundred families, there was given unto the bishop the land of three hundred families ; and the portion which he thus received he intrusted to the care of a certain one of his clergy—Bernuin, his sister's son ; and he gave him a priest named Hildila, that he might preach the word, and administer the waters of life to those who should desire salvation.

A.D. 686.

" Now I think it should not be passed over in silence that, amongst the firstfruits of those who were saved in that island by belief, were two princely youths, the brothers of Arvald, king of the island, who were crowned with the special grace of God ; inasmuch as when the island was menaced by the enemy, they took to flight, and crossed over into the next province of the Juti, and being conveyed to a place which is called *Ad Lapidem* (Stone, or Stoneham), where it was thought they might be hidden from the search of the victorious monarch, were foully betrayed, and doomed by

him to death. Whereupon a certain abbot and priest, named Cyniberct, who governed a monastery not far distant, at a place which is called *Hreutford*, that is, *Reedford* (Redbridge), went to the king, who was then concealed in that neighbourhood, that he might be healed of wounds received while fighting in the Isle of Wight, and besought of him, that if it needs must be that the young princes should die, at least he might first be suffered to administer to them the sacraments of the Christian religion. To this the king consented ; and the priest having taught them the word of truth, and washed them in the waters of salvation, rendered them sure of admission into the kingdom of heaven. And so, when the doomsman appeared, they gladly endured a temporal death, not doubting that thereby they would pass to the eternal life of the soul. Thus it was, that after all the provinces of Britain had accepted Christianity, the Isle of Wight also received it, though, on account of the heaviness of foreign domination, no one was appointed to the ministry thereof, nor to the bishop's seat, until Danihel, now bishop of the East Saxons."—*Bede, Ecc. History,* iv. 16.

The island became the seat of the bishopric alluded to by Bede, about A.D. 730, when Daniel, bishop of Winchester, obtained its jurisdiction ; and it has ever since remained a portion of that wealthy see. To Winchester, in 826, Egbert, king of Wessex, granted, by a charter still extant, a portion of the lands of "*Cawelburne,*" or Calbourne, which remained for many years in its possession.—*Hillier.*

Another gap in the island history now confronts us, which we can only fill up from the conjectures suggested by an examination of the Saxon antiquities of the island. These are remarkably numerous, and point to the existence among our Saxon forefathers of a very high degree of luxury.

The principal *tumuli* or *barrows*, identified as Saxon in their origin, are to be found on Arreton and Chessel Downs, and have been examined with great care, on different occasions, by competent authorities. The first recorded discovery of Anglo-Saxon remains occurred in the month of April 1815, and from that date to the present, the discoveries have been numerous, and their results considerable. Relics have been obtained which indicate, with remarkable force, the gradual progress of the Saxon islanders from barbarity to civilization. The bone combs, iron buckles, rude spears, and coarse urns of the early race, contrast very vividly with the gold fibulæ and armlets, the polished weapons and artistic ornaments of their descendants. Among these strange memorials of the fathers of modern England are beads, finger-rings, buckles, childish toys, and armlets—swords, spears, and knives—hair-pins, ear-rings, and needles—arrow heads, bowls, buckets, and pails; and the curious observer, by spending an hour or two at either of the island museums, where many of these relics are preserved, will gather a more distinct idea of the manners and customs, the mode of life, and even the character of the Anglo-Saxons, than from long and patient perusal of volumes of studied description.

There is, indeed, sufficient evidence that the islanders had attained to a very considerable degree of refinement. They had learned the manufacture of glass, and the construction of stone edifices. Something, too, of workmanship in metals must have been generally known. The articles of domestic adornment, discovered by various explorers in their researches into the *tumuli*, so numerous on the island, are often distinguished by their elegance of design and superiority of workmanship. The wealthier Saxons appear to have delighted in the decoration of their persons; they girded their tunics round the waist by a belt which probably held their swords or knives,

and which was gaily adorned with buckles of bronze or silver. They fastened their cloaks at the neck with bronze-gilt fibulæ, or clasps of precious metal, sometimes enriched with ruby-coloured glass. Globelets of crystal of great value they suspended round the neck. Their fingers sparkled with rings of gold, and gems set with no common skill. The females had their beads of glass and amber, their bronze pins, their 'spindle balls.' The Saxon boy and girl played with their rattles, and strung their perforated cards together, like the children of a later race. In many of his domestic articles the Saxon displayed a refined taste, absent, perhaps, from our modern households. His bronze bowls, his wine cups, his funeral urns were characterized by a graceful simplicity of design. And when he committed to the earth the bones of his friends or neighbours, the sepulture was marked by a decency, we might almost say a splendour, which of itself would be a sufficient proof that the Saxon dwellers in the Isle of Wight were acquainted with many of the arts and customs of civilized life.

The Danes appear to have first planted their ominous standards in the island in the year 897, when " there came six ships and did there serious harm. . . . . Then King Alfred commanded nine of the new ships (long galleys, which he had built to compete with the swift, narrow *esks*, or war ships, of the Danes) to go thither, and they obstructed their passage from the port towards the outer sea. Then went the Danes with three of their ships out against them, and three lay in the upper part of the port in the dry, for the men were gone ashore. But the Saxons took two of the three ships at the outer part of the haven, and slew the men, and the other ship escaped ; but in that also all the crew were slain except five, who got away because the other ships were aground. The Saxon vessels were also aground very disadvantageously; three lay ashore on that side of the deep where lay the Danish ships, and all the rest upon the opposite bank, so that none could reach the other. But when the water had ebbed many furlongs from the ships, the Danes crossed from their three ships to the three which were left by the tide on their side, and then they fought against them." Of Saxons there fell in the struggle 72; of Danes, 120. And when the flood-tide rose, it reached the Danish ships before those of the Angles, and so they rowed out to sea, but "were so injured that they could not row round the Sussex land, where the sea cast two of them on shore."—*Saxon Chronicle.* And the crews were brought before King Alfred at Winchester, and by his decree most righteously were hanged.

About 998 the Danes again visited the Isle of Wight, and the chronicler records that whenever they occupied it, "they obtained supplies from the South Saxons and the county of Southampton."— *Florence of Worcester.* In 1001 they ravaged the unfortunate island with even more than their ordinary ferocity. "They roved about even as they pleased, and nothing could withstand them, nor durst any fleet by sea oppose them, nor land forces either, howsoever far into the land they penetrated. Then was it in every way a grievous time, inasmuch as they never rested from their evil doings."—*Saxon Chronicle.* "Therefore," says Florence of Worcester, "no slight grief affected the king, and a sadness, not to be described, the people." In this incursion the Danes destroyed a town which the Saxon Chronicle calls *Waltham,*—supposed by some authorities, though on slight grounds, to have occupied the site of the modern *Werrow,* near Thorley,—and many "cotlifs," or villages. Then a treaty was entered into with them; a certain ransom was paid, and a temporary peace prevailed.

Prevailed, however, for five years only. In 1006 they once more more plundered the ill-fated island, and again in 1009. In 1013 they obtained, under Sweyn,

such an ascendency in southern England that Ethelred the Unready, the unfortunate king of the Saxons, was compelled to fly, and "at midwinter" betook himself "into Wiht-land," where he remained during the winter months, departing in the spring of 1014 to the court of Richard, Duke of Normandy.

Sweyn was succeeded on the English throne by the sagacious Cnut, who appears to have visited the island in 1022 —the last occasion on which it trembled before "the Raven" of the Norsemen. The Saxon Chronicle, indeed, records that, in 1048 "Sandwich and the Isle of Wight were ravaged, and the chief men that were there were slain;" but we opine that this passage refers to an incursion made by the great Earl Godwin, or his son Harold, in revenge for the maltreatment they had received at the hands of Edward the Confessor and his Norman favourites. The Danes have left no trace of their frequent occupancy of the island, unless we except a small intrenchment on the elevation called Castle Hill, near the Longstone, in the parish of Mottistone.

In the struggle between Earl Godwin and the Norman court, which clouded the later years of Edward the Confessor's reign, the Isle of Wight, from its position, naturally became a favourite rendezvous of the powerful Saxon chief. There he obtained provisions, sheltered his ships, and re-inforced his crews. He probably visited it in 1050, when he was at Bosham with his ships. In 1052, with his sons, Sweyn and Harold, he landed there, and according to the Saxon Chronicle, "did not much evil except that they seized provisions; but they drew unto them all the land-folk by the sea-coast, and also up the country." Another version, it is true, paints their proceedings in blacker colours.

In 1066, "on the 8th of the Kalends of May, there was such a token seen in the heavens as no man ever before saw. Some men said that it was the star

Cometa, which others call *the hairy star,* and it shone seven nights. And soon after came Tostig the earl (the victorious brother of King Harold), from beyond sea into the Isle of Wight, with as large a fleet as he could draw together; and there they yielded him money as well as food." And during "the summer and harvest" of the same year, King Harold gathered together his fleet in the secure waters of the Solent, and went himself into the Wight, keeping his royal state, it may be, in the Keep of Carisbrooke. This was the prelude to that decisive battle of Hastings, which has exercised so remarkable an influence, not alone upon the fortunes of England, but the destinies of the world.

SECTION IV.—CONDITION OF THE ISLAND AT THE PERIOD OF THE NORMAN CONQUEST.

From the curious but valuable compilation, known as the *Domesday Book,* made by order of William the Conqueror, we may gather some interesting facts in illustration of the condition of the Isle of Wight, at the epoch of its occupation by the Normans. It is true that the Domesday Book was not compiled until 1086, but there is no reason to believe that any material changes were made in the general arrangements of the island by the Conquest, which there affected only the landed proprietary. Apparently the island passed into the hands of the stranger without let or hindrance, and it may well be that the spirit of its inhabitants had been completely broken by the long tyranny of the Danish sea-chiefs. Probably they submitted to the Norman invaders with instant readiness; at all events, they could not have been in a position to withstand them with the scantiest prospect of success.

At the date of the Norman conquest, the Isle of Wight then possessed a population of between 6000 and 7000. The Domesday Book thus registers the number of villeins, borderers, and serfs employed upon the lands of the different proprietors :—

On the CROWN LANDS were 198 villeins, 191 borderers, and 142 serfs.

On WILLIAM FITZ-STUR's lands were 36 villeins, 56 borderers, and 24 serfs.

On WILLIAM FITZ-AZOR's lands were 16 villeins, 75 borderers, and 16 serfs.

On GOZELIN FITZ-AZOR's lands were 30 villeins, 44 borderers, and 18 serfs.

On lands belonging to the CHAPEL of ST. NICHOLAS (in Carisbrooke Castle) was 1 borderer.

On lands belonging to the ABBEY of ST. MARY of LIRE in Normandy were 5 villeins.

On lands belonging to the ABBEY of ST. MARY of WILTON were 7 villeins and 12 borderers.

On lands belonging to the SEE of WINCHESTER were 30 villeins, 38 borderers, and 23 serfs.

On lands belonging to the KING'S THEGNS (or immediate·retainers of the Crown) were 33 villeins, 47 borderers, and 11 serfs.

TOTAL, 355 villeins, 464 borderers, and 234 serfs; in all, 1053 souls.

Allowing, therefore, for armed retainers of the feudal chiefs, the garrison of Carisbrooke, women, and children, the population of the island may fairly be estimated as between 6000 and 7000, or, in fact, at about the same number as when, three centuries before, it was converted to Christianity.

The Domesday Book also records, as existing in the island, nine churches, three parochial—Calbourne, Carisbrooke, and Shalfleet; and six, bestowed by William Fitz-Osbert upon the Abbey of Lire, Arreton, Freshwater, Godshill, Newchurch, and Niton.

A toll existed at Bowcombe: there was a *bake-house,* belonging to Count William, at Chiverton (Cevredone), and a *fishery,* in connection with the mansion —*piscaria ad aulam*—at Periton (Prestitone).

No less than thirty-three *mills* are spoken of; two at Avington, one at Alverston, two at Sandford and Week, five at Shide, two at Sheat, one at Wroxall, four at Whitfield, one at Shalcombe, one at Ford, one at Horringford, one at Brooke, one at Kingston, two at Bowcombe, two at Calbourne, one at Gatcombe, one at Westover, one at Woolverton, three at Whitfield, one at Yaverland, and one at Shorwell.

Three *salterns* are mentioned: at Whitfield, Bowcombe, and Watchingwood; nine *woods, feeding thirty-seven hogs,* at Shalfleet, Wroxall, Bowcombe, Heldelie, Watchingwell, Periton, Selins, Brading, and Shalcombe; six *woods* or copses "*furnishing wood for making fences,*" at Lemerston, Shorwell, Shide, Calbourne, Gatcombe, and Chiverton; and three *small woods, free from pannage,* at Sandford and Week, Hardley and Lepene.

There was a *park,* supposed to be the first in England, at Watchingwell.—*Sir R. Worsley.*

From these particulars the reader may gather some idea of the condition of the Isle of Wight, when it first passed into the hands of William of Normandy's knights; and the contrast between the past and the present, in this instance as in all others, cannot fail to prove as instructive as it is interesting.

SECTION V.—THE LORDS OF THE ISLAND, FROM WILLIAM FITZ-OSBERT TO ISABELLA DE FORTIBUS.

WILLIAM FITZ-OSBERT.

The Isle of Wight, after the conquest of England by William the Norman, A.D. 1066. fell to the share of his kinsman and chief councillor, WILLIAM FITZ-OSBERT, or FITZ-OSBORNE, of whom an old chronicler speaks, as "a man of vast influence, note-worthy for his intellectual powers, as well as personal strength" (*Guil. Gemett. Hist. Normann.*), and whom the conqueror, from his boyhood, "had loved and favoured beyond all other Norman barons."—*Guil. Pictaviensis.* Of the spoils of unhappy England, indeed, his share was such as to indicate the esteem in which he was regarded by his sovereign. He was created Count of Hereford, Seneschal and Marshal both of Normandy and England, Chief Justiciary of the north of England, Governor of the castles of York and Winchester; and, finally, the Isle of Wight was bestowed upon him "for his own use and profit." These favours, indeed, his courage and prudence merited, and were but a just recompence of his important services; for "by his advice William was encouraged to invade England, and by his valour was assisted to preserve it."—*William of Malmesbury.* Not but what, at times, his wrathful sovereign could hold him in disfavour; on one occasion when, as steward of the household, he served the Norman duke "with the flesh of a crane scarcely half-roasted, William was so highly exasperated, that he lifted up his fist and would have struck him, had not Eudo, appointed *dapifer* (or napkin-bearer), immediately warded off the blow."—*Warner.*

He divided the Isle of Wight among his principal followers—the Fitz-Azors and Fitz-Sturs—reserving some of the richest manors for his own behoof, and bestowing others upon the Benedictine Abbey of Lire (in the diocese of Evreux, in Normandy), which he had founded, and which he liberally supported. With six of the island-churches he endowed this priory. He strengthened and, perhaps, enlarged the castle, and founded and endowed the priory of Carisbrooke, conferring the latter upon the monks of Lire. He appears to have exercised an absolute supremacy in the island, and to have dispossessed without remorse all the

Saxon landholders, but those who, as the king's thegns, had held their feofs directly from the crown.

The history of the great Norman's chequered career has no relation with that of the Isle of Wight, and we shall content ourselves, therefore, with recording his death on Septuagesima Sunday, 1070, in a skirmish at Cassels, in Flanders.

He was twice married. By his first wife, Adeliza, daughter of Roger de Toëni, standard-bearer at Hastings, he had three sons,—William, who succeeded to his estates in Normandy—Ralph, who became a monk in the Abbey of Cormeilles, which Fitz-Osbert had also founded—and Roger, surnamed De Breteuil, or Bretteville, who became Count of Hereford, and second Lord of the Isle of Wight. He had also a daughter, Adeliza.

His second wife was Richildis, daughter of Reginald, Count of Hainault, and to his passionate love for this lady his death is attributed by the ancient annalists. " For a long time had Flanders been disturbed by intestine commotions. This could not Fitz-Osbert, who was much enamoured of Richildis, endure; but he entered Flanders with a body of troops, and being warmly welcomed by those he came to protect, after some days had passed he rode hastily from castle to castle, with but a few attendants. Then Friso, being aware of this imprudence, decoyed him into an ambuscade, and slew him—fighting bravely but in vain—together with his step-son, Ernulph." — *William of Malmesbury.*

ROGER DE BRETEUIL.

The sole circumstance that connects Roger de Breteuil, so named from the place of his birth, with the Isle of Wight, is an entry in Domesday Book to the effect that Raynauld, son of Croc, held a portion of the lands of Wilmingham, which Count Roger had given to his father.

A.D. 1070.

In 1075 Count Roger incurred the wrath of the Conqueror, and broke out into a rash revolt, which ended wofully for him and his race. The circumstances are so graphically detailed by the chroniclers, and so vividly illustrate the peculiar manners and customs of the time, that the reader may not be displeased to have them placed before him at greater length than their slight connection with the island history of itself would warrant.

As guardian of his youngest sister, Emma, whose dowry he had undertaken to provide, Roger de Breteuil contracted for her a marriage with a potent noble of Bretagne, one Raulf de Gaël, created by the Conqueror Count of Norfolk. But King William fearing, perhaps, that the intimate alliance of two nobles of such vast power and haughty spirit might be fatal to the peace of the realm, or for some other weighty reason, sent over from Normandy expressly to forbid the nuptials. The proud counts, however, thought fit to despise their monarch's prohibition, and the marriage was celebrated at Norwich, the chief city of De Gaël's earldom, where—

" Was held that bride-ale
The source of man's bale,"
Saxon Chronicle—

a nuptial feast fatal to all who attended it. There came to it many bishops, abbots, and barons, and many stalwart warriors. There were Normans, and Saxons allied by marriage to those Normans, and Welshmen, the good friends of Count Roger of Hereford and Count Waltheof, who ruled the fair earldoms of Huntingdon, Northampton, and Northumberland. And the tapers shone merrily on the knightly throng, and the red wine glowed brightly in the golden goblets. And lo, the heart was opened, and the tongue loosened, and out spake Count Roger in fierce denunciation of the tyranny of King William in seeking to prohibit his sister's alliance. It was an affront, he cried, to the memory of his father, who had won for the bastard his kingdom.—*William of Malmesbury.*

Then out spake the Saxons, who, indeed, had received far deeper injuries, and on all sides arose fierce expressions of wrath : "They began unanimously, and with loud cries, to plot the betrayal of their king."

Said a Norman : "He is a bastard, and hath no right to a crown."

"He poisoned Conan, our gallant Breton count," muttered a Breton.

"He hath rashly invaded the noble realm of England," cried a Saxon; "hath unjustly slain the true heirs thereof, or cruelly forced them into exile."

"And those who aided him," was the reproach of others, "and through whose valour he is raised higher than all his race, he hath treated with cold ingratitude. To us, victors and wounded, he gave but sterile fields, and these he has taken away, or diminished, at the dictates of his avarice." So they protested solemnly that he was abhorred by all men, and that many would rejoice were he but to perish.

Whereupon Count Roger spake boldly unto the powerful Count Waltheof : "Brave Saxon," said he, "now is the much longed-for hour for thy revenge. Do thou unite with us, and we will establish the English monarchy even as it was in the days of Edward. One of us shall be king, and the other two shall be his generals, and we will govern all. William assuredly will not return here, seeing that in Normandy he hath enough upon his hands. Unite then with us, O Saxon Earl, and do that which is good for thee, and thy family, and thy fatherland, down-trodden under foot."

And these words were hailed with a mighty shout of applause, and Normans and Saxons sware to aid each other, and to overthrow King William.

But this conspiracy was crushed before it was fairly afoot, by the energy and vigour of Lanfranc the primate, Odo of Bayeux, and William de War-

renne. Levying a numerous army, they attacked De Gaël's forces at a place called *Vagadune,* and completely defeated them—cutting off, it is said, the right foot of every prisoner they captured. In the west, the king's troops also defeated the army of Count Roger, and he himself was taken prisoner.

Then King William hastily returned to England, and held a court at Westminster, where the Count of Hereford appeared, and was unable to deny his treason. Therefore, in accordance with the Norman laws, he was condemned to lose his hereditary estates, and to be imprisoned for life in one of the royal prisons. But still haughty was the spirit, and unconquerable the pride of Count Roger, and in his dungeon he derided the king, and by his contumacy implacably offended him ; for once upon a time, at Easter tide, King William, desirous, it may be, of soothing the haughty baron, sent unto him a complete suit of costly stuffs. Straightway Count Roger ordered his attendants to kindle a great fire before him, and into the flames he cast the royal gifts,—a silken tunic, and a mantle, and a short cloak made of precious furs. When the king heard thereof, he was justly angered, and swore, "Very proud is he who hath done me this dishonour, and by the splendour of God out of my prison while I live he shall not go !" And the oath was kept.

Count Roger died in 1086, and the vast estates of the Fitz-Osberts, and their sovereign rights in the Isle of Wight, were resumed by the crown.

On one occasion only did the Conqueror visit his island-fortress, and that was in an hour of peril A.D. which vividly brought out the 1085. manly qualities of his kingly mind. His half-brother, Odo, bishop of Bayeux, half-warrior half-priest, who had received from King William the province of Kent, and fat estates and manifold honours, collected during the

Conqueror's absence in Normandy a large and powerful following in the Isle of Wight, with the view of going forth into Italy and intriguing for the Popedom.

The king, apprised of his brother's ambitious design, suddenly returned, and summoned to Carisbrooke Castle his knights and men-at-arms, and other vassals.

They met in the Royal Hall (*regalis aula*), by the shifting lights of a hundred torches, which wavered and flickered merrily enough upon the glittering armour of the knightly throng. William, with moody brow and angry eye, sate in stern silence upon the dais; and when the murmur of voices was hushed, he recounted, one by one, the offences which Odo had done against him :—

"Excellent peers," he cried, if we may believe the old historian, "I beseech you hearken to my words, and give me your counsel. At my sailing into Normandy I commended England to the government of Odo, my brother, the bishop. In Normandy my foreign foes have risen up against me,—yea, and inward friends, I may say, have invaded me; for Robert my son, and other young lords whom I have brought up, and given arms, have rebelled, unto whom my false clients, and other bordering enemies, have given their assistance. But they have not prospered, God (whose servant I am) even defending me; neither have they gotten anything of mine besides iron in their wounds. They of Anjou prepared against me whom, with the fear only of war, I have pacified. These businesses, you know, have drawn me into Normandy, where I have stayed long, and employed my painful endeavours on public behoofs. But, in the meantime, my brother hath greatly oppressed England, spoiling the Church of lands and rents; hath made it naked of ornaments given by our predecessors, and hath seduced my knights, with purpose to train them over the Alps, who ought to defend the land against the invasion of the Danes, Irish, and other enemies overstrong for me; but my greatest dolour is for the Church of God, which he hath afflicted, and unto which the Christian kings that reigned before me have given many gifts, and with their loves honoured; for which now (as we believe), they rest, rejoicing with a happy retribution in a pleasant state. But my brother, to whom I committed the whole kingdom, violently plucketh away their goods, cruelly grindeth the poor, and with a vain hope stealeth away my knights from me, and by oppression hath exasperated the whole land with unjust taxations. Consider thereof, most noble lords, and give me (I pray you) your advice what is herein to be done."—*Speed, Book* ix.

But Odo was a prelate, and sacred—a noble wealthy and powerful, and not over-slow in his punishment of an enemy. What marvel, then, that out of all that knightly gathering not one dared raise his voice against him?

"Seize him!" shouted the Conqueror, as if resolved to construe their silence into an acknowledgment of his brother's offences,—"seize him, and let him be closely guarded."

But not a knight laid his finger upon the prince of the Church. All stood mute and aghast at the king's wrath. With instant decision, he sprang from his seat, strode through his astonished followers, and grasped his brother's robes.

Whereupon Odo exclaimed, "I am a priest and a servant of the Lord! None but the Pope has the right to judge me."

The monarch, prepared for the crafty excuse, replied, "I do not punish thee as a priest, but as my own vassal, and a noble whom I myself have made."

And Odo was surrounded by armed men, and borne from his sovereign's presence; and in due time he was despatched across the seas to wear out many years in a Norman fortress.

Great spoil fell into William's hands. "Heaps of yellow metal did move admiration in the beholders, and many of his bags were taken up out of the bottom of a river (the Medina ?), where they were hidden, full of gold ground into powder."
—*Speed.*

RICHARD DE REDVERS I.

There lived in these times a potent knight, RICHARD DE REDVERS, *de Riviers,* or *de Ripariis,* so named from Riviers, near Creuilli, in Normandy, who safely sided with King Henry I. in his contest with his brother Duke Robert, and whose loyalty so won that monarch's favour, that, in addition to the honours and estates which had descended to him from Count Baldwin, his father, he created him Count of Devon, with a yearly pension of one-third the revenue of the county, and bestowed upon him the town of Tiverton, the honour of Plympton, the manor of Christ Church, and finally, the LORDSHIP OF THE ISLE OF WIGHT.

A.D. 1101-2.

He enjoyed his honours until his death in 1107. By his wife Adeliza, daughter of William Fitz-Osbert, he left issue, and his son, Baldwin de Redvers. succeeded to his power and titles.

BALDWIN DE REDVERS I.

COUNT BALDWIN, fourth Lord of the Island, was a true type of the true Norman Baron : restless, gallant, impatient of control, but a pious son of the Church, ever ready by the gift of a fat acre to deserve its blessings. He lived and reigned in the Isle of Wight, and probably in such state as romancists and poets have loved to paint, weaving their thick fancies upon the scanty details afforded by the ancient chroniclers. He founded *Quarr Abbey,** a monastery of the Cistercian

A.D. 1107.

order, choosing for it a delectable site in an ample meadow-land, bordered by a thick wood, and opening out upon the blue waters of the Solent. There he placed a colony of monks brought over from Savigni, in Normandy, and he liberally endowed the monastery he had founded (A.D. 1135). Upon the town of *Eremuth* or *Yarmouth,* situated at the mouth of the Yar, he conferred a charter—thus creating the first municipality in the Isle of Wight.

Count Baldwin espoused the cause of the Empress Maude, in her struggle with Stephen for the English crown, and suffering a severe defeat in the fens of Ely, betook himself with great haste (A.D. 1139–40) to his island fastness. He greatly strengthened and enlarged Carisbrooke Castle, and invented, we are told, many new and surprising engines of war for its defence. But this did not avail him against the superior military skill and strength of Stephen, who drove him from the island, and confiscated all his possessions. Nor were they restored to him until 1153, when peace was made between Stephen and Henry Plantagenet. Then the Count returned from Normandy to his Castle of Carisbrooke, and there abode in the tranquil enjoyment of his almost regal powers, until his death in 1155.

His wife, Adeliza, bore him three sons—Richard, William, and Henry—and a daughter, named Adewisia, or Hadewisa, who is recorded to have possessed lands in the island. Baldwin, his Countess, and his son Henry were buried at Quarr Abbey.

RICHARD DE REDVERS II.

The fifth Lord of the Island, and third Count of Devon. was RICHARD DE REDVERS, eldest son of Count Baldwin, who married Dionysia, daughter of Count Reginald of Cornwall; begat two sons, Baldwin and Richard; followed his father's excellent example in enriching the Abbey of St.

A.D. 1156.

---

* *Quarr,* from *Quarrariis,* in allusion to the quarries in its vicinity, which had been worked as early as the preceding reign, and were perhaps not unknown to the Romans.

Mary of Quarr; and bestowed a charter upon the rapidly rising town of Newport.

He died in 1161, at Cenomanes, in France, leaving a son, Baldwin, still a minor.

And here we pause to enumerate, very briefly, some of the privileges of the Lords of the Island. They themselves held their estates and honours from the crown, and owed it military service, being bound in *escuage* at fifteen knights' fees and a half (about 4700 acres). They alone possessed dominion in the island. Their tenants could not be taxed by the crown, but held their lands of the castle, or, as it was sometimes termed, the *honour* of Carisbrooke. When the lord's eldest son was admitted to the order of knighthood, or when his daughters were married, they were bound to defray the attendant expenses. If the castle were besieged, his tenants were bound to defend it, at their own cost, for forty days. When he visited the island, they were required to receive him; when he left it, to attend him to the place of embarkation. All minors were placed under his guardianship. He had the return of the king's writs, appointed his own constable and bailiffs, and was coroner within the island. For his pleasaunce, he had a chase in the forest of Parkhurst, and free warren over the lands lying east of the Medina. All wrecks on the coast, all waifs and strays, were his; and the tolls of the fairs and market at Newport and Yarmouth. Finally, he had his own judicial tribunal in the *Knighten Court*, or *Court of Knights*, established by William Fitz-Osbert, and continued until a comparatively recent period, where he and his knights presided, and adjudicated on all insular claims without let or hindrance from superior authorities. — *Worsley.*

BALDWIN DE REDVERS II.

The second COUNT BALDWIN, sixth Lord of the Wight, who had married Avicia, daughter of Ralph de Dol, died, without issue, one year after the death of his father, and was buried at Christ Church.—*Lansdowne MSS.* 40, art. iv. A.D. 1162.

RICHARD DE REDVERS III.

Of this COUNT RICHARD DE REDVERS, the historian of the Wight has nothing to record, save that he first assumed the De Redvers' coat of arms, *or*, a lion rampant, *azure*. He died without issue, and was buried at Mantzbourg, in Normandy. A.D. 1163.

WILLIAM DE VERNON.

One of the most illustrious of the Lords of this Island was WILLIAM, surnamed DE VERNON, from a town in the Cotentin, where he was born, or, according to some authorities, educated. He was the second son of the first Baldwin, Count of Devon and Lord of the Wight, and succeeded to the dignities and estates of the De Redvers, in default of male issue to his nephew Richard. A.D. 1184.

A gallant baron was William de Vernon, and loyal to his king, the famous Cœur de Lion. At whose second coronation, celebrated on his return from his Austrian prison (A.D. 1194), Count William was one of the four barons who supported the silken canopy over the royal head.

As a firm adherent to King Richard he was necessarily an object of suspicion and hatred to the crafty John. In the first year of *his* reign, therefore, the Count—fearing confiscation of his estates —made over to Hubert de Burgh, the Grand Justiciary of England (who had wedded his daughter Joanna), the Lordship of the Island and the manor of Christ Church. This, however, was but a nominal surrender; and on the death of Hubert de Burgh, in 1206, De Vernon obtained the restitution of his honours on payment to the crown of the enormous fine of 500 marks, and placing his grandson as a hostage in the king's hands.

De Vernon was one of the great barons who wrested from the reluctant monarch that famous title-deed of English freedom, *Magna Charta*,*—animated, perhaps, by personal animosity as much as by public spirit.

He chiefly resided, it is believed, in his Castle of Carisbrooke, which had undergone many changes since the days of Fitz-Osbert. Here he exercised, we may well suppose, the splendid hospitality of a feudal chieftain, and gathered about him his knights and vassals to hold high revel or enjoy the vigorous pleasures of the chase. The squire, under his regal roof, may have learned those principles of chivalry which made the civilization of the feudal times; and have practised those athletic exercises which strengthen the frame and sharpen the intellect. Here the page may have waited on the lady of the island, have whispered love to her maids of honour, or at the banquet ministered to the service of his lord.

> The fretted wall,
> Beneath the shade of stately banneral,
> Was slung with shining cuirass, sword, and shield:
> Light-footed damsels moved with gentle graces
> Round the wide hall, and showed their happy faces.
> *Keats.*

William de Vernon imitated his predecessors in liberal donations to the Abbey of Quarr, within whose stately walls he raised a mausoleum for his father and himself at a cost of £300, or nearly £6000, computed at the present value of money. He died on the 14th September 1216, and was therein interred. His son BALDWIN— the *third* De Redvers of that name—had "passed away" a few days before him (1 Septem-

ber), and his titles, honours, and estates, therefore, devolved upon his grandson,

BALDWIN DE REDVERS IV.

This BALDWIN, the son of Baldwin de Redvers and Margaret Fitzgerald, had been placed, as we have shown, in the hands of King John as a hostage for his grandfather's fidelity. A.D. 1216. On the death of his kinsman, being still a minor, the king placed him as a ward in the care of the notorious Fulk de Breauté, whom his mother had been compelled by the king to marry—an unnatural union which excited the disgust of all thinking men. Thus, "this high-minded lady," says one, "became the wife of a murtherous traitor. The noble was linked to the ignoble ; the pious to the blasphemous ; the beautiful —against her will indeed, and constrained by the tyrant John—to the base. So that of this marriage, a certain poet has sang with sufficient elegance :—

> ' By law, by love, by household feelings bound—
> Yet say, what law is this ? what love, or peace ?
> Law without law, and love that hate hath found,
> And concord strange whose discords never cease.' " *
> *Matthew Paris.*

But this unworthy minion fell from his proud estate in 1224, was deprived of his ill-gotten treasures, and banished the country. Whereupon the wardship of the young Count Baldwin was entrusted to Richard, Count of Cornwall, the able brother of Henry III., by whose influence a marriage was contracted between his ward and Amicia de Clare, daughter of Gilbert, Count of Gloucester (A.D. 1227),—the latter being constrained to pay to the royal treasury a fine of 2000 marks on the union of his daughter with so wealthy a young noble.—*Rotul., xi. Henry III.* A son, Baldwin, was born to them in 1235, and a daughter, Isabella, in 1237.

At Christmas tide, in 1240, when the

---

* After signing this charter, King John fled to the sea-shore, and it has generally been asserted that he retired to the Isle of Wight. But the king's Itinerary, or journey book (edited by Mr. Hardy), conclusively shows that the statement is erroneous.

* Lex connectit eos, amor, et concordia lecti.
  Sed lex qualis? amor qualis? concordia qualis?
  Lex exlex; amor exosus; concordia discors.

third Henry held a brilliant court at Winchester, Baldwin, *adolescens primæ indolis, miles elegantissimus,* a youth of noble disposition, and skilfully practised in all martial exercises, was knighted, and formally invested with the lordship of the Wight (*Matthew Paris*),—the privileges of that high dignity having been previously enjoyed by his guardian, the Count of Cornwall. Five years later, and Count Baldwin died (15th February, 1245) still in the prime of his chivalrous manhood.

AMICIA DE CLARE.

At the period of Count Baldwin's decease, his son Baldwin, the fifth De Redvers of that name, was only ten years old, and his wardship was entrusted to one Henricus de Wengham. He married at the early age of fifteen or sixteen, Avicia of Savoy, a cousin of Queen Eleanor; had a son John, who died at the early age of ten; was knighted on the occasion of the nuptials of King Henry's daughter Beatrice with the Duke of Brittany; and died in September 1252, of poison administered to him at the table of Peter de Savoy, Earl of Richmond, when Richard of Gloucester also met his death by the same foul means. He was buried at Breamore.

A.D. 1245.

The lordship of the Isle of Wight formed a portion of the dowry of his mother AMICIA DE CLARE, who enjoyed it from the death of her husband until her own decease in 1283, when the estates and honours of the De Redvers became the undisputed inheritance of her daughter, the celebrated Lady of the Island.

ISABELLA DE FORTIBUS.

ISABELLA, daughter of Baldwin de Redvers and Amicia de Clare, married, in her early youth, William de Fortibus, Count of Aumerle or Albemarle, and at the age of twenty-three was left a widow, her husband dying at Amiens in 1260. She

A.D. 1283.

had had by him three sons — John, Thomas, and William; and two daughters, Alice and Aveline. The latter alone survived her; the others died in infancy.

On the death of her mother she succeeded, at the mature age of forty-six, to the vast inheritance of the De Redvers, while in right of her marriage she enjoyed the large estates of the Aumerles. Her abilities, and administrative capacity, appear to have been considerable, and she supported her weighty honours with becoming dignity. She resided principally in her Castle of Carisbrooke, where she maintained an almost regal splendour. With knights and pages in her train, and a bodyguard of men-at-arms, we may imagine that she swept in exceeding pomp along the broad highways of her island realm; often visiting, we may be sure, that new and important borough of *Medina* or *Newport,* upon which she had conferred extensive privileges, and the municipalities of Yarmouth and Francheville (Newtown), founded by her ancestors.

She was very bountiful to the Abbey of Quarr, bestowing upon it several manors, and fully confirming the donations of her predecessors; and on the Norman Abbey of Mantzbourg, she conferred her possessions at Appuldurcombe and Week. To other religious foundations she was equally liberal, but nevertheless she knew how to preserve her own dignities from ecclesiastical encroachment. She claimed certain lands enjoyed by the Abbey of Quarr, and so prompt were her proceedings that the monks were forced to seek the protection of the Crown, and Edward I. to entrust their defence to William de Braybœuf, Sheriff of Hampshire. She quarrelled also—history does not record the *why*—with the convent of Breamore, which received *gravissima damna,* such heavy damages in the strife, that the king judged it right to command the Bishop of Winchester, in consideration of its losses, to endow it with the church of Brading. "On the vacancy of a prior of Christ Church, she assumed the power of holding the lands of the convent in her hands; and a prior of Carisbrooke being elected without her approbation, she summoned him to answer in her court."

Isabella de Fortibus died at Stockwell, in Surrey, in 1293, aged 56. On her deathbed she executed a deed by which, for the sum of 6000 marks—upwards of £60,000—she parted with all the powers, privileges, and lands of the lordship of the Wight to Edward I.[*] The king had previously sought the concession from her daughter, the Lady Eveline, but her untimely death abruptly terminated the negotiation.

Henceforth, then, we are to regard the Isle of Wight as an appanage of the Crown, whose lordship "was rarely granted, except for life or during pleasure, to such as the king delighted to honour."

SECTION VI.—FROM ISABELLA DE FORTIBUS TO SIR JAMES WORSLEY.

THE WARDENS OF THE ISLAND.

THE government of the Isle of Wight, under Edward I. and his successors, was, with few exceptions, administered by WARDENS, or *Custodes Insulæ*, appointed by the Crown, and removable at the Sovereign's pleasure. With these were often joined in commission the constable of Carisbrooke Castle, the Bishop of Winchester, or some one or two notable knights, for the purpose of regulating and investigating its defences. For the Wight, during the stormy reigns of the Plantagenets and their incessant wars with France, was necessarily a position of considerable military importance.

The first Warden appointed by Edward I. was JOHN FITZ-THOMAS, A.D. 1393. of whom "nothing further is known, but that he was also steward of the New Forest." He was succeeded in 1295 by RICHARD DE AFFETON (*Afton*), with whom was joined in commission HUMPHREY DE DONASTERRE, constable of Carisbrooke. And, in the following year, another commission was appointed for the purpose of examining into the defensive forces of the island,—Sir RICHARD DE AFFETON, the BISHOP of WINCHESTER, and ADAM DE GOURDON.

This Adam de Gourdon, we may observe *par parenthèse*, had been a famous freebooter, and in the days of the feeble Henry III., the terror of the Hampshire hinds. His bands ravaged the shire from east to west, issuing forth, ever and anon, from their strongholds in the bowery glades of the New Forest, where their leader maintained a sovran state, to carry off the beeves, the corn, and, it may be, the brown - cheeked daughters of the panic-smitten farmers. Against this redoubtable robber-knight Prince Edward at length led a troop of men-at-arms, and came up with him at Alton; but it was agreed, in accordance with the chivalrous spirit of the times, that the fortunes of the day should be decided by a passage-at-arms between the two leaders. So the sword of the rebel crossed the sword of the heir of England. Sharp and obstinate was the combat,—long afterwards sung of by the old ballad minstrels,—but the prince succeeded in disarming his opponent, and brought him to the ground. He spared his life, with a rare generosity, and procured him the royal forgiveness. Finally, recognising in him certain chivalrous qualities, he appointed him to a post near his own person; and a trusty servant of

---

[*] Hugh de Courtney, her heir, the founder of the Courtneys of Devon, disputed the testament of the countess, and declared it a forgery. His charges were formally investigated by the Parliament, and pronounced unfounded.— *See Parliamentary Rolls, ix., Edward II.*

King Edward was the rebel whom Prince Edward had doubly vanquished.

From 1302 to 1307, Sir JOHN DE LISLE, of Wootton, surnamed *De Bosco* (of the Wood), was warden of the island, and also held the constableship of the Castle of Carisbrooke. This John de Lisle was a knight of weight and influence, and appears to have been, so to speak, "the representative man" of the island-chivalry. "With divers other great men," he was summoned (23 Edward I.) "to consult of the important affairs of the realm." He accompanied the great Plantagenet, "well fitted with horse and arms," on his expeditions into France and Scotland. His son, John de Lisle, was one of the many noble youths who received the honour of knighthood with Prince Edward—"by bathing, and divers sacred ceremonies"—at "the famous solemnity," held by King Edward in the thirty-fourth year of his reign.—*Dugdale.*

NICHOLAS DE LISLE, in 1307, the year of Sir John's death, was appointed to the wardenship, and commanded by Edward II. to place the island in the possession of his infamous minion, Piers Gaveston, Earl of Cornwall. But the gentlemen of the Wight, and the English nobility, remonstrated so strongly against this appointment that the weak king was compelled to rescind it, and he shortly afterwards bestowed the lordship, with all its privileges, and the Castle of Carisbrooke, on his eldest son, the gallant EDWARD, then styled EARL of CHESTER. "That prince kept them in his possession as long as he lived, governing by wardens, as had before been practised by his grandfather; these he generally chose out of the chief gentlemen of the island, judging them the fittest to defend their own lands."—*Worsley.*

Sir JOHN DE LISLE, son of the former warden, was appointed to this important office in 1310. He was succeeded in 1321 by Sir HENRY TYES, who was be-

headed for treason in the following year; in 1325, the wardens were JOHN DE LA HURE and JOHN LISLE; in 1336, JOHN DE LANGFORD, Lord of Chale, and, in 1338, THEOBALD RUSSEL, Lord of Yaverland.

And here we propose, in accordance with our general plan, to pause for awhile in this arid summary of names and dates, and to put before the reader, with such skill as we can command, a view of the curious defensive military arrangements of the Wight under the Plantagenet. At the present time, such a subject cannot be without interest, and may not be without profit.

It is difficult, however, to approximate to any correct estimate of the number of men which formed the militia of the island. Every able-bodied inhabitant was liable, in the event of its invasion, to be called upon to bear arms; and those were the days when the English peasant knew how to draw "the tough bowstring" with a strength and a skill which rendered it a formidable weapon. From various ancient rolls we also gather that the Earls of Devon, in right of their feudal service, contributed to the insular forces 70 men-at-arms; the king, 100 bowmen; the City of London, 300; while several religious houses and the principal land-owners together supplied 127 men-at-arms, and 141 bowmen. Every person owning land of the yearly value of £20, was bound to provide a horseman fully armed. The island was parcelled out into *nine* military districts, over each of which was set its principal land-holder or most distinguished knight. If the reader will take his map, and follow upon it this arrangement as we are about to indicate it, he will see that the division was ordered with considerable skill :—

1. *Yaverland, Bembridge, Northill,* and *Brading* were under WILLIAM RUSSEL, Lord of Yaverland.
2. *Stenbury, Whitwell, Wroxall, Bonchurch, Cliff, Apse, Niton, and Sandown,* under PETER DE HEYNO, Lord of Stenbury.

3. *Knighton, St. Helen's, Kerne, Ryde, Quarr, Binstead,* and *Newchurch,* under THEOBALD DE GORGES, Lord of Knighton.

4. *The Borough of Newport,* under the BAILIFF of NEWPORT.

5. *East Standen, Arreton, Whippingham, St. Catherine's, Rookley, Nettlecomb,* and *Wootton,* under JOHN URRY, Lord of East Standen.

6. *Kingston, Shorwell, Carisbrooke, Park, Northwood.* and *Watchingwell,* under JOHN DE KINGSTON, of Kingston.

7. *Brixton, Calbourne, Mottistone,* and *Newtown,* under THOMAS CHYKE, Lord of Mottistone.

8. *Brook, Shalfleet, Thorley,* and *Yarmouth,* under the LORD of BROOK.

9. *Compton, Afton,* and *Freshwater,* under ADAM DE COMPTON, Lord of Compton.

On the chief eminences and exposed points of the coast, watches were stationed by day and night, and beacons* kept in readiness. Thus, in the East Medina, were thirteen of these stations; in the West Medina, sixteen. If a hostile squadron sailed up the eastern entrance of the Solent, straightway the lurid beacon blazed upon St. Helen's Hill, meeting with instant response from the ready sentinels who kept watch on the heights of Shanklin—on the down which towers above Appuldurcombe—at Niton, and rocky Atherfield. Thence the balefire streamed far into the very heart of the island, to Standen and to Avington; and so away on the one hand to Ryde, Wootton, and Cowes; on the other, to Freshwater and Mottistone, and "the sea-shore at Brighstone."

> And soon a score of fires, I ween,
> From height, and hill, and cliff, were seen,
> Each with warlike tidings fraught,
> Each from each the signal caught;
> Each after each they glanced to sight,
> As stars arise upon the night.

Other regulations made by the inhabitants for their security have been preserved by Sir Richard Worsley (*History,*

p. 31), and are curious enough as illustrations of the iron conditions under which the islanders then "held their own:"—

1. That there should be but three ports in the island, namely, La Riche (Ryde), Shamblord, and Yarmouth.

2. That three persons should be appointed wardens of these ports, who were to prevent any one from retiring from the island, or exporting provisions from thence without licence.

3. That none but licensed boats should be permitted to pass, except the boat belonging to the Abbot of Quarr; a boat belonging to Sir Bartholomew de Lisle, and another belonging to Robert de Pimely.

The WARDEN of the ISLAND possessed extensive powers,—could array, at his pleasure, the horse and foot forces; could raise new levies, if necessary; could provide them with weapons; could draw additional men from Hampshire; could compel the return of all absentees on pain of forfeiture of their lands, tenements, goods, and chattels; and, in case of non-compliance, provide men to supply their places. The king supplied the Castle of Carisbrooke with ten tuns of wine, one hundred quarters of wheat, the same quantity of malt, and oats; fifty quarters of pease and beans; with coals, wood, salt, and other munitions. And to encourage the military spirit of the inhabitants, he conferred upon them great and peculiar privileges.

We may add that the landholders of the island were compelled, by the conditions on which they held their estates, to defend the Castle of Carisbrooke, in time of war, at their own expense (*sumptibus propriis*) for forty days.—(7 Edward III.)

A few words* in elucidation of the ecclesiastical condition of the island at this period may, perhaps, be permitted

---

* These beacons were "a long and strong tree set up, with a long iron pole across the head of it, and an iron brander fixed on a stalk in the middle of it, for holding a tar barrel."

* From a *Return made by the Dean of the Island* to Henry Woodlock, Bishop of Winchester, in 1305.

us before resuming our historical narrative. Most of those quiet village churches which lend such a charm to its picturesque landscapes — nestling away in shadowy combes, and among leafy copses, or looking out afar from lonely heights upon the distant sea—echoed with matin and with vesper, in the days of the haughty Normans. But the chapels, or oratories, which existed in connection with their stately mansions, have passed away ; passed away like the names of their founders, like the brave old manorial houses which once were so numerous in the island, but of which not a grey stone or ivied buttress can now be traced.

Thus, of the chapels once existing at *Alfredston* (Alverston), *Briddlesford*, *Lymerston*, *Whitfield*, and *Standen*, the antiquary cannot now detect a relic. Much must the pilgrim of the isle regret that memorials of the past so full of interest have not been spared by Time and "sacrilegious hands." But at *Arreton* still rises the gray old tower. There is still a church at *Binstead*, though of recent erection, the former building having been removed in consequence of its extreme dilapidation. At *Chale*, bleak, desolate, and lonely—in the leafy village of *Brighstone*—on the abrupt hill of *Carisbrooke*—at *Godshill*, towering above the fertile mead—at *Thorley*, *Shalfleet*, sequestered *Shorwell*, and pleasant *Gatcombe*—at quiet and sequestered *Mottistone*, still stand the churches, repaired, "restored," and somewhat changed in aspect, it is true, which gave up their revenues, five centuries and a half agone, to the Norman Abbey of Lire, and the Island-Abbey of Quarr. The hamlet of *St. Helen's*, now as then, supports a church, though the *Priory* long ago passed from the memory of man. *Carisbrooke's* rich *priory*, the small "*cell*" of monks at *Appuldurcombe*, and the *priory* of *St. Cross* at *Newport*, have utterly vanished from the earth. But the churches of *Calbourne*, *Yarmouth*, *Freshwater*, *Newchurch*, *Brading*, and *Wootton*, and the dependent chapels of *Northwood*, *St. Lawrence*, and *Newport*, are still among the ecclesiastical edifices of the island. Within the walls of Carisbrooke Castle was a small, but parochial church, that of *Sanctus Nicolas in Castro*, whose memorials now-a-days are without importance or interest.

In the Isle of Wight, then, about this time, there existed no less than 16 churches and 11 chapels, many of them possessed of considerable wealth and some degree of architectural beauty. There were also an opulent abbey, that of Quarr ; the priories of St. Helen's, Carisbrooke, and St. Cross ; the cell of Appuldurcombe, and a chantry at St. Catherine's. Altogether, a liberal ecclesiastical provision for a population which, probably, did not exceed 12,000.

The courage of the islanders, and the value of their military preparations, were first tested in the year of grace 1340, when a French force landed at St. Helen's point, and rapidly pressed forward into the interior. Sir Theobald Russell, at the head of the insular forces, coming up with them, drove them back to their ships, but unfortunately fell in the brief though sanguinary action. Stow, by the way, calls him *Sir Peter*, a pregnant illustration of the truth of Byron's dictum,—

" Thrice happy he whose name has been well-spelt,
    In the despatch !"

In 1377 the French again invaded the island, and succeeded in forcing their way as far as Newport. The inhabitants retired for shelter to Carisbrooke Castle, which, says Stow, Sir Hugh Tyrill "kept manfully." A body of the invaders, approaching the castle, were decoyed into an ambuscade, and so completely cut up that the exulting islanders named the place where they fell " Noddies' Hill " (now *Node Hill*), and "Deadman's Lane." — *Worsley.* Unable to capture the castle, and, perhaps, apprehensive of the besiegers receiving formidable reinforcements, the French retired, "taking of the inhabitants 1000 marks to spare their houses unburnt."—*Stow.* In this invasion the towns of Yarmouth and Francheville were completely destroyed, and the whole island appears to have been in the temporary occupation of the enemy.

The lordship of the Isle of Wight, and the Castle of Carisbrooke, were bestowed by Richard II., in the ninth year of his reign, on a potent and splendid noble, WILLIAM DE MONTACUTE, EARL OF SALISBURY, who fills no unimportant niche in English history. This lord had enjoyed the special favour of Edward III., having fought with him at the siege of Caen and the battle of Crecy. He won two memorable sea fights; defeating the Spaniards, off Winchelsea, in 1351, and burning seven large Spanish ships at St. Malo, in 1373. At the battle of Poictiers he commanded the rereward of the English army, "in the heat of which fight, it is said that he strove with the Earl of Warwick which of them should most bedew the land of Poictiers with French blood."—*Dugdale.*

A.D. 1386.

This gallant baron, who was one of the first knights of the most noble Order of the Garter, was wont to maintain on ship-board, 300 men-at-arms, 300 archers, 20 knights, and 279 esquires—a magnificent contribution, assuredly, to the naval strength of England.

Edward III., in 1377, made him admiral of the fleet, and he was present at Sheen, in the June of the same year, when the great sovereign, who had so liberally recompensed his services, "passed away." Never resting on his arms, we hear of him in the following year as harassing the French coast with his ships, and capturing Cherbourg. Shortly afterwards he was appointed Governor of Calais.

A terrible calamity befell him in 1383.

"In a tilting at Windsor," charging in the melée, he accidentally slew his only son, a misfortune which clouded all his latter years. In 1386 Richard II. bestowed upon him "the Isle of Wight and the Castle of Carisbrooke," with all their royalties, rights, and privileges, "without paying any rent;"[*] honours which the magnificent earl enjoyed eleven years, dying at Christ Church Twyneham, on the 3d June 1397.

On the death of this earl the *constableship* of *Carisbrooke* was bestowed, for his life, upon THOMAS, EARL OF KENT; the *lordship* of the *island* was conferred upon EDMUND, EARL OF RUTLAND, fifth son of Edward III., a man whose ambition, valour, and sagacious intellect enabled him to hold his own, even in the stormy days of Henry IV.

A.D. 1397.

Against Richard II. and his brothers of Lancaster and York, a conspiracy was formed, in 1397, by the Earls of Derby, Arundel, and Warwick, the Duke of Gloucester, and certain dignitaries of the church, from which this Earl Edmund gained a great advantage. For the plot being discovered, and the leaders beheaded, Earl Edmund received a large share of the spoil of their vast estates. The Earl of Warwick was suffered to escape with banishment to the Isle of Wight, his sentence being pronounced in this quaint fashion,— "Earl of Warwick! this sentence is very favourable, for you have deserved to die as much as the Earl of Arundel, but the handsome services you have done in time past to King Edward, of happy memory, and the Prince of Wales, his son, as well on this as on the other side of the sea, have secured your life;

---

[*] A great French invasion being apprehended in 1386, the Earl of Salisbury, inasmuch as "his lands were in the Isle of Wight, was ordered thither to guard and protect it with its men-at-arms and bowmen."—*Froissart.*

but it is ordered that you banish yourself to the Isle of Wight, taking with you a sufficiency of wealth to support your state so long as you shall live, and that you never quit the island."—*Froissart.*

The Earl, created Duke of Albemarle, played an important part in the shifting drama of the reign of Henry IV.; but his treason and his ambition, his deeds of valour and wisdom, his subtilty and courage, rather belong to the History of England than to the Annals of the Isle of Wight.

Having received his hereditary title of Duke of York, he accompanied Henry V. in that famous invasion of France A.D. which closed so gloriously with 1415. the battle of Agincourt, and upon that historic field terminated his turbulent career. "It is said that he desired of King Henry, that he might have the fore-ward of the battle that day, and had it, and that by much heat and thronging, being a fat man, he was smothered to death."—*Dugdale.*

> "Suffolk first died, and York, all haggled over,
> Comes to him, when in gore he lay insteep'd,
> And takes him by the beard; kisses the gashes,
> That bloodily did yawn upon his face;
> And cries aloud,—Tarry, dear cousin Suffolk!
> My soul shall thine keep company to heaven:
> Tarry, sweet soul, for mine, then fly abreast;
> As, in this glorious and well-foughten field,
> We kept together in our chivalry!"
>   SHAKSPEARE.

During the lordship of Earl Edmund the French made another descent A.D. upon the island. The old chro-1404. nicle thus tells the tale: "Waleram, Count de St. Pol, assembled at Abbeville, in Ponthieu, about 1600 fighting men, among whom were many men of noble birth, who had largely provided salted meat, biscuits, brandy, flour, and other things necessary for use at sea. From Abbeville the count led them to Harfleur, where they found all sorts of vessels ready to receive them. Having there abode some days to perfect their arrangements, and commend

themselves to St. Nicholas, they embarked on board these vessels, and sailed straight for the Isle of Wight. Landing there, they assumed a bold face to meet their enemies, of whom, on their landing, they had seen but little; most, or all, of them having retired to the woods and fastnesses. And now the count made several new knights; namely, Philippe de Harcourt, Jean de Frosseux, Le Seigneur de Guiency, and several others, who went to burn some paltry villages, and set on fire some other places. Meanwhile, there came to them an astute priest of the country to treat for the ransom and safety of the isle; and he gave the count to understand that to him and his knights would be paid a very considerable sum of money. To this did the count lend an eager ear; but it was simply a deception on the part of the priest, so that their movements might be interrupted until the strength of the island could be got together. Now of this plot Waleram at length was advised, but too late for him to avenge himself; and re-embarking his men with all speed, he set sail, and returned home without effecting anything more. Then were his lords sore displeased with him, inasmuch as they had invested largely in provision for this expedition, which had thus been utterly overthrown by a solitary priest."—*Monstrelet*, c. xix.

Earl Edmund's widow obtained from the king a grant, for life, of the lordship of the island, the castle and A.D. manor of Carisbrooke, the manor 1416. of Bowcombe, and the tithes of the church of Freshwater. She also possessed, as a portion of her dowry, the manors of Thorley, Whitfield, Pann, and Niton, so that she specially deserves a line of record among the historic men and women of the Wight. She died in 1430.

"Towards the latter end of this year a body of Frenchmen landed on the island, and boasted that they would keep their Christmas there; but as near a thousand of them were driving **A.D. 1418.** cattle towards their ships, they were suddenly attacked by the islanders, and obliged to leave, not only all their plunder, but also many of their men behind."

In the following year, or "about that time," they came again "with a great navie, and sent certayne of their men to demand in the name of King Richard, and of Queen Isabell, a tribute or subsedie of the inhabitants; who answered that King Richard was dead, and the queen, some time his wife, was sent home to his parents, without condition of any tribute; but if the Frenchmen's minde were to fight, they willed them to come up, and no man should let (*hinder*) them for the space of five hours to refresh themselves, but when that time was expired, they should have battayle given to them, which, when the Frenchmen heard, they went away and did nothing." —*Stow.* Such confidence in their own valour had the battle of Agincourt, and the victories of Henry of Monmouth, excited in the men of the Wight.

The lordship of the island, "by virtue of a grant of the reversion thereof," **A.D. 1439.** passed into the hands of the famous HUMPHREY, DUKE OF GLOUCESTER, (17 Henry VI.), on the decease of the Duchess of York. There is no reason to suppose that he ever set his foot upon its shores, and we, therefore, content ourselves with this brief notice of his temporary connection with it. During his lordship, Henry Trenchard, an island-gentleman, held the post of warden.

A singular event in our annals is here to be noted. Upon HENRY BEAU- **A.D. 1443.** CHAMP, DUKE OF WARWICK, King Henry—"to whom he was very dear"—bestowed the nominal dignity of KING OF THE ISLE OF WIGHT, and placed the mimic crown with his own hands upon his youthful brow. "He had the Castle of Bristol given

him, with the islands of Guernsey and Jersey, the patronage of the Church and Priory of St. Mary Magdalene of Goldcliff, with leave to annex it to the Church of Tewkesbury. He confirmed the grants made by his predecessors to the Church of Tewkesbury; gave all the ornaments he wore to purchase vestments for the monastery; died in the twenty-second year of his age, and was buried in the middle of the choir." **A.D. 1446.** Though titular king, he enjoyed neither power nor profit from his dignity, the lordship remaining with "the good duke" until his death in 1447.

Henry Trenchard then received from King Henry a grant of the constableship of Carisbrooke.

RICHARD PLANTAGENET, DUKE OF YORK, father of EDWARD IV., was the next lord of the island; **A.D. 1449.** and one John Newport, and Henry Bruin were successively his lieutenants. Against the illegal oppressions of the former, the inhabitants remonstrated forcibly, and laid their complaints both before the Duke and the Parliament. Duke Richard fell in the battle of Wakefield,—one of the most sanguinary of the great fights of the White and Red Roses,—in 1460.

EDMUND, DUKE OF SOMERSET, in 1453, obtained a grant of the island, and the Castle of Carisbrooke, for him- **A.D. 1453.** self and his heirs-male, in satisfaction of certain sums of money due to him from the crown. He was slain in the skirmish at St. Albans, May 22, 1455.

His son, HENRY, DUKE OF SOMERSET, succeeded to his honours, but revolted from the Yorkish party, to **A.D. 1455.** which his father had clung so stoutly. Thereupon, being taken by Lord Montague, at the battle of Hexham, fought upon the banks of the Dilswater, May 15, 1464, his head was struck off without the formality of trial or sentence.

The gallant ANTHONY, LORD SCALES,[*] next received a dignity illustrated A.D. 1467. by so many of the heroic leaders of feudal England. His royal brother-in-law, in recognition of his eminent services, bestowed upon him "a grant in special tail of the Isle of Wight, with the castle and lordship of Carisbrooke, and all other the castles, manors, and lordships in the island." The next year he was despatched as ambassador to Charles, Duke of Burgundy, to negotiate a marriage between the Prince and the Lady Margaret, sister to Edward IV. In return, came to Edward's court a chivalrous nobleman, the Count de Charolois, or the Bastard, "having in his retinue divers brave men, expert in all feats of chivalry, and to the number of 400 horse in his train," and great festivities were prepared for his welcome.

And here the reader will permit us to introduce a brief episode in illustration, not only of Lord Scales' mighty merits, but of the manners of the age wherein he lived. We shall borrow the words of a famous historian, but the lover of fact arrayed in splendid fiction will find the scene we are about to quote charmingly painted in glowing colours, by Sir E. Bulwer Lytton, in his "Last of the Barons." The king decrees a grand tourney, or tilting match, "whereupon lists were set up in West Smithfield, and upon Thursday next, after Corpus Christi Day (1467), the king being present, they ran together with sharp spears, and parted with equal honour. Likewise, the next day, on horseback; at which time, this Lord Scales his horse, having a long sharp jute of steel on his chaffron,[†] upon their coping together it ran into the nose of the Bastard's horse. Which making him to mount, he fell on the one side with his rider. Whereupon this Lord Scales rode about him, with his sword drawn, till the king commanded the marshal to help him up, no more being done that day.

"But the next day coming into the lists on foot, with pole-axes, they fought valiantly, till the point of this lord's pole-axe entered the sight of the Bastard's helm. Which being discerned by the king, he cast down his warder, to the end the marshal should sever them. Hereupon the Bastard requiring that he might go on of his enterprise, and consultation being had with the Duke of Clarence, then constable, and the Duke of Norfolk, marshal, whether it might be allowed or not, they determined that if so, then, by the law of arms, the Bastard ought to be delivered to his adversary *in the same condition as he stood* when the king caused them to be severed. Which, when the Bastard understood, he relinquished (very wisely!) his further challenge."—*Dugdale, Baronage,* vol. ii.

Lord Scales, on the death of his father, became Earl Rivers, but did not enjoy the earldom many years. Being a formidable obstacle in the upward path of Richard of Gloucester, he was foully murdered at the ill-omened Pontefract Castle, on the 13th or 14th of June, 1483.

"O Pomfret! Pomfret! O thou bloody prison,
Fatal and ominous to noble peers!"
                                        SHAKSPEARE.

On the death of Earl Rivers, Richard III. bestowed the captaincy of the island on Sir WILLIAM BERKE- A.D. LEY, and shortly afterwards, on Sir 1483. JOHN SAVILE. The battle of Bosworth Field, however, summarily disposed of King Richard's servants, and, in 1485, the lordship and captaincy of the Isle of Wight was granted by Heny VII. to his wife's brother.

---

* Edward IV., in the first of his reign, conferred the captainship, for life, on Sir Geoffrey Gates, who surrendered it in 1467 and received in compensation the governorship of Calais.

† *Chevron,* a head-piece, the head armour of the horse.

SIR EDWARD WOODVILLE,

"A stout man of arms," and of famous excellence in all knightly exercises, who appears to have gained considerable influence over the knights and gentlemen of his miniature realm.[*] For being much affected towards the Duke of Brittany, who was then at war with the King of France, Sir Edward determined to lead a body of men-at-arms to his assistance. "And having plain repulse and deniall of the king, could not rest, but determined to work his business secretly without any knowledge of the king, and went straight into the Isle of Wight, whereof he was made ruler and captain, and there gathered together a crew of hardy personages, to the number of 400."—*Hall*, folio xv. So, with forty gentlemen in four vessels, he set sail from St. Helen's for Brittany; joined the duke's forces, and marched against the French army, with whom they came into collision at St. Aubin. "To make the Frenchmen believe that they had a great number of Englishmen, they apparelled 1700 Bretons in coats with red crosses, after the English fashion. The Englishmen shot so fast, that the Frenchmen in the fore-ward were fain to recede to the battaile, where their horsemen were." But they were finally outnumbered and out-generalled, and notwithstanding the courage of the islanders, the Bretons were totally routed. So terrible, truly, was the carnage, that out of the 400 Englishmen who had followed Sir Edward's standard, only one—a boy—escaped to relate the sad history of their misfortunes; their leader, and "many noble and notable persons" were among the slain. And there was scarcely a family in the island which had not cause to rue the fatal battle of St. Aubin's! (A. D. 1488).

SIR REGINALD BRAY, a trusty servant of King Henry's mother, who had been "most happily instrumental in advancing King Henry to the royal throne by his faithful and sedulous transacting in that affair" (*Dugdale*), received a lease of the island, with the castle of Carisbrooke and its appurtenances, the crown lands, and the manors of Swainstone, Brighstone, Thorley, and Wellow, on the condition of making a yearly payment to the crown of 307 marks (£205, nearly £2500 at the present value of money). It must have been during Sir Reginald's administration that Edward IV.'s daughter, LADY CICELY, retired to the Isle of Wight, and spent there the last years of her singularly chequered life, of which so little is known to the general reader, that a brief memoir may not be unacceptable. *A.D. 1495.*

THE PRINCESS CICELY.

Cicely, or Cecilia, the third daughter of Edward IV., and Elizabeth his wife, was born towards the close of 1469. Her first years were years of storm and shadow; for she was scarcely a twelvemonth old when her royal mother, on the outbreak of the Lancastrian rebellion, was compelled to fly with her to sanctuary at Westminster; and she had but just attained her fifth year, when she was betrothed by proxy (26th December, 1474), to James, the son of James III. of Scotland.

The contemplated marriage, however, was not carried out, King Edward's ambitious designs preventing its consummation; and the Lady Cecilia, instead of a throne and probable unhappiness, was left to consult at a future period the modest wishes of her loving heart, and to furnish English history with the rare instance of a daughter of one of its kings wedding "a man of mean estate."

---

[*] He repaired and strengthened the castle of Carisbrooke, and erected its noble gatehouse, with its circular towers, still bearing the scutcheon of the Woodvilles, and the white rose of York.

On the decease of Edward IV., and the gradual development of Richard of Gloucester's ambitious designs, Cecilia and her elder sister were placed in sanctuary at Westminster. A scheme devised by their adherents for their escape to the Continent was betrayed to Richard, and he immediately placed a strong guard round the sanctuary, under the command of one of his creatures, John Nesfield. Thus imprisoned, the royal ladies and the queen-mother remained for nine months, negotiating meanwhile with the subtle Richard relative to his proposed alliance with the Princess Elizabeth. His "messengers, being men of gravity, handled the queen so craftily, that anon she began to be allured, and to hearken unto them favourably."—*Harding.*

Richard at length solemnly undertook
A.D. to provide for their safety, to put
1485. them "in honest places of good name and fame;" to marry "such of them as were then marriageable to gentlemen born," and to provide each with a dowry of lands and tenements of the yearly value of 200 marks.—*Harl. MSS.*, 433. On these conditions the queen gave up her daughters, who received apartments in the palace, and "familiar loving entertainment."

It was, however, very speedily reported that Richard designed to marry her beneath her condition, so that her offspring might not prove troublesome candidates for the crown; and when Henry of Richmond landed in England, resolved to wed her if her sister Elizabeth were already married to King Richard, he received assurance that this dishonouring marriage had really been contracted, and was "sore amazed and troubled" at the tidings. But their falsity was soon detected, and after the victory of Bosworth, and Henry's subsequent marriage to Elizabeth, she
A.D. resumed her proper position in the
1486. royal court, and was treated with the distinction due to her birth and personal attractions.

At Elizabeth's coronation, in November 24, 1487, she also bore her sister's train; and her loveliness made her "the observed of all observers." Amongst these was a certain gallant soldier, a kinsman and favoured servant of the king's, John, Lord Wells, who immediately proffered his suit to the beautiful princess; and though he was more than twice her age, was accepted by her, and, with the king's consent, they were straightway wedded. As husband and wife they attended the Christmas revels at Greenwich, which were held that year with extraordinary magnificence.

By Lord Wells the Lady Cicely had two daughters, Elizabeth and Anne, whose education, it is recorded, she sedulously attended to, while her lord waited upon his royal nephew in his expedition to France, and his progresses through his dominions. About 1495 or 1496—the date is uncertain—she lost her eldest daughter, and, in 1498, her husband died of pleurisy, "at Pasmer's Place, in Saint Swithin's Lane," bequeathing to his well-loved wife the whole of his large possessions. Shortly afterwards her sorrows were much increased by the death of her younger daughter.

We next find mention of the widowed lady as figuring in the grand pageantry of the bridals of Prince Arthur and Catherine of Arragon, whose train she bore; and the day afterwards, diligent chroniclers record, she performed "two bass dances" with Prince Arthur (Nov. 14, 15, 1501).

Two years later, and she suddenly retired from the splendour of the court into the obscurity of a private condition, wedding—from true love, we may surely presume—one John, or Thomas Kyme, of the Kymes of Kyme Tower, Lincolnshire, a gentleman by birth, but whom the old annalists, stout upholders of feudal distinctions, disdainfully speak of as "a man of mean degree." This singular event took place about the close of 1503, or the beginning of 1504. This gentleman is differently styled as "John *Keime*, of the Isle of Wight, Knight," and "Sir John *Kime* of the Isle of Wight" (*Harl. MSS.*, 1139), and is reputed to have had two children by the Lady Cicely, named Richard and Margerie. With his wife he retired to East Standen, near Newport, where for a few brief years "the daughter of England" secluded herself among her quiet household joys, dying on the 24th of August, 1507, in her thirty-eighth year. She was buried in the Abbey of Quarr, and a stately monument erected to her memory. But of this "HIC JACET" not a stone now remains.—*Miss Roberts' Houses of York and Lancaster*, ii., &c.

Returning to our narrative, we can but barely record the captaincy of SIR NICHOLAS WADHAM, who came of an ancient Devonshire family, and held, by virtue of his patrimonial inheritance, certain manors in the Isle of Wight. His second wife, Margaret, sister of the Jane Seymour who wedded Henry VIII., died at Carisbrooke, and was buried in the parish church, where her monument may still be noted. Sir Nicholas himself died in 1511, when the captaincy was conferred upon a gallant and distinguished knight, SIR JAMES WORSLEY, whose career we shall briefly indicate in our next Section.

SECTION VII.—FROM SIR JAMES WORSLEY TO COLONEL HAMMOND.

SIR JAMES WORSLEY.

Sir JAMES WORSLEY was a younger brother of the Worsleys of Lancashire, who rose into high repute at the courts of Henry VII. and Henry VIII., and who, as page to the former, and keeper of the wardrobe to the latter, enjoyed considerable distinction, and received much of their confidence.

A.D. 1511.

By his marriage with Anne, daughter of Sir John Leigh, and heiress of the Hackets of Woolverton, he had become possessed of Appuldurcombe, and other large estates in the Isle of Wight, occupying a position among its gentlemen which abundantly justified the king's choice of him for their captain. .

He was appointed Captain-General for life, at a salary of 6s. 9d. per day (nearly £5, according to modern computation), and was made, moreover, Constable of Carisbrooke ; keeper of the forest ; steward, bailiff, and surveyor of the crown lands ; clerk of the market ; sheriff, and coroner of the island. These weighty offices he held until his death in 1538.

SIR RICHARD WORSLEY

succeeded to all his honours, trusts, and estates, and maintained the dignity of his office with becoming splendour. At his mansion of Appuldurcombe, he entertained, in 1540, King Henry, his minister Cromwell (then constable of Carisbrooke Castle), and a splendid retinue. What occasioned the royal visit it is difficult to conjecture, unless it was for the purpose of enjoying the pleasures of the chase in Parkhurst Forest.

Five years later, and the French made their last descent upon this "invincible isle." The circumstances are related with singular vigour by *Mr. J. A. Froude* in his *History of England*, and we need not apologize to the reader for illustrating our pages with his graphic pictures.

A.D. 1545.

"With July," he says, "came the summer, bringing with it its calms and heat ; and the great armament,* com-

* The French fleet, under Claude D'Annebault, consisted of 150 large ships, 25 galleys, and 50 small vessels and transports.—*Archæologia*, il. The English fleet, under Lord Lisle, was far inferior, but his ships were larger and better manned.

manded by D'Annebault in person, sailed for England. . . . . The king was at Portsmouth, having gone down to review the fleet, when, on the 18th of July, two hundred sail were reported at the back of the Isle of Wight. The entire force of the enemy, which had been collected, had been safely transported across the Channel. With boats feeling the way in front with sounding lines, they rounded St. Helen's Point, and took up their position in a line which extended from Brading Harbour almost to Ryde. In the light evening breeze fourteen English ships stood across to reconnoitre; D'Annebault came to meet them with the galleys, and there was some distant firing; but there was no intention of an engagement. The English withdrew, and night closed in.

"The morning which followed was breathlessly calm. Lisle's fleet lay all inside in the Spit, the heavy sails hanging motionless on the yards, the smoke from the chimneys of the cottages on shore rising in blue columns straight up into the air. It was a morning beautiful with the beauty of an English summer and an English sea; but, for the work before him, Lord Lisle would have gladly heard the west wind among his shrouds. At this time he had not a galley to oppose to the five-and-twenty which D'Annebault had brought with him; and in such weather the galleys had all the advantages of the modern gunboats. From the single long gun which each of them carried in the bow they poured shot for an hour into the tall stationary hulls of the line-of-battle ships; and keeping in constant motion they were themselves in perfect security. According to the French account of the action, the *Great Harry* suffered so severely as almost to be sunk at her anchorage; and had the calm continued, they believed that they could have destroyed the entire fleet. As the morning drew on, however, the off-shore breeze sprung up suddenly; the large ships began to glide through the water;

a number of frigates—long, narrow vessels—so swift, the French said, that they could outsail their fastest shallops —came out with 'incredible swiftness;' and the fortune of the day was changed. The enemy were afraid to turn lest they should be run over; and if they attempted to escape into the wind, they would be cut off from their own fleet. The main line advanced barely in time to save them; and the English, whose object was to draw the enemy into action under the guns of their own fortresses and among the shoals at the Spit, retired to the old ground. The loss on both sides had been insignificant; but the occasion was rendered memorable by a misfortune. The *Mary Rose*, a ship of six hundred tons, and one of the finest in the navy, was among the vessels engaged with the galleys. She was commanded by Sir George Carew, and manned with a crew who were said, all of them, to be fitter, in their own conceit, to order than obey, and to be incompetent for ordinary work. The ports were open for the action, the guns were run out, and, in consequence of the calm, had been imperfectly secured. The breeze rising suddenly, and the vessel lying slightly over, the windward tier slipped across the deck, and, as she yielded further to the weight, the lee ports were depressed below the line, the ship instantly filled, and carried down with her every soul who was on board. Almost at the same moment the French treasure-ship, *La Maitresse*, was also reported to be sinking. She had been strained at sea, and the shock of her own cannon completed the mischief. There was but just time to save her crew and remove the money-chest, when she, too, was disabled. She was towed to the mouth of Brading Harbour, and left on the shore.

"These inglorious casualties were a feeble result of the meeting of the two largest navies which had encountered each other for centuries. The day had as yet lost but a few hours, and

D'Annebault, hearing that the king was a spectator of the scene, believed that he might taunt him out of his caution by landing troops in the island. The sight of the enemy taking possession of English territory, and the blaze of English villages, scarcely two cannon-shot distance from him, would provoke his patience, and the fleet would again advance. Detachments were set on shore at three different points. Pierre Strozzi, an Italian, attacked a fort, perhaps near Sea View,* which had annoyed the galleys in the morning. The garrison abandoned it as he approached, and it was destroyed. M. de Thais, landing without resistance, advanced into the island to reconnoitre. He went forward till he had entangled his party in a glen surrounded by thickets; and here he was checked by a shower of arrows from invisible hands. The English, few in number, but on their own ground, hovered about him, giving way when they were attacked, but hanging on his skirts, and pouring death into his ranks from their silent bows, till prudence warned him to withdraw to the open sands. The third detachment was the most considerable; it was composed of picked men, and was led by two of the most distinguished commanders of the galleys. These must have landed close to Bembridge. They were no sooner on shore than they were charged by a body of cavalry. There was sharp fighting; and the soldiers in the nearest ships, excited at the spectacle of the skirmish and the rattle of the carbines, became unmanageable, seized the boats, and went off without their officers to join. The English being now outnumbered, withdrew; the French straggled after them in loose order, till they came out upon the downs sloping up towards the Culver Cliffs; and here,

being scattered in twos and threes, they were again charged with fatal effect. Many were cut in pieces; the rest fled, the English pursuing and sabreing them down to the shore; and but few would have escaped, but that the disaster was perceived from the fleet, large masses of men were sent in, under shelter of the guns, to relieve the fugitives; and the English, being badly pressed in return, drew off, still fighting as they retreated, till they reached a stream (the Eastern Yar, probably), which they crossed, and broke the bridge behind them."—*Froude,* iv. 423–427.

The evening had now come on, and D'Annebault had to determine whether he should attack Portsmouth, or seize upon the Isle of Wight. The former plan was at once rejected, on account of the difficulty of the entrance to the harbour. "It remained, therefore, to decide whether the army should land in force upon the island and drive the English out of it, as they might easily do. They had brought with them 7000 pioneers, who could rapidly throw up fortresses at Newport, Cowes, St. Helen's, and elsewhere; and they could have garrisons strong enough to maintain their ground against any force which the English would be able to bring against them. They would thus hold in their hands a security for Boulogne; and as the English did not dare to face their fleet in the open water, they might convert their tenure into a permanency.

"D'Annebault, however, had received discretionary powers; and, for some unknown reason, he determined to try his fortune elsewhere. After three days of barren demonstration, the fleet weighed anchor and sailed. His misfortunes in the Isle of Wight were not yet over. The ships were in want of fresh water; and on leaving St. Helen's he went round into Shanklin Bay (July 21), where he sent his boats to fill their casks at the rivulet which runs down the Chine. The stream was small, the task was

---

* The headland at Sea View still bears in ancient maps the appellation of Old Fort. M. Thais probably landed at Brading, and penetrated into the Barnsley woods.

tedious, and the Chevalier d'Eulx, who, with as few companies, was appointed to guard the watering parties, seeing no signs of danger, wandered inland, attended by some of his men, to the top of the high down adjoining. The English, who had been engaged with the other detachments two days before, had kept on the hills, watching the motions of the fleet. The chevalier was caught in an ambuscade, and, after defending himself like a hero, he was killed, with most of his followers."

This invasion was productive of good fruits, as far as the island was concerned, by inducing the king to order the construction of several forts for its defence. These were circular towers, with a platform, mounting two or three guns, and accommodating a small garrison, on which modern engineers would look with a great deal of contempt. At East and West Cowes, at Sandown, Yarmouth, and near Freshwater, these fastnesses were erected under the superintendence of Richard Worsley,— the latter being named after him, Worsley's Tower. The indefatigable captain also persuaded the islanders to provide a train of artillery at their own expense, every parish providing their own gun.

In September 1547, the first of the reign of Edward VI., a return was made to the crown of the condition of these fortresses, from which we shall extract a few details:—At Yarmouth, under the command of Captain Richard Ewdall, were two guns of brass, and eight small guns of iron, nineteen hagbuts, and one hundred and forty-one bows. At Sharpnode, under the charge of Nicholas Cheke, were two brass guns. At Carisbrooke, under Richard Worsley himself, were five iron "slynges, fowlers, and double basses," one hundred and forty hagbuts, and a tolerable provision of powder, bows, arrows, javelins, and bills. At Sandham (*Sandown*), under the care of Peter Smythe, were three

pieces of brass, and eight of iron, seventy-eight hagbuts, one hundred and twenty bills, and a chest of bows and arrows. And at West Cowes, under Robert Raymond, captain, were two brass guns, eleven of iron, several basses "not liable to serve," and a small provision of bows, bills, and pikes. The Sandham captain received four shillings *per diem;* his under captain, two shillings; thirteen soldiers, sixpence each; one porter, eightpence; the master gunner, eightpence; and seven gunners, sixpence each. At West Cowes, the captain received but one shilling daily; two soldiers, one porter, and six gunners, were paid the same rates as their comrades at Sandham.—*Harl. MSS.*

When Queen Elizabeth came to the throne she placed the defensive establishment of the island on a safer basis, as may be gathered from the instructions issued to the captain of the Island in the second year of her reign, which we now condense :—

The said captain shall forthwith put in order and array the whole people of the isle as shall seem meetest for the defence of the said isle.

He shall cause every "centoner," twice a year, to call together the whole "centon," and bring together to such place within the said isle as by the said captain shall be appointed, "there to consult what is to be done for the better fortification and strength of the said isle."

He shall cause the able men in these centons twice a year to muster for practice.

He shall prohibit that neither timber, wood, nor coal shall be carried out of the isle to any place.

All manners of persons having lands to the clear yearly value of twenty marks, should find one "hasquebutier" furnished in time of war to remain in the isle under the rule of the captain during the time of war. And every other person having land valued at 40 shillings shall join so many together as shall amount to the yearly value of twenty marks, and so be jointly charged with one hasquebutier.

It was also ordered by the queen that fire-arms should be introduced into the island, and an arquebus-maker was settled in Carisbrooke Castle to keep them in order.

Richard Worsley was one of the commissioners for the sale of church plate on the suppression of the religious houses, and therefore, on the accession of Queen Mary, found it necessary to resign all his offices—a Mr. Girling, of whom history says nothing, succeeding him. In 1556, the captain of the island was one Nicholas Uvedale. He joined the Dudley conspiracy, and undertook to betray the island and Hurst Castle to the French, who were to assist in deposing Queen Mary. The plot was betrayed to government, and Uvedale tortured into making a full confession.— *Froude.* When Queen Elizabeth came to the throne, Worsley was reinstated, and employed by her in several important commissions. He died, full of honours, in 1565.

SIR EDWARD HORSEY.

EDWARD HORSEY was descended from a reputable Dorset family, of Melcombe-Horsey, and as a gallant sea-chief did good service against the French, clearing the Channel from their piratical cruisers. He was held in high esteem by the great Earl of Leicester, and at his patron's secret nuptials with the Lady Douglas Sheffield, gave away the bride; though we do not find, when, at a later period, the ambitious noble denied the marriage, that Sir Edward vindicated the lady's fair fame.

His government of the island was marked by energy and foresight. He encouraged trade, while he kept alive a military spirit among those he ruled. From certain MSS. still extant in that wonderful store-house of unpublished history—the British Museum—it is, however, to be inferred that his sway was somewhat lax; and we read of piratical doings in the Medina, wherein "Sir Edward Horsey's men" were openly concerned. Mr. Froude has shown us that their leader shared the audacious mor-

ality of Drake, Frobisher, and Hawkins, —believing it to be a religion and a policy to oppress and defraud the Frenchman and the Spaniard. He was implicated in the Dudley conspiracy, which made Lady Jane Grey a "ten days' queen," but contrived to escape punishment.

It is recorded of this gallant sea-rover that he mightily interested himself in the preservation of game, and that he gave a lamb for every hare brought into the island. Sir Richard Worsley states that "he lived in perfect harmony with the gentlemen there;" and we may fairly suppose that his sea-life would give him a frankness of speech and manners calculated to render him popular.

He died of the plague at Haseley, on the 28th of March 1582, and was buried in Newport Church, where a handsome monument was erected to his memory. Sir Philip Sidney, our English Bayard, is said to have held the captaincy of the island about this period.

SIR GEORGE CAREY

was appointed soon after the decease of Sir Edward. It was his misfortune to succeed a popular governor, and the inhabitants accordingly drew a contrast by no means to his advantage. A preacher at Newport added fuel to the flame by conferring upon him, in the prayer before the sermon, the unauthorized title of "Governor." He stretched his authority, moreover, to an illegal extent at the epoch of the apprehended invasion of the Spanish Armada; but he probably was only desirous of adopting necessary precautions, which the ill feeling of the inhabitants seized upon as arbitrary measures justifying an appeal to the Lords in Council. The commotion, however, appears to have subsided, and Sir George to have withdrawn his excessive pretensions; for Sir John Oglander eulogizes his splendid hospitality, and commends him for his constant residence at Carisbrooke Castle.

A.D. 1588.

" I have heard," says Sir John, "and partly know it to be true, that not only heretofore there was no lawyer nor attorney in oure island, but in Sir George Carey's time, an attorney coming in to settle in the island, was, by his command, with a pound of candles hanging att his breech lighted, with bells about his legs, hunted oute of the island; insomuch as oure ancestors lived here so quietly and securely, being neither troubled to London nor Winchester, so they seldom or never went oute of the island; insomuch as when they went to London (thinking it an East India voyage), they always made their wills, supposing no trouble like to travel."

Sir John Oglander paints the condition of the island at this period in glowing colours. "Money was plenty in the yeomen's purses, and all the gentry full of money and out of debt; the markets full, comodities vending themselves at most high rates. Prizes and men-of-warre at the Cowes, which gave great rates for our comodities, and exchanged other good ones with us. If you had anything to sell, you should not have needed to have looked for a chapman, for you could not almost ask but have. All things were exported and imported at your heart's desire, your tenants rich, and a bargain could not stand at any rate." In another part of his Memoirs, he states that he has seen 300 ships at one time in Cowes Harbour.

During Sir George Carey's captaincy, Carisbrooke Castle was thoroughly repaired and considerably enlarged, under the direction of Gianibelli, an Italian engineer, who had planned the fortifications of Antwerp, and who destroyed the Duke of Parma's fire-ships in 1585.—*J. L. Motley.* Towards the outlay the queen gave £4000, the gentry £400, and every able-bodied man his labour. The other island-fortresses were strengthened, and *Carey's Sconce* erected near Yarmouth.

In 1585, Newport, Yarmouth, and Newtown, first sent members to Parliament.

Sir George Carey, on the death of his father, succeeded to the title of Lord Hunsdon. He was a kinsman of the queen, and much favoured by her, receiving from her hands the Order of the Garter and the Lord Chamberlainship of her household. Died on the 9th of September 1603.

THE EARL OF SOUTHAMPTON.

The next Captain and Governor—for this title was now regularly assumed — was HENRY EARL OF   A.D. SOUTHAMPTON, known in history   1603. as the patron of Shakspeare and the friend of Essex. He regularly resided in his island-palace, and held, conjointly with the chief knights and gentlemen of the island, "an ordinary, twice every week," on St. George's Down, near Arreton, where they diverted themselves with the then popular game of bowls.

The *Free Grammar School* at Newport was established during his governorship; and to the same period may be referred the erection of those manorial houses, of which, at Yaverland and Mottistone, two notable examples may still be admired.

King James visited the island twice or thrice during Lord Southampton's rule. He was at Beaulieu, the seat of Lord Chancellor Wriothesley, in August 1607, and during his stay there knighted an island gentleman, Bowyer Worsley. "It is highly probable that the king was afterwards in the Isle of Wight, and was then entertained at Nunwell, the seat of Sir W. Oglander" (*Nichols*); for Mr. William Knyveton, his attendant, wrote to the Dowager Countess of Shrewsbury on the 22d of June, "that his Majestie intends a progresse into the Ile of Wight;" and there yet lingers a tradition that the king (and Queen Elizabeth) honoured Nunwell with a visit. Notwithstanding his timidity, he was passionately fond of the chase, and Parkhurst Forest could not fail to supply him with abundant sport. And, at all events, the parochial register of Carisbrooke proves that he hunted there in 1609. "King James," runs the record, in the vicar's own hand-writing, "landed at the Cows, and saw a muster at Hony Hill, and saw in the afternoon most of the iland, with Prince Charles his sonne, and hunted in the park, killed a buck, and so departed again to Bowly, the 2d of August, Ann. Dom. 1609, being Wednesday.—*J. Baker.*" And a later entry records a visit from Prince Charles: "Prince Charles landed at the Cowes, and came into the forest, and saw a skirmish there, and went from thence to Alvington Down, and looked over the island, and so thence to Newport, where he dined at Mr. James's house; and so his grace departed to the Cowes, and tooke ship and went to Portsmouth, in the year 1618, the 27th of August, being Thursday." — *Carisbrooke Parochial Muniments.*

At this time the principal gentry of the island were, Sir Robert Dillington;[*] Sir Richard Worsley; Sir Thomas Fleming; Sir Richard White, "a soldier and follower of the Earl of Southampton;" Sir John Meux; Sir John Leigh; Sir William Lisle; Sir John Richards; Sir John Oglander; Sir William Oglander; and Sir Edward Dennis; tne Chekes of Mottistone; the Bowermans of Brook; the Urrys of Thorley; the Worsleys of Gatcombe; and the Lisles of Bridlesford.—*Sir J. Oglander.*

The Earl of Southampton died in December 1625, and the government of the island passed into the hands of—

EDWARD LORD CONWAY.

This gallant gentleman was knighted by the Earl of Essex at the sacking of Cadiz in 1596, where he commanded a regiment of foot. He served under King James as one of his principal Secretaries of State, was created Baron Conway in 1625, and appointed Captain of the Isle of Wight on the 8th December in the same year. — *Dugdale.* King Charles continued him in his Secretaryship, and bestowed upon him an Irish viscountcy. As a further proof of the royal favour, he was created, in 1628, Viscount Conway of Conway; and shortly afterwards appointed Lord President of the Council.

He never resided in his government, but administered its affairs through his lieutenants, Sir Edward Dennis and Sir John Oglander.[*] Partly to this circumstance, and partly to the troubles which had already clouded the reign of the unfortunate Charles, must be attributed the declining prosperity of the island, and the decay of its gentry—bitterly bewailed by the gossipping knight whose MS. Memoirs we have so frequently quoted. "It grieved me," he exclaims, "to hear and see the poverty and complaint of our poor island, April 1629. No money stirring, little market, a small assembly of the gentlemen, less of the farmers and yeomanry. Our ordinary down for want of company; little resort to our lecture (the weekly lecture at Newport); the comely visages and wonted carriage of it clean altered." "The Isle of Wight, since my memory, is infinitely decayed;

---

* Sir John Leigh was knighted at Beaulieu by James I., August 30, 1606; Sir W. Oglander at Hampton Court, September 1606; Sir John Oglander at Royston, December 22, 1615; Sir W. Mewys at Hampton Court, June 26, 1606; Sir. J. Mewys, May 22, 1605, at Greenwich; Sir R. White at Whitehall, December 1605; Sir W. Lisle, May 14, 1606, at Whitehall; Sir R. Worsley at Whitehall, February 8, 1611; and Sir E. Dennys, February 20, 1607, at Oatlands.

* Sir John Oglander collected valuable MS. memorials of his native isle, which have never yet been published *in extenso*, but were made much use of by Sir R. Worsley, in the compilation of his heavy but valuable History. He was not only Deputy-Governor of the Isle of Wight (1624), but also of Portsmouth (1620). In 1637 he served as Sheriff of Hampshire. He married Frances, daughter of Sir George More, of Loseley, Surrey, knt.; and had several children by her.

for either it is by reason that so many attorneys have of late made this their habitation, and so by suits undone the country ; . . . . or else wanting the good bargains they were wont to levy from men-of-war, who also vended all our commodities at very high prices, and ready money was easy to be had for all things. Now peace and law hath beggared us all, so that within my memory many of the gentlemen and almost all the yeomanry are undone."—*Sir J. Oglander.*

Lord Conway died in 1631, and was succeeded by—

RICHARD LORD WESTON,

whose " wisdom and integrity" were abundantly tested in the high offices of state which he held under James and Charles.   He was created Earl of Portland in 1633, and died at Wallingford House, Westminster, March 1634.   He was followed in the government by his son,—

JEROME, EARL OF PORTLAND,

who held it, much to the satisfaction of the island gentry, until removed by the parliament, on the ground that he was "popishly affected," but in reality because his loyalty to the crown could not be misunderstood.   They further objected against him "all the acts of good fellowship, all the waste of powder, and all the waste of wine, in the drinking of healths, and other acts of jollity, which ever he had been at in his government, from the first hour of his entering upon it."—*Clarendon.*

During his captaincy an anonymous traveller, passing through the island in 1635, wrote down in plainest words his impressions of what he saw ; and the narrative is curious enough, we fancy, to justify us in now, for the first time, embalming it in type.

THE ISLE OF WIGHT IN 1635.

" From this rich merchant and sweet maritime town [Southampton] I crossed over that broad stream [Southampton Water] to Heath [Hythe], which is almost a league, with a blustering passage ; and so, by a knight's place, leaving Calshot Castle, running with a hook a mile into the sea ; and so, leaving Leap on my left, I there, with much ado, leapt my nag into the boat, and got passage to cross over that three miles' rough and untoward channel to Garnard [Gurnard Bay], and there set footing in that strong, healthful, and pleasant island of Europe. I hastened through a little forest to the chief town thereof, and to the chief inn in the town, where one of the captains of the island, with some merry Londoners, kept his quarter that night, and kept *me* sentinel—for rest I could not take more than *they* must upon their resting posture.

" The next morning I marched a short mile from this town to a spacious, strong, and defensible castle, which was built by a Saxon, but hath now a young lord to its governor [*the Lord Weston, son to the Lord of Portland, Lord Treasurer.* Sic in margine.]   It is mounted on a hill, with long, deep ditches round about the walls, whereunto I was suddenly admitted by a brave old blade (the residing Deputy-Governor thereof), over a stately large bridge, through a strongly-built gate-house—the Deputy's lodgings—and within, thus I found it :—

" In that corner next Newport, on a mounted hill, stands a round strong tower, called the keep, to which I ascended by 60 stairs, wherein hath been watching and lodging rooms.   Nothing therein now but the wall, and a deep well of water in the midst thereof.

" As I marched with my old keeper the rounds upon the walls, I viewed the large chambers [guns so named] and lodgings, the platforms, counterscarps, casemates, bulwarks, and trenches without the walls, whereupon were mounted many pieces of ordnance.   I found it well guarded with arms, though not with men ; for in the armory, which is over against the chapel, in one room, were 500 good corselets; and in another room, by the other, 700 or 800 muskets.

"By this time I was pretty well informed of the strength of this castle and her warlike munition; and so I hastened back again to the rendezvous, where I left that mad captain, and in the same place I found him, fully resolved, by laying in good store of provision in his camp, to have lain leaguer there, if his nimble-spirited wife had not come and taken up the bucklers, and fetched him home, for his leading staff failed him.

"I found this town [Newport] governed by a mayor, and twelve aldermen, and two captains; and but one church, wherein is a fair monument for a knight [Sir Edward Horsey] who had been governor of the island.

"This fertile and pleasant island, for her martial discipline, I found her most bravely and prudently guided by the government of two generous knights [Sir E. Dennis and Sir J. Oglander], lieutenants, and fourteen gentle and expert captains [see *post*], most of them all worthy knights and gentlemen, having pleasant situations in this isle; and having under their command 2000 foot soldiers, of ready exercise and well disciplined, trained men—most of them as expert in handling their arms as our artillery nurseries; which skill they attain to by taking pleasure in that honourable exercise, and training, and drilling, from their very infancy. Every captain hath his proper field-piece, which marches and guards him into the field, where they all often meet together, and pitch an equal battle of 1000 on each side, with an equal distribution of the captains—eight of each party, with the two lieutenants, who are also captains; the East against the West Mede, on St. George's Down, by the river that runs down to Cowes Castle. A brave show there is, and brave service performed, by thundering echoes from those valleys by that sweet stream. They have, be-

sides, in this island arms for 2000 more, if need should require. A safeguard for so small an island—of twenty miles in longitude, and but ten in latitude—to be so securely furnished with.

"As this precious island is well strengthened and fortified inwardly, so is she also well guarded and defended outwardly by Yarmouth Castle (*Captain Burley*), Cowes Castle (*Captain Tarry*), by the Needles, and Sandown Fort (*Captain Buck*); having no place of invasion either in or out, but such places as are safely defended: as Yarmouth against Hurst Castle (*Lieutenant Gorge*), Gurnard (*Captain Barret*) against Leap, Cowes against Calshot Castle (*Captain James*), and Ryde against Portsmouth—so as no daring approaching enemies can pass those channels, without thundering gun-shot from those commanding castles.

"I could willingly have spent some longer time in such a stately, safe, hedged-in paradise, but that it jogged me along by that sweet and delicate stream, to their new, white-built maritime town of Cowes; from whence, after I had spent a little time in viewing that strong-built castle and her ordnance, I sailed thence with a fine gale of wind, over the still and quiet waves to Southampton."[*]

THE EARL OF PEMBROKE

received the appointment of the captaincy in 1642. He immediately demanded from one Sir John Dingley, who had been Deputy-Governor, a report upon the condition of the island, and was presented with it on the 31st March, couched in sufficiently unsatisfactory terms.

In this interesting document Sir John points out that the park belonging to the Captain is three miles in circuit; that there is a common for the whole country, to put in horses or beasts without stint,

---

[*] *A Relation of a Short Survey, &c.* By a Lieutenant of the Military Company at Norwich, August 1635. *Lansdowne MSS.* 218.

which is called by the name of Park-hurst Chase; that the said chase has been grievously neglected by its keeper and ranger; that Sandham Fort, though of great consequence, is but "poorly manned;" that Cowes Castle, also, is insufficiently garrisoned, and Yarmouth in like condition; that Worsley's Sconce had been taken down by order of Lord Conway; that the train bands are much weakened and decayed, and the island nearly depopulated by reason of the lords of manors and the farmers getting together as many farms as they can; that there is a town called Newport, made by King James, a municipal town ("mare-town"), which will not now be governed like other towns, and "hinder men from buying and selling at their pleasure;" and, finally, that the clergy of the island, for the most part, are "loose and idle livers, and neglect their charge."—*Worsley*, 111–114.

The militia of the island numbered at this time about 2000 men, divided into two divisions and fourteen companies— eight in the West Medine, six in the East Medine—led by fourteen captains, and commanded by the two lieutenants of the island. Of these 2000, nearly 1100 handled arquebuses; 33 had charge of the culverins or small cannons; 263 bore corslettes; 196, pikes; 10, halberds; 297 were unarmed;[*] and 133 were officers.

The watches and wards that were kept in the island (September 20, 1638) are shown in a MS. of Sir John Oglander's:—

EAST MEDINE.—At *St. Catherine's*, a ward with two men; on the *Hatton Night-onfield*, a watch with two men .... under Captain Rice. A watch at *Lane's*, of two men, and another on *Wroxall Down* .... in Sir Edward Dennys' district. On *Ashey Down*, a ward of one man and a watch of two; and at *St. Helen's Point*, a watch of two .... under Sir J. Og-

lander. On *Knighton*, a watch of two men, and at *Ryde*, a similar watch .... under Sir R. Dillington. On *Appuldur-combe*, and at *Cripple*, near *Niton*, a watch of two men .... under Sir Henry Worsley. A similar watch at *St. George's Down* .... under Captain Cheke. A ward of one man and a watch of two men on *Bembridge Down* .... under Captain Basket. A watch of two men at *East Cowes*, at *Wootton*, and at *Fish-house* .... under Sir W. Lisle.

WEST MEDINE.—The usual watch at *Ramsey Down* and *Chale Down* .... under Mr. Meaux. On *Lardon Down* and at *Atherfield* .... under Sir John Leigh. On *Harborough Down* and on the sea-shore at *Brixton* .... under Captain Urry. On *Avington Down*, on *Gatcombe Down*, and at *Northwood* .... under Captain Harvey. On *Freshwater Down*, a ward and watch of two men each, and a watch on *Mottistone Down* .... under Captain Bowerman. At *Hamstead*, a watch of two men .... under Captain Hobson. In *Newport*, two companies, which patrolled the town.

If the reader will take his map, and mark each of these stations with some distinguishing sign, he will, at a glance, perceive how skilfully they were distributed in reference to the general defence of the island.

Though much dissatisfaction, when the Earl of Portland was removed from the captaincy, was expressed by the knights and gentlemen who had served under him, it could scarcely have arisen from any feeling of wounded loyalty. On the contrary, from the very outset of the great civil war, the inhabitants of the Wight sided with the parliament, and so secured an immunity from the tumults and distractions which fell with such heaviness upon other parts of England. They were, indeed, so vehement in their zeal for the parliamentarian party, that they could not suffer the Countess of Portland to abide peaceably in the castle, where she had taken refuge with her five

---

[*] These men were soon afterwards armed.

children and her husband's brother and sister, under the protection of Colonel Brett, the recently appointed custodian of Carisbrooke. The Mayor of Newport, Moses Read, at the head of the Newport train bands and 400 naval auxiliaries supplied by the men-of-war in the Solent, and inspired by Harby, a stout Puritan and minister of Newport, besieged the castle, wherein Colonel Brett had but 20 men, and provisions for 3 days. The brave countess, however, made her appearance on the ramparts with a lighted match in her hand, and declared that she herself would fire the first cannon, and that the garrison would hold out to the last extremity, unless they were granted easy and honourable terms of surrender. A pacification was soon arranged, when, as we may reasonably conclude, neither party was very much in earnest. Colonel Brett, his comrades, and their attendants, were permitted to go where they would, except to Portsmouth, then held for the king by dissolute Goring; and after a day or two's delay, the countess and her family were removed from the island.

The other fortresses, in like manner, were seized for the parliament, and the Earl of Pembroke, on his arrival at Cowes, was received with a cordial welcome by the leading inhabitants, who proffered him, in behalf of the good cause, their heartiest services.

The *Journals of the House of Commons* present numerous indications of the watchfulness exercised by the parliament in reference to the safety of the Isle of Wight; and though it is not our province to enter fully into these details, it may be permitted us to place a few significant passages before our readers in illustration of the remarkable contrasts existing between the present and the past.

We read on the 13th of August 1642 :—

"ORDERED, that it be recommended to the Earl of Warwick to furnish the town of Newport in the Isle of Wight with thirty barrels of powder, with all convenient speed, to be disposed of as the Mayor of Newport, Mr. Bunckley, Mr. Thomas Boreman, and Mr. Robert Urry of Freshwater, shall think fit, for the safeguard of that place and island.

"And it is further Ordered, That Mr. Venn and Mr. Vassall do write a letter of thanks to the Mayor of Newport, and those that joined with him in the certificate to the House of the state of that town, for their care of the safety of that place, and respects to this House; and to assure them that this House hath, in some measure, already taken care, and will take further care, in providing for the safety of that island."

We read on the 18th of February, 1645 :—

"ORDERED, that there be forthwith provided and furnished out of the public stores, for the service of the Isle of Wight, forty barrels of powder, one ton of match, three hundred culverin shot, one thousand demi-culverin shot, one thousand Saker shot, and two tons of lead: And the Lieutenant of the Ordnance is required to take notice thereof, and to furnish these provisions accordingly."

The Earl of Pembroke was withdrawn from the captaincy in 1647, and Colonel ROBERT HAMMOND, a soldier of good repute, appointed (6th September 1647). The colonel was a nephew of Dr. Henry Hammond, one of the king's chaplains, but he owed his rise to Cromwell's favour, and was married to Hampden's daughter. At the early age of twenty-two he had entered the army, and fought against the Royalists. His sympathies, therefore, were naturally with the parliamentarian leaders, and justified the confidence of those who intrusted to him so important a command.

SECTION VIII.—CHARLES I. IN THE ISLE OF WIGHT.

ARRIVES IN THE ISLAND.

Whilst pent up in Hampton Court, and surrounded by the soldiers of the parliament, Charles I. could not but feel that he was in reality a closely-watched and suspected prisoner. He felt, too, that the great Roundhead leaders, however sincere in their desire, would soon be without the power, to assist him; that they themselves were, in fact, the servants of their army. He had reason, perhaps, to dread the secret dagger. At all events, he was on the brink of an imminent peril; and he might justly conclude that his escape would leave the Puritan chiefs at greater liberty to carry out their professed designs of serving him, while placing himself in a position to act with fuller confidence and freer energy.

So, on the evening of the 11th of November 1647, attended by Legge, the groom of the chamber, he effected his escape from the palace, and being joined by Berkeley and Ashburnham, crossed the Thames at Thames Ditton, and rode with fiery speed through the dark and cloudy night to Titchfield House, a fair seat of the Earl of Southampton. The Dowager Countess welcomed him gladly, and spread before him the refreshment he needed.

He now deliberated with his attendants whither he should next proceed, and great confidence being professed by Ashburnham (a man apparently of very sanguine temperament) in the good intentions of Colonel Hammond, it was resolved that Ashburnham and Berkeley should repair to the island, and sound the colonel cautiously upon his feelings and sympathies. They bore a complimentary message from his sovereign; and were required to insist upon a pledge, that if the king placed himself under his protection, he would not surrender him to the army or the parliament, but provide him with an opportunity of effecting his escape. And if he refused that undertaking, they were not to disclose the secret of the king's present concealment.

They started from Titchfield on a windy and violent morning; they reached Lymington, but could not make the passage of the Solent on account of the stormy weather, and were detained there the whole day. They arrived at Carisbrooke on the following morning, but Colonel Hammond had set out for Newport on matters of importance, and they were forced to follow him thither. When, at length, they found themselves in the presence of the governor, and explained their errand, he expressed considerable apprehension, but finally determined upon repairing with them to the king's retreat. Ashburnham and Berkeley weakly consented to this proposal, and by so doing, betrayed their unfortunate sovereign into the hands of the very men he had endeavoured to avoid. There is no room, however, to suppose—in fact, their whole future conduct negatives the suspicion—that they were actuated by any traitorous motives. They confided too implicitly, not in Hammond's honour, which they had no reason to doubt, but in his power to secure the king's person for any length of time from the machinations of his bitterest enemies.

Colonel Hammond's letter to the Speaker of the House of Peers sets forth the circumstances under which King Charles entered the island :—

"MY LORD,—I hold it my duty to give your lordship an account of the king's unexpected coming into this island, and of the manner of it, which was thus,—

"This morning, as I was on the way passing from Carisbrooke Castle to Newport, Mr. Ashburnham and Sir John Berkeley overtook me: and, after a short discourse, told me that the king was near, and that he would be with me that night; that he was come from Hampton Court upon information that there were some intended to destroy his person, and that he could not with safety continue any longer there; and that, finding his case thus, chose rather to put himself in my hand, being a member of the army; whom, he saith, he would not have left, could he have had security to his person, than to go to any other place. Being herewith exceedingly surprised at present, I knew not what course to take; but upon serious consideration, weighed the great concernment that the person of the king is of, in this junction of affairs, to the settlement of the peace of the kingdom, I resolved it my duty to the king, to the parliament, and kingdom, to use the utmost of my endeavours to preserve his person from any such horrid attempt, and to bring him to a place of safety; where he may also be in a capacity of answering the expectation of parliament and kingdom, in agreeing to such things as may extend to the settlement of those great divisions and distractions abounding in every corner thereof. Hereupon I went immediately with them over the water, taking Captain Basket, the captain of Cowes Castle, with me, and found the king near the water side; and, finding myself no way able to secure him there, I chose, he desiring it, to bring him over into this island, where he now is.

"My lord, my endeavours, as for my life, shall be to preserve and secure his person. And I humbly desire I may receive the pleasure of the parliament in this great and weighty matter; and that the Lord will direct your counsels to his glory and the kingdom's good and peace, shall be my prayer; and my endeavour shall be ever to express myself in all things in my power.—My lord, your lordship's and the kingdom's most humble and faithful servant,   ROBERT HAMMOND.*

"Cowes, Nov. 13, 1647."

The doomed king, with Hammond, Captain Basket, Legge, Berkeley, and Ashburnham in attendance, landed in the island on the 22d day of November,

* The Houses duly thanked Colonel Hammond, and issued instructions for his guidance, besides voting £5000 for "His Majesty's present necessities and accommodation,"—£10 daily for his table, and a provision yearly of £5000,—and liberally rewarding the Governor on account of his increased responsibilities with a gratuity of £1000, and an annuity of £500 for himself and his heirs.

and, passing the night in a small and obscure ale-house, made their way towards Carisbrooke on the following day, being Sunday. He was received with respect by all, with scarcely-concealed affection by a loyal few. "A gentlewoman,* as he passed through Newport, presented him with a damask rose which grew in her garden at this cold season of the year, and prayed for him, which his Majesty heartily thanked her for."—Herbert. And so the king passed onwards into the Castle of Carisbrooke.

PRECAUTIONS.

Meanwhile the Parliament, who had received, as we have seen, due information from Colonel Hammond A. D. of these remarkable proceedings, 1647. had issued, on the 16th of November, instructions for his guidance. They ran as follows:—

"RESOLVED by the Lords and Commons in Parliament assembled.

"1. That the securest place during the time the king shall think fit to continue him in the Isle of Wight be Carisbrooke Castle.

"2. That noe person who hath bin in armes, or assisted in this unnatural war against the parliament, be permitted to come or remain in the said isle during the king's residence there, unless they be inhabitants of the isle, and have compounded with the parliament.

"3. That no person who hath bin in armes, or assisted, &c., shall be permitted to come into the king's presence, or into any fort or castle in the said isle, during the king's residence there, although he be an inhabitant and hath compounded with the parliament.

"4. That no stranger, or person of a foreign nation, shall be permitted to come into the king's presence, without the directions of both houses, except such as have warrant from the parliament of Scotland, or from the committee of that parliament thereunto authorized, and are not disabled by the propositions agreed on by both kingdomes.

"5. That a sufficient guard be appointed by Colonel Robert Hammond, governor of the said isle, for security of the king's person from any violence, and preventing his depart-

* It is said her name was Frances Prattle. —Hillier.

ing the said isle without the direction of both houses."—*Journals, H. of Commons.*

Colonel Hammond's position had thus become peculiarly difficult. If he neglected his trust, he could expect but little from the tender mercies of the Roundhead chiefs; if he performed it faithfully, though mildly—if he "did his spiriting" ever so gently—he could not but incur the hatred of the Royalist party. He appears to have adopted that "golden mean" the Roman poet unwisely commends, and with the scanty success he might reasonably have expected. The Royalist news, letters, and pamphlets of the period load him with the foulest abuse; and later writers, taking up the unjust prejudices conceived in a time of violent excitement, have shown his memory but little indulgence. Nevertheless Sir Thomas Herbert, the most chivalrous of the king's adherents, who had opportunities of observing him closely, speaks of him in honourable terms, and confesses that the Roundheads suspected him of being "too much of a courtier." And Tailor, "the water-poet," a zealous Royalist, warmly vindicates him from the aspersions of his enemies. He says that he will speak of him without flattery, and, he continues, "The plaine truth is, that myself, with many others, did hate him so much, that he was very seldom or never prayed for. The reasons and motives which possest most men with this mistaking and misapplied inveterate malice, was upon the flying lying reports that the governour had behaved himself most coarsely, rigid, and barbarously unrespective to his Majesty. The false weekly pamphlets and pamphleteers (being inspired by their father, the devil), were not ashamed to publish in print that the governour had proceeded so far in incivility, as to immure, or wall his Majesty in a small, close roome, under many bolts, bars, grates, locks, and keys, and debarred him the comforts of his soule, and of the society of men; and

further, it was often printed (by severall lying villaines) that the said Governour Hammond did strike the king on the face, and gave him a black eye. These reports being invented by the devil's imps (the firebrands of contention), printed and published by needy, greedy knaves and varlets, and believed by too many fooles and foolish Gotehamists (amongst which number I, with much simplicity, was one); and as by oath and duty I am bound to save, love, and honour my soveraigne lord and master, so (on the contrary) myselfe, with all true and loyall subjects, had no cause to be well affected to any man that should dare to affront his Majesty with such transcendent base indignities.

"But to give the world satisfaction of the truth, it is certaine that all these aspersions and rumours against the governour are most odious, scandalous, and malicious lies; for, according to the trust reposed in him, he hath always carried himselfe with such deportment and humblenesse of dutifull service to his Majesty, that he hath gained much love and favour from his soveraigne, and such good regard from all knowing men, as belongs to a gentleman of his place and quality."—*Journal of the Brit. Archæol. Association,* Dec. 1853.

Considerable liberty was allowed to the king and his attendants for the first few weeks of his detention. He was permitted to pursue the chase in the green arcades of Parkhurst, to receive the visits of the gentry of the island, to enjoy the services of his most devoted adherents, and the ministrations of his chaplains, Drs. Sheldon and Hammond. The respect, and something of the etiquette of a court were maintained about his person. Colonel Hammond's mother, a lady of good family, superintended his household arrangements, and the king's own furniture was brought from his palaces, to give an air of splendour to the bare, bleak chambers of the castle.— *Herbert, Clarendon, and others.*

a
i
l
c
s
c
h
A
F
t
tl
te
is
ha
de
ar
th
m
th
m
ur
we
(b
de
pr
so
r

CARISBROOKE CASTLE

DARK TIMES.

While the king was thus sheltered within the walls of Carisbrooke, and his partizans were everywhere scheming and designing his speedy restoration to power, the triumphant parliament—or rather, that imperious majority which controlled its proceedings—was busied in endeavouring to bring to some conclusion the troubles of the nation, and finally, on the 14th December, passed four resolutions to which, as to an ultimatum, they required the assent of the king as a preliminary to entering upon a personal treaty with him.—*Lingard*, x. c. 4, and *Journals*, vol. ix. These resolutions, in effect, placed the royal prerogative in the hands of the Parliament, vesting in it the command of the army for twenty years; limiting the creation of peers; empowering the Houses to adjourn from place to place as they might deem it best; and insisting upon the king's acknowledgment of the justice of their cause. Buoyed up by the promises of his supporters, and by a treaty secretly agreed upon with the Scotch commissioners, the king warmly protested that "neither the desire of being freed from that tedious and irksome condition of life which he had so long suffered, nor the apprehension of anything that might befall him, should ever prevail with him to consent to any one Act till the conditions of the whole peace should be concluded."—*Clarendon*.

His adherents, meanwhile, had been concerting a plan of escape, and a ship, provided by the queen, had for some time been hovering off the coast. The evening of the day on which he forwarded to the parliament his peremptory refusal of their ultimatum, was appointed for the enterprise; but Hammond obtained some inkling of it, and proceeded to enforce restrictions which he had hitherto avoided. His suspicions were further aroused by a singular *émeute* which took place in Newport itself.

There lived in that busy borough at this unquiet time one Captain Burley, who had served in the royal army, and afterwards had holden a military command in the island. As if seized by a sudden frenzy, or acting on some preconcerted plot whose particulars were never known, he caused a drum to be beaten, and drawing together a small gathering of curious and adventurous citizens, declared himself their leader, and proposed to attempt the rescue of the royal captive. But Berkeley and Ashburnham, apprehending no good consequences to the king, made haste to dismiss to their homes the noisy crowd. A company of soldiers was drawn out from Carisbrooke, Burley taken prisoner, and the riot abruptly terminated. A commission of Oyer and Terminer was instantly appointed by the Parliament to sit at Winchester, under Chief Baron Wilde (January 22, 1648). The result may easily be guessed. Burley was found guilty of high treason, and on the 3d of February expiated his loyalty by a terrible death. He was hung, drawn, and quartered; but suffered with invincible courage, exclaiming to the last, "Fear God, and honour the king!"

To take measures * for the monarch's safe custody was now appointed a special commission, known—from the place of their meetings—as the *Derby House Committee*. It included seven peers,—the Earls of Kent, Manchester, Northumberland, and Warwick, and the Lords Roberts, Say, and Sele, and Wharton; and thirteen commoners,—Sir William Armine, Sir John Evelyn, Sir Gilbert Gerrard, Sir Arthur Haselrig, and Sir Harry Vane; the Lieutenant-General Cromwell, and Pierpoint, Harry Vane the younger, Fiennes, Brown,

---

* Sir William Constable, Lieutenant-Colonel Goffe, and Lieutenant-Colonel Salmon, were sent from the army to the Isle of Wight. Reinforcements of troops were poured in; the ports garrisoned and victualled; and Vice-Admiral Rainsborough's fleet ordered to cruise off the island.

Crew, H. John, and Wallop. They communicated direct with Hammond, the correspondence being conducted in cipher; and such was the subtlety of their measures, such the skill of their agents, that they learned every movement of the royalists, and often apprised Hammond of plots hatched in his very neighbourhood, to which he himself could gain no clue.

The appointment of this committee immediately affected the conditions of the king's imprisonment, and compelled Hammond to watch his captive with a closer vigilance.

Four conservators were appointed,—Herbert, Mildmay, Captain Titus, and Preston, who alternately, two at a time, guarded the doors of the royal apartments. When the king went abroad for a walk he was always accompanied by Colonel Hammond; and his exercise was strictly confined within the limits of the castle walls. Most of his attendants were dismissed, and—what the king felt sorely—his chaplains were ordered to leave the island (February 1648).

Nevertheless, the governor did what he could to lessen the discomfort of this close confinement. He converted the barbican, or place of arms, of the castle "into a bowling green, scarce to be equalled, and at one side built a pretty summer house for retirement."—*Herbert.* His own manner was marked by a courteous deference, and he never intruded upon the monarch's privacy.

King Charles's daily life,[*] during this period, if monotonous, was not altogether an unpleasing one, and is curiously illustrative of his peculiar character.

He rose betimes, prayed devoutly and read the Scriptures, then breakfasted, and afterwards took exercise "within the works, a place sufficiently large and convenient for the king's walking, and having good air, and a delightful prospect both to the sea and land." When he had dined—and during his dinner, always a temperate one, he entered into familiar converse with those who waited on him—he withdrew to his private chamber, and read or wrote until the evening meal. Then he took further exercise, and so, at an early hour, retired to rest.

His chief favourites among his books have been carefully recorded. "The Sacred Scriptures he most delighted in; read often in Bishop Andrews's Sermons; Hooker's Ecclesiastical Polity; Dr. Hammond's Works; Villalpandus upon Ezekiel, &c.; Sands's Paraphrase upon King David's Psalms; Herbert's Divine Poems; and also Godfrey of Bulloigne, writ in Italian by Torquato Tasso, and done into English heroic verse by Mr. Fairfax, a poem his majesty much commended, as he did also Ariosto, by Sir John Harrington, a facetious poet, much esteemed of by Prince Henry his master; Spenser's Fairie Queen, and the like, for alleviating his spirits after serious studies." He likewise amused himself also in composition; wrote some dreary verses,—the *Suspiria Regalia,* or *Royal Sighs,* and *Majesty in Misery*; and translated from the Latin Dr. Sanderson's book, *De Juramentis.* Of his little library the faithful Herbert was the custodian.

The king was fond of writing Latin and Greek mottoes in his books, and especially affected the significant epigraph, *Dum spiro, spero*—"While I breathe, I hope;" and in one he wrote the following distich:—

"Rebus in adversis facile est contemnere vitam;
Fortiter ille facit qui miser esse potest."[*]

---

[*] "His majesty takes usually every morning a walk about the castle wall, and the like in the afternoon, if fair; much time spent every day in private; he speaks most to us at dinner. . . . . His majesty is as merry as formerly; all quiet and fair between his majesty and Colonel Hammond."—*Rushworth's Collections,* iv. 2.

[*] It is an easy matter to speak slightingly of life when we are in sore distress; but the brave man is he who can calmly endure to be wretched.

His scholarship was, indeed, considerable; and he was well acquainted with Latin, Greek, French, Spanish, and Italian.—*Herbert.*

He told Sir Philip Warwick that his best companion was "an old, little, crumpling man," who "for three months together made my fire;" but this statement was either exaggerated, or misunderstood by Sir Philip, for Sir Thomas Herbert continued in close attendance upon him.—*Godwin.* From the time that he was deprived of his usual retinue, "he would never suffer his hair to be cut, nor cared he to have any new cloaths; so that his aspect and appearance was very different from what it had used to be; otherwise, his health was good, and he was much more cheerful in his discourses towards all men than could have been imagined after such a mortification of all kinds. He was not at all dejected in his spirits, but carried himself with the same majesty he had used to do. His hair was all grey, which, making all others very sad, made it thought that he had sorrow in his countenance, which appeared only by that shadow."—*Clarendon.*

THE FIRST ATTEMPT AT ESCAPE.

Such was the quiet tenor of the royal prisoner's daily life; but as the political complications of the kingdom rapidly increased in difficulty, and hourly became more ominous, his adherents bent all their energies to the perfection of a plan of escape.

Amongst the household was a gallant and ingenious man named Henry Firebrace,[*] who, having resolved upon opening a communication between the king and his friends in the island, contrived to secure the confidence of Captain

Titus, one of the conservators or wardens already named, who was a loyal servant of the king's at heart. Charles was wont to retire "into his bed-chamber as soon as he had supped, shutting the door to him. I offered my service," says Firebrace,[*] " to one of the conservators (Captain Titus) to wait at the door opening into the back stairs whilst he went to supper—I pretending not to sup—which he accepted of; by which means I had freedom of speaking with his majesty." When Firebrace had any letters to deliver, they were placed in a certain concealment in the royal chamber, where, in due time, the king's answer was also deposited. In the wainscot, which was covered by thick hangings, an aperture was made, so that the king might privately communicate with his attendants, and on the approach of any suspicious person, instantly let fall the hangings.

The plan, at length determined upon, seemed feasible enough, and to present every prospect of a successful issue.

One of the attendants placed about the king, by order of the parliament, was a *Mr. Richard* March 20, *Osburne,* a "gentleman of an 1648. ancient family, and singular good parts," but of lax morals, having been educated by Lord Wharton, widely known as a nobleman of dissolute life. This Osburne had been converted into a zealous adherent of King Charles by the influence of the monarch's stately presence and fascinating manner. There were also *Mr. Edward Worsley* of Gatcombe, a gentleman of good descent, and *Mr. John Newland* of Newport, eager with life and purse to serve their king. With *Captain Titus* and *Mr. Henry Firebrace,* they formed the adventurous design so unfortunately frustrated.

The king, at a certain signal made by Firebrace (to toss a stone against his

---

* He was known to the king, and privately enjoined by him to repair to the island. To effect this, he applied to the speaker and to other commissioners for permission to wait upon the king as page of the bed-chamber. His prayer was readily granted.

* *Letter to Sir George Lane.* Published at Whitehall, 1675.

bed-room window), was to force himself through the window, and let himself down by a stout cord. [Firebrace had much misdoubted that the king would be able to make his way through so narrow an opening; but Charles declared that where his head would pass, surely his body would follow.] Firebrace, it was agreed, should then receive him, and conduct him across the court, where no sentinel was stationed, to the great wall. This the king would descend by means of a thick rope, with a stick fastened to it for a seat, and climbing the counterscarp, which was very low, would find a horse ready saddled, boots and pistols, with Osburne and Worsley, well mounted, to escort him. Riding across the island in the deep night shadows, they would speedily gain the sea side, and join Mr. Newland, who held in readiness a properly furnished boat. The monarch's safety was then ensured.

The night came; the king dismissed his attendants. Worsley and Osburne stealthily led their horses into the neighbourhood of the castle, and John Newland, on the bleak sea-shore, eagerly awaited his sovereign's coming. Firebrace took up his station beneath the memorable window, and gave the appointed signal. Then "his Majesty," says Firebrace, "put himself forward, but, too late, found himself mistaken, he sticking fast between his breast and shoulders, and not able to get backward or forward, but that, at the instant before he endeavoured to come out, he mistrusted and tied a piece of his cord to a bar of the window within, by means whereof he forced himself back. Whilst he stuck, I heard him groan, but could not come to help him, which (you may imagine) was no small affliction to me. So soon as he was in again, to let me see (as I had to my grief heard) the design was broken, he set a candle in the window. If this unfortunate impediment had not happened, his majesty had certainly then made a good escape."

Firebrace warned his confederates of the failure of their scheme, by flinging stones from the high wall at the place where the king should have descended. They took the alarm, and got away quietly and without discovery.

Some hints of the intended escape, however, reached the Derby House Committee, and Cromwell wrote to Hammond in reference to it, expressly naming Firebrace "as the gentleman who led the way," and cautioning the governor against Captain Titus, Dowcett, and others of the king's household. Firebrace was shortly afterwards dismissed, though not before he had succeeded in arranging a mode of communication between the king and his friends, and rendering some help towards a future attempt at escape. He wrote to a Mrs. Whorwood "a tall, well-fashioned, and well-languaged gentlewoman," a staunch loyalist, residing in London, and desired her to forward some files and aquafortis to sever the window-bars. She immediately betook herself to the famous astrologer, Lilly, who, in his turn, had recourse to one George Farmer, a locksmith in Bow Lane. Of these fantastic devices the Derby House Committee obtained information, and warned Hammond to be upon his guard. The aquafortis, therefore, never reached the king, being "upset on the road," but a hacker, intended to convert into saws two knives which the king had concealed, in spite of all his jailer's precaution, safely reached him.[*]

Charles was now removed from the apartments he had occupied since his entrance into the castle, to the chief officer's "in a building on the left side of the first court." As the window contained but one bar, a second was in-

---

* In Mr. Hillier's "Narrative of the Detention of Charles I." will be found by the curious reader a very full account of these matters, with some interesting letters and novel details.

serted by Hammond's orders, having scarcely five inches between each bar, and the stone mullions. Beneath it was thrown up a platform of earth, where a sentinel was stationed, and ordnance was so placed as to command the various approaches.

Nevertheless, the king, under certain restrictions, was still permitted to receive those who waited upon him. He often discoursed with a Mr. Troughton, chaplain to the governor, and an anti-episcopalian, a young man of good parts, "who," says Herbert, "could argue pretty well." On one occasion, whilst disputing with him warmly, Charles suddenly took a sword from a lieutenant of foot who was in waiting, and drew it, much to the alarm of the young debater; but a gentleman present, better interpreting the monarch's intention, bent his knee, received the honour of knighthood, and rose "Sir John Duncomb." The king told him he had then no better method of acknowledging his services.

He sometimes received books proffered to him by their authors. Thus, one Mr. Sedgwick posted down from London to present him with his "Leaves of the Tree of Life." The king accepted it for perusal, read it, and returned it, ironically remarking, "that, by what he had read in that book, he believed the composer stood in some need of sleep."

THE SECOND ATTEMPT AT ESCAPE.

The project next designed for the king's release was simple in its details.

May 1648. The king, with a file or some aquafortis, was to sever the iron window-bars, let himself down, and crossing the bowling-green, descend the counterscarp, mount a horse ready saddled, and accompanied by Osburne and Worsley, ride across the island to the sea-shore, then into Newland's boat, and so to the coast of Hampshire. There he would find horses in readiness to convey him to Sir Edward Alford's seat, near Arundel in Sussex, whence, at a fitting opportunity, he might proceed to Queensborough, and take ship for Holland.

But of this well-devised scheme Rolfe, Hammond's chief officer, "a fellow of low extraction and very ordinary parts," a fierce republican, and a brutal soldier, obtained information, so that when, on the evening of Sunday, May the 20th, the king made the attempt, he found, on coming through the window, more persons in waiting than he had been led to expect, and apprehending danger, closed the windows, and tranquilly retired to his rest. Rolfe had stationed, at a suitable spot, a soldier in whom he could trust, with orders, it is asserted by some authorities, to fire at the king if he got through the window; others armed with pistols, stood in convenient proximity. Osburne and Worsley, taking the alarm, rode off, escaping uninjured the fire of the musketeers placed in readiness to intercept them;[*] but on reaching Newland's boat, the master refused to take them on board because they were unaccompanied by the king, so leaving their horses on the shore, they concealed themselves in the woods of Gatcombe for several days, finding means in the night, by the assistance of a kinsman of Mr. Worsley's, to obtain provisions, and at length to leave the island. They effected their escape to London, where Firebrace contrived to conceal them.

Osburne immediately addressed a letter to Lord Wharton declaring his conviction that Rolfe had designed to murder the king, and repeating certain conversations to that effect, which Rolfe had held, when he believed him to be in the interest of the parliament. Lord Wharton treated the letter with silent indifference, whereupon Osburne laid his

---

[*] It is said that one of the sentinels was afterwards fired at and killed, by whom was never discovered.—*Hillier's King Charles in the Isle of Wight.*

complaint before parliament, and the Peers received it in so serious a spirit as to desire the House of Commons to join with them in the necessary investigation.

Abraham Dowcett, whose fidelity to the parliament had previously been suspected, and who had assisted in the project of escape, was examined in support of Osburne's statement before the bar of the House of Peers; and, being "imperfect in the English language," was permitted to put in the following written declaration (3d July, 1648):—

"1. I am ready to make oath that Mr. Richard Osburne told me the king's person was in great danger, and that the said Rolfe had a design on foot for the conveying his majesty's person to some place of secrecy, where *onely three* should go with him, and where they might dispose of his person as they should think fit; which information from Mr. Osburne, and the assurance I had of his majesty's intentions forthwith to come to his parliament, was the cause of my engagement in this business.

"2. I am ready likewise to depose that the said Rolfe came to me (when I was a prisoner in the castle), and, in a jeering manner, asked me why the king came not doune according to his appointment; and then, with great indignation and fury, said he waited almost three hours under the new platform, with a good pistol ready charged, to receive if he had come."

To which Major Rolfe put in a counter-statement, which we abridge :—

"MY LORDS,—Knowing myself (I speak in the presence of that God who searcheth all hearts) to be perfectly clear and innocent of that foul and horrid crime charged upon me—that I abhor the very thought of it; earnestly desiring an opportunity of appearing for vindication of my innocency, or whatever else malice in wicked men can lay against me; resting fully assured that, whatsoever award I shall find at the hands of men, I shall enjoy the happiness of an upright and peaceable conscience with the same God in whose presence I stand.

"EDWARD [EDMUND ?] ROLFE."

The charge brought against him by Osburne and Dowcett is improbable enough, or, at all events, not substantiated by any evidence we know of. Is it to be supposed he would indulge in such dangerous confidences with men whose attachment to the king had so long been suspected? Nor, at that time, would the king's death have been an event by which Rolfe's party could have profited. His guilt, however, was very generally credited by the Royalists, and provided the news-writers and pamphleteers of the day with a fertile and inexhaustible subject. Thus a rhymster exclaims—

"That he [the king] hath 'scaped the cursed plot,
  Thanks, Osburn, unto thee !"
      Mercurius Bellicus, 11th July, 1648.

Another—

"Now if the people do proceed to sing,
  God curse the parliament and bless the king;
If they continue their unpleasant notes—
Give us our prince or els we'll cut your throats;
Then there may hap a treaty, Rolf may die,
Else Osburn's trust for his discovery."
      Mercurius Psittacus, 10th July.

A third relates an incident of the king's captivity in the most exaggerated form—

"And were it but onely for abusing their soveraigne Lord the king in so vile and transcendant manner, they [the Puritan chiefs] could not but full expect the strictest vengeance, while, contrary to their oathes, their frequent solemn protestations, their publishing to the world in print that they intended nothing but his preservation, with the supportance and backing him in all his just privileges, they have shut him up in prison, put so strict a guard upon him that he enjoyeth not the liberty of the meanest of his subjects; have accused him for poisoning his father, thereby endeavouring as much as in them lay not onely to render him odious in the eyes of his subjects, but also to take away his life; have limited his meales, so that the meanest gentleman is served with more varieties; and, which is worst of all, have made Hammond, the worst of villaines, his jailor, whom they countenance—yea, authorize—to revile him on all occasions to his face; which hell-hound, the other day, upon a pretended order from them, in the dead of night, came and knockt at his majestie's doore; and when the king, all amazed, demanded who was there, he told him it was he, and he must come in. His majestie desired him to put off the business till the morrow; but he replied he neither could nor would, and that if he opened not the doore he would break it open. Whereupon the meek prince presently arose, and easting his cloak about him, admitted him. Being in, he told him he had an order from the Houses to search his cabinet for letters; whereupon his majestie, opening his cabinet, took thence two letters, and left him to view the rest, which the traytor perceiving, demanded them also. The king told him he should not have them, and, with that word, threw them into the fire; when Hammond endeavouring to gain them, the king tripe up his heeles, and laid him on the fire also. Whereupon the villaine bauld out for aide, when presently came in a ruffian, and laid hands on the king in such a rude manner as he would have strangled him, and, striving with him, pusht his face upon the hilt of Hammond's sword, whereby it was extremely bruised; and, attempting him further, hit him also against the pummel of a chaire, whereby his majestie's eye is black and blew; but maugre the utmost of the two devils, the letters were burnt, and Hammond, rising up, threatened his majestie in very approbrious language, and so departed at that present."— *Declaration from the Isle of Wight*, 1648.

Another example must content us—

"They have any time this six months frequently solicited Hammond (a mercenary slave, a fellow whose litterature lies in his heeles, and whose nature is so flexible that with small allurement he may be woo'd to act any kind of villanie), his majestie's demoniacall jaylor, to convey his majestie's person out of the Isle of Wight to some more obscure place (perhaps to immure him in some hollow cave cut out of from the intrailis of the earth), and there to dispatch him by poyson, to depresse him beneath a feather-bed, or as hell should prompt his executioner."— *Mercurius Bellicus*, 5th July.

Rolfe was tried at Winchester on the 28th of August, acquitted, and shortly afterwards discharged from custody, when the Commons ordered him, as a recompense for his imprisonment, a gift of £150. He returned to the Isle of Wight, and resumed his position at Carisbrooke Castle.

THE TREATY OF NEWPORT.

" What though the faction are agreed
The kingdom still to cheat ?
Doe what they can, it is decreed
The king shall come and treat."
Mercurius Pragmaticus.

On the 3d of August it was resolved by the two Houses of the Legislature, that a personal treaty should be entered into with the king, in the hope of securing a settlement for the distractions of the realm ; and after much debate and conference with the royal prisoner, it was agreed that the negotiation should be conducted at Newport, the chief town of the Isle of Wight.

Fifteen commissioners were appointed to transact this important matter : *five lords* —the Earls of Middlesex, Northumberland, Pembroke, and Salisbury, and Lord Say and Sele ; *ten commoners*—Thomas Lord Weuman, Sir Harbottle Grimston, Sir John Potts, Sir Harry Vane, Samuel Brown, John Bulkley (or Buckley), John Crew, Denzil Holles, William Pierrepoint, and John Glynn, the Recorder of London. It was estimated that £10,000 would defray the expenses. £3000 were allowed the commissioners towards their outlay, and Messrs. Marshall and Rye were appointed chaplains. The restrictions upon the king's personal liberty were to a great extent removed ; horses were provided for his pleasure, and a certain number of lords, prelates, clergy, and gentlemen, reputed for their loyalty, were permitted to repair to the Isle of Wight and attend upon him. Amongst these attached adherents were the Duke of Richmond, the Marquis of Hertford, the Earls of Lindsey and Southampton, who were named gentlemen of the Bedchamber ; the Bishops of London and Salisbury, the Dean of Canterbury, Drs. Sanderson and Heywood, his chaplains ; Nicholas Oudart, Charles Whitaker, Sir Edward Walker, and Sir Philip Warwick, his secretaries ; Henry Firebrace, clerk of the kitchen, and Anthony Mildmay, his carver. Drs. Brian Duppa and Juxon were also in attendance.—*Oudart's Diary.*

The royal household was accommodated in Mr. Matthew Hopkins' house, near the *Grammar School*, at Newport ; the *Bull* (now the *Bugle*) Inn was placed at the disposal of the parliamentary commissioners; and the conferences were held in the *Town Hall*.

The king sat upon a raised canopy under a dais, attended by his lords, chaplains, and secretaries. The commissioners were seated on each side of a long table, at a convenient distance from him. When he sought to consult with his attendants, or to refresh himself, he retired to the adjoining chamber. The negotiations were conducted with much gravity, the king displaying so vigorous an intellect and so keen an apprehension as to astonish his foes and delight his friends. Even Sir Harry Vane pronounced him "a person of great abilities." "The Earl of Salisbury," says Clarendon, "thought him ' wonderfully improved of late.'"

This important conference, on which the eyes of all parties in the nation were fixed with intensest eagerness, was protracted for three months. A minute report of each day's transactions is preserved in Oudart's Diary (vide *Peck's Desiderata Curiosa*, b. ix.); but with most of its details we must not here concern ourselves. They relate to the history of the Wight, only so far as that history is involved in the history of England.

We learn from this Diary, however, and from Herbert's Memoirs, in what manner the monarch passed his days at Newport. He rose early; performed at some length, as he was wont, his religious duties; breakfasted, and devoted the morning to discussions with the commissioners. Then he gave audience to the island gentry, to his friends, to poor invalids afflicted with *the king's evil*, and desirous of receiving his healing touch. (Seven of these cases are recorded by Tailor, the water poet.) Having dined, he conversed with his chaplain, and the bishops in attendance, upon national affairs, or the progress of the treaty. After supper he withdrew to his own apartment, to record the events of the day and dictate letters to the Prince of Wales.[*]

On Sunday, one of his chaplains, or some reverend prelate, performed divine service in the chamber in the Grammar School, now occupied as the school-room, and he listened with that devoutness which always characterized his religious exercises. Oudart furnishes us with the names of the preachers, and notes of their discourses :—

Sunday, the 8th October,	Dr. T. Turner,	*Text*, John v. 14.
„ 15th „	Dr. Heywood.	
Wednesday, the 25th October, Fast Day, }	Dr. R. Baylie,	„ Psalm xlii. 5, 6.
Sunday, the 29th October,	Dr. T. Turner,	„ Matt. xi. 28.
„ the 5th November,	Dr. Heywood,	„ Psalm lxviii. 1.
„ the 12th „	Dr. Jos. Gulson.	
„ the 19th „, The King's Birthday }	Archbishop of Armagh,	„ Gen. xlix. 3.
Sunday, the 26th November,	Dr. Sanderson,	„ Heb. xiv.

[*] A curious anecdote is recorded in "Rushworth's Collections," which may be quoted in illustration of the feeling prevalent in the town itself: "His majesty last night at supper, the Bishop of London waiting on the right hand of his chair and the Bishop of Salisbury next to him, as usual, all were put into a great fear by reason of a fire near the court; but soon after came news that it was only a chimney, and quenched; but the same night one of the soldiers on the guard, and one of the king's footmen, broke out into a great flame, and were parted, but so that the footman put a second affront upon him afterwards, and they were then a second time appeased; and that night his majesty's health went round lustily in the *George* cellars, whither some of the cooks and others came over from the court."— *Rushworth's Collections*, vol. iv., pt. 2.

Oudart also preserves two quaint couplets, "written about this time in the king's own hand," and which were found among the royal MSS. :—

" A coward's still unsafe, but courage knows
No other foe but him who doth oppose."

And—

" A pickthank and a picklock, both are alike evil,
The diff'rence is, this trots, that ambles to the devil."

Meanwhile the army had grown more powerful than the parliament, and its leaders were evidently determined to get the person of the king into their own power. Fairfax summoned Hammond, whose fidelity to his trust was a weighty obstacle in their way, to the headquarters at Windsor; and Colonel Eure was ordered to repair to the island, to take charge of the king, and remove him again to Carisbrooke.

But Colonel Hammond, though compelled to obey the general's orders in a matter of military discipline, refused to give up the trust placed in his hands by the parliament; and before he repaired to Windsor, intrusted the government of the island and the security of the royal person to three deputies—Major Rolfe, Captain Bowerman, and Captain Hawes. He gave them strict injunctions to prevent the removal of the king.

On the 27th November the treaty was signed by Charles, but with manifest reluctance, for it bestowed all the prerogatives of the Crown upon the parliament; and the commissioners, accompanied by Colonel Hammond, immediately set out for London. The king, a prey to bitter apprehensions, returned, with his suite, to Carisbrooke.

REMOVAL FROM THE ISLAND.

The leaders of the army, however, were not to be baulked of their prey, and secretly despatched a troop of horse and a company of foot, under Lieutenant-Colonel Cobbit, to seize the Stuart, and

repair with him to Hurst Castle.[*] Of their arrival one of the king's attendants was informed by a person in disguise, and much alarm was consequently excited in the king's mind. He summoned to his presence the Duke of Richmond, the Earl of Lindsey, and Colonel Cooke, one of Cromwell's soldiers, but attached to the king. As the result of their deliberations, Cooke repaired to Rolfe, and acquainted him that the king wished to know whether the army had resolved to seize him that night?

"Not that I know of," replied Rolfe, and added, "You may assure the king from me that he may rest quietly *this night.*"

Colonel Cooke, observing the emphasis placed upon these words, pressed him further on the intentions of the army, but without obtaining any satisfactory answer. Rolfe promised, however, to give the king due notice of what they might purpose in reference to his removal.

Having acquainted the king with what had passed, Colonel Cooke, "though the night was extraordinarily dark," and the rain fell heavily, made his way to Newport. There he speedily found his worst fears confirmed. The streets were alive with soldiers—with faces of men whom he well knew; and he soon ascertained that every officer who was suspected of entertaining friendly feelings for the king had been removed, and his place supplied by a less scrupulous instrument. "The governor (Captain Bowerman) plainly told him he was no better than their prisoner in his own garrison, for they had threatened him with immediate death if he but so much as whispered with any of his own servants."—*Colonel Cooke's Narrative.*

During his absence Firebrace had

---

[*] On their arrival Captain Bowerman sternly refused them admission into the castle; but Rolfe, who commanded at Newport, proffered his assistance.

vainly endeavoured to persuade the king to take advantage of the confusion which prevailed, and make his escape—reminding him that Mr. John Newland's boat might easily be procured. But the king having given his word of honour not to attempt an escape,* persisted in his refusal.

On Colonel Cooke's return to the castle, "he found," he says, "a great alteration at court. Guards not only set round the king's lodgings, and at every window, but even within doors also; nay, sentinels on the king's very chamber door, so that the king was almost suffocated with the smoke of their matches." After much entreaty, Colonel Cooke succeeded in relieving him from the intolerable nuisance.

Having related what he had seen and heard, the faithful colonel, conjointly with the Duke of Richmond and the Earl of Lindsey, besought the royal prisoner, while he had yet time, to accomplish his escape. But though they showed it was perfectly feasible, and adduced many serious arguments why it should be attempted, the king replied, "They have promised me, and I have promised them; and I will not break first."

So, after a while, King Charles retired to rest—his sorrowful attendants holding themselves in readiness for whatever might occur. "It was then about one o'clock; and though Colonel Cooke went not to bed all that night, yet all things were carried with such secrecy and quiet, that not the least noise was heard, nor the least cause of suspicion given.

"But next morning, just at break of day, the king, hearing a great knocking at his outward door, sent the Duke of Richmond to ask what it meant; who, demanding, *Who was there?* he was answered, *My name is Mildmay*. (One of the servants the parliament had put to the king, and brother to Sir Henry).

"The duke demanded, *What he would have?* Who answered, *There were some gentlemen from the army, very desirous to speak with the king.*

"Which account the duke gave the king; but the knocking rather increasing, the king commanded the duke to let them into the room. No sooner was this done, but before the king could get from his bed, these officers rushed into his chamber, and abruptly told the king they had orders to remove him.

"*From whom?* said the king. They replied, *From the army.*

' The king asked, *To what place? To the Castle,* said they.

"The king demanded, *To what castle!* Again they answered, *To the Castle.*

"*The Castle,* said the king, *is no castle;* and added, he was well enough prepared for any castle, requiring them to name the castle.

"After a short whisper together they said, *Hurst Castle.*

"*Indeed,* said the king, *you could not have named a worse.* Whereupon immediately the king called to the Duke of Richmond to send for the Earl of Lindsey and Colonel Cooke.

"At first they scrupled at the Earl of Lindsey's coming; but the king saying, *Why not both since both lie together?*

"Then having whispered together, they promised to send for both, but sent for neither."—*Col. Cooke's Narrative.*

Meanwhile, Firebrace, by the king's desire, had caused a breakfast to be prepared;* but the rough soldiers hurried him into the coach which was in waiting without suffering him to taste it. After

---

* "Not to go out of the island during the treaty, nor twenty days after, without the advice of both Houses of Parliament."—*Rushworth.*

* "The king said to me, ' I know not where these people intend to carry me, and I would willingly eat before I go, therefore get me something to eat.' "—*Firebrace's Narrative.*

he had taken his seat Lieutenant-Colonel Cobbit,[*] "with his hat on," attempted to jump in, but Charles stoutly pushed him back, exclaiming, "It is not come to that yet; get you out." And so the lieutenant-colonel was forced to content himself with a seat beside the driver, while Herbert, Harrington, and Mildmay entered the coach. Then the king hastily bade his servants farewell, with an evident presentiment of coming evil. "At other times," says Herbert, "he was cheerful; but at his parting from his friends he showed the sorrow in his heart by the sadness of his countenance—a real sympathy."

Through the shadows of the sullen night the coach, escorted by two troops of horse, "went westward, towards Worsley's Tower, in Freshwater Isle, a little beyond Yarmouth Haven." Having rested there an hour, the king and his attendants went on board of a small sailing vessel, crossed the narrow sea, and landed at Hurst Castle.

And here we must necessarily conclude our narrative of the monarch's imprisonment in Carisbrooke.

SECTION IX.—THE PRINCESS ELIZABETH.

On the removal of Colonel Hammond, the government of the island A.D. was conferred upon Colonel William 1649. liam Sydenham, a zealous parliamentarian soldier, who had stoutly defended Weymouth and Melcombe Regis against the royal forces. He was a brother of the famous physician, and a kinsman of Dr. Hopton Sydenham, for a brief time Rector of Brighstone. Cromwell trusted him so thoroughly as to appoint him one of his council, and at a later period to raise him to the House of Peers which he attempted to establish.[†]

During his government Carisbrooke again became a royal prison, and received within its precincts two of the lineage of its late captive—the PRINCESS ELIZABETH and the DUKE of GLOUCESTER. As the former died within its walls, and as her dust still lies in the church at Newport—as her history, moreover, has all the pathos of a tender romance—we apprehend that the reader will not look with disfavour upon the brief memoir we subjoin.

THE PRINCESS ELIZABETH.

Doomed in her opening flower of life to know
All a true Stuart's heritage of woe.—
Agnes Strickland.

This hapless scion of the fated race of Stuarts was born at St. James's Palace, on the 20th January 1635. She was the second daughter and fifth child of Charles I. and Henrietta Maria, and seems to have inherited the melancholy temperament of the one, and something of the delicate loveliness of the other. Her birth called forth a special embassy of congratulation from the States of Holland, and costly presents were forwarded to the royal mother: "a massive piece of ambergris, two fair and almost transparent china basins, a curious clock, and of far greater value than these, two beautiful originals of Titian, and two of Tintoret, to add to the galleries of paintings, with which the king was enriching Whitehall and Hampton Court."
—*Strickland.*

---

* Cobbit, according to Herbert; Rolfe, according to Firebrace.

† A contemporary writer gives a concise sketch of this Puritan leader: "Colonel Sydenham, a gentleman of not very much *per annum* at the beginning of the wars, was made governor of Melcombe Regis in the West; became one of the Long Parliament, and hath augmented his revenue to some purpose; he helped, in question, to change the government, and make those laws of treason against kingship; was also of the Little Parliament, and those that were since; one also of the Protector's council, hath a princely command in the Isle of Wight, is one of the commissioners of the treasury; by all of which he is grown very great and considerable."—*A Second Narrative, &c.,* A.D. 1658.

As she grew out of infancy into childhood a notable resemblance was observed between her and her sister, the Princess Mary, so that the poet Crashaw likened them to "two silken sister-flowers." Her portrait, painted by Vaughan when she was five years old, represents her as very fair, with long loose ringlets, and a tender expression of countenance. Beneath an engraving from this portrait, which was inserted in "The True Effigies of the Royal Progeny," are written some complimentary lines, justified, certainly, by her girlish beauty:—

" Here is the grace of Nature's workmanship,
Wherein herselfe herselfe she did outstrip.
Elisabeth the fair, the rare, the great,
In birth, and blood, and virtues full replete;
An high prized jewel, an unvalued gem,
Of more worth than a kingly diadem."

But from her earliest years her constitution seems to have been very delicate. She was "sad, and somewhat liable to complaints of the spleen;".* and when but nine years old (1643), she met with an accident while running across a room, which caused a fractured leg. But the debility of her frame was contrasted by the vigour of her intellect. "She proved a lady of parts beyond her age; the quickness of her mind making recompense for the weakness of her body." Her physical infirmity preventing her from joining with any vigour in the pastimes of her brothers and sisters, she sought recreation in letters; and so great was her progress, that before she was eight years of age she could read and write five languages besides her own,— Hebrew, Greek, Latin, Italian, French. To the study of the two first her earnest and devout mind led her to apply with singular enthusiasm, and she read the Scriptures—an exercise in which she especially delighted—in their original tongues. Her theological acquirements

must have been extensive, if she was able to understand the work which William Greenhill dedicated to her in 1644, an "Exposition of the first five chapters of Ezekiel." At a later period she accepted the dedication of Alexander Rowley's "Scholar's Companion," an English-Latin Lexicon of Hebrew and Greek words employed in the Bible. Rowley speaks of "the fame of her great inclination to the Study of the Book of Books, and of its two original languages, the Hebrew and Greek." And Greenhill says, "Your desire to know the original tongues, that you may understand the Scriptures better, your resolution to write them out with your own princely hand, and to come to the perfect knowledge of them, breed in us hopes that you will exceed all your sex, and be without equal in Europe."

Her first gouvernante was the Countess of Roxburgh; and for a few years, while under her care, she enjoyed the companionship of her brothers and sisters. But in February 1642, the queen set out for Holland with her eldest daughter Mary, betrothed to the Prince of Orange, to raise supplies for her husband's assistance in his struggle with the parliament. Neither her mother nor her sister, therefore, did sad Elizabeth ever meet again. Her royal father's visits were necessarily few; with her brothers, Charles and James, it is doubtful if ever she felt much sympathy. So, lone and still, she brooded in the darkness of the time over the fate that dogged the steps of her unhappy sire. The battle echoes of Marston and Naseby broke in upon her solitude like death-music; and as earth grew more and more repulsive to her saddened soul, she turned with the greater eagerness to the consolations of heaven.

In October 1642, the plague becoming epidemical in the vicinity of St. James, it was resolved by the Commons that her household should be removed to a suitable mansion in a more healthy locality, and for that purpose Lord Cottington's

* When, in 1640, there was some design of betrothing her to the Prince of Orange, the Secretary of State wrote that she might probably die before the contract was completed.

house in Broad Street was finally engaged.

Her establishment at this time was not on a scale of ordinary comfort, such as might be found in a tradesman's modest family, and she was so hedged round with rigorous restrictions that she could neither speak with, nor write to any of her royal father's friends. The Countess of Roxburgh at length addressed an urgent remonstrance to the House, and due inquiry being made, the Speaker himself acknowledged its justice, by declaring that her poverty was such "he should be ashamed to speak of it." A monthly payment of £800 was, therefore, ordered to Colonel Holland to defray the expenses of her household, and at a later period a larger allowance was made.

In 1643 the Commons removed her gouvernante and servants, and placed her under the care, at first, of Lady Vere, and shortly afterwards of the Countess of Dorset. The princess remonstrated in a letter addressed to the Peers, which is pathetically simple :—

"MY LORDS,—I account myself very miserable that I must have my servants taken from me, and strangers put to me. You promised me that you would have a care of me ; and I hope you will show it in preventing so great a grief as this would be to me. I pray, my lords, consider of it, and give me cause to thank you, and to rest your loving friend,

"ELIZABETH.
" *To the Right Hon. the Lords and
Peers in Parliament.*"

The Lords objected to these proceedings, and appointed a committee of inquiry, but without effect. The Commons would brook no interference from the Upper House, even in so small a matter, and of themselves determined upon the number of the royal lady's servants. Two cofferesses, four chamber women, a laundress, and starcher ; two physicians (of whom the senior was the eminent Mayerne) ; six chaplains, and one house chaplain ; two gentlemen ushers, one French master, four pages, &c. They also ordered that prayers should be read twice every day, and two sermons preached on every Sunday ; the gates were to be locked at sunset, and on no occasion opened after 10 P.M., without the special license of the chief resident officer. For the house expenses £100 monthly were voted, and an additional sum for apparel.

In July 1644 she was removed to Sir J. Danver's house at Chelsea, and in September to Whitehall, where she received the instructions of Mrs. Makin, a noted linguist.

Early in 1645, on the death of the Countess of Dorset, her brother (the young Duke of Gloucester), and herself, were placed under the care of the Earl of Northumberland, and resided for a few weeks at pleasant Sion House, on the banks of the Thames. He was allowed £3000 per annum for his labour, and £9500 for the diet of his wards. From Sion House they returned to St. James's Palace, where they were joined by the young Duke of York, after the fatal issue of the siege of Oxford. Weary days dragged on, each marked by the shadow of some dread disaster to their father's cause, until the tidings of his capture at Holdenby reached the ears of his unhappy daughter. Her sympathy for him, however, was reciprocated by his paternal love, which prompted him, at considerable risk, to seek an interview with her.

On the 16th July, therefore, the Earl of Northumberland accompanied the princess and the young princes to Maidenhead. Through streets gaily strewn with flowers they passed, until they reached the *Greyhound* inn, where, about eleven o'clock, they were joined by King Charles. The interview was an affecting one. To the Duke of Gloucester, then a lad about seven years old, the

king said, " Do you know me, child ?"
And when the little prince replied, " No,"
he continued, " I am your father, child ;
and it is not one of the least of my
misfortunes that I have brought you,
and your brothers and sisters, into the
world to share my miseries."—*White-
locke*, 259.

From Maidenhead the royal children
went to Caversham, a quiet village on
the green banks of the Thames, and
stayed there two days, mightily enjoying
themselves the while.

During the king's detention at Hampton Court, he was several times permitted to see them. On these occasions
Cromwell was often present, and it is to
be noted that he alone, of all the stern
Puritan leaders, bent the knee to the
sons and daughters of King Charles. A
longer interval than usual having at one
time occurred, the princess, it would
appear, affectionately complainèd, and
the king soothed her in thèse loving but
guarded words :—

> " HAMPTON COURT,
> 27*th Oct.* 1647.

" DEAR DAUGHTER,—This is to assure
you that it is not through forgetfulness,
or any want of kyndenes, that I have
not, all this tyme, sent for you, but for
such reasons as is fitter for you to imagen
(which you may easily doe), than me to
wryte ; but now I hope to see you, upon
Fryday or Saturday next, as your brother
James can more particularly tell you, to
whom referring you, I rest your loving
father, CHARLES R."

Equally tender in spirit is the following, written at a later period, but which
may here be fitly introduced :—

> " NEWPORT, 14*th October* 1648.

" DEAR DAUGHTER,—It is not want of
affection that makes me write so seldome
to you, but want of matter such as I
could wishe, and indeed I am loathe to
write to those I love when I am out of
humore (as I have beene these dayes by

past), least my letters should troble those
I desyre to please ; but having this opportunity, I would not loose it, though,
at this time, I have nothing to say, but
God bless you. So I rest, your loving
father, CHARLES R.

" Give your brother my blessing with
a kisse ; and comend me kyndly to my
Lady Northumberland by the same
token."—*Ellis's Orig. Letters*, 2d series,
ii.

The aspect of affairs was now so
menacing, that the partizans of the
royal family thought it advisable to
remove the young Duke of York out of
the reach of the parliament. The king,
while at Hampton Court, had foreseen
that this would be necessary, and had
enjoined him, "when a fit opportunity
offered, to make his escape beyond the
seas." They were, at this period, residing at St. James's, " where," says Clarendon, " they had the liberty of the garden and park to walk and exercise themselves in, and lords and ladies, and other
persons of condition, were not restrained
from resorting thither to visit them."
One Colonel Bamfield, " a man of an
active and insinuating nature," availed
himself of this permission to devise
means of escape, and the princess providing the duke with female apparel,
when joining, as they were wont to do,
in " hide and seek,"—a favourite pas-
time of their younger brother, the Duke
of Gloucester,—he made his way unperceived into the garden, and thence
by a private door into the park, where
Colonel Bamfield met him, and conducted him to the river (April 21,
1647). He afterwards reached Holland
in safety.

His escape caused considerable excitement, and the parliamentary proceedings
in consequence are thus alluded to by
Rushworth :—" *April* 22, 1647. A
message came from the Lords to the
Commons, desiring a conference in the
Painted Chamber, concerning the escape

of the Duke of York last night from St. James's. At this conference report was made that the duke, with his brother the Duke of Gloucester, and his sister the Lady Elizabeth, being sporting by themselves after supper, the duke privately slipt from 'em down the back stairs, without either cloke or coat; and having the key of the garden door, passed through the park, and so away."

Shortly afterwards, however, the royal children were intrusted to the guardianship of the Countess of Leicester, much to the relief of the Earl of Northumberland, whom nature had ill fitted to play the part of jailer. An allowance was made to the duke of £2500 per annum, and a suitable number of attendants was appointed to wait upon them. They had previously been removed to Sion House, where they remained in a captivity but thinly disguised, until, on the fatal morning of the 29th of January 1649, they were summoned to take their last farewell of their martyr-father.

Some lives are long, not from years but events; the heart grows aged, and the mind matured, while the eyes are still full of the light of youth. It was so with the child-princess. She counted but thirteen summers, and yet she possessed the intelligence, and, alas! had undergone the experience of a woman thrice as old. In simple but expressive language she recorded, during her imprisonment at Carisbrooke, the particulars of this last sad interview between the children and the father,—an interview which the shadow of the coming death must have darkened unto their souls. This remarkable narrative runs in simple fashion, thus :—

"*What the king said to me 29th of January last, being the last time I had the happiness to see him.*

"He told me that he was glad I was come, for, though he had not time to say much, yet somewhat he wished to say to me, which he could not to another, and he had feared ' the cruelty' was too great to permit his writing. 'But, sweetheart, he added, ' thou wilt forget what I tell thee.' Then shedding abundance of tears, I told him that I would write down all he said to me. ' He wished me,' he said, ' not to grieve and torment myself for him, for it was a glorious death he should die, it being for the laws and religion of the land.' He told me what books to read against Popery. He said, that ' he had forgiven all his enemies, and he hoped God would forgive them also;' and he commanded us, and all the rest of my brothers and sisters, to forgive them also. Above all, he bade me tell my mother that ' his thoughts had never strayed from her, and that his love for her would be the same to the last;' withal, he commanded me and my brother to love her, and be obedient to her. He desired me ' not to grieve for him, for he should die a martyr; and that he doubted not but God would restore the throne to his son, and that then we should be all happier than we could possibly have been, if he had lived;' with many other things, which I cannot remember.

"Then, taking my brother Gloucester on his knee, he said, ' Sweetheart, now will they cut off thy father's head;' upon which the child looked very steadfastly upon him. ' Heed, my child, what I say.; they will cut off my head, and perhaps make thee a king. But mark what I say: you must not be a king as long as your brothers Charles and James live; therefore, I charge you, do not be made a king by them.' At which the child, sighing deeply, replied, ' I will be torn in pieces first.' And these words coming from so young a child, rejoiced my father exceedingly; and his majesty spoke to him of the welfare of his soul, and to keep his religion, commanding him to fear God and he would provide for him. All which the young child earnestly promised.

"His majesty also bid me send his

blessing to the rest of my brothers and sisters, with commendations to all his friends. So after giving me his blessing, I took my leave." *—*Reliquiæ Sacræ*, 337, 338.

Many kisses, many embraces—such kisses, such embraces as Love on the threshold of the grave well may bestow upon the loved ones—the royal sire lavished on his children, already fatherless in his sad eyes. And then he called to good Bishop Juxon to lead them from him. They sobbed bitterly. The father—still a man, still a king—leant his head against the window, and strove to keep down his tears; but as they passed through the door, his eyes chanced to light upon them, and hastening from the window, he folded them in one last, long embrace, and pressed upon their lips his last, long kisses, and then—cast himself upon his knees, and told his sorrow and his love to God!

At this interview he gave to Elizabeth two seals, wherein were set two diamonds, and a yet more costly gift—a Bible, saying, "It had been his great comfort and constant companion through all his sorrows, and he hoped it would be hers." And it *was* hers: she died, with her pale cheek resting on its open page.

After the execution of King Charles, his children were removed to Penshurst; thus adding another historic association to the home of Sir Philip Sidney. The allowance received from the parliament was now reduced to £1000 per annum

each; and their household was greatly curtailed. Orders were given "that they should be treated without any addition of titles, and that they should sit at their meat as the children of the family did, and all at one table." At Penshurst they were carefully tended by the Countess of Leicester—the mother of Algernon Sidney—who " observed the order of the parliament with obedience enough, and," says Clarendon, with a somewhat ungenerous sneer, " treated them with as much respect as the lady *pretended* she durst pay to them."

While residing in this—"the fitting abode of the noble Sidneys "—the malady of the princess, which had lurked so long in her feeble frame, rapidly grew upon her, necessitating the constant attendance of her physician, Dr. Treherne. Otherwise, her situation was pleasant enough ; and, doubtlessly, to her cultivated mind, the historic and poetic associations of " the ancient pile " which Ben Jonson had celebrated in stately verse, had a constant charm. The massive oaken table, whereat she took her place " with the children of the family," had been graced with the presence of " the chivalrous author of the Arcadia,"—that virtuous Countess of Pembroke, whom the poet's epitaph* has immortalized,—the amiable Edward VI., —the royal Elizabeth,—the magnificent Leicester,—Cecil, astute, unscrupulous, and able,—her grandfather, the pedantic James,—and " the martyr-king" himself, while yet in his grave and decorous youth. There is still at Penshurst a relic of the times of our ill-fated maiden Stuart. In the south court, on a very simple frame of wood, hangs a great bell, bearing an inscription in raised letters to this effect:—*Robert, Earl of Leicester, at Penshurst*, 1649. The princess and her brother probably witnessed the ele-

---

* " He bad her remember to tell her brother James, 'twas his father's last desire that he should no longer look on Charles as his eldest brother only, but be obedient to him as his sovereign ; and that they should love one another, and forgive their father's enemys, but not trust 'em, seeing they had bin false to him, and he feared also to their own souls. He bid her read Bishop Andrew's Sermons, Hooker's Ecclesiastical Polity, and Bishop Laud's Book against Fisher, to ground her against Popery."—*Rushworth's Collections.* vl. 604.

* Underneath this marble hearse
Lies, the subject of all verse,
Sidney's sister, Pembroke's mother.
Ben Jonson.

vation of this bell, and heard its earliest tones swell over the old pleasaunce, and float far away down the waters of the Medway.*

From "the broad beech and the chestnut shade," from "the mount to which the Dryads did resort" (*Ben Jonson*), the Princess Elizabeth,—her health being sufficiently restored,—and her brother, were removed to Carisbrooke Castle, in pursuance of an order made by the parliament for the removal of "the two children of the late king, out of the limits of the commonwealth."—*Journals, House of Commons.*

They landed at Cowes on Thursday, the 13th of August 1650, having left Penshurst on Friday, the 9th, and reached Carisbrooke, after some delay, on Saturday, the 16th. The apartments allotted to them were elegantly furnished, and their charge was intrusted to Mr. Anthony Mildmay (see *ante*, p. 50), who, according to royalist testimony, was "an honest and faithful gentleman." In attendance upon them were Mr. Lovel, the young duke's tutor; John Barmiston, gentleman-usher; Judith Briott, her gentlewoman; Elizabeth Jones, her "laundrie-mayde;" and John Clarke, groom of her chamber. To add to their comforts, Mildmay sent to Penshurst for a large quantity of their father's household furniture; but probably it "did not arrive at its destination sufficiently early to afford any comfort to the princess."— *Journal, British Archæol. Association,* Sept. 1855.

It is almost unnecessary to state that there exists no foundation for Hume's assertion, that the leaders of the commonwealth designed to apprentice the princess to a button-maker at Newport, and the young duke to a shoemaker. Reports to this effect, however, reached

Queen Henrietta, and caused her much uneasiness. In the House of Commons, indeed, a debate arose on the question of providing for the maintenance of the royal captives, and Cromwell bluntly said, in that rough, vigorous way of his, that "as to the young boy, it would be better to bind him to a good trade;" but the parliament carried their severity no further than to enjoin that "no person should be allowed to kiss their hands, and that they should not be otherwise treated than as the children of a gentleman."

The confinement of the princess was of briefest duration. On the Monday following her admission into Carisbrooke (August 19th), while playing at bowls, there fell a sudden shower, and the princess being of an infirm and debilitated body, "it caused her to take cold, and the next day she complained of headache and feverish distemper, which by fits increased upon her; and on the first three or four days she had the advice of Dr. Bagnell, a worthy and able physician of Newport, and then care was taken by Dr. Treherne, in London, to send a physician and remedies of election [an astrological nostrum] to her. But notwithstanding the care of that honest and faithful gentleman, Anthony Mildmay, Esq., and all the art of her physicians, her disease grew upon her; and, after many rare ejaculatory expressions, abundantly demonstrating her unparalleled piety, to the eternal honour of her own memory, and the astonishment of those who waited on her, she took leave of the world on Sunday, the 8th September 1650."

The Père Gamache, a capuchin attached to the court of Henrietta Maria, gives in his memoirs a somewhat different account of the last scenes of this sad drama, based, of course, upon the rumours which travelled from England, and accumulated in monstrosity on the way: "The princess, then about twelve years old, endowed with an excellent understanding, and justly appreciating her

* We may here notice that at Penshurst Parsonage long dwelt Dr. Hammond, one of Charles I.'s chaplains, and uncle of Colonel Hammond, the Governor of Carisbrooke.— See *ante,* p. 48.

high birth, vexed at being obliged to leave the royal residence of St James, was absorbed in melancholy thoughts on approaching the castle to which she was going. There she made many doleful reflections, and they made such deep impression on her heart, and so heated her blood, that a violent fever ensued. It seemed at first that it was too violent to last long, but the event proved otherwise ; for the disorder kept increasing, resisted all remedies, and at length put an end to the life of the afflicted princess."—*Court and Times of Charles I.* According to Sir Theodore Mayerne, who was summoned to her assistance, but did not reach the castle until after her decease, " she died of a malignant fever, which constantly increased, she being far distant from physicians and remedies." Heath's account is somewhat more minute : "The princess Elizabeth, coming from bowls with her brother, the Duke of Gloucester, complained first of her head, and having lain sick a fortnight, died. Little care was there taken of her, the place affording no learned physician, yet Dr. Mayerne sent out some fitting cordials." But this accusation, as we have shown, was incorrect, Drs. Bagnell and Treherne being in constant attendance upon her, and Sir Theodore Mayerne's aid was immediately sought. The progress of her disease, however, anticipated his arrival. She expired in solitude, sitting in her apartment at Carisbrooke, "her fair cheek resting on a Bible, which was the last gift of her murdered father, and which had been her only consolation in the last sad months of her life."—*Strickland.*

From a recent examination of her remains, it has been satisfactorily shown that the princess died of a disease just introduced into England, and comparatively unknown to English practitioners, *Rachitis* or *Rickets.** To natural causes,

---

* See Adams's *History, Topography, and Antiquities of the Isle of Wight.*

therefore, and 'not to the effects of a romantic melancholy, must her early death be ascribed by the impartial historian.

The princess's body was first embalmed, and then carefully disposed of in a leaden coffin. It lay exposed to the sorrowing gaze of her attendants for some fourteen days, and on Wednesday, the 24th of September, " was brought (in a borrowed coach) from the castle to the town of Newport, attended thither with her few late servants. At the end of the town the corpse was met and waited on by the mayor and aldermen thereof in their formalities to the church, where, about the middle of the east part of the chancel in St. Thomas's Chapel, her highness was interred in a small vault purposely made, with an inscription of the date of her death engraved on her coffin." Quaint old Fuller, who has preserved this simple narrative, makes thereupon a characteristic comment : " The hawks of Norway, where a winter's day is hardly an hour of clear light, are the swiftest of wing of any fowl under the firmament, nature teaching them to bestir themselves, to lengthen the shortness of the time with their swiftness. Such the active piety of this lady, improving the little life allotted to her 'in running the way of God's commandments.'"

The coffin was made of strong lead, ridged in the middle. On the lid was placed a brass plate, with the inscription,—

"Elizabeth, Second Davghter
of ye late King Charles,
dece'd Sept. viii., M.D.C.L."

It was interred in the middle of the east part of the chancel, and the letters, E. S., were cut in the adjacent wall. But, in the course of time, the vault and its memorable occupant were forgotten, until, in Oct. 1793, some workmen employed in opening a new grave discovered the coffin.

" In order that the spot might not be

again overlooked, a plate with a simple inscription was placed on the stone covering of the vault, and advantage was taken of the opportunity to remove from the wall of the church-yard, where it had long administered a silent, but potent rebuke of the then very prevalent practice of burying in the church, a tablet bearing the following singular inscription: 'Here lyeth y⁰ body of Master George Shergold, late minister of New Port, who, during sixteen years in discharge of his office, strictly observed y⁰ true discipline of y⁰ Church of England, disliking that dead bodies should be interred in God's house, appointed to be interred in this place. He died, universally lamented and esteemed, January xxiii., 1707.' This old inscription being placed with the face to the stone, and economically supplying, by the reverse, the tablet for the more interesting record."—*Journal, Brit. Arch. Association*, Sept. 1855.

When the new Church of St Thomas was erected in 1856, the princess's remains were therein interred, and a graceful monument, with a graceful inscription (see *post*), was raised within its walls to the daughter of the Stuart by her Majesty the Queen.

SECTION X.—A SUMMARY FROM 1651 TO 1867.

Carisbrooke, during the commonwealth, was the prison of many A.D. gallant cavaliers and independent 1651. spirits, whose loyalty rendered them obnoxious to the ruling powers, but none of these is it needful we should notice. At Cowes Castle, however, was confined a poet, a wit, a soldier, and a man of letters—Sir William D'Avenant, the godson—by scandal said to be the son—of William Shakspeare.

While imprisoned at Cowes, and awaiting trial on a charge of high treason, he finished the first portion of his great poem, "Gondibert," of which a brother poet warmly sang:—

> " Here no bold tales of gods or monsters swell,
> But human passions such as with us dwell;
> Man is thy theme, his virtue or his rage,
> Drawn to the life in each elaborate page."
> *Waller.*

He says, in the postcript to the first edition, "I am here arrived at the middle of the third book. But it is high time to strike sail and cast anchor, though I have run but half my course, when at the helm I am threatened with *death*, who, though he can visit us but once, seems troublesome; and even in the innocent may beget such a gravity as diverts the music of verse." It is pleasant, however, to know that after his removal from Cowes to the Tower, to be tried, his life was saved by the good offices of two aldermen of York whom he had once obliged, and that he lived to interfere, in his turn, on Milton's behalf with Charles II. He has been characterized by the elder D'Israeli as "a poet and a wit, the creator of the English stage with the music of Italy and the scenery of France, a soldier, an emigrant, a courtier, and a politician!" Aubrey, in his own quaint fashion, describes the circumstances which led to D'Avenant's imprisonment. The anecdote is worth extracting: "He laid an ingenious design to carry a considerable number of artificers, chiefly weavers, from France to Virginia, and by Mary the queen-mother's means he got favour from the King of France to go into the prison and pick and choose; so when the poor wretches understood what his design was, they cried, *uno ore*, ' *Tous Tisserans*'—We are all weavers. Well, he took thirty-six, as I remember, and not more, and shipped them; and as he was on his voyage to Virginia, he and his weavers were all taken by the ships then belonging to the parliament of England. The French slaves, I suppose, they sold, but Sir William was brought prisoner to England. Whether he was at first a prisoner at Carisbrooke Castle,[*] in the Isle of Wight, or at the Tower of London, I have forgotten. He was a prisoner at both. His 'Gondibert' was finished at Carisbrooke Castle."

GOVERNORS OF THE ISLE OF WIGHT SINCE THE RESTORATION.

When Charles II. was welcomed back to the throne he was so soon to disgrace, the old things passed away with a wonderful celerity, and dashing cavaliers speedily usurped the seats of stern-browed Puritans. Colonel Sydenham, therefore, was compelled to quit his island-captaincy, and Lord Culpeper "reigned in his stead."

A.D. 1660.

1. *Thomas, Lord Culpeper* (A.D. 1660), had been of some service to the Royalist cause, and was a gallant, but imperious soldier, better fitted to shine in the arts of war than in those of peace. His government was so excessively unpopular from its arbitrary character, that the islanders appealed to the king for redress, but obtained scant satisfaction from Lord Clarendon. Their principal grounds of complaint were—that he had enclosed a considerable portion of Parkhurst Forest, imprisoned several loyal subjects in "a noisome dungeon" in Carisbrooke Castle, neglected the defences of the island, and assumed the title of "governor" in addition to that of "captain." They also remonstrated, and with justice, against the piratical doings of his kinsman and deputy, Captain Alexander Culpeper, who plundered foreign vessels which put into "the Cowes" in distress, and committed other enormities recorded in the MS. history treasured up in the British Museum.

Though shielded by Lord Clarendon, the cavalier-captain of the Wight deemed it advisable to surrender his appointment, and was succeeded—much to the joy of the islanders—by the famous sea-chief—

2. *Admiral Sir Robert Holmes* (A.D. 1667), whose rise in the service had been as rapid as his courage and skill were eminent. In 1661 we first hear of him as the commodore of a small squadron of four frigates despatched to the African coast to make reprisals on the Dutch, an expedition in which he was completely successful. Two years later, as captain of the *Jersey*, a 50-gun ship, he was again on the coast of Africa, and captured Goree.[*] He next reduced Cape Corse Island (A.D. 1664), and sailing to America, joined Sir Robert Carr's squadron, and subdued the Dutch settlement of New York.

His successes gained him the appointment of captain to a fine new vessel, the *Defiance*, of 66 guns, and on its launch at Woolwich he received the honour of knighthood from his royal patron, Charles II., who was present (27th March, 1665). In the two great naval actions with the Dutch, which illustrate with a lurid splendour the dark pages of Charles II.'s reign (June 3, 1665, and June 25, 1666), he bore himself as became an English seaman, and won "golden opinions" from his countrymen.

He was selected by Albemarle to command the squadron destined to operate on the Dutch coast, and with a squadron of boats and fire-ships entering the channel (between the islands of Vlie and Schelling), where lay the Baltic fleet in fancied security, he achieved a most brilliant success—burning two men-of-war, 180 merchantmen, and the town of Brandaris, with a loss of only twelve men killed and wounded.—*Charnock, Biographia Navalis.*

---

[*] Aubrey was in error; the postcript to "Gondibert" is dated from *Cowes* Castle.

---

[*] Dryden says of him in the *Annus Mirabilis* :—

" And Holmes, whose name shall live in epic song,
  While music numbers, or while verse has feet.
Holmes, the Achates of the general's fight,
  Who first bewitched our eyes with Guinea gold."

Sir Robert Holmes was now appointed commander-in-chief of the Portsmouth squadron (answering to the modern dignity of port-admiral), and appointed to the vacant governorship of the Isle of Wight.[*] He immediately took up his residence in the island, building himself a stately mansion at Yarmouth † (then a strongly-fortified and well-garrisoned town, approached from the east by a draw-bridge). Here, in July 1671, he entertained King Charles, the Duke of York, Prince Rupert, and a brilliant company; and again in 1675 he was honoured by a royal progress. The Duke of York visited him in 1673.

He acquired great popularity in his government from his zeal in furthering the interests of the island. His deputy-governor was the Sir Edward Worsley who so loyally served King Charles I. during his imprisonment at Carisbrooke.

Sir Robert Holmes died at Yarmouth, full of years and honours, on the 18th November 1692. He was buried in Yarmouth Church, and a splendid monument erected to his memory by his son.

3. *John, Lord Cutts* (A.D. 1693), was appointed governor in the year after Sir Robert's death. During the interval, it would seem from the inscription on the monument in the church of Yarmouth, that Henry Holmes, Sir Robert's eldest son, administered the affairs of the island.

Lord Cutts was of an ancient Cambridgeshire family; had been liberally educated; was a polished scholar, and a most daring soldier. In the Irish and Flanders campaigns of King William his heroic bravery was frequently displayed, and raised him, step by step, to the rank of lieutenant-general and the colonelcy of the Coldstream Guards. In the camp, where he spent the prime of his years, he acquired an imperiousness of temper, and a habit of command, which, when brought to bear upon his administration of the government of the Wight, involved him in ceaseless conflicts, and rendered him singularly unpopular. He interfered in the management of the corporations, disfranchised several burgesses of Newtown, threw a clergyman into the dungeon of Cowes Castle, and raised a feud between himself and the island gentry that promised to result in serious consequences.

Lord Cutts, however, had the frank heart as well as the rough hand of the soldier, and perceiving the difficulties in which he was involved, had the candour to withdraw his more objectionable pretensions. The gentry of the island were equally ready to lay down their arms; and in March 1697, a solemn pact or treaty was concluded between the governor and his subjects at Appuldurcombe (the seat of Sir Robert Worsley), which proved the commencement of a lasting peace. Lord Cutts grew excessively popular, and maintained a splendid hospitality. And at Carisbrooke Castle, already falling into pitiful decay, he caused to be repaired and refitted the governor's apartments.

This gallant soldier, whose bravery at the siege of Namur is historically famous, served under Marlborough in the glorious campaign of 1704, and on the field of Blenheim commanded a brigade of infantry. His successful attack upon the village of Blenheim greatly contributed to the completeness of that splendid victory.

For his services he was appointed Commander-in-Chief of the Forces, and one of the Lords Justices of Ireland; where he died, while yet in the prime of manhood, in 1706.

4. A civilian was selected to succeed the brilliant soldier in his island-government,—*Charles, Duke of Bolton* (then Marquis of Winchester), a knight of the Garter, Warden of the New Forest, and

---

* In the preceding year he had been appointed governor of Sandown Castle.
† Now the *George Inn*.

Lord-Lieutenant of Hampshire and Dorsetshire; and, in 1706, one of the commissioners for negotiating the union between England and Scotland. As he was, emphatically, "an absentee," a Lieutenant-Governor was now formally appointed. Colonel Morgan was the first to fill the office, at a salary of £365 per annum.

5. In 1710 the Duke of Bolton retired, and *John Richmond Webb*, Lieutenant-General and Colonel of Foot, one of the soldiers of fortune, bred up by William III. and the great Marlborough, who fought gallantly at Blenheim, and defeated La Mothe at Wynendale, was appointed to the governorship. He was superseded, in 1715, by—

6. *William, Earl Cadogan*, whose services form a portion of British history, and need not here be recapitulated. A brother soldier of Cutts and Webb, he shared with honour in almost all the campaigns in Flanders and the Netherlands. At Oudenarde and Malplaquet he specially distinguished himself. On the death of Marlborough in 1722, he succeeded to his dignities as Commander-in-Chief, and Master General of the Ordnance. He died in August 1726.

7. *Charles, Duke of Bolton*, held the governorship, rapidly becoming a sinecure, until 1733, when opposing the excise scheme of Walpole, he was forced by that powerful minister to resign all his offices, and the governorship was bestowed on a more tractable peer.

8. *John, Duke of Montague*, whose reign was a very brief one, inasmuch as in July 1734 he surrendered his appointment.

9. *John Wallop, Lord Viscount Lymington*, was forced to resign the governorship, and vice-admiralty of the island, in July 1742, on the fall of Walpole, whose cause he had espoused. He was, however, rewarded by George II. with the earldom of Portsmouth, and *re-appointed* to the governorship of the Isle of Wight, in 1745, *on the dismissal* of—

10. *Charles, Duke of Bolton*, who had enjoyed it for three years.

11. After the death of the Earl of Portsmouth, aged 72, on November 23, 1762, the government of the island, for a brief interval, was administered by the lieutenant-governor. *Thomas, Lord Holmes,* Baron Kilmallock of the kingdom of Ireland, was appointed to the post in April 1763. Lord Holmes was the son of Henry Holmes, formerly lieutenant-governor of the island, and Mary, daughter of Admiral Sir Robert Holmes. He was born in 1699, and died, without issue, in 1764. During his year-long governorship he chiefly resided in the island, where he was well beloved. He was wont, it is said, to entertain his friends in two caverns in the cliffs of Freshwater, still traditionally known as *Lord Holmes's parlour* and *Lord Holmes's kitchen.*

12. He was succeeded by *Hans Stanley, Esq.*, a Lord of the Admiralty, and a gentleman of considerable property, who built, and splendidly fitted up, a cottage ornée at Steephill. The sad tale of his daughter's early fate is alluded to by the poet Thomson in the second book of "The Seasons."[*]

13. *Harry Powlett, Duke of Bolton,* superseded Mr. Hans Stanley in 1766, and was in his turn superseded by Mr. Stanley in 1770, who held it until his decease in 1780. The House of Industry at Parkhurst, a species of prototype of the modern Poor Law Union, was founded, we may here notice, in 1770.

14. *Sir Richard Worsley, Bart.*, Comptroller of the Royal Household, and a Privy Councillor, descended from one of the most influential of the old island families, and possessing large estates at

---

[*] "And art thou, Stanley, of that sacred band ?
Alas, for us too soon !" &c.—*Thomson's Seasons.*

She died in 1738, at the early age of 18, and was buried in Holyrood Church, Southampton, where there is a monument to her memory. Thomson wrote the epitaph.

Appuldurcombe and St. Lawrence, was next appointed. To his industry and research we are indebted for a ponderous, but very valuable history of the island, published in 1782, and dedicated to King George III. He was removed from the government in 1782, and the Duke of Bolton re-appointed.

15. In 1791 the office was bestowed upon the *Right Honourable Thomas Orde*, in whose patent it was first provided that the appointments to the military commands of Yarmouth, Cowes, and Sandown, should be vested in the Crown. Mr. Orde built a house at Fern Hill, near Wootton, where he frequently resided. In 1795 he assumed the arms and name of Powlett, on succeeding, in right of his wife (a natural daughter of the last Duke of Bolton) to large estates; and, in 1797, he was elevated to the peerage with the title of Lord Bolton, of Bolton Abbey, Yorkshire. He is spoken of as "a man of very powerful talents, great industry in business, extensive political knowledge, and many amiable moral qualities."—*Collins*.

16. *John Harris*, first *Earl of Malmesbury*, a distinguished English diplomatist, Ambassador to the Courts of Paris and St. Petersburgh, was appointed August 22, 1807.

17. The *Right Hon. W. H. Ashe A'Court Holmes, Earl of Heytesbury* (d. 1860), formerly Lord Lieutenant of Ireland, received the appointment in 1841, on the understanding that the salary previously attaching to it (about £1300) would no longer be allowed. He resigned it in 1857, when the honour was conferred upon—

18. *Charles Shaw Lefevre, Viscount Eversley*. This distinguished statesman was born in Bedford Square, in 1794; was educated at Winchester, and afterwards at Trinity College, Cambridge, where he graduated as Master of Arts in 1817. In the same year he married Helena, youngest daughter of the late S. Whitbread, Esq., and shortly afterwards entered parliament.

From 1839 to 1857 he held the high office of Speaker of the House of Commons, and discharged its responsible and sometimes difficult duties with a dignity and courtesy which won him "golden opinions" as well from his friends as his political opponents.

Governor and Captain of the Isle of Wight.

Right Hon. the Viscount Eversley, G.C.B., P.C.

Member of Parliament for the Island—Sir John Simeon, Bart., M.A.

(1867) Registered electors, 2362.

Members of Parliament for Newport { R. W. Kennard, Esq.
C. W. Martin, Esq.

(1867) Registered electors, 643.

Coroner for the Island—F. Blake, Esq.

PART II.

A DESCRIPTION OF THE ISLE OF WIGHT;

ITS

TOWNS, VILLAGES, MANSIONS, AND ANTIQUITIES.

And Wight who checks the western tide."—COLLINS.

DISTRICT I.-NORTH.

EAST AND WEST COWES.

THE tourist may enter the Isle of Wight either at Ryde *via* Portsmouth, at Cowes *via* Southampton, or at Yarmouth *via* Lymington. The former is the most popular, but the Cowes route, as the most central, is, perhaps, the most convenient for the tourist who intends to examine the island thoroughly, and does not visit it simply *pour passer le temps* during the season which fashion loves to spend at the sea-side.

The passage from Southampton, the fable-city of Sir Bevis, to West Cowes, occupies about an hour, and on a bright summer noon is not without a certain agreeable character. The banks of Southampton Water are beautiful with associations of "antique verse and high romance," and as the rapid vessel bears him past the ruins of Netley, Hythe, Calshot Castle, and Eaglehurst, the traveller will not fail to recall historic memories and legendary fancies which will pleasantly beguile the time. As he approaches the mouth of the Medina, he will observe with pleasure the picturesque aspect of its banks, crowned by the gardens, and villas, and winding streets of the two Cowes,—

" The two great Cowes that in loud thunder roar,
This on the eastern, that the western shore,
Where Newport enters stately Wight."—*Leland*.

Each of the sister-towns stands on a gently-sloping hill, well surrounded with fresh green foliage. In the back-ground of East Cowes rise the Palladian towers of Osborne. The river is always thronged with vessels of different sizes and rigging. The shore is busy with shipwrights, and crowded with the skeletons of unfinished craft. Altogether, a picture of varied and animated life.

WEST COWES,

(*Hotels* — Marine, Fountain, Gloster, Vine; *Railway* to Newport; *Steamers*, for South-ampton, or Ryde and Portsmouth,)

Is a town of considerable antiquity, and has always been the chief port of the island. In the days of Elizabeth and the earlier Stuarts, its harbour was constantly frequented by English and foreign masts. "Prizes and men-of-war which gave great rates for its commodities."—*Sir J. Oglander, MSS.*

1. *West Cowes*, in 1861, had a population of 5482 souls (2647 males + 2835 females). In 1841 it had a population of just 4107. Against 814 inhabited houses, and 70 uninhabited, in 1851, it could place, ten years later, 1015 inhabited houses, and 80 uninhabited. The town is included in the parish of Northwood, and, for municipal purposes, in the borough of Newport. Its government is in the hands of a local board, annually elected by the rate-payers, under the provisions of the "Health of Towns" Act.

2. *Cowes Harbour* is an estuary formed by the junction of the Medina, here half a mile wide, with the Solent. It is commodious, sheltered, and capable of admitting vessels of heavy tonnage. During the yachting season (May to November) it is the favourite rendezvous of the yacht clubs of the south of England, and then presents a peculiarly attractive aspect. The customs levied here in 1865 amounted to £3499. 805 vessels entered *inwards*, having an aggregate tonnage of 57,161; while 256 vessels, representing 11,459 tons, cleared *outwards*. In 1866 the number of vessels registered as belonging to the port was 215, of 10,992 tons; in 1846 there were only 171 (of 8357 tons), so that the increase is eminently satisfactory. A new pier is in course of construction (1866-7) opposite Gloucester House.

3. *West Cowes Castle* was one of the circular forts built by Henry VIII., about 1538-9, for the defence of the southern coast. Its materials were brought across the Solent from the ruins of Beaulieu Priory; so that the spoils of the Church furnished the arms by which the Pope and his allies were to be defied. During the Commonwealth and Protectorate, it was much used as a prison, and here D'Avenant, the poet, dramatist, and father of English Opera, was confined in 1651, and wrote a portion of his epic of "Goudibert." Its inutility as a fortress having become apparent after the formation of the stronger defences at Hurst and Yarmouth, it was sold by the Government, in 1856-7, to the Royal Yacht Club, who repaired and refitted it at considerable expense, and now employ its miniature battery for peaceful ceremonials.

4. *The Royal Yacht Club*, to which, undoubtedly, the town owes much of its prosperity, was founded in June 1815. It includes 150 members, and on its lists are enrolled about 120 yachts, employing 1500 seamen, with an aggregate of 11,000 tons. The entrance fee is £15, 15s.; the annual subscription £8. No yachts under 40 tons are enrolled in the club. The annual regatta, one of "the sights" of the season, usually takes place the third week in August, and receives the patronage of the Queen and the Royal Family. A plate of 100 guineas is given by her Majesty. The club is entitled to carry the St. George's ensign. The yachting season extends from May 1st to November 1st.

5. The *Dockyard* and *Shipbuilding Establishment* of the Messrs. White, first established in 1815, has attained a worldwide reputation, having contributed approved vessels to almost every foreign navy as well as to our own. Many of our swiftest yachts have been launched at these yards, where the Messrs. White employ throughout the year nearly 400 men.

6. The *Streets* of Cowes are mostly narrow and hilly, with few large shops or good houses. But the environs are very beautiful, and crowded with pleasant villa-gardens; and near the castle there is *one* good row of houses, built by the late Sir Charles Fellows, and appropriately named the *Marine Parade*. A pleasant promenade has been laid out, and a handsome fountain erected, at the expense of Mr. R. Stephenson, the eminent engineer. The bathing here is very good, from the excellence of the beach, and was famous even in 1760, when an enthusiastic rhymster exclaimed,—

" No more to foreign baths shall Britain roam,
  But plunge at Cowes, and find rich health at home."
                              Vectis, a poem, *H. Jones*.

West Cowes has not given birth to any literary or artistic celebrity. Almost the only associations of this sort which it enjoys are connected with the residence, in 1799, at the house of a surgeon named Lynn, of Morland the painter, who produced here some of his cabinet pictures; and the memory of the late eminent antiquary and traveller, Sir Charles Fellows, who died at his seat near the town.

7. There are two places of worship in the town connected with the Church of England,—*West Cowes Church*, situated on the summit of the hill, and remarkable as one of the few churches built during the Commonwealth; and the *Church of the Holy Trinity*, which occupies a prominent situation on the West Cliff, and has recently been improved by the addition of a new chancel.

There stands a *Roman Catholic Church* in Carvel Lane; a *Wesleyan Church*, Medina Road; and *Independent Church*, Sun Hill. The *Athenæum* is a well-conducted literary society.

SUB-ROUTES.

In laying down these day-journeys we shall endeavour to point out to the tourist all the fair nooks and "angles of this isle," that lie *out* of the beaten guide-book-track, as well as the show-places and tame lions which are the peculiar property of excursionists, and "the flymen" in whom they generally confide. *a.* Along the Parade to Egypt (a villa seated on the most northern point of the island), and thence by Debourne and Gurnard Farm to Gurnard Bay (where Charles II. landed in 1671, on a visit to the governor of the island). Southward, past Rew Street (notice traces of ancient Celtic-Romano Road), to Mark's Corner; then into the Newport Road, and homeward to Cowes along the river-bank. *b.* By the bank of the Medina to Newport, 5 miles, passing Northwood Church, and (about a mile from Newport) Parkhurst Prison, Barracks, and House of Industry. Return through the forest, by the Signal Staff to Mark's Cross, reversing the order of sub-route *a*. *c.* Through Fiddler's Green, and Cockleton, keeping on the skirts of the forest, to Shalfleet, 5 miles, and then, by road on the right, to Newtown, 1½ mile. Return by Clamerkin's Ford and Coleman's Farm, crossing the south-western angle of the Forest to Hedge Corner, reaching the Newport Road near the Parkhurst Reformatory. By the high road back to Cowes. *d.* Through the forest to Bowcombe Down (notice barrows and traces of Roman road), to Carisbrooke Castle, returning *via* Newport. *e.* Cross the river by the ferry to East Cowes, and passing Osborne, take a bridle road through the royal estates from Barton to Wootton Church. Descend the hill to Wootton Bridge (a causeway over a considerable creek), and through Quarr Wood and Binstead into Ryde, 7 miles. Return by the main road to Newport, and back to Cowes *via* Parkhurst. *f.* From Cowes to Northwood, and *via* Parkhurst to Newport. Through the town, and take the right bank of the Medina, passing Fairlie (notice the ancient house and fine glimpses of well-wooded country), to Whippingham, a quiet village with an interesting church; and *via* East Cowes, across the river, home.

EAST COWES (ANCIENTLY SHAMBLORD).

Straggles along the left bank of the river, and up a tolerably steep hill, where it forms a collection of elegant villas, called East Cowes Park,—the unfortunate speculation of an enterprising builder, who relied too confidently on the attractions of its proximity to Osborne. From the summit may be enjoyed a panorama of exquisite beauty,—the mouth of the river with its numerous masts, the town of West Cowes rising in a succession of terraces among

" No
Bu

V
lite
only
e jo
in 1
Ly
duc
and
qua
wh
7
the
En
on
abl
dui
Ch
pie
Cli
the

in
dir
Su
coi

we
tou
of
gui
pla
lia
fly
fid
vil
of
an
(w
vis
So
tia
to
poi
the

WEST COWES.

leafy trees, the green landscapes beyond, the foliage of the New Forest, and the ripples of Southampton Water. About 30 acres were here arranged with taste and effect as a botanic garden. The park itself covered nearly 160 acres. The wood ascending the hill debouches, if we may use the term, opposite the principal entrance to Osborne,—a picturesque archway with handsome iron gates. Observe, too, the entrance to East Cowes Castle, apparently intended as an imitation or a rival of that of Osborne.

Of the castle erected by Henry VIII., from the ruins of a religious house at East Thamblord, not a vestige exists.* It is referred to by Leland: "Ther be two new castelles sette up and furnishid at the mouth of Newporte; that is the only haven in Wighte to be spoken of. That that is sette up on the este side of the havin, is caullid the Est Cow; and that that is sette up at the west syde is caullid the West Cow, and is the bigger castelle of the two."

1. *East Cowes Chapel*, dedicated to St. James, (perpetual curate, Rev. W. V. Hennah, 1839; chapelry to Whippingham Rectory; income £135), a plain, uninteresting building with a square tower. There are, also, places of worship in connection with the chief dissenting denominations.

2. The *Trinity House* has here a district station, with a rather handsome frontage.. The Queen's private landing-place is approached through it.

3. *Population* of East Cowes, in 1795, 300; in 1851, 1440; and in 1861, 1954. The only hotel (well situated on the bank of the river, with a fine view), is the *East Medina*.

SUB-ROUTES.

There is much pleasant rambling to be enjoyed in the neighbourhood, which is thickly wooded, and alternates agreeably between hill and dale,—the river, from many points, producing a charming effect. *a*. From East Cowes through Barton, 1½ mile, to Wootton Bridge, 2 miles, and thence to the venerable ruins of Quarr Abbey, 2 miles, returning through Wootton to Whippingham, 4 miles, will offer a most attractive day's journey. *b*. Or by the river side to Newport, 4 miles, passing a little inn where oysters may be enjoyed, fresh from their "beds" in the Medina, and through Newport to Carisbrooke, 1 mile, thence returning by way of Northwood and West Cowes, about 5 miles. "The rambler may very well keep beside the river to Whippingham, occasionally ascending the uplands; and if he be a lover of river scenery, he will not regret the devious course it has led him. The broad sweep of the stream stretches before you in bold sweeping curves, its clear green water curling into light ripples, and reflecting in long tremulous lines the white sails that are gliding rapidly along; on each side are fine hanging woods, or slopes of 'glad light green;' in front the view is bounded by softly swelling uplands, or when a turn in the path brings into sight the broad opening where the river falls into the sea, by the silver Solent, and the hazy coast beyond." —*Knight*. *c*. A boat voyage up the Medina, taking care to start just before high water so as to secure each way the advantage of the tide, is very enjoyable. *d*. From Cowes, through Wootton and Binstead, adopting the foot path that passes Quarr Abbey, to Ryde (6 miles), and back, will give the pedestrian a day's experience of the finest scenery of this part of the island.

ENVIRONS OF WEST COWES.

Northwood is the name of a village and parish in the West Medina liberty of the Isle of Wight. The parish is bounded north and north-west by the sea; west

---

* "This has been long totally demolished; the materials have from time to time been carried away; some within the memory of persons now living, in order to build a house at Newport, and for other erections."—*Grose, Antiquities*, ii. (A.D. 1776.)

by Calbourne parish ; south by Shalfleet parish, and part of Parkhurst Forest. Contains (including West Cowes) 5122 acres ; 1217 inhabited houses, 86 uninhabited, and 5 building. Population in 1801, 2771 (1318 males + 1453 females); in 1811, 3325 (1598 males + 1727 females); in 1821, 3579 (1703 males + 1876 females); in 1831, 4491 (2097 males + 2394 females); in 1841, 5147 (2377 males + 2760 females); in 1851, 6049 (3155 males + 2894 females; and in 1861, 6534.

The church, dedicated to *St. John the Baptist,* was a chapel of ease to Carisbrooke until the reign of Henry VIII. (A.D. 1545), when parochial privileges were granted to it. There stood in its vicinity before the time of the great destroyer, Henry VIII., a small religious house of " Brothers and Sisters of the fraternity of John the Baptist in the church of Northwood; " but not a trace of it is now discernible, nor is anything known of its history.

Gurnard Bay, a small cove with pleasantly-wooded banks, is well worth a visit. The view of the Hampshire coast, and the mouth of the Beaulieu River, of the bold reach of the Solent, and the distant western heights of the island, is full of variety and interest. " Between Rue Street and Thorney is a small farm called *Whippence,* which deserves some notice, from its being finely shaded by a considerable range of tall elms, that are so disposed as to form a rich boundary to a wide and semi-circular lawn, which gradually descends from the farm-house towards the shore."—*Wyndham.* *Thorness* has also the charm of leafiness, and of an extensive range of wood and water. From the sea *Gurnard Bay* offers a delightful prospect. Roman ruins have been recently found here.*

* It is the traditional site of a seaport to which the tin was brought from Leap, on the opposite coast. Charles II. landed here in 1671, on his visit to Sir Robert Holmes at Yarmouth.

ENVIRONS OF EAST COWES.

Whippingham is a parish and village in the East Medine liberty, evidently so named from its original Saxon holders,—the Wepingas' *ham,* or *home.* Called *Wipingeham* in Domesday Book. The parish is bounded, east by Wootton, west by the Medina, south by Arreton, and north by the Solent, as far as King's Quay. Contains 5208 acres ; and (in 1861) 710 inhabited houses, 58 uninhabited, and 11 building. The population was 3915 (1936 males + 1979 females).

Whippingham church stands on a gentle eminence just above the river, its tower forming a prominent landmark to all the country-side. Near it is the New Cemetery, which has been arranged with much taste, and contains some interesting memorials.

The present building was erected at the cost of the Queen and the late Prince Consort, from the designs of Mr. A. J. Humbert. The first stone was laid by the Queen, May 23, 1860. The style is Norman. The stained glass windows are of good design and colour, and the decorations in admirable taste ; but the most notable feature is Theed's marble monument to the Prince Consort, bearing the following inscription :—" To the beloved memory of Francis Albert Charles Emanuel, Prince Consort, who departed this life December 14, 1860, in his 45th year. This monument is placed in the church erected, under his directions, by his broken-hearted and devoted widow, Queen Victoria, 1864." There is also a memorial to Dr. Arnold's father.

Whippingham is a rectory, valued in the Clergy List at £757, occupied by the Rev. George Prothero, B.D., one of the Queen's chaplains, appointed in 1857. The parsonage commands a beautiful and extensive landscape. It was rebuilt, or modified, by Dr. Ridley, Lord Eldon's brother-in-law, and Dr. Hook, Dean of Worcester, son of the once popular musical composer, and brother of Theodore Hook, of pleasant memory.

Barton, or Burton, is an ancient manor, now forming a portion of the royal demesne of Osborne, between which and King's Quay it lies. After the conquest it belonged to the Fitz Sturs, whose heiress, in the reign of Henry III., married Walter de Insula. Shortly afterwards (A.D. 1282) John de Insula, Rector of Shalfleet, and Peter de Winton, Rector of Godshill, founded here a religious house, and liberally endowed it, dedicating it to the Holy Trinity. The constitution and regulations of the society, which consisted of an arch-priest, five other priests, and a clerk, are preserved in the Winchester registers (A.D. 1259), and are exceedingly curious:—

"1. There shall be six chaplains and one clerk, to officiate both for the living and the dead, under the rules of St. Augustine. 2. One of these shall be presented to the Bishop of Winchester to be the arch-priest, to whom the rest shall take an oath of obedience. 3. The arch-priest shall be chosen by the chaplains there residing, who shall present him to the bishop within twenty days after any vacancy shall happen. 4. They shall be subject to the immediate authority of the bishop. 5. When any chaplain shall die, his goods shall remain in the oratory. 6. They shall have only one mess, with a pittance at a meal, excepting on the greater festivals, when they may have three messes. 7. They shall be diligent in reading and praying. 8. They shall not go beyond the bounds of the oratory without licence from the arch-priest. 9. Their habits shall be of one colour, either blue or black ; they shall be clothed *pallio Hiberniensi de nigra boneta cum pileo* (in the Irish vestment of a black bonnet and a cloak). 10. The arch-priest shall sit at the head of the table, next to him those who have celebrated the great mass, then the priest of St. Mary, next the priest of the Holy Trinity, and then the priest who says mass for the dead. 11. The clerk shall read something edifying to them while they dine. 12. They shall sleep in one room. 13. They shall make a special prayer for their benefactors. 14. They shall, in all their ceremonies, and in tinkling the bell, follow the use of Sarum. 15. The arch-priest alone shall have charge of the business of the house. 16. All of them, after their admission into the house, shall swear to observe these statutes. *Further Ordered :*— After a year and a day from entering into the oratory, no one shall accept of any other benefice, or shall depart the house."— *Journal, Brit. Arch. Association.*

The patronage of the Oratory was bestowed on the Bishops of Winchester. In 1439 the Oratory and its endowments were entirely surrendered into the hands of Cardinal Beaufort, then bishop. William of Waynflete conferred it on Winchester College. It was dissolved by Henry VIII.; but the lands remained in possession of the college, until purchased, about twenty years ago, by her Majesty.

Barton Court House was probably built in the reign of Elizabeth, and some portions of the Oratory used in its construction. When demolished by the Queen's orders, a very solid wall, the sole remainder of the original building, was brought to light. "One peculiarity of the house was, that it contained a room about twelve feet square, known as the Chapel, which had been apparently fitted up as a secret chapel for the performance of mass subsequent to the Reformation, and which, within the memory of living individuals, retained its altar, crucifix, and other Catholic accessories."—*Moody.* Two of the fronts, the southern and eastern, have been preserved in the new building, and are worth inspection as specimens of Tudor domestic architecture.

Osborne, a "household word" with Englishmen, was formerly called *Austerburne*, East Bourne, or the Eastern Brook. After being held for many years by an ancient island-family, the Bowermans, it passed into the hands of the Arneys; then the Lovibonds; and, *temp.* Charles I., was purchased by Eustace Mann, who, according to a vulgar tradition, buried a large sum of money, during the troubles of the civil war, in an adjacent wood (still known as *Money Coppice*), and not marking the spot, was never able to recover his treasure. Mr. Mann's grand-daughter and heiress married a Mr. Blachford, whose son built *Osborne House*, then a plain but commodious mansion of stone. Their descendant, Lady Isabella Blachford, transferred the estate to her Majesty in 1840, who has enlarged it by later purchases, until it comprises 5000 acres, and stretches from the Medina west to Brock's Copse east. The old house was pulled down, and the present mansion built, from the designs of T. Cubitt, Esq., assisted, it is said, by the late Prince Consort. The architecture is Palladian in character, with a campanile or bell-tower 90 feet high, and a flag-tower 107 feet. The Queen occupies the apartments in advance of the latter. The rooms are crowded with objects of taste and *vertu*, sculptures by our most eminent artists, rare specimens of the modern painters, and all the refinements which a cultivated taste could suggest. The gardens are arranged in terraces, with a lawn sloping to the water's edge, where there is a small jetty for her Majesty's convenience. The estate comprises many delightful varieties of scenery,—woodland, meadow, valley, glen, and broad, rich pastures. The Prince Consort's agricultural experiments were here conducted with skill and vigour. The *Model Farm* is arranged with excellent taste. There are spacious kennels on the estate, and numerous excellent cottages for labourers and others, constructed on the most approved sanitary principles. The *lodges* on the East Cowes road are of fanciful design. We may add, that from the grounds and palace visitors are rigorously excluded.

King's Key, about two miles from Osborne, and three south-east from East Cowes, is a narrow but picturesque creek, formed by the small stream of Palmer's Brook, jutting in between high, sloping banks, crowned with thick masses of wood. Its name is connected with a tradition that King John dwelt in its retired neighbourhood for three months, after the signature of Magna Charta (A.D. 1215). "Here he led," says Grafton, "a solitarie lyfe among reivers and fishermen;" but the King's *Itinerary*, or *Journey Book*, lately edited by Mr. Hardy, satisfactorily proves that the tradition cannot be supported by any historical evidence. It was formerly known as Shofleet Creek, and was a favourite resort of the sea-rovers in Elizabeth's reign.

SEATS OF THE GENTRY.

Fairlee lies in the parish of Whippingham, though it is scarcely a mile from Newport. The position is an admirable one, commanding a fine view of the Medina valley and the surrounding country, here eminently sweet and pastoral. The house is a substantial, unadorned building of glazed brick, fronting an ample lawn, which stretches down to the river. —*Maule.*

Padmore House, near Whippingham Church, was formerly a farm, but is now a comfortable family mansion, enjoying broad reaches of woodland, vale, meadow, and water. *Woodhouse Farm*, on the western bank of King's Key, and *Woodside*, a delightful little villa, nestling down amid fine old trees near the Wootton river, are only to be discovered by the tourist who leaves the well-trodden highway for "fresh fields and pastures new." He will gain, for instance, a very delightful day's strolling by taking a bye-way on the left of the East Cowes road, a little below Osborne, and winding through the copses, past Barton Farm, Brook Copse, and Palmer's Farm to Wootton Church, whence he may make his way into the high road, and keeping

Fern Hill on his left, after a mile or two of pleasant country lanes, cross Stapler's Heath, and so into Newport. He can then return to East or West Cowes by one of the sub-routes previously detailed.

Northwood (near West Cowes) is a large stone building, with wings, seated in a considerable park, and commanding a fine prospect of wood and water. It is the seat of G. H. Ward, Esq., formerly well known as the author of a curious book, entitled "The Ideal of a Christian Church." His brother was Sir H. G. Ward, the late governor of Madras.

Norris Castle, finely situated on the brow of a hill which slopes gently to the marge of the Solent, and commands the most beautiful views conceivable of land and sea—of Stokes Bay on the opposite coast; Portsmouth and the sail-thronged roadstead of St. Helen's, with the wooded shore of the Wight away to the glittering villas of Ryde; Northwood, the broad waters of Southampton river, and the masts and roofs of Southampton; and to the west, the abrupt headland of Calshot Castle and the green masses of the New Forest. Norris Castle was built for Lord Henry Seymour by Mr. James Wyatt, and is an adaptation of castellated Gothic to modern purposes. The front is bold and picturesque, and admirably diversified with thick clusters of ivy. A stout sea-wall, built of Swanage stone, at a cost of £2000, has been erected by the present proprietor, Mr. R. Bell. Here George IV. was entertained in 1819, and here the Queen (then Princess Victoria) and the Duchess of Kent resided in 1831. *East Cowes Castle*, in the immediate neighbourhood of Norris Castle, "combines the features of the castellated mansion of a late date, with those of the baronial fortress of a much earlier period;" was rebuilt in its present rococo style by the architect John Nash (1798); and passed through the hands of the Earl of Shannon, R. Barwell, C. R. J. Sawyer, to George Tudor, Esq., whose relict now occupies it. Many of the rooms are fitted up in a style of great magnificence. Observe especially the library and picture gallery. The conservatory is a fine one, 250 feet in length, and the gardens are picturesquely laid out. *Slatwoods* (Mrs. Shedden) is noticeable as the birth-place of Dr. Arnold, the eminent historian, and reformer of our public school discipline. His father was the collector of customs, and died here in 1801. He himself was born at Slatwoods, June 13, 1795, and always looked back to it with singular affection. From "the great willow-tree" in the grounds, he "transplanted shoots successively to Laleham, to Rugby, and to Fox How."—*Stanley's Life of Dr. Arnold.* He revisited it in 1836, and wrote to his sister, Mrs. Buckland: "Slatwoods was deeply interesting. I thought of what Fox How might be to my children forty years hence, and of the growth of the trees in that interval. But Fox How cannot be to them what Slatwoods is to me—the only home of my childhood."—*Stanley.* Arnold died June 13, 1842.

DISTRICT II. (C).—NEWPORT AND ITS ENVIRONS.

NEWPORT,

(*Hotels:* The Bugle; Green Dragon; Star; Wheat Sheaf *Inn*),

Is the metropolitan town of the island. Seated on the Medina river, in a pleasant valley, it is almost surrounded by lofty calcareous downs, whose grassy slopes are always chequered with shifting lights and shadows. It is a market town and a borough, returning two members to parliament. The market is held every Saturday, and brings together the whole produce of the island. The cattle market is held every other Wednesday. A fair is held on Whit-Monday and the two following days. Though almost surrounded by the West Medina liberty, Newport has a jurisdiction of its own; a court of borough petty sessions, which sits every Monday; and county petty sessions every Saturday. The County Court for the island is held here monthly.

THE MUNICIPALITY.

1. Newport, at the instance of Sir George Carey, Governor of the Wight, was summoned to return two representatives to the parliament holden in the 27th Queen Elizabeth, 1585, and from that date has been regularly represented. The right of voting, however, was first restricted to the free burgesses; and as their number was limited to twenty-four, it was essentially a close borough until thrown open by the Reform Act. The ancient borough comprehended the whole of the chapelry of Newport, a part of the parish of St. Nicholas called Castle Hold, the river Medina and harbour of Cowes from the town to a shoal out at sea called the Brambles, and all the land on the contiguous banks where the tide has ever flowed. In the *new* borough, the old districts are included, and also a large part of the parish of Carisbrooke, "completely surrounding the ancient limits, except down the river."

Among its representatives have been the famous Lord Falkland (1640), Admiral Sir Robert Holmes (1678–1689), gallant Lord Cutts (1648), Lord Palmerston (1790 and 1807), and the Right Hon. George Canning (1826). Since the *Reform Bill* the following have been its members:—December 12, 1832—*Thomas Hawkins*, 216 votes; and *Thomas Ord*, 204. January 8, 1835—*Thomas Ord*, 235; and *Thomas Hawkins*, 233. July 26, 1837—*Thomas Hawkins*, 264; and *James Blake*, 263. June 30, 1841—*C. W. Martin*, C., 254; and *J. J. Hamilton*, C., 252. July 30, 1847—*G. Plowden*, C., 262; and *C. W. Martin*, C., 252. July 9, 1852—*W. Biggs*, 310; and *W. N. Massey*, 306. February 10, 1857, on resignation of Mr. Biggs—*R. W. Kennard*, C., 270. March 28, 1857—*Captain C. E. Mangles*, 305; and *Charles Buxton*, 296. April 1859—*R. W. Kennard*, C.; and *W. L. Powys*, C., unopposed. July 1866—*C. W. Martin*, L.; and *R. W. Kennard*, C.

2. The registered electors number 662. Population in 1861, of the town, 3819 (1881 males + 1938 females), with 730 inhabited houses, and 79 uninhabited; of St. Nicholas parish, 183 (74 males + 109 females), with 37 inhabited houses, and 2 uninhabited. Population of the borough in 1861, 7934. Annual value of property, £31,556.

3. The *Income* of the Corporation amounted in 1865–6 to £1011, 12s. 8¼d. The *Expenditure* was £503, 12s. 8¼d. From *Cowes Harbour Duties* was received in 1866, £65, 11s. The *Newport and Cowes Railway* paid £800. The *Poor Rates*, in 1866, amounted to nearly £1800.

4. The *Fire Brigade* consists of a superintendent, three engineers, three foremen, and five firemen. Annual cost, £60.

The town is well lighted, there being about 165 *street lamps* within its precincts. Yearly cost, £360. The *Borough Police* consists of an inspector, at £75 per annum, and four constables, at 18s. per week. The *Hants Constabulary Police* is under the direction of one superintendent, at £120 per annum, three sergeants, and thirty-seven constables paid at the rate of 17s. weekly.

PUBLIC BUILDINGS.

1. The *Town Hall* is situated in the High Street, and faces a large open area or square. It was erected in 1816, from the designs of the architect Nash, at a cost of £10,000, and though heavy in character, is a noticeable building. "The basement is opened on two sides by arches, surmounted by Ionic columns, which support a pediment in front. The columns only are of stone, the remainder being stuccoed." Here are held the weekly sittings of the magis-

trates, the meetings of the Corporation, and all public ceremonials. The council-chamber has a portrait, by Owen, of the late Sir Leonard Worsley Holmes, recorder of the borough. Observe, also, a fine statue (12 feet high) of James I.'s Lord Chief Justice, Sir Thomas Fleming, presented to the town by his descendant, Mr. Fleming, of South Stoneham. Underneath the Town Hall, and in the open place before it (St. James Square), is held the weekly market, which always presents a lively and animated scene.

2. The *Free Grammar School* (St. James Street), a plain stone mansion of the Tudor era, is note-worthy for its historical associations. Here Charles I. met the parliamentary commissioners in the autumn of 1648 (see *ante*, p. 56), and in the room now used as the school-room divine service was performed every Sunday before him and his *suite.** The school was established in 1614–19 by Sir Thomas Fleming, Sir John Oglander, Edward Cheke, of Mottistone, and others of the island gentlemen, for the education on the foundation of fifteen (now twenty) boys, entering at seven or eight years of age, and remaining until they are fifteen. Thirty day scholars are also admitted, and the master may receive boarders. The income is derived from the rents of three houses in Newport, and about 35 acres of land, at Hunny Hill. The master's yearly salary is £120, and he has also a house and garden, rent free. — *Carlisle's Endowed Schools.*

3. The *Isle of Wight Museum* is an interesting collection of antiquities and relics, chiefly local, commenced in 1852, and sheltered in somewhat inconvenient apartments in a house in Lugley Street. It may be inspected gratuitously, but as the funds are derived from voluntary subscriptions, a visitor's small offering will be judiciously bestowed. We extract from a MS. catalogue, drawn up by the curator, the following particulars :--

" The historical and antiquarian department contains : CASE I. A large funereal urn, taken from a British or Celtic *barrow* on Shalcombe Down, measuring 16 inches by 14; several incinerations from similar barrows opened in various parts of the island; ancient Celtic torques; *celts* found at Binstead, Watchingwell, Billingham, &c.; a large collection of pottery from a Romano-British manufactory discovered at Barnes, near Brixton, consisting of fragments of urns, pateras, and other utensils, some specimens being nearly entire. The most interesting feature is its variety, the collection appertaining to several historical eras. The earliest specimens are of a coarse, slightly baked pottery, similar to that of the British or Celtic period. A second variety is Samian ware. The third differs in no respect from the urns found in various Saxon barrows in the island. Many are plain; a few rudely ornamented, coloured either brown, black, red, red and green, or pale blue; Roman bricks and tiles from Carisbrooke; several Romano-British and Anglo-Saxon urns, found in different parts of the island.

" The contents of a Romano-Saxon cemetery, discovered on the estate of Sir John Simeon, Bart., and excavated under the superintendence of the Museum Committee. This collection consists of a Roman (late) brooch, representing a hare, enamelled; a bronze tag sword-belt, buckle, iron dagger, coin of Constantine found at the mouth of an urn, several urns (plain or rudely ornamented, the largest measuring 8 inches by $10\frac{1}{2}$ in width), a few beads, fragments of iron weapons or ornaments, several incinerations, a headless skeleton, &c. Other skeletons were discovered which had been interred without heads, but they were again buried. Arrow-heads, spear-heads, and a gilt spur, from Carisbrooke Castle; a bellarmine from Freshwater, of a blue and white colour; ancient spoons, fetters, &c., dug up near Newport; a collection of quaint shoe-buckles of the last century, and of early clay tobacco-pipes; antique boots, &c.

" CASE II. contains fragments of Celtic funereal urns, with incinerations, found near Yafford and on Compton Down; an ancient British or Celtic bronze instrument, or dagger, and pottery found in a barrow opened on Arreton Down; a collection of Anglo-Saxon remains discovered in various island

---

* The king occupied Sir William Hopkins' house; the cavaliers made merry at the George Inn (long since pulled down); and the parliamentary commissioners stayed at the Bull (now the Bugle) Inn.

barrows, and in the cemetery on Chessell Down, and presented by the late Sir Leonard Worsley Holmes, Mr. Dennett, and other gentlemen. The most interesting are iron swords and knives; iron spear-heads for warfare, and the sports of the chase; a funereal urn, and fragments of others found scattered in the graves; fragments of glass vessels; fibulæ and buckles of bronze and iron, some thickly gilt; gilt earrings, or pendant ornaments; finger-rings of bronze and silver, some gilt; bronze tweezers, a small tooth-comb, and a measuring rule ornamented in ivory or bone; beads of amber-glass, and terra cotta, with various other articles; human skulls, and other bones; horses' teeth; a coin of Marcus Aurelius, and ornamented Roman tile, dug up on Bowcombe Down; a bronze (Roman) armlet, found on a skeleton near Ventnor; contents of an Anglo-Saxon barrow, opened in Arreton Down, by Thomas Cooke, Esq., namely, iron spear-head, small bronze tool or celt, iron knives, iron axe, fragments of pottery, boars' and horses' teeth; several ancient deeds and papers bearing signatures of English sovereigns, &c.

"ANOTHER CASE contains Isle of Wight trade-tokens; English local tokens and half-pence; large and small brass coins, Roman and Greek, not discovered in the island.

"CASE IV. contains 170 silver, and large and small brass Roman and Greek coins (from Augustus Cæsar, A.D. 31, to Gratian, A.D. 313), found in various parts of the island.

"In A RECESS are various interesting relics of the ancient chapel of St. Thomas, Newport, and a collection of human bones of former Anglo-Saxon inhabitants.

"In A ROOM adjacent is a model of old St. Thomas Church; specimens of Roman sculpture found among its materials; Roman tiles, bricks, and mortar from Carisbrooke; steel dies of a sixpence and a shilling formerly coined in Newport; a collection of ancient weapons: ancient sword. &c., &c., &c."

4. The *Isle of Wight Institution* is an elegant structure, erected in 1811, at a cost of £3000, from Nash's designs, and fronts the open area of St. James Square, where the cattle market is held. It contains an excellent library of upwards of 5000 volumes, and a reading-room well supplied with magazines and newspapers. Members are elected by ballot, and pay an admission fee of one guinea and a half, and a yearly subscription of two guineas. The annual income is about £180.

ITS ANNALS.

The *corporation* of Newport consists of a mayor, six aldermen, and eighteen councillors (out of whom the aldermen are chosen), appointed under the provisions of the 6th and 7th William IV. There are also a town-clerk, treasurer, and clerk to the justices. The mayor is elected on Michaelmas day, and sworn in at Carisbrooke Castle before the steward of the governor of the island.

The municipal constituency numbers about 600.

The town (then called *Meda*) received its first charter from Richard de Redvers, Lord of the Island, *temp.* Henry II. A second and fuller charter, very liberal in its provisions, was granted by Isabella de Fortibus, to her "new borough of Medina." Fifteen charters, confirming and amplifying the above, were granted by different English sovereigns from Richard II. to Charles II. They are extant, in excellent preservation among the muniments of the borough, and many are adorned with well-executed portraits of the monarchs who bestowed them.

The first charter of incorporation was given by James I., and substituted for the bailiff of the town a mayor, twenty-four burgesses, and a recorder. The seal then used was of copper, and presented a figure of James I., in royal robes, and crowned. On one side of him the initial J., on the other R., and round the seal the legend, "S'statvtorvm Mercator' Capt, Infra Bvrgvm de Newport in Insvla Vect."

A second charter of incorporation was granted by Charles II., and constituted a corporation of mayor, aldermen, and burgesses; the twelve aldermen elected from the twenty-four burgesses. A recorder was also appointed.

The history of Newport presents some details of interest and importance. It was probably founded by the Romans as a port to their town at Carisbrooke, and was known to them by the name of *Meda*.

What position it held at the epoch of the Norman Conquest it is impossible to ascertain; but it must have acquired some degree of prosperity in the days of Richard de Redvers, when the chapel of St. Thomas was erected at the cost, and by the labour, of its inhabitants.

In 1377 it was captured by the French who had invaded the island, and was so ruthlessly devastated that it remained unoccupied for two years afterwards. They next proceeded to assault the castle of Carisbrooke, but were repulsed by Sir Hugh Tyrril with such signal success, that the localities where the slaughter chiefly occurred were named (it is said) by the exulting islanders *Node* (or *Noddies'*) *Hill* and *Deadman's Lane.*

Newport was again set on fire by the French in the reign of Edward IV., when its church was somewhat injured.

It was almost decimated by the plague in 1582 and two following years, when the captain of the island, Sir Edward Horsey, was one of the victims. The road to Carisbrooke was blocked up by the dead-carts, and so crowded was the cemetery, that licence was accorded to the inhabitants of Newport to form a grave-yard round their own church.

Not the less the town continued to grow in prosperity and increase in influence. A town hall was built, and a jail, and an ordinary established, at which Sir John Oglander had known "twelve knights and as many gentlemen" to attend. In a report of the condition of the island in 1642, drawn up for the Earl of Pembroke, occurs a curious passage :—" Since yᵉ coming of King James," he says, " there is a toun in the island (called Newport) made a mare-toun, which heretofore was only a bayly-toun, and then yᵉ live-tenants and justices had yᵉ same power there they had in yᵉ rest of yᵉ country. But now they have gotten a charter to be a mare-toun and have justices, a recorder, aldermen, &c., which yᵉ other two mare-towns have not, as Yarmouth and Newtoun; they

will not be governed as those two mare-touns and yᵉ rest of yᵉ island are, which is very prejudiciall to yᵉ country, and I wish it might be regulated. And in that toun of Newport yᵉ captain of yᵉ island is clerk of yᵉ market, and hath yᵉ ordering of yᵉ country; this toun, notwithstanding, will take yᵉ power to themselves, and hinder men from buying and selling at their pleasure."

Camden speaks of it as, in his time, "a toun well seated and much frequented, populous with inhabitants, having an entrance into the isle from the haven, and a passage for vessels of small burden unto the key."

In the reign of James I., indeed, some considerable men dwelt in Newport and its vicinity. The James family, at whose house the king refreshed himself when he visited the island in August 1618 ; the Fleming family, whose head was then Lord-Chief-Justice of England ; the Marchs, and the Stephens. In 1614–19, the *Free Grammar School* was established.

In 1623 leave was obtained from the corporation, by Mr. Andrew James, to establish *water-works* for the supply of the town. His scheme never came into full operation, and " the principal part of the water used by the inhabitants was brought in water-carts from Carisbrooke" for more than a century later. But he probably commenced it, inasmuch as an historian, writing about 1796, says, " In digging lately in the beast market for stone to pave the town with, a large reservoir was discovered, and several pipes have likewise been found in the road from Carisbrooke, leading in a direct road to Newport."—*Tomkins.*

The privilege of carrying on a trade in the borough was chiefly confined, in the "good old times," to those who had served their apprenticeship within its limits, and were, so to speak, "native and to the manner born." Thus we find it recorded in the corporation books, Nov. 13, 1629, how the corporation determined that one John Wavell should be " opposed and resisted as farre as lawe and the charter of the borough would afford. And the charge thereof should be borne by the whole corporation." Nor was he allowed to open his store until he had ultimately paid a fine.

Here are two or three extracts illustrative of men and things·as they were :—

"*September* 3, 1624.—It is thought fitt and agreed, that part of the vestrie where the mortar is usuallie made, shall serve to make a prison for the toun, if yt male be admitted by the Chauncellor.

"In 1625, we find 'it being reported that King James is deceased, watch and ward are to be kept daily until the certaintie of the report be known, and longer if need require.'

"*May* 28, 1628.—It is reported 'that the plague is suspected to be in some tounes whereof the inhabitants might have recourse to this toune at Whitsun fair,' and therefore the said fair is not to be holden.

"*September* 20, 1654.—Every house is to provide a watchman at the householder's expense (except the minister and schoolmaster), or to pay double watch for every default.

"*April* 8, 1656.—'A disperse and sale of goods and chattels' to be levied on those citizens who have not duly paid their subscriptions towards 'the maintenance of Mr. Robert Tutchin, the minister.'

"*August* 18, 1656.—A dinner is to be given to the governor, and 'the whole charge of it shall be borne by the toun, for that it is intended the governor shall be moved about some things for the public good of the toun.'

"*March* 13, 1647.—All the able inhabitants to be called together 'to set down what each will give yearly towards the support of a godly minister.'

"*April* 1648.—A monthly taxation of £208 2s. 6¼d., imposed by ordinance of parliament on the Isle of Wight for six months ending the 20th September last, is to be 'set on the town for three months more.' It is agreed that a petition shall be presented to the Houses, praying that Newport, may be relieved from so onerous a burden.

"*August* 25, 1651.—A proclamation is received 'from the parliament of the commonwealth of England, declaring Charles Stewart and his agents, abettors, and complices, to be traitors, rebels, and public enemies.'

"*March* 3, 1661.—It is resolved that three aldermen and three chief burgesses *in their gowns*, attend the mayor to church every Sunday.

"*October* 14, 1662.—The two seats before the governor's seat (in the church) are 'to be left to the disposal of Thomas, Lord Culpeper, to be reduced into a pew for his lady to sit in during the time of his government.' "

1. *Honours of Newport.* — Montjoy Blunt was created Earl of Newport, in the fourth year of Charles I. Succeeded, in 1655, by his son, also Earl of Newport. Charles Blunt died in 1665, and Henry Blunt died 1679. In the reign of Anne, a Lord Windsor was created Baron Newport, succeeded by his son Herbert, who died 1758.

2. *Charities of Newport.*—The *Blue School*, in Lugley Street, was founded in 1761, for the education and maintenance of twenty poor girls born in Newport, who are properly fitted for servants, and made "good Christians and useful subjects." Supported by voluntary subscriptions, and the interest of certain sums of money, bequeathed by Benjamin Cooke, Esq., and Mrs. Martha Cooke, in 1764. The school is regulated by the minister of Newport and six ladies. Every girl, on leaving, is presented with suitable clothing, a Bible, and a prayer-book. If she retains for one year the situation with which she is provided, she is rewarded with the gratuity of a sovereign.

Worsley's Almshouses were founded in 1618, by Sir R. Worsley, in pursuance of the will of one Giles Kent; they consist of six small tenements of one room each, inhabited by six poor widows.

The Upper Almshouses are four tenements, occupied by deserving families, established in 1623 by Daniel Serle of Westmill, in the parish of Carisbrooke.

Widow Roman's Almshouses were erected in 1752, in pursuance of the provisions contained in her will :—" I bequeath to such six widows as shall inhabit the Charity House in Newport, called the Lower Almshouse, situated in Crocker Street, and shall not receive alms from the town, the sum of £10 every year for ever, after the decease of my brother-in-law W. Roman, from my property at Yafford, free from all taxes and deductions whatever; by equal portions, by the churchwardens and overseers of the poor of the parish of Newport, to be disposed of to the six widows equally, share and share alike." Each widow, therefore, at Michaelmas and Lady Day, receives 16s. 8d.

Bowle's and *Ruffin's Gifts* are two sums of £5 each, distributed yearly to the poor on Christmas Eve. The first £5, Bowle's gift, are expended in bread; Ruffin's donation, in bread and beef.

3. *Religious Edifices.*—There is a picturesque new church in Newport, dedicated to *St. Thomas a Becket,* whose spire is everywhere so prominent a landmark, that the tourist cannot fail to find its locality without difficulty. *St. John's Church* (perpetual curate, Rev. R. Hollings), is situated on St. John's Hill. There are also a *Catholic Chapel* in Pyle Street; a *Baptist Chapel* in Castle Hold; *Primitive Methodist,* in Holywood Street; *Wesleyan,* in Pyle Street; *Independent,* at Node Hill, and in St. James's Street; and *Unitarian,* in High Street. Of these full particulars will be found in Part III.

4. " Newport stands nearly in the centre of the island, in a spot apparently marked out by nature for the site of the miniature capital. It is built on a gentle slope rising from the west bank of the Medina, which is navigable for vessels of considerable burden up to the town; and the nature of the surrounding hills allows of easy lines of communication to radiate from it to every part of the island. The town itself is neat, clean, cheerful-looking, and apparently flourishing. The streets are well paved and lighted, and filled with good, well-stored shops."—*Thorne.* " Newport is essentially a domestic town—the heart and centre of the Isle of Wight. Its streets are laid out with great regularity, the largest ones lying east and west, with cross ones north and south, dividing the area into chequers. The two principal ones are those which connect the great roads—St.

James's Street, from Cowes road, to that which leads by Niton to the Undercliff; and High Street, which connects the Ryde road with the road to Carisbrooke, and the western roads which diverge from them."—*Mudie.* The original plan of the town appears to have contemplated three large squares, or piazzas, for markets of poultry, cattle, and corn, to be formed by the intersection of the main streets. In one of these now stands St. Thomas's Church; the Town Hall has encroached upon another; and a third is irregular enough, though not diverted from its original purpose.

At high water there is a depth, at the town-quays, of about six feet; but at low water it does not exceed two feet. Many plans have been devised for deepening and widening the channel of the river —one by Sir John Rennie, the eminent engineer—but the estimated outlay has always deterred the inhabitants from embarking in the enterprise. And, assuredly, the railway now in course of construction between Cowes and Newport will afford a more convenient mode of transit.

" Set in the midst of our meridian Isle,
By wandering heaths and pensive woods embraced,
With dewy meads, and downs of open smile,
And winding waters, naturally graced,
The rural capital is meetly placed.
Newport, so long as to the blue-eyed deep
Thy river by its gleamy wings is traced,
Be it thine thy portion unimpaired to keep!"
Edmund Peel.

5. *Extinct Ecclesiastical Foundations.* —At *St. Cross* (long the seat of G. Kirkpatrick, Esq.), there was formerly a small *priory,* dependent upon the French abbey of Tiron, and afterwards, on the dissolution by Henry V. of the alien priories, bestowed upon the college of Winchester. It was in existence before 1155, as the name of " Gerard, Prior de Sancta Cruce," occurs among the witnesses to a grant made by William de Vernon to the monks of Quarr. It is mentioned in the Lincoln Taxation, 20 Edward I., and amongst the alien priories, 25 Edward. In part 1. Richard

II., it is called the *Hospital* of St. Cross, " Rex dedit Johanni de Coweshall custodiam hospitalis Sanctæ Crucis in insula Vectis ad totam vitam." (The king gave the charge of the Hospital of St. Cross to John de Coweshall for his whole life).—*Dugdale*, and *Tanner*.

The Chantry was founded by one John Garston, and dedicated to the Blessed Virgin. There is still a house in Newport—the Chantry House—which preserves its-memory.

At *Marvel*, near Standen, was a small college of secular priests, founded by Henry of Blois, Bishop of Winchester.

6. There has been little alteration in the ground-plan of Newport in the last two centuries and a half. In Speed's " Theatre of Great Britaine's Empire " (1635), there is a plan of the town " described by William White, senior," which might almost be used by the modern tourist. The five principal streets running from east to west, or rather south-west, are " Lugley Street, Crocker Street, High Street, Pile Street, and Cosham Street." These are crossed by " Holyrodde Street," and " St. James's Street." The key is connected with " Holyrodde Street," by Key Street, and with Lugley Street by " Shospoole Street." Sea Street connects Shospoole Street with High Street. " Sainte Cross," Castle Hold, and the Church-yard are also indicated.

SUB-ROUTES.

a. " The walks in the immediate vicinity of Newport are many of them very beautiful ; but there is one spot in particular which affords so pleasant a prospect that it should on no account be left unvisited. We refer, of course, to Mountjoy, the lofty hill on the south of the town. From the summit of this hill you see, on a clear day, the whole lower valley of the Medina and the surrounding country,—a rich, undulating tract, where shining meadows alternate with dusky lines of sombre foliage,

and the broad Medina, winding through the midst, leads the eye along the curves of the valley to its union with the sea, where a forest of small craft and a light hazy vapour mark the site of Cowes. Bounding the valley on the right is a range of low hills, from the highest of which the town of Osborne rises out of a dense mass of trees. On the left another range of uplands terminates near you in the brown, heathy tract of Parkhurst Forest. In the extreme distance are the purple hills of Hampshire ; between which and the northern side of the island the Solent breaks upon the sight at intervals, between the depressions in the uplands, gleaming in the sunshine like a number of small lakes. And at the foot of the hill on which you stand lies the town of Newport, its regular rows of plain houses and dark red roofs partly concealed by noble trees, which, with the grey tower of the old church and the masts of the ships that are lying by the town quay, not only break the uniformity and loneliness of the buildings, but render the little town a bold and striking relief to the open country beyond, and assist it in throwing the whole landscape into exquisite harmony."—*Knight*. This, indeed, is " a morning walk " which we stoutly recommend to the pedestrian tourist. *b.* From Newport to Carisbrook, 1½ mile, and view the famous old castle (see *post*, p. 90) ; thence, through a pleasant valley with sloping downs on each side, to one of the prettiest of the island churches, Shorwell, 4 miles (notice the fine old mansion of Northcourt); to the leafy village of Brixton, or Brighstone, with its memories of Ken and Wilberforce, 2 miles ; back to Newport by the same road. *c.* Or, continue from Brixton to Mottistone, 2 miles, and across the downs to Swainston and Calbourne, 2 miles (see Route IV.); homeward *via* Parkhurst, 4 miles. *d.* Or, from Newport to Wootton Bridge, 4 miles; Quarr Abbey, 1 mile; Binstead, 2 miles; and Ryde, 1 mile; returning to Wootton Bridge, 4 miles; by a road to the left to Arreton, 3 miles; and by a most picturesque road into Newport, 4 miles. *e.* A delightful day may be spent in an excursion to the wild beauties of the Undercliff, thus: Newport to Standen, 1½ mile; Pidford, 1½ mile; thence by Rookley, keeping the left road, to Godshill, its quaint village and fine church, about 4 miles; from Godshill, passing Appuldurcombe — the ancient seat of the Worsleys, to Steep Hill, Ventnor, and Bonchurch, 5 miles. Return through St. Laurence, 2 miles, to Whitwell (notice ruined church), 1 mile; then, *viâ* Whitcomb, Black Down, and Appleford, to Kingston, one of the smallest of parishes, by a romantic and heathy road, 5 miles; from Kingston, passing Billingham House, across the chalky height of Chillerton Down, 2 miles, to Gatcombe, a delectable little hamlet, nestled away amidst bright waters and green trees, 1 mile; and homeward, *viâ* Marvel and Watergate to Newport, 3 miles. A long tour, but a surprising one, opening up the widest contrasts of scenery, and the amplest possible reaches of landscape and seascape. *f.* We must also recommend to the tourist our *hill-route,* as we were wont to call it in the days of our island pedestrianism. Leave Newport by "The Long Lane" (it well deserves its name), and cross Arreton Down, 4 miles (notice the fine panoramic interchange of hill and dale spread out around you). Then across by Messly Down, to Ashey Down, 3 miles, known afar off by its sea-mark, and from whose summit may be enjoyed *the* view in the island, which lies beneath you, spread out like a many-coloured map. From Ashey Down a road bending slightly to the south leads to Brading Down, 2 miles; descend into the valley, and take the Brading road to Yarbridge (where Izaak Walton's disciples will find good carp and dace), 1½ mile. Then, up a steep lane which winds between blooming banks and chalky rifts, *viâ* Yaverland (notice Norman church), to Bembridge Down, 1½ mile (notice its obelisk). Return through Yaverland, keeping the coast-road, to Sandown, 3 miles, and its lovely bay; and thence, through the fair valley of the Yar, *viâ* Lake, 1 mile, and Borthwood, 1½ mile, to Newchurch, 2 miles. Descending the hill, keep by the base of the downs to Arreton, 2½ miles, and go into Newport, *viâ* St. George's Down and Shide, or *viâ* Long Lane, 4 miles. *g.* A short but pleasant walk may be enjoyed from Newport, across Staplers' Heath, and through or by Briddlesford to Haven Street, returning *viâ* Combley Wood into Long Lane. *h.* Or, a well-trodden route is that which conducts the Newport flyman through Shorwell to Brighstone, and then away south to Chale and Blackgang (notice chine), returning *viâ* Kingston, Chillerton, and Gatcombe. *i.* The walks to West Cowes, or to East Cowes and Osborne, or *viâ* Parkhurst Forest to Newtown, Shalfleet, and Yarmouth, or by Calbourne, over a wonderfully picturesque and breezy road, which crosses Chessel, Shalcombe, and Afton Downs, to Freshwater-Gate (about 13 miles), will naturally suggest themselves to the intrepid tourist, who is advised to determine for himself *where* he will go, and by *what road* he will go, for if he confides in the mercies of the Newport flyman, he will see "the show-places," and miss the rarest beauties of the island. *k.* The tourist should devote a day to an examination of the curious pit-villages of the Celts still discernible at Gallibury, Rowborough, and Newbarns (see *post*). Rowborough and Gallibury are easily reached by the road to Shorwell, *turning off to the right* at Rowborough Farm. He may then cross Brixton Down to Mottistone Down, and in a little shadowy combe on its slope towards Mottistone, inspect the *Long Stone,* a curious cromlech or Celtic memorial (see *post*).

Many of the places mentioned above

will be
tricts I
sketch 1
rate dist
port.

I. A:
the Isle
8833 a
habited
Popula
in 1821
1964 ;
female
lage is
from V
Bou
Newch
ton an
and Ca
The
valley,
pastur
winds
Richm
while
covere
with a
blue v
The
of sca
small,
and p
situat
distar
On
Georg
in the
died
ward
d'Eve
tion v
read a
ably
ficel
b

ths ago.
n, to the right, seat of a branch of the De Lisles, one of
whom, Sir John de Lisle, built here a

chapel, dedicated to St. Martin ; *West Standen*, near Long Lane, formerly included among the possessions of Isabella de Fortibus ; *Haseley*, granted by one Engelgerius de Bohun to the monks of Quarr, and by them converted into a pleasant grange, sold, with Quarr Abbey, to John Mills, a Southampton merchant (*temp.* Henry VIII.), and by his descendants to the father of Sir Thomas Fleming, James I.'s Lord Chief Justice, — here Sir Edward Horsey died of the plague, 1582 ; *Merston, Periton, Budbridge, Pidford, Stapler's Heath,* from which there " is a very fine view ;" and *Blackwater*, or *Blackbridge*, at the head of Wootton River, " a region of the thickest shade, where antique and decayed oaks expose their half naked roots from both the banks."—*Wyndham.* We may add that *Haseley* belonged to the great Harold who fell at Hastings,— " the last of the Saxon kings."

ARRETON is a vicarage in the gift of the Fleming family (Rev. J. B. Snow, presented 1843 ; Rev. H. Brooks, curate), valued in the Clergy List at £220 *per annum.* The church was one of the six bestowed by William Fitz-Osbert on the abbey of Lire. The manor was conferred by Baldwin de Redvers upon his new foundation at Quarr. At the dissolution of the Religious Houses Sir Levinus Bennett became possessed of it, and his son sold it to Lord Culpeper (or Colepeper), whose daughter and heiress bought it into the Yorkshire family o Fairfaxes, now represented by the present owner, Charles Wykeham Martin, Esq.

Arreton Farm-house is a good specimen of the Jacobean domestic architecture, in the occupancy of F. Roach, Esq. .... *Stickworth* is a considerable seat, south of Arreton, 5 miles south-east of Newport..... *Fern Hill* (J. J. Galt, Esq.) is in this parish, but more conveniently visited from Ryde. Its position, on the brink of a declivity, well-wooded, and commanding a fine view of the broad sweep of the Wootton River,

and the blue sheeny Solent, renders it a noteworthy mansion. It was built by Lord Bolton, when governor of the island, and " appears to have been erected upon the plan of a church ; a lofty and handsome tower rises from one end, with a large Gothic window near its base, while a single room annexed to the other end, of an inferior height and breadth to the rest of the building, denotes the chancel of it."

II. GATCOMBE.—The fair village of Gatcombe (the *gate* or *opening* of the *valley*) lies 3½ miles S.S.W. of Newport, 11 from Ryde, and 7½ from Ventnor. The parish contains 1392 acres, and, in 1861, possessed a population of 201 (110 males + 91 females) ; in 1841, 306 ; in 1831, 263 ; in 1821, 247 ; in 1811, 239 ; and in 1801, 222. There were 40 inhabited and 4 uninhabited houses in 1861. Boundaries :—northwest and south, parish of Carisbrooke ; Arreton, east. A portion of Chillerton hamlet is included in this parish.

In Domesday Book the manor is mentioned among the possessions of the Norman knight, William Fitz-Stur. A younger branch of the Worsleys enjoyed for centuries this most agreeable estate.*

Gatcombe House (Mrs. Bidgood) is a large stone mansion, built about 1750, by one of the Worsley family. "The tower of the adjoining church, just showing its top and pinnacles from above the grove in which it is embosomed, ... the high knolls of timber that back and flank the building, and a range of coppice that covers the steep precipice of a lofty hill on the south side, sufficiently mark out its beautiful situation."—*Wyndham.*

Gatcombe is a rectory (Rev. J. Barrow, 1854 ; Rev. J. Back, curate), in the presentation of the University of Oxford, who purchased it in 1821.

III. CARISBROOKE (*Six Bells Inn*, and

* Of this branch of the Worsleys came the gallant Sir Edward, who attempted to release Charles I. from his imprisonment at Carisbrooke.

New Inn), anciently Beaucombe, Bowcombe, or Buccombe, *the fair valley*, is one of the largest, most fruitful, and most populous of the parishes of the island. It includes 7409 acres, and a population, in 1861, of 7502 (4072 males + 3430 females), against 6712 in 1851, 5613 in 1841, 4713 in 1831, 4670 in 1821, 2811 in 1811, and 2353 in 1801,—having nearly trebled in half a century. According to the present rate of increase, its population, in 1871, would be 8550, nearly. In 1861, there were 1196 inhabited houses, 67 uninhabited, 9 building. [The parish of Carisbrooke includes the hamlets of Bowcombe, Billingham, and part of Chillerton; also Parkhurst Forest, containing 2 houses. Part of Parkhurst Prison, containing 315 persons in 1861; and the Isle of Wight House of Industry, containing 461 persons in 1861, are in this parish."—*Census Comm.* 1863.] A considerable portion of the town of Newport is also within it. The value of rated property has largely increased of late years.

1. There anciently stood here, on the summit of the hill, and facing the stately castle—pleasantly enough placed among bowery trees and green uplands, and with a fine view northward of busy Newport, and the broad lights of the rippling Medina—a goodly PRIORY of Benedictine monks, associated with the famous Abbey of Lire. This wealthy house was founded by William Fitz-Osbert, about 1070, and endowed with six of the richest island churches,—Arreton, Whippingham, Newchurch, Godshill, Niton, and Freshwater—the neighbouring pile of Carisbrooke being added at a later period, besides fair lands and liberal revenues. Successive lords of the island followed in Fitz-Osbert's pious footsteps, and Carisbrooke Priory became second only to Quarr Abbey in wealth and influence. When Edward III., in want of funds to support his wars with France, seized upon all the alien priories—that is, upon those which were connected with religious houses abroad—Carisbrooke also passed into his hands, and, after a brief time, was bestowed upon the Abbey of Mont Grace, in Yorkshire.

Henry IV., in 1399, desirous of confirming his friendly relations with the French court, restored the priory to the Abbey of Lire; but it was again resumed by Henry V., and conferred upon the new abbey which he had founded at Sheen. After Henry VIII.'s celebrated *coup-de-grace*, the Sheen monks leased Carisbrooke, worth about £270 yearly, and the tithes of Godshill and Freshwater, to Sir James Worsley for £105, 6s. 2d. per annum,—a considerable sum in those days. A renewal of the lease was granted to his son Richard, on whose death it passed to the celebrated Walsingham, Elizabeth's great statesman, with the hand of the Worsley's widow. It is said that he destroyed the offices of the monks. From him it was purchased by Sir Thomas Fleming, at the same time that he obtained possession of Quarr Abbey; and the stately structure speedily fell into utter and lamentable decay. The site is now occupied by a farm, into whose walls, apparently, have been built some portions of the ancient building, which "probably extended itself as far as the church, and had an entrance into it."—*Tomkins.*

A *chapel*, dedicated to St. Augustine, and mentioned in the Cartulary of Carisbrooke (which is still extant, and contains upwards of 200 deeds, records, grants, and papers) as "a chapel for lepers," formerly stood near the priory; but not a vestige of it remains.

2. CARISBROOKE CASTLE.—The great glory and chief boast of Carisbrooke, however, is the famous pile, so grand even in its very decay, whose crown of towers circles the artificial mound rising with such abruptness out of the fertile valley, 239 feet above the sea. Between this mound, and the hill up whose ascent straggles the long street of Carisbrooke village, winds a branch of the Medina,

—noted for the excellence of its shining waters,—and spreads a pleasant sweep of grassy plain. Against the horizon—southward and westward—towers a range of lofty downs. At the foot of the hill clusters the town of Newport, with its church spires and tiled roofs presenting a curious picture; in the mid-distance rise the masts of Cowes Harbour, and still further off, the blue hills of Hampshire. The massive tower of Carisbrooke Church, and the green masses of Parkhurst Forest, relieve the view in another direction. And so—

" The pastoral slopes in noonday quiet sleep,—
Green lanes run down into the valley green,
Or climb, 'mid gleamy brooks, a bosky steep,—
Towers over hill and dale the castle's haughty keep ! "
Edmund Peel.

In fact, CARISBROOKE, from " the bravery " of its position, and the extent of its ruins, as well as its pregnant historical associations, cannot fail to impress the thoughtful observer with peculiar force. " I do not think," wrote Keats, " I shall ever see a ruin to surpass Carisbrooke Castle." And he proceeds with some lively details : " The trench is overgrown with the smoothest turf, and the walls with ivy. The keep within side is one bower of ivy ; a colony of jackdaws have been there for many years. I daresay I have seen many a descendant of some old cawer who peeped through the bar at Charles I., when he was there in confinement. "—*Keats' Life and Letters.*

The tourist from Newport proceeds along the ancient Mall, and crossing the *brooke* which, with the *caer* (a stronghold or fort) above it, gives name to the village, laboriously ascends the steep eminence on which the venerable pile is based. He then finds himself opposite the entrance, an archway of picturesque character, of the reign of Elizabeth, for it bears her initials, and the date 1598, on a stone shield over the arch. Crossing a stone bridge which spans the moat, now filled with wild flowers and verdant turf, he reaches the *Gate-house*, built by gal-

lant Antony Woodville, a stately machicolated structure, still boasting of its ancient, cross-barred, ponderous gates, and adorned with noble circular towers, which have been grooved for two portcullises. Not long ago these towers were nearly shrouded in the most luxuriant ivy, but during the recent repairs their rich overgrowth was carefully removed, much to the detriment of their picturesque character, though an advantage in the way of insuring them a longer existence. The Woodville escutcheon is discernible over the gate, flanked on each side by the " White Rose " of the house of York.

Having entered the castle area you see, on your left, the ruins of the apartments which formed the *prison of King Charles* during so many months of heart-weariness and impending peril. The cicerone points out a window as that from which the unhappy monarch sought to escape, —but this is a pleasant fiction. The *true* window was an aperture " blocked up in after alterations, but nevertheless easily recognisable in the exterior of the wall, as it nearly adjoins the only buttress on this side of the castle."—*Hillier.* This part of the ruins is of the architecture of the 15th century.

To the right lie the scanty ruins of the *Chapel of St. Nicholas.* The fane was only erected in 1738, during Lord Lymington's governorship, but it has been suffered to moulder into complete decay. It was built on the site of a former chapel, or oratory, founded by Fitz-Osbert. Over it there was formerly an armory, dismantled by orders of Lord Cadogan.

The *Tilt-yard*, or *Bowling Green*, was converted by Col. Hammond out of the ancient place of arms, for the amusement of Charles I. " The bowling green on the barbican with its turf steps, the walls of the old castle frowning above it, and its beautiful marine view, is as perfect at the present moment as if it had been laid down but yesterday,"—as perfect as when the Stuart walked there to and fro attended by Col. Hammond, or the Princess Elizabeth played "at bowls, a sport she much delighted in."

The plain, indeed, the somewhat ugly mansion which faces you as you enter appears to have been modernized out of the original *Hall*, and divided into two stories. It was formerly connected with the keep by a strong wall. During the recent repairs,—ably directed by Mr. Hardwicke, the architect,—many interesting details, hitherto concealed, have been discovered. A stalwart chimney, and one of the ancient windows on the side opposite to the keep, may now be seen. The *smaller* of the *two* chapels which once existed within the castle precincts,—the chapel erected by Isabella de Fortibus,—has been brought to light. The side window remains, and the beautiful arcade on both sides, but of the east window there is no trace but the position of the sill; it is now occupied by the great staircase which Lord Cutts put up when he repaired the governor's residence.— *The Builder*, No. 739. "Adjoining the chapel, south, was the principal apartment of the castle, communicating with the chapel by means of a hagioscope. In this room is a very fine ancient staircase."—*Murray*. Some of the apartments in the governor's residence are worth examination, with the coved ceilings of "the Georgian era."

The massive and venerable *keep* lies to the north-east, and stands upon an artificial mound, bravely overlooking the rest of the castle, and commanding a grand panorama of the surrounding landscape. It is reached by a weary flight of 74 rather difficult steps, leading to a stout gateway grooved for a portcullis. The keep is a Norman erection, of what date is uncertain. In the interior there is a smaller flight of steps, leading to the irregular polygon, 60 feet broad, formed by the massive walls of the old Tower. The donjon well (for there were two wells in the castle),—of a fabulous depth, according to tradition,—has long been choked up.

"One of the most curious things in the castle is *the* other well, which is above 300 feet deep" (really, 144 feet deep, with 37 feet depth of water). "The visitor is shown into the well-house (near the entrance); and while he is noticing the singular appearance of the room, one side of which is occupied by an enormous wooden wheel, a small lamp is lighted; and after being told to mark the time that elapses before a glass of water that is thrown down strikes against the bottom of the well, the lamp is lowered by means of a small windlass, making, as he watches its descent, a circle of light continually lessening till the lamp is seen to float on the surface of the water, at a depth that makes him almost dizzy. A grave old donkey is then introduced, who quietly walks into the huge treadwheel, which he anon begins to turn,—as curs in days of yore turned spits,—whereby the bucket is lowered and drawn up again, which feat being accomplished, Jacob very soberly walks out again."— *Knight*. The building over the well (of the date of the 15th century), has been carefully repaired and restored by Mr. Hardwicke. The well itself probably reaches the chalk-marl, which is in general the first water shed when the white chalk is perforated.

We need not dwell upon the history of Carisbrooke Castle, which is, in fact, the history of the island, as we have already given it at considerable detail in the earlier pages of our little volume. Its name is said to have been corrupted from that of the old Jutish stronghold, whose site it probably occupies,—Wihtgarabyrig, Garsburg, Garsbrook, Carisbrooke. Warner claims for it a yet more fanciful derivation,—*Cuerbroc*, the town among the yew trees. But its real etymology seems to us sufficiently obvious: *Caer*, the fort; *brooke*, on the brook or stream, an appellation clearly descriptive of its peculiar situation.

There can be little doubt but that Carisbrooke was originally a British settlement, and that it commanded or overawed the great highway of the tin trade which crossed the island from Gurnard Bay to Puckaster Cove. By the Romans its eligibility as a military position was immediately recognised, and there is evidence enough to prove that with them it was the principal island-settlement, only pushed from its pride of place by Newport, when the situation of the latter, on a navigable stream, rendered it commercially of greater importance. The old Roman road—laid down, we fancy, on the line of the British traject—may still be traced upon Buccombe Down. The recent discovery of a large Roman villa, adjoining the parsonage, confirms the truth of this hypothesis.

William Fitz-Osbert commenced the erection of the present stronghold, and some parts of his handiwork are, probably, still extant. Richard de Redvers largely repaired and rebuilt it, inventing, we are told, many new engines of war, and raising, perhaps, the glorious massive keep, evidently of early Norman architecture. By Isabella de Fortibus it was completely repaired, and considerably strengthened. In a recent work a very curious statement of the expenditure she incurred has been published— from the original document—and there is extant an *inquisition*, or *survey of the island*, taken shortly after her death, which affords an interesting view of the then condition of the castle :—" The jury say, upon their oath, that the advowson of the free chapel of the blessed Nicholas, in the Castle of Carisbrooke, belongs to the abbot and convent of Quarrera. A house in the same castle, to wit, one hall, four chambers for straw adjoining the hall, with a solar (upper chamber) ; one small church, and another great church, which churches are supported at the expense of the Abbot of Quarrera ; one large kitchen ; one chamber for the constable, with a solar to the same : one small chamber

beyond the gate, and another under the wall ; one great chamber with a solar ; one house which is called the ' Old Chapel;' one larder ; one great house which is called ' the bakehouse and brewhouse,' in which there is a granary at one end ; two great stables for corn and forage ; two high towers, built with the chamber for straw, and other two towers built under the wall ; one house, with a wall for a prison ; one chamber near the same. Richard le Porter hath the custody of the prison in the castle, and of the castle-gate, for the term of his life, by charter of Isabella, formerly Countess of Albemarle, and receives yearly, from the manor of Buccombe, his pension." The chapel recently brought to light by Mr. Hardwicke is the " small church " herein mentioned, and was built by Isabella de Fortibus; for in the accounts already alluded to occurs an entry, " For cleansing and making a foundation for the new church."

The castle-walls, at this period, only included an area of an acre and a half, and were nearly "in figure a rectangular parallelogram, having the angles rounded." — *Worsley*. Montacute, Earl of Salisbury, did something towards its repair in the 9th year of Richard II., and great additions were made to its strength and beauty by Antony Woodville, better known as Lord Scales, during his captaincy of the island. At a later period it was thoroughly repaired by order of Henry VIII. When the alarm of invasion by the Spanish armada echoed through the land, the fortifications were completely remodelled on the plan of those of Antwerp, by Genebella, the Italian engineer, who constructed Tilbury fort. The ramparts erected by him are still in some degree of preservation, and include twenty acres of ground, their circuit being nearly a mile. The Queen contributed £4000, the gentry of the island £400, and the commonalty their personal labour, by digging the

outward ditch without fee or payment.
The present building is, in fact, the
Castle of Carisbrooke, as enlarged and
strengthened in the days of Elizabeth.
The works occupied 245 days (25th March
to 24th November, 1587), and the manual labour and materials cost £470,
18s. 5d., nearly £6000 at the present
value of money.

The governor's residence within the
castle was repaired and rebuilt by Lord
Cutts, and afterwards by Lord Bolton,
during their respective governorships of
the island. Their successors being
"non-resident," took but little heed of
the condition of the grand old stronghold, and it gradually mouldered away
into grievous dilapidation, until two
years ago Mr. Hardwicke was commis-
sioned to check the decay, and effect
what reparation he could.

And so, let us hope, this famous pile,

> Whereon the men of other times
> Have stamped their names, and deeds, and crimes,

will raise, for many a long year, its gray
keep and ivied buttresses upon the height
of Carisbrooke, a splendid memorial of
the historic past. *

3. *The Roman Villa.* (See *Appendix.*)

4. CARISBROOKE CHURCH (see *Pt.* iii.)
is a very fine specimen of early English,
and its noble tower is an admirable landmark for all the country side.

5. A *Roman Catholic Nunnery* has
recently been erected in the vicinity of
the village, by the Countess of Clare, at
a cost of £18,000. The buildings possess
no particular architectural pretensions,
but are simple, and even elegant in design.

6. *Carisbrooke Cemetery*, a spot to
make one, as Shelley says, "in love with

---

* In 1807, Sir Walter Scott (then writing
the first part of "Marmion"), visited Carisbrooke in company with his friend, W. Stewart
Rose, who alludes to the journey in his poem
of "Gundimore:"—

> "Bound to the gloomy bower
> Where Charles was prisoned in yon island tower."

death," was formed in 1858, at a cost of
£4500. Its two chapels are in the Early
English style.

IV. PARKHURST. — At Parkhurst
three considerable buildings attract the
attention of the tourist : the *Barracks*,
the *Prison*, and the *House of Industry*.

1. The *Barracks* lie to the left of the
road connecting Newport with West
Cowes, about half a mile from the former. They were established in September 1798, and were originally called
Parkhurst Barracks; but their name was
afterwards changed to *Albany*, in com-
pliment to the then Commander-in-chief,
the Duke of York and Albany. They
occupy an area of 1211 feet by 700—or
about 100 acres—and include five officers'
houses, eight large and twelve small
barracks, a house for the commandant,
another for the chief accountant, a
chapel, necessary offices, and a large
parade ground, next in completeness to
that of Chatham. There are three
excellent wells worked by means of
engine-pumps. Altogether, the arrangements of the Barracks, which will accommodate about 2000 men, are excellent,
and their sanitary condition superior to
that of most of our English barracks.
The depots of several regiments are
always stationed here. Lt.-Col. Jeffrey
is the present commandant, and the
number of troops stationed here in 1861
was 849.

2. In 1838 the government converted
the hospital portion of the Barracks into
a *reformatory prison* for juvenile offenders, and the experiment answered so
admirably as to lead to the construction
of a second prison, a little higher up the
hill. Together the two buildings would
contain 700 prisoners, but the average
number of inmates at one time is 400.
The system adopted is a combination of
punishment and prevention,—"the prevention of crime in the unconvicted, and
the reformation and punishment of the
convicted offender,"—objects sought to
be attained "by moral and religious in-

struction and industrial employment. The penal discipline consists of deprivation of liberty, wearing an iron on the leg, a strongly-marked prison dress, and a regular diet reduced to its minimum. Silence is enforced, and the prisoners are subjected to uninterrupted surveillance." From a recent *Parliamentary Report* we extract a few additional particulars: During 1856, 201 prisoners were received into the prison, in addition to 429 remaining on the 31st December 1855. Of these 10 were discharged on the expiration of their sentence, 106 liberated on licence, 5 pardoned, 30 transferred to Pentonville, 429 remained in prison on the 31st December, and the remainder were removed to other jails. At the probationary schools 580 boys received instruction during the year; 115 petty offences by them were entered in the school-book; 64 were reported to the governor for punishment, leaving 516 not reported, and 465 not complained of for petty offences. Out of 282 boys received, on their entrance, into the senior school, 42 could not read at all, 49 scarcely at all, and 151 imperfectly; 70 could not spell, 61 could not write, 138 could not cypher, and 158 were entirely ignorant in Scriptural and general information. At the close of the year *all* the 282 could read a little, 103 *well;* all could spell tolerably, and 67 excellently; 108 could write well, and only 4 wrote badly; 119 could cypher well, and only 15 indifferently. Out of 201 boys received in one year (1856), 27 were under 14 years of age, 48 were 14 years of age, 69 were 15 years old, and 54, 16, while 3 were aged 17. The expenditure of the prison for the year ending March 31, 1857, amounted to £13,867, 13s. 0½d. The productive labours of the prisoners, and other receipts, amounted to £1755, 2s. 5½d., leaving a charge upon the state of £12,112, 10s. 7d. The average annual cost of each prisoner is £24. The governor of the prison is G. Hall, Esq.; the chaplain, Rev. H. Smith Warleigh,

M.A. Admission to inspect it can only be obtained from the Secretary of State for the Home Department.

3. The *House of Industry* was established by the gentlemen of the island in 1770, and is managed under a local Act. In some measure its system of management was the forerunner of that of the new Poor Law, and it has undoubtedly proved a great boon to the pauper population of the island. A grant of 80 acres of the waste lands of the forest was obtained from the crown, and the present building erected at a cost of £20,000, which will accommodate 700 inmates, though in 1861 it only contained 434. They are supported by a rate levied, rather unequally, on the different parishes, and amounting to a considerable yearly income, and the management rests in the hands of a corporation styled *guardians of the poor*, consisting of landowners rated at £50 per annum, heirs-apparent to £100 per annum, and occupiers of land rated at £100 per annum. Out of these are annually elected 24 directors and 36 acting guardians.

The whole frontage of the house is about 300 feet in length and 27 in depth, with a wing ranging southwards 170 feet by 24. The dining-hall is 118 feet long.

The grounds are divided into fields and gardens, and tended and cultivated by the inmates. There are also workshops for artizans and tradesmen, whose productions are regularly sold for the benefit of the institution.[*]

V. In the vicinity of Newport and Carisbrooke are many fine farms, numerous villas, and seats of the gentry, to which it is impossible for us to allude in our limited space. The *Parsonage* at Carisbrooke is most agreeably situated. *Shide House* is a respectable mansion; while, east of the town, on the Ryde road,

[*] Parkhurst Forest is now under the control of the Chief Commissioner of Works. The annual receipts amount to about £1200; the expenditure to £950.

are *Bellecroft*, well worthy of its significant name, and Mr. Nunn's *Lace Manufactory*, famous for the production of the Isle of Wight lace, " extensively patronized by her Majesty and the court."

At Rowridge, near Apes Down, 2½ miles west, Sir David Brewster and other eminent naturalists discovered, in 1841, the *flowering calamint*, previously supposed to be confined to Switzerland.

"The country around Carisbrooke is very lovely. There are delicious green lanes, where the trees interlace overhead and form an exquisite roof to the informal avenue ; there are again lone farmhouses, shaded by lofty, spreading elms, and environed by broad tilths of wheat ; little playful brooks running wild among the alder spotted meadows, and downy heights with wide-spread prospects, and shadowy copses, peopled only by the merry song-birds. You might roam about here for weeks, and not exhaust the affluence of gentle pastoral loveliness."—*Thorne.*

Places to be visited by the pedestrian—Apes Down, 2½ miles ; Clatterford, 1 mile, where Roman relics, especially the ruins of a villa, have been discovered ; Bowcombe Down, and traces of a Roman road ; Park Cross, 2 miles, a lovely nook ; Chillerton and its chalky down, 4 miles ; Marvel, 1 mile, the site of an ancient religious house ; Rowborough (see *post*); and Newbarns, for Celtic earthworks, 2½ miles, at the foot of Gatcombe Down (see *post*).

DISTRICT III. (S.W.)—BRIGHSTONE AND ITS ENVIRONS.

HAVING taken COWES and NEWPORT as the centres of *two* considerable districts of the island, we shall select, as the best starting-point for our *third* great division, the delightful village of BRIXTON or BRIGHSTONE, situated on the main road from Ventnor to Freshwater, and Newport to Freshwater Gate, at a distance of 7 miles south-west of Newport, 14 miles south-west of Ryde, 11 north-west of Ventnor, and 9 miles south-east of Yarmouth.—(*Inns :* New Inn, and Five Bells.)

" A cheerful little village, on the sunny side of the Isle of Wight, sheltered from cold winds by overhanging hills, with a goodly church, and a near prospect of the sea "—(*Life of Ken*)—is not an inaccurate description of this pleasantest of the pleasant places on the south-western coast of the island ; for it lies on a sunny table-land, open to the warm breezes of the south, and defended against bitter winds by a range of lofty downs, whose green sides are for ever dappled with changing shadows. All about it are blossomy gardens and clumps of green elms, and sequestered bowers hidden away among silent hills, and " eternal whisperings around " of the distant sea. And ever the wind goes—

> " With a musical motion towards the west,
> Where the long white cliffs are gleaming ! "
> *Owen Meredith.*

And the birds whirr from copse to copse, and the soft rosy haze rises above the ample meadows, and onwards to the furthest angle of the isle rolls the great chain of abrupt hills whose summits, we may fancy, are guarded by the spirits of those who sleep within their bosom ! So it lies—

> " Deep-meadowed, happy, fair with orchard lawns
> And bowery hollows crowned with summer sea."
> *Tennyson.*

BRIGHSTONE,

(From *Ecbright's town*, the manor having been conferred on the see of Winchester by King Egbert (Ecbert or Ecbright) in A.D. 326,)

Is a parish in the West Medine liberty, containing 3251 acres, and a population, in 1861, of 630 (337 males + 293 females), with 128 inhabited houses, and 6 uninhabited. A great portion of the land consists of bare chalky downs, and the population, therefore, is chiefly centred

In the hamlet of Brighstone, which is one of the largest in the island. On the west the parish is bounded by Mottistone, on the east by Shorwell, north by Calbourne and Carisbrooke, south by the British Channel. It includes Lymerston, part of Chilton, Atherfield, and Uggeton (now called Muggleton), formerly a possession of the Knights Templars.

Brighstone Church is an interesting edifice, which has recently been restored with considerable taste. Bishop Ken, the sweet singer of the "Morning" and "Evening Hymns," the honest prelate who refused to receive Nell Gwynne into his house at Winchester, held the rectory from 1667 to 1669. His yew-hedge is still shown as "a cherished memorial" in the rectory garden; and his name imparts to the church and village "a sweet savour of holy things." The present Bishop of Oxford was the incumbent from 1830 to 1840; and his father, the illustrious William Wilberforce, spent several months of the last year of his life in the pretty and cozy parsonage-house. A walk in the garden is still associated with his name. In this delightful neighbourhood he spent the summer of 1832, "climbing with delight to the top of the chalk downs, or of an intermediate terrace, or walking long upon the unfrequented shore."

The rectory is now held by the Rev. Dr. Moberley, long head master of Winchester School.

Lemerston or *Lymerston* lies about one mile eastward of Brixton village. The manor was anciently in the possession of the crown, but soon after the Conquest was bestowed upon a family who took their name from it—De Lymersi, or De Lymerston. They founded here a chapel of the Holy Ghost for three priests, who were to officiate both for the living and the dead, under the rules of St. Augustine.

After two or three generations male issue failed the family, and the manor was purchased about the middle of the last century by George Stanley, the father of the Right Hon. Hans Stanley. It lately belonged to S. Stanley, Esq., of Paultons, Hampshire.

The oratory was in existence in 1349, but probably soon afterwards perished, as it was a private chapel, and the Tycheburnes did not maintain any state at Lymerston.

SUB-ROUTES.

1. The tourist who takes up his abode at Brighstone for a week will find six days' ample occupation in the following excursions: *a.* Passing Lemerston, and the pleasant old mansion of West Court, to the village of Shorwell, 2½ miles; let him then ascend the hill, by Sir Henry Gordon's seat, North Court; turn to the right, and take the Chillerton road, which opens up some fine bursts of scenery, *via* Gatcombe, 3½ miles, to Newport. Return by Carisbrooke and Rowborough (See District II., Subroute *b*). *b.* From Brighstone to the west, by a picturesque road which winds up steep hills and down into green vales, with agreeable alternations; passing Mottistone, 1 mile (notice a steep lane, by the church, which leads to the *Long Stone*, or Druidic *cromlech*), Brook, 2 miles (notice the chine, and petrified forest), and taking the road to the north, *via* Shalcombe and Afton Downs to Freshwater Gate, 3½ miles. Returning, if the tide permits, by the sands, past Brook Point—with its petrified forest—Brook Chine, Chilton Chine, and Grange Chine, about 7 miles. *c.* From Brighstone, by Mottistone Mill, through Calbourne Bottom, and to Westover (formerly the seat of the Holmes family), to Calbourne, 3½ miles, and Newtown, 3 miles. Returning by Swainston (notice the seat of Sir John Simeon, M.P.), over the downs. *d.* From Brighstone to Woolverton, an old gabled mansion, and across a wild moorland country to Kingston, 4 miles. Then by way of Stroud Green, 1 mile, passing Chale Farm, 1 mile,

with its bits of early English architecture, to Chale, half a mile, and Blackgang Chine, half a mile. Ascend St. Catherine's Hill, and cross into Niton, whence the tourist may continue his tour to Godshill and Ventnor, or return *via* Atherfield, to Brighstone. *e.* A walk along the cliffs, passing Barnes Chine, Cowleaze Chine, Atherfield Point, Whale Chine, Walpan Chine, St. Catherine's Point, and Lighthouse, to Puckaster Cove. Returning by Sub-route *d.* *f.* A walk along the cliffs, westward, observing Grange Chine, Chilton Chine, Bull Rock, Brook Chine, Brook Point, and Compton Bay, to Freshwater Gate. Then across a delightful country to Freshwater and Yarmouth, returning *via* Calbourne, by Sub-route *c.*; or, from Freshwater Gate to Alum Bay and the Needles, returning *via* Afton Down, by Sub-route *b.*

ENVIRONS OF BRIGHSTONE.

1. MOTTISTONE, a parish and village in the West Medine liberty. The parish contains 1107 acres; population in 1861, 160 (86 males + 74 females); in 1851, 143. Inhabited houses, 27; uninhabited, 1. Bounded north by Calbourne, south by the Channel, east by Brighstone, west by Shalfleet. Most of this parish lies between the sea and the green slopes of Mottistone Down (698 feet in height), and possesses a good arable soil. The scanty population (9 to an acre) is chiefly occupied in agricultural pursuits. There is here, north of the church, a large farm; the farm-house, formerly the *manor-house* and residence of the Cheke family, an excellent specimen of the Tudor domestic architecture. It was built in 1557, and is popularly, though erroneously, supposed to have been the birth-place of Sir John Cheke,—

Who taught Cambridge and King Edward Greek,—
Milton.

and who really *did* belong to the Mottistone family. "Mottistone Church is

worth turning aside to see : it is of different dates, and has the peculiar picturesqueness that so many of these old churches possess, which have thus grown into their present form by the addition of new limbs in different ages."—*Thorne.* The internal fittings are of cedar, obtained from a vessel which was wrecked on the neighbouring coast. *Pitt Place* (S. E. Walmisley, Esq.), a little beyond the village, lying left of the road, is a commodious mansion, enjoying a fine sea prospect.

The tourist, however, will visit Mottistone chiefly for the purpose of examining the singular relic of bygone days known as the *Long Stone*, which probably gives its name to the village. "It is a huge quadrangular mass of stone, bearing upon it no marks of the chisel, though somewhat rudely formed. It consists of stratified iron sandstone, from the lower greensand formation,—the prevailing stone in that neighbourhood, abundance of which might be had from Compton Bay Cliff. The height of the upright stone is 13 feet, its widest side 6½ feet, its circumference 20 feet." Its depth is supposed to be considerable. At a slight distance from it there is a recumbent stone: "its length 9 feet 3 inches; its width, at the widest part, 4 feet; and its height, at the thickest end, 2½ feet. Besides these two contiguous stones, there is another, of a similar kind, about 300 yards distant from Longstone, to the east, on the wayside. This stone is 4 feet 3 inches wide, and 2 feet 2 inches thick. Another stone lies near the gate from the Calbourne and Mottistone road to the pathway to Longstone, from which it is distant 570 yards." By some authorities Longstone has been considered as simply a landmark; others have looked upon it as place of public meeting, from the Saxon *mote,* as in the word, "wardmote;" but the general opinion pronounces it a *cromlech,* or Druidic funeral-stone.

About 200 yards north-east of it is

Castle Hill, where stands an ancient earthwork, or fort, nearly square, probably of British origin. Its length, from north to south, is 191 feet; its breadth, from east to west (on the north side), 177 feet; and on the south side, 168 feet. The bank which surrounds it is 21 feet broad and 3 feet high. There are other earthworks in the neighbourhood which the tourist may easily light upon, and from almost every point he will, at least, enjoy a delectable sweep of lea, and dale, and grove, farmstead and grange, white cliff and sparkling sea.

2. BROOK, 3 miles from Brighstone, lies in a hollow betwixt the hills, looking out upon a rough and pebbled beach. The parish contains 713 acres, 32 inhabited houses, and 2 uninhabited houses. Population, in 1861, 156 (90 males + 66 females). Boundaries:—N., Thorley; S., the Channel; E., Shalfleet; W., Freshwater. The church, a lonely building, has been recently rebuilt, after being destroyed by fire on the 16th of December 1863. The manor was in the possession of the Bowermans, an ancient island family, for many years, and afterwards of the Howes; but was recently purchased (about 1856) by C. Seely, Esq., M.P., whose seat, *Brook House*, upon the uplands, is a noble mansion, finely situated. It was here that Dame Joanna Bowerman received, in 1499, King Henry VII.; who, in acknowledgment of her hospitality, presented her with a drinking-horn, long preserved in the family. And here, in 1864, Mr. Seely entertained Garibaldi, who planted some trees in the ground, and also at Faringford.

From Brook Down there is a goodly prospect. There is perhaps even a finer one from Afton Down (500 feet in height). " Freshwater Bay stretches round in a splendid curve, the chalk cliffs rising perpendicularly to a height of some 500 or 600 feet from the sea, which rages constantly against their base, and crowned by the Needles' lighthouse. Beyond is the broad belt of the channel. along which ships of all sizes are constantly passing to and fro. In the extreme distance lies the coast of Dorset, which is visible from Poole Harbour to Portland Bill; while the foreground obtains boldness and strength from the shattered and detached masses of rock that lift their heads far above the water at Freshwater Gate. Nor, though less grand, is that inland view less pleasing where the Yar winds ' its silver winding way ' along the rich valley to which it gives its name, enlarging rapidly from a scarcely traceable rivulet, till, in a mile or two, it has become a goodly estuary."— *Thorne.*

There is a life-boat station at Brook, supplied by two-and-twenty men, besides the coxswains.

3. SHORWELL.—We now suddenly return to the pastures and green dells of the grateful inland village of Shorwell, which boasts one of the fairest of the island churches. The parish derives its name from a brook (*Shere-well*) which runs through it, rising on the grounds of Northcourt. It contains 3685 acres, and had in 1861 a population of 612 souls (324 males + 288 females), 113 inhabited houses, and 9 uninhabited. Boundaries: N., Carisbrooke; S., Brighstone; E. and partly S., Godshill, Niton, and Chale; W., Brighstone. Shorwell is 5 miles south-west of Newport, and 12 of Ryde. It lies in an agreeable valley, which forms the only pass or opening in the range of downs from Gatcombe to Freshwater, and which debouches, so to speak, upon the table-land which skirts the chalk cliffs of Brighstone and Chale Bays.

The church is certainly an interesting edifice; has been restored within the last few years with commendable care; contains an interesting brass or two, and some monuments to the Leigh family. It dates from the reign of Edward III., when the parish was taken out of that of Carisbrooke, on the complaint of the inhabitants that they had to carry their dead five miles to burial, and when "the waters were out," in winter, the death of one person was the occasion of many more. There are two schools in the village, and in the neighbourhood are the handsome seats of *Northcourt, Woolverton,* and *Westcourt.*—(See *post.*)

4. BARNES is a cluster of small cottages south of Brighstone, which gives name to a considerable chine, opening upon Brighstone Bay. It is noticeable on account of the remains of a *Romano-British pottery* which once existed here, and must have been of an important character, but has gradually been washed away with the crumbling cliff by the continual agency of the undermining waves of the British Channel. Fragments of urns, drinking vessels, and other pottery, were excavated here some four or five years ago.

5. KINGSTON, anciently *Chingeston,* or the King's Manor, lies about 5½ miles south-south-west of Newport, 4 miles south-east of Brighstone, and about 2 miles from Shorwell. It contains 883 acres, 10 inhabited houses, and a population of 68 souls (40 males + 28 females). The church is one of the smallest and plainest in the island, dating from the fourteenth century.

6. CHALE is a very pretty village, 8½ miles south-south-west of Newport, lying, a short distance from the sea, at the foot of Chale Down. The name is derived by some from *Schiele,* the hollow of a bowl or cup, in allusion to the shape of the bay, or perhaps of Blackgang Chine.—*Knight's Journey-Book.* The parish contained, in 1861, 180 inhabited houses, and 584 inhabitants (300 males + 284 females), having increased from 391 in 1801 to 406 in 1811, 473 in 1821, 544 in 1831, and 610 in 1841. Acreage, 2375. The church is a good thirteenth century building, well restored, with a noble Perpendicular tower.

Chale Farm, on the left, is a picturesque building, with several relics of decorated architecture wrought into it, and a fine barn, 100 ft. by 30. The *Parsonage*

on the right (from Kingston) is a pleasant house pleasantly placed.

"Here the country begins to expand itself into more level and extensive fields, and to disclose the boundless view of the British Channel, the proximity of which prevents the few trees that are scattered through this open region from showing any signs of luxuriance."—*Wyndham.*

Blackgang Chine, one of the lions of the island; *St. Catharine's Hill;* and *Atherfield Point,* we shall describe in their proper places.

In *Chale Church-yard* lie buried eighteen of the victims who perished by the wreck of the *Clarendon* in Chale Bay, October 11, 1836.

ALONG THE COAST.

From Brighstone Westward.—The road to be pursued by the tourist along the cliffs has been agreeably described by a traveller who wrote and travelled half a century ago. His sketch is still correct in its details:—"Our track was mostly over extensive sheep-walks, fragrant with thyme crushed under the wheels of the carriage. Rich farms and neat cottages adorned the valleys. The meanest of the cottages, and those inhabited by the poorer class, were buried in roses, jessamine, and honeysuckle, and often large myrtles, which, on the southern coast, bear the winter out of doors."—*Simond.* He crosses an extensive table-land, sheltered from the north by a long and lofty range of undulating downs. Occasionally he comes to a thick cluster of branching elms, or a lone farm-stead nestling away in a quiet valley—"an ancient grange half-hid in harvest-home." There are rivulets, too, meandering slowly through the plain, until lost in the deep savage ravines, or *chines,* which their agency has worn in the yielding soil. Far away to the westward he sees a wall of precipitous chalky cliff, gleaming and flashing with a wonderful brilliancy, and beyond, against the horizon like a bank of white cloud, lie the steep bulwarks of the Isle of Portland. To the south stretch the shifting waters of the famous Channel.

> Outspread is seen
> Ocean's blue mantle, streaked with purple and green;
> Now 'tis he sees a canvas'd ship, and now
> Marks the bright silver curling round the prow;
> Now sees the lark down-dropping to his nest,
> And the broad-winged sea-gull, never at rest—
> For when no more he spreads his feathers free,
> His breast is dancing on the restless sea."
>
> Keats.

"The villages along the summit of these cliffs have some attractions in point of beauty, and are full of interest to the antiquary. Mottistone Church is worth turning aside to see. The little secluded village of Brooke, lying in a hollow betwixt the hills, close by the chine of the same name, and looking upon a rough, rock-strewn beach, might also be seen; but it will be well to ascend the Downs at Mottistone, and proceed along them to Freshwater. The views from these grounds are of vast extent, and are hardly surpassed in the island in any respect. The prospects from Afton Down have always been famous; the view over Freshwater is especially striking. Freshwater Bay stretches round in a splendid curve, the chalk cliffs rising perpendicularly to a height of some 500 or 600 feet from the sea, which rages constantly against their base, and crowned by the Needles' lighthouse. Beyond is the broad belt of ocean, along which ships of all sizes are constantly passing to and fro. In the extreme distance lies the coast of Dorset, which is visible from Poole Harbour to Portland Bill, while the fore-ground obtains boldness and strength from the shattered and detached masses of rock that lift their heads far above the water at Freshwater Gate. Nor, though less grand, is that inland view less pleasing where the Yar wends 'its silver winding way' along the rich valley to which it gives its name, enlarging rapidly from a scarcely traceable rivulet, till, in a mile or two,

it has become a goodly estuary."— *Thorne.*

Freshwater Gate, with its singular rocks, and deep, shadowy caverns, will engage our attention hereafter. We now proceed on our homeward route—from Freshwater Gate to Brighstone; and, as the tide permits—time and tide always wait for the scribe!—make our way along the firm red sands.

1. *Compton* * *Bay* will first attract the tourist's attention. The *Chine* is "a deep chasm worn in the ferruginous sands by a stream that falls from the summit of the cliff," which is here, and as far as Atherfield Point, composed of the clays, shales, and sands of the Wealden formation. The Wealden points are consequently very abundant along these shores, and petrified hazel nuts, called by the islanders *Noah's nuts*, are often met with.

2. The eastern extremity of Compton Bay is *Brook Ledge*, or *Brook Point*, and "at its base a dangerous reef of rocks extends seaward to a considerable distance. If the tide is very low, a succession of ledges of this kind are visible along the shore, stretching out to the distance of half a mile or more from the land, and indicating the former extent of the southern coast of the island, at a comparatively very modern period. These reefs and rocks consist of the harder masses of the Wealden sandstone, which have resisted the destructive effects of the waves, after the clays, sands, and softer materials have been swept away."—*Mantell.* Many disastrous wrecks have occurred upon this dangerous coast.

Here the attention of the tourist will be arrested by the remains of a singular and vast petrifaction—petrified trunks and branches of huge trees; which "evidently originated in a raft composed of a

---

* Compton (*combe* and *ton*), the settlement in the hollow. Afton (*af, avon*), the settlement by the stream.

prostrate pine-forest, transported from a distance by the river which flowed through the country whence the Wealden deposits were derived, and became submerged in the sand and mud of the delta, burying with it the bones of reptiles, mussel-shells, and other extraneous bodies it had gathered in its course."—*Mantell.* To the geologist this scene, a sort of glimpse of a pre-Adamitic world, cannot but suggest the most interesting conclusions. "The trees appear to have been submerged when arrived at maturity, and while fresh and vigorous. On a late visit there were two stems which could be traced to a length of 20 feet; and they were of such a magnitude as to indicate the height of the trees when living at from 40 to 50 feet. Many stems are concealed and protected by the fuci, corallines, and zoophytes, which here thrive luxuriantly, and occupy the place of the lichens and other parasitical plants, with which the now petrified trees were doubtless invested when flourishing in their native forests, and affording shelter to the Iguanodon and other gigantic reptiles."—*Mantell.*

The sea-beach in Compton and Brixton Bays chiefly consists of chalk flints broken and rounded by attrition into boulders, pebbles, and gravel. Some of these are transparent, with bands and veins of quartz and chalcedony. There are "silicified chalk sponges," called by the lapidaries moss-agates; and the beautiful *choanites* (petrified sea-anemones), which are simply characteristic zoophytes of the white chalk. Pebbles of pure transparent quartz, others of jasper—dark-brown mottled, and opaque white, and boulders of petrified bone and wood, are also found here in considerable numbers.

Passing Brook Chine, we notice, at low water, the ominous reef of *Bullface Ledge,* and find ourselves in the small cove, or hollow, of Brighstone Bay, as it is somewhat grandiloquently called. The cliffs are completely scored with *chines*

of various degrees of interest; most of them, however, being fully as deserving of examination as the show-chines at Blackgang or Shanklin. The tourist will come to them, and other note-worthy points, in the following order:—

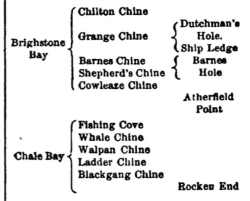

From Brighstone Westward. — At *Chilton Green* (*chil,* chalk, and *ton,* the settlement) rises a small stream which works its way to the cliff, and produces a chine of noticeable extent, and even sublimity. Near *Grange Chine* is a cavern of considerable height, called *Dutchman's Hole,* from a Dutch galliot having been hurled into it. *Barnes Hole* is also a tolerably extensive cavern. *Cowleaze Chine* is worth notice. The rivulet to which it owes its formation does not reach the cliff directly, but runs parallel with it for some distance. Here "the Wealden clay and its passage to the sands beneath are better displayed than in any other locality."— *Dr. Fitton.*

Walpan Chine (about 1½ mile from Blackgang), is worth visiting for the different shapes of its winding sides. It is 184 feet in height.

Ladder, or *Chale Chine,* is an excavation in the black clay cliffs, which, in this place, are about 200 feet in height. It runs deep into the land, is extremely narrow, and its sides in many places are perpendicular. "It is as naked as Blackgang Chine, and though much less deep, is more gloomy; but the most striking peculiarity of its character is the copious exudation of chalybeate springs from its sides, which are stained with ochreous tints to a very great extent, and their dusky red on the black clay ground gives the appearance of a vast extinguished furnace to the deep hollow."

Whale Chine, described by Sterling as resembling "a mighty gash inflicted by the sword of an Orlando," is 180 feet wide at its mouth, and extends inland for nearly two-thirds of a mile.

Atherfield Point (*Aderfeldt*, the veined or streaked field) throws out a dangerous ledge of rocks into the sea—the scene of several wrecks, and the whilom haunt of a gang of smugglers. The cliffs at the point are about 150 feet in height, and almost entirely consist of the green-sand strata. The Wealden clay begins here, and stretches as far as Bullface Ledge, in a layer about six feet deep. "Near this place, after recent slips of the cliff, and the removal of the fallen debris by the waves, the uppermost of the Wealden deposits and the lowermost of the green-sand may be seen in juxtaposition; in other words, the line of demarcation between the accumulated sediments of a mighty river — some primeval Nile or Ganges, teeming with the spoils of the land and the exuviæ of extinct terrestrial and fluviatile animals and plants—and the bed of a vast ocean, loaded with the debris of marine organisms, of genera and species unknown in the present seas."—*Mantell*.

Blackgang Chine (Black gang, the *black way*, or *path*) is the most famous of the island curiosities, and has been *lionized* in the guide-books *usque ad nauseam*. Viewed from the sea, its aspect is wildly picturesque, and not without a certain savage grandeur. Viewed from a resting-place about half-way down, there is something exceedingly effective in the irregular combination of bare, bleak down, iron-coloured rock, abrupt precipitous cliff, and boundless sea, which the view

presents. There is neither tree nor shrub; no bright masses of foliage relieve its sombre sides; and on a breezy day, when the south wind brings up the foamy waters with a heavy *thud* upon the shore, filling the dark hollow with its dreary echoes, anything more desolate or sorrowful it is impossible to conceive.

"The chine is on the west declivity of St. Catherine's Hill (769 feet[*]), and its upper appearance is not far below its high summit; two currents, from distant parts of this hill, have made their way to its brow, and from this height have excavated two large separate chasms, but their waters form a junction at the top of a high prominent point, the sides of which have been torn away by their respective torrents. The chasms at this junction become one, and consequently much deepened; from whence the united waters more rapidly hurry down the steep channel for about 200 yards, till they arrive at an impenetrable precipice of rock (a layer of ironstone grit), from whence they fall in a perpendicular cascade of 70 feet upon the shore."—*Wyndham*. There is, however, very little water in the chine except after heavy rains. The cliff sides are but "of mean height and lumpish form," but above them tower majestic broken cliffs, 400 feet in height; and as a background to the singular picture, above *these* rises "the majestic escarpment" of St. Catherine's Hill.

"The country people in these parts once thought that they were possessed of a Pactolian sand, for they obtained for a certain time some gold dust from the sand of the bay; but, from a number of dollars having been from time to time cast on shore, it was justly suspected that it came from the wreck of some unfortunate Spanish ship."—*Pennant*.

Chale Bay was the scene, on the morning of the 11th of October 1836, of a

---

[*] Some authorities place its height at 830 feet.

BLACK GANG CHINE.—ISLE OF WIGHT.

terrible wreck,* which has long held a prominent place in the dark roll of these mournful disasters. The good ship *Clarendon*, a West Indiaman of 345 tons, with a crew of 17 men and boys, and 11 passengers, was driven in-shore by a tremendous gale, and immediately went to pieces. Only three lives were saved. Of the drowned, five bodies were never recovered; the rest were either decently interred in Chale church-yard, or in the church-yard at Newport.

From the beach at Blackgang Chine the tourist ascends to the upper cliff by a rough flight of steps, formed by small logs of wood imbedded in the earth at somewhat irregular distances. At the summit there is a "bazaar," with a collection of many-coloured bottles of Alum Bay sand, curious pebbles, agates, and fossils. Within a species of tent is preserved the skeleton of an enormous whale, stranded at some time or other in Gurnard Bay. A commodious hotel and some lodging-houses are seated in excellent positions upon the cliff; very pleasant in the genial months of summer and autumn, but a little too exposed for winter residence.

The tourist will next ascend *St. Catherine's Hill*, the loftiest elevation in the island, which, with its two towers, offers for so many miles around a conspicuous and splendid landmark. Here, at least as early as the beginning of the 14th century, was a hermitage—strange solitude, on the summit of this precipitous height, where even on the stillest day the winds hover and whistle as they list! One Walter de Godyton also built here a chantry (A.D. 1323), and dedicated it to St. Catherine, who, in the Roman Hagiology, is invariably the patroness of hills and mountains. In the registry of the diocese of Winchester, however, there is an entry referring to the hermitage:—

"Walter de Langstrell, admissus ad hermitorium supra montem de Chale, in insula Vectis, idib. Octobris, A.D. 1312;" which shows that it was erected prior to the foundation of the chantry. The good knight Walter also provided an endowment for a man priest, who should chant masses, and maintain a burning light at night for the safety of mariners who passed that dangerous coast. This duty was duly performed until the dissolution of the minor religious houses, when the priest was swept away, though the chantry, built of stone and massive masonry, remained, and may still be inspected by the curious. Many years since it was strongly repaired, in consideration of its value as a landmark, when "the foundation of the whole chapel was also cleared and levelled; by which, not only its figure was discovered, but also the floor and stone hearth of the priest's little cell at the south-west corner."—*Worsley.* Its height is 35½ feet; its form octagonal. Almost adjoining it is the shell of a lighthouse, erected in 1785 by the Trinity Board; but speedily discontinued, the mists which so often crown the summit of the hill rendering it of little service. A beacon was also established here, under the charge of a lieutenant, a midshipman, and two seamen. St. Catherine's is "the western extremity of the southern range of chalk downs, which is separated by a considerable district of green-sand from the central chain of hills. This system of chalk downs varies in breadth from half a mile to 3 miles, and extends 6 miles in a direction E.N.E. and W.S.W., from St. Catherine's Hill to Dunnose, its eastern termination, which is 771 feet high. The intermediate parts of this range maintain an elevation of from 650 to 800 feet, with the exception of a deep valley on the east of St. Catherine's, through which the road to Niton passes, and another at Steep Hill, called the Shute, or Shoot, above Ventnor, traversed by the road to Appuldurcombe and Newport."—*Mantell.*

---

* Here, also, in 1830, was wrecked a Dutch the *Diana Frau* but the crew were

BLACK GANG CHINE—ISLE OF WIGHT.

The splendid prospect to be enjoyed, on a clear sunny day, from the summit of this lofty down, has often been expatiated upon by enthusiastic travellers. "This view is really of wondrous extent —reaching over by far the larger part of the island, and including the New Forest and the hills of Hampshire, and the south coast as far as Beachy Head. In the opposite direction, the high lands about Cherbourg are said to have been occasionally seen, but it is a very rare occurrence. On a calm, clear day, the better part of the island lies spread like a map at your feet: its bare hills, and its long valleys dusky with the thick foliage that everywhere crowds them; the villages and the towns marked by the lighter or denser smoky vapour that hangs above them; the winding streams, growing sometimes into lakes ere they fall into the sea; and the silver ocean that encircles it, alive with mighty ships of war, and every kind of smaller craft; and, beyond that again, the far distant hills, losing themselves in a soft purple haze."—*Thorne.* Such a scene, in fact, as the poet has touched with a glowing pencil in the following lines:—

" A land of streams ! some, like a downward smoke,
Slow-dropping veils of thinnest lawn, do go ;
You see the gleaming river seaward flow
From the inner land. . . . . .
            Through mountain clefts the dale
Is seen far inland, and the yellow down
Bordered with trees, and many a winding vale
And meadow, set with slender galingale ;
A land where all things always seem the same ! "
                                            Tennyson.

SEATS OF THE GENTRY.

In that portion of the island which we have now surveyed,—a triangle, as it were, whose three points are indicated by Rocken End, Freshwater Gate, and Gatcombe Down,—there are half a dozen ancient mansions which cannot fail to attract the tourist's attention.

Northcourt, the seat of Sir H. P. Gordon, Bart., lies on the right of the road from Newport to Shorwell, about half a mile from the latter village, in a position of singular beauty. The house was begun in the reign of James I. by Sir John Leigh, and completed by his son, Barnaby Leigh, from whose descendant the manor was purchased by R. Bull, Esq. His eldest daughter, to whom it was bequeathed, devised it to her half-brother, R. H. C. Bennet, Esq., of Beckenham, Kent, whose widow became the possessor on the death of their eldest son. From the Bennets it passed by marriage into the hands of General Sir James Willoughby Gordon, Bart., a distinguished Peninsular soldier, who died in 1851 ; and it is now in the possession of his son, Sir H. P. Gordon, Bart., one of the magistrates for the county. " The front of the house is adorned with a handsome central porch. On either hand is a large window, and beyond them, semi-octagon bows, two storeys high, terminated by a battlement and pinnacles. Beyond these, to the right, the front terminates with a projecting building, which is wanting to the left. All these parts severally finish in gables, ornamented with slender pinnacles rising from projecting corbels."—*Neale.* The east front is the only portion of the ancient mansion which remains in its original purity, and with its square projecting windows, its casements pendent on their stone mullions, its seated porch, and gable-end roof, has a very picturesque appearance. Over the porch is a scutcheon, and the date 1615. The gardens are admirably laid out in terraces, and from certain points command the finest conceivable views of the English Channel. In a woody hollow, formerly a chalk pit, and overhung by a large ash tree, is a low stone building like a Gothic chapel, with a thatched roof and painted windows, containing a stately sarcophagus of white marble, on whose front are carved, in bas relief, a male and female figure hanging over an urn. This was erected to the memory of Miss Catherine Bull by her sister.* On a tablet, beneath

---

* On the neighbouring down there is a small stone obelisk, also dedicated to this lady's memory.

the urn, are inscribed some mediocre lines by her father, R. Bull, Esq. :—

> " Oft, in this once beloved retreat,
> A father and a sister meet ;
> Here they reflect on blessings past,
> On happiness too great to last :
> Here, from their fond endearment torn,
> A daughter, sister, friend they mourn ;
> Soothing the mutual pangs they feel,
> Adding to wounds they cannot heal.
> Strangers to grief, while she survived
> In her their every pleasure lived ;
> She was their comfort, joy, and pride—
> With her their every pleasure died !
> Ah, shade revered ! look down and see
> How all their thoughts ascend to thee !
> In scenes where grief must ever pine,
> Where every bursting sigh is thine,
> Prostrate they bow to God's behest,
> Convinced whatever is, is best :
> In trembling hope they may be given
> With thee, blest saint, to rest in heaven !
> If, reader, thou canst shed a tear
> At sorrow's asking, drop it here ! "

On another tablet, detached from the monument, is an inscription to the *genius loci* :—

> " Sweet Peace, that loves in placid scenes to dwell,
> Extend thy blessings to this quiet dell ;
> Bring resignation to the wounded breast,
> And Contemplation, Reason's favourite guest ;
> Restore that calm Religion only gives,
> Correct those thoughts desponding Grief conceives ;
> So shall these shades a brighter aspect wear,
> Nor longer fall the solitary tear ;
> So shall Content from tranquil pleasures flow,
> And Peace, sweet Peace, best happiness bestow ! "

In the grounds a small stream rises, which, running southward through the village, has given to it the appellation of *Shorwell*. The main road passes through this pleasant estate, and over it has been thrown a picturesque rural bridge to connect the divided portions.

Westcourt, or South Shorwell, on the Brighstone road, is probably of the same date as Northcourt, and, though of smaller size, was evidently at one time the residence of a considerable family. This ivy-shrouded house derives its name from its position with regard to—

Woolverton (Wulfere's town), 1 mile south of Northcourt, a large mansion of the date of James I., which contains some good carvings, and is agreeably surrounded with luxuriant foliage. Near it may be traced the site of a more ancient house.

No buildings are visible, but " a broad and deep moat, enclosing a square area, is entire. This was evidently the principal seat in the parish."—*Englefield*.

Waitscourt, a pleasantly-situated mansion, lies to the south of Brighstone Church, on a road to the left of the Parsonage.

To *Mottistone Farm, Pitt Place*, and *Brook House*, we have already alluded.

PLACES TO BE VISITED BY THE PEDESTRIAN.

Chilton Green, 1 mile south of Brighstone ; *Yafford*, 1 mile south-west of Shorwell; *Down Court*, and *The Hermitage*, "the Dene " of Miss Sewell's *Ursula*, situated at the foot of St. Catherine's Down ; the *Alexandrian Pillar*, on the north-west extremity of St. Catherine's Down, and best reached from the Hermitage. This pillar, 72 feet high, was erected by a Russian merchant, Michael Hoy, while living at the Hermitage, to commemorate the visit to England, in 1814, of the Czar Alexander. A tablet to the memory of the heroes who fell in the Crimean war was placed on the base of this handsome column, in 1857, by Lieut. Dawes ; *Stroud Green*, 2 miles north of Chale ; *Ivy House*, a picturesque farm half a mile north-east of Kingston; *Rowborough* and *Gallibury*, about 3 miles from Brighstone, by a breezy route across the downs, or by the road to Newport, striking off to the left at Rowborough Farm. " This collection of ancient British pits may be regarded as constituting two villages, divided by natural boundaries, though connected by the intermediate pits and defences on the downs."—*Rev. E. Kell*. *Gallibury* means the *burgh* or fastness of the Gaels (Kelts) ; *Rowborough*, the *village* in a *row* or *line*. The Rev. E. Kell, F.S.A., who carefully examined these ancient British habitations in 1854-5, measured sixty-two of these pits, or hollows, " some round, the majority oval, and a few double pits." He also observed noteworthy traces of the Celtic fortifications,—in particular, an embankment at the head of the valley on the side of Brighstone Down, 175 feet in length, 40 in breadth, and 8 in depth. . . . . There is another and larger British settlement, about a mile distant, at the foot of *Newbarns Down*, which the tourist should examine. " This ancient village is located in three small valleys running from Newbarns Down into a larger valley, encircled by high hills. Through the centre of each of these valleys are pits, in number thirty-four; and nearly at the base, where the three valleys unite, is a pond of very considerable dimensions, which received its supplies from the neighbouring hills. Besides these thirty-four larger pits, there are in the basin of the valley sixty or seventy generally of a smaller size."—*Rev. E. Kell.* On the neighbouring downs are many other pits, barrows, embankments, and ditches, memorials of the earlier inhabitants of this beautiful isle.

DISTRICT IV.-NORTH-EAST.—RYDE AND ITS ENVIRONS.

[The district of which we design the popular and populous town of Ryde to form the *point d'appui*, will include a part of the extensive parish of Newchurch, Brading, Wootton, and St. Helen's,—in a word, the north-eastern angle of the Isle of Wight, included within a line drawn from Wootton Bridge to Newchurch, a base line from Newchurch to the Culver Cliffs, and the coast line, marked by Wootton Creek, Ryde, the Foreland, and White Cliff Bay.]

RYDE

Is the fashionable watering-place of the island, and the chief resort of summer visitors, for whom it is equally eligible as a place of residence, and as a starting point whence all the beauties of the Undercliff and the picturesque scenery of the East Medine may conveniently be reached. Its growth during the last sixty years has been extraordinary. In 1801 the population was only 900 or 1000; in 1811, 1601; in 1821, 2876; in 1831, 3676; in 1841, 5840; in 1851, 7147; and in 1861 was 9269. It is now (1867) probably upwards of 11,000. In 1841 it contained 1000 inhabited houses, and 63 uninhabited; in 1851, 1265 inhabited, and 66 uninhabited; and in 1861, 1734 inhabited and 57 uninhabited. It now contains about 1900 houses.

The administration of the town is placed in the hands of a Board of Commissioners, twenty-seven in number, annually elected by the rate-payers. Each commissioner must possess property worth £700, or be rated at not less than £20 per annum. The commissioners appoint their own chairman, town-clerk, auditor, road surveyor, inspector, and other officials, and work under the provisions of a local Act, obtained in 1854. Nine commissioners go out yearly. It is proposed, however, to convert Ryde into a municipal borough, which will probably be effected in the course of the session of 1867.

The *income* of the town, in 1866, amounted to about £14,550; £7032 being raised for *general purposes*; £7179 on the Water-works' account; and £345 on the Town Hall account. The *expenditure* reached the amount of £13,800; of which £6508 were absorbed by the Water-works' account, and £267 by the Town Hall account. The ratable property in Ryde is valued at £44,460. Owing to the great improvements effected during the last few years, the town is considerably in debt, having borrowed on mortgage a sum of £46,730. The Burial Board receives about £576 yearly, and expends about £517.

[We jot together a few memoranda of interest both to the resident and tourist:—The average yearly expenditure of the town, on strictly local matters, exceeds £2800. The poor-rates, in 1866, produced £3000. There are no manufactures carried on; 92 colliers visit it annually, and import 13,750 tons of coals. The principal landed proprietors in the manors of Ryde and Ashey are members of the Player family. Communication with Portsmouth is maintained by the handsome and commodious vessels of the United Steam Packet Company; with Cowes and Southampton, by another line of steam-packets. Principal hotels: The *Pier Hotel*, close to the pier; *Royal Eagle*, opposite to it; *Yelf's*, and the *Royal Kent*, in Union Street; the *York*, in George Street; *Sivier's* in Pier Street; *Salter's Belgrave Family Hotel*, in Nelson Street; *Kemp's Esplanade Hotel*, on the Esplanade; and the *Crown (Commercial)*, in High Street. There are numerous excellent inns (the *Star, Vine, Castle*), and almost every house is a lodging-house, "with a fine sea view." The season lasts from June to October. There are stage-coaches, several times daily to Newport and Cowes; and railway communication with Brading, Sandown, Shanklin, and Ventnor. It is also intended to bring the Isle of Wight Railway and the Ryde Pier into immediate communication, and to lay down a direct line between Ryde and Newport, with a branch from Newport, *via* Wroxall, to Ventnor. Ryde rejoices in an abundance of the usual watering-place accommodations,—libraries, news-rooms, and bazaars. The Theatre is generally open during the season, and concerts are numerous, and usually good. Excursions round the island, occupying about six hours, are made by swift steamers twice a-week. The bathing is excellent, and there are bathing establishments, of all sizes and at all prices, from the pier eastward to Appley.]

The principal objects which will attract the tourist's attention during his residence in Ryde may be briefly noticed.

PUBLIC BUILDINGS.

1. *The Pier* is, of course, the great "lion" and main attraction of the place. Previous to its erection, there existed only a small and dilapidated jetty, so that, at low water, visitors were conveyed from their boats by a horse and cart, or in sedans supported by a couple of sailors,—a *désagrément* of which both Fielding and Marryatt have complained. In 1813 a local Act was procured, and the construction of a pier commenced, by a company whose funds were supplied by 2400 shares of £50 each. At first 1740 feet in length, it grew in 1824 by 300 feet, and in 1860 and 1863 by other extensions, so that it is now about half a mile long, affording a delightful promenade, from which may be obtained a sea view of no ordinary beauty, including, as it does, the whole sweep of the Solent, from Osborne on the west to the Nab light-vessel on the east; Spithead, with its men-of-war; the Motherbank, with its merchant sail; Portsmouth Harbour, mast thronged, and backed, as it were, by the blue Hampshire hills; the sunny Hampshire coast; and the well-wooded shores of the island stretching away, with many a gentle curve, on either hand. From the pier-head, looking back upon the town, the spectator may enjoy another attractive picture: the villas of Ryde rise one above another like an amphitheatre, diversified by clusters of foliage, by two or three tall church spires, and long lines of streets winding up the steep hill on which the town is built. The shores of the island assume the shape of a crescent, whose eastward point is the wooded headland of Sea View, and the western, that sloping ridge on whose crest arise the stately towers of Osborne.

2. *The Esplanade* is another promenade, not an unworthy rival of the pier. It is of comparatively recent construction (1855-6), and provides a broad, straight, and open parade, defended from

the sea by a wall of excellent masonry—length 1200 feet, and breadth, at the widest, 150. The sea wall is 19½ feet in depth, and coped with Swanage stone.

3. Almost parallel with the Pier, and opening upon the Esplanade nearly opposite George Street, is the *Tramway*, or *Pier*, of the extinct "Isle of Wight Steam Ferry Company," whose managers proposed to furnish an easier communication with the mainland, in connection with the Stokes Bay Railway,—a feeder of the London and South-Western, which avoids the unsavoury town of Portsmouth. The Dock is used by small vessels. The Pier, about 700 feet long, is unfinished, and now belongs to the Old Pier Company, but will probably be removed in a few months.

4. The *Town Hall*, in Lind Street, erected in 1829–31, at a cost of £5000. The frontage, including the wings, measures 198 feet. The centre has a slight projection, and forms a vestibule with a columned pediment, of elegant design. A handsome clock-tower is in course of erection; the clock, a gift to the town, cost £400. A portion of the right wing is occupied by the Literary Institute; the left wing forms a market. The Town Hall, properly so called, forms the centre of the building, and consists of a spacious apartment, 60 feet long and 26 wide.

5. The *Yacht Club House* is an ornamental building west of the Pier, with a small battery sea-ward, and interior appurtenances of considerable elegance. The foundation-stone was laid by the late Prince Consort, March 1846, and the Club House opened in the following year. It was enlarged, and a new Italian façade erected in 1864.

The *Royal Victoria Club* was established May 24, 1845, and, by Admiralty warrant of July 29, in the same year, was entitled to bear the St. George's ensign. The Club now enrolls 80 yachts, with an aggregate of about 8000 tons. The entrance fee is £5, 5s., and the annual subscription, £5, 5s.;—commodore, Captain Thellusson; vice-commodore, Lord Burghley. The annual regatta is held about the second week in August, and is followed, after a short interval, by a town regatta for the encouragement of the Ryde boatmen.

6. The *Royal Victoria Arcade*, in Union Street, is a covered promenade, with handsome shops on each side, and a sort of circular recess or show-room at the end of it. The design was furnished by Westmacott, and carried out at a cost of £10,000.

7. The *Isle of Wight Philosophical and Scientific Society* have established a *Museum* and *Lecture Room* in a building in Melville Street, formerly occupied by the National Schools. The Museum was opened November 2, 1857, and contains a large and valuable collection of the antiquities, and specimens of the zoology and natural history of the island, with natural and scientific curiosities brought together from every part of the wide world. Visitors are gratuitously admitted on Tuesdays, Wednesdays, Thursdays, and Fridays, from 10 A.M. till 4 P.M. The Society, which includes about 90 members, is under the patronage of the Bishop of Winchester and the Right Hon. Viscount Eversley, governor of the island.

8. The *Royal Isle of Wight Infirmary* is situated in the Swanmore Road, on ground presented by the lord and lady of the manor. It owes its prosperity to the exertions of the late Dr. Dodd, and has undoubtedly been of great advantage to the island poor. Its income in 1865–6 was £1507. The total number of cases treated in the twelvemonth was 1050 (167 in-patients, and 883 out-patients).

9. The *Water-works*, which supply the town, are placed at the foot of Ashey Down, nearly 4 miles from Ryde, and cost the large sum of £22,500. They were constructed under the superintendence of Messrs. Easton and Amos, a well-known hydraulic engineering firm.

The reservoir will hold 504,000 gallons, and is about 250 feet above low-water mark.

10. The Ryde *Theatre* is a small and rather ugly building, in St. Thomas's Square, between High Street and Union Street. Its single association of any interest is with the well-remembered actress, Mrs. Jordan, who, on her way to France in 1816, made her last public appearance upon its miniature stage.

Ryde is bountifully provided with *places of worship*, and members of every denomination will find here ample accommodation. The Church of England has four edifices. The oldest is *St. Thomas's*, recently erected into a parish church, in St. Thomas's Street. The ugliest is *St. James's*, near the Town Hall. The handsomest, *Holy Trinity Church*, in a commanding position, eastward, on the summit of the hill; this is a proprietary and district church. *St. Michael and all the Angels*, at Swanmore (Rev. R. H. G. Wix), was built in 1862, from the designs of R. J. Jones, Esq. Its interior is picturesque, and owing to its choral services, the church is much frequented. The *Roman Catholics* have a richly-decorated chapel in High Street; the *Independents*, a pretentious building in George Street; the *Baptists*, a New Church, in George Street, built at the cost of Sir Morton Peto, from Mr. Francis Newman's designs; and the *Wesleyans*, a chapel in Nelson Street. The *Cemetery*, with a chapel dedicated to St. Paul, lies north of the town. It was consecrated in 1842, and enlarged in 1862. Some of the monuments are worth notice, such as General Sir J. Caldwell's, Captain Wyatt's, and the Rev. J. Telford's. The late Mrs. Wilder established, in memory of her husband, some Alms-houses of picturesque design in the Newport Road.

The town of Ryde can scarcely be said to have a history, its growth is of such recent date. The old town, *La Rye*, or *La Riche*, was a cluster of cottages upon the summit of the hill, with perhaps a few fishermen's huts straggling along the shore. It was burnt by the French in the reign of Edward II.; was one of the places where a watch and ward were maintained for the safety of the island; and one of the three ports to which all communication with the mainland was restricted. About the close of the 18th century it began to struggle out of its insignificance, and many pleasant seats were erected in its neighbourhood. Its increase was such as speedily to necessitate the accommodation of a church, and the lord of the manor, in 1719, founded the chapel of St. Thomas.

Fielding, the inimitable creator of "Parson Adams" and "Joseph Andrews," on his voyage to Lisbon in 1753, was detained here for several days, and to his lively pen we are indebted for a picture of singular force and humour. He was then a dying man, and in a condition of deplorable weakness; but it was considered desirable that he should leave the wind-bound vessel, and enjoy, while he could, the repose and refreshment of a residence on shore. To leave the ship, and get on board a hoy was possible, but from the hoy to reach the land was a task of surprising difficulty. For "between the sea and the shore," he says, "there was at low water an impassable gulf, if I may so call it, of deep mud, which could neither be traversed by walking nor swimming; so that, for one-half of the twenty-four hours, Ryde was inaccessible by friend or foe." He was, therefore, rowed in a small boat as near the shore as possible, and then "taken up by two sailors, who waded with him through the mud, and placed him in a chair on the land." At a later period, for this human vehicle was substituted a more suitable conveyance; "the wherries came in as far as they could, and were met by a horse and cart, which took out the passengers, and carried them through the mud and water to the hard ground."—*Marryatt, "Poor Jack."*

In Fielding's time the town could only boast of one butcher, but, according to Fielding's landlady, "he was a very good one, and one that killed all sorts of meat in season—beef two or three times a year, and mutton the whole year round." When the great satirist wanted a cup of tea, he discovered that "the whole town of Ryde could not supply a single leaf; for as to what Mrs. Humphreys (his landlady) and the shopman called by that name, it was not of Chinese growth," but "a tobacco of the mundungus species."

Notwithstanding these *désagréments*, the beauty of the place made a great impression upon Fielding's fancy. "Its situation," he exclaims, "is most delightful, and in the most pleasant spot in the whole island. It is true it wants the advantage of that beautiful river which leads from Newport to Cowes; but the prospect here extending to the sea, and taking in Portsmouth, Spithead, and St. Helen's, would be more than a recompense for the loss of the Thames itself, even in the most delightful part of Berkshire and Buckinghamshire." Again: "This pleasant village is situated on a gentle ascent from the water, whence it affords that charming prospect I have above described. Its soil is a gravel, which, associated with its declivity, preserves it always so dry, that immediately after the most violent rain a fine lady may walk without wetting her silken shoes. The fertility of the place is apparent from its extraordinary verdure, and it is so shaded with large and flourishing elms that its narrow lanes are a natural grove or walk, which in the regularity of its plantation vies with the power of art, and in its wanton exuberancy greatly exceeds it."—*Fielding.*

The progress of the town since the days of Fielding may best be understood from a brief chronological summary:—

1. The Pier, built 1814
2. Steam packets established 1825
3. St. Thomas's Church, rebuilt 1827
4. St. James's Church, built 1829
5. Town Hall and Market 1831
6. Gas introduced 1838
7. Holy Trinity Church, and the ⎫
8. Roman Catholic Church,   ⎬ 1845
                                               ⎭
9. Yacht Club established 1846
10. Isle of Wight Infirmary, built 1847
11. New Local Act passed 1854
12. The Esplanade, built 1855–6
13. The Waterworks, built 1855 6
14. Railway to Ventnor opened 1866

[The manor of Ryde and Ashey belonged to the Abbey of Wherwell; at the dissolution of religious houses was sold to the Worsley family; next became the property of the Dillingtons, and by Sir John Dillington was sold to Henry Player, Esq., whose descendants (Player, Lind, Brigstocke) still enjoy it.]

SUB-ROUTES.

The neighbourhood of Ryde is peculiarly attractive to those who love a calm and gentle beauty—the loveliness of broad meadows and plashing runlets, of leafy copses and balmy lanes, of wooded slopes washed by a sunny sea. There is nothing of sublimity, nothing of grandeur, but all is picturesque and blooming, like the garden-bowers of Armida. The hedge-rows are prodigal of fragrance; the banks are loaded with primroses and cowslips, so as to justify the poet's exclamation, "This island ought to be called Primrose Island; that is, if the nation of cowslips agree thereto."—*Keats.* At one time the traveller finds himself in a pleasant reach of woodland, musical with the song of birds; at another,—

"In a dell mid lawny hills,
Which the wild sea-murmur fills,
And the light and smell divine
Of all flowers that breathe and shine."
Shelley.

In a word, the scenery in this angle of the isle has been faithfully reflected in the language of a graphic writer:—" It possesses much of that kind of beauty which seldom sinks into tameness on the one hand, or rises into sublimity on the other. It is almost always such as to produce only placid and gentle emotions. Its charms arise from the sight of verdure and fertility spread over an undulating and often well-wooded surface, many points commanding fine views of the sea, and particularly of the strait which separates the island from the coast of England."—*Edinburgh Review.*

In every direction the tourist may open up a score of pleasant rambles; but the sub-routes we are about to indicate will embrace nearly everything which is worth seeing.

a. Leaving Ryde by the Spencer Road (notice Sir Augustus Clifford's elegant seat of *Westfield,* and Miss Player's, *Ryde House*), by a pretty lane to Binstead, 1 mile, and its picturesque little church (notice *Binstead House,* and the quaint old *Parsonage,* Rev. P. Hewitt); then through Quarr Wood to the ruins of Quarr Abbey, 2 miles, and by a pathway through a small coppice to Wootton Bridge (notice *Kite Hill,* D. Hollingsworth, Esq.). Return by the turnpike road to Binstead, 2 miles (notice *Stone Pitts,* Captain Brigstocke's pretty villa, lying in a hollow, left of the road, and *Corstorphine Hill,* . . . .) and into Ryde; or, turning to the right at Kite Hill, go through Firestone Coppice, across the meadows to Haven Street, 1½ mile, and back to Ryde, *via* Pound Farm. *b.* From Ryde to Wootton, 4 miles; and turning to the left, take the road to Arreton, 3 miles; and crossing the slopes of Arreton Down, reach Newchurch, about 2¼ miles. Then, return *via* Knighton (notice ruins of an ancient manorial mansion), across Ashey Down, 2 miles (notice the Ryde Waterworks on the right); and over Ashey Common, into Ryde, 2 miles. *c.* From Ryde to Appley (notice *Appley,* Mrs. Tredwell; and *Appley Tower,* G. Young, Esq.), and keeping the sea-wall, to Springvale. Pass the ancient salterns to Sea-View, 3 miles; and by the sands, which here are very fine, to Priory Bay. St.

Helen's Bay (notice portion of old St Helen's Church, now used as a sea-mark), and Brading Haven. Cross by ferry to Bembridge, 2 miles, and thence to White Cliff Bay and Culver Cliff, 2½ miles. Climb Bembridge Down, (now surrounded with military works: Bembridge Fort, on the summit; Red Cliff Fort, near the cliff edge; Yaverland Fort, just below; and Sandown Fort, on the beach,) descend into Yaverland (notice manor-house and church), and by a "leafy lane," to Yar Bridge, 2 miles. Then, by road to the right into Brading (notice church, and, at a short distance northwest, *Nunwell,* seat of Sir H. Oglander), and return by the main road to St. John's. Enter Ryde by the *Duver.* [*Duver,* or *Duyver,* land once overflowed by the sea. Here were buried the bodies of the ill-fated mariners of the *Royal George,* which foundered off Spithead, August 29, 1782. A line of handsome houses (*the Strand*) is now built upon this charnel-ground.] *d.* From Ryde, *via* St. John's Hill, to Appley Tower; then by a picturesque road, with fine views of the Hampshire coast, leaving *St. Clare,* 1½ mile (Colonel F. Vernon Harcourt), and *Puckpool* (from *Puck,* the fairy), with its new fort; on the left, to Westbrook, 1 mile (notice *Westridge* J. Young, Esq., a large white house embowered amidst magnificent trees), and through Nettlestone, 1 mile (notice, to the left, on the road to Sea-View, the beautiful seat of *Fairy Hill,* W. A. Glynn, Esq.), passing St. Helen's Church, half a mile (notice the fine prospect on every side), and the *Priory* (Henley Smith, Esq.), to St. Helen's village, half a mile. Return by the sea-shore to Ryde. *e.* From Ryde by the usual coach-road to Sandown, 6 miles (notice new Sandown Fort), and *via* Lake, 1 mile, through Cheverton to Apse, 1 mile (notice here an ancient farm-house). From Apse, *via* Whiteley Bank, to *Appuldurcombe,* 2½ miles. From Appuldurcombe and its Park, passing

Park Farm, to Godshill, 2 miles, and return *via* Bottlebridge and *Stickworth* (R. Bell, Esq.), through Horringford, into Newchurch, or (leaving Newchurch to the south-east) to Hasely; and by Knighton, 6 miles, and Ashey 1 mile, to Ryde, 4 miles. *f.* As above, *via* Sandown, 6 miles, to Shanklin, 2½ miles (notice Shanklin Chine); and back by a delightful route, to a sequestered nook, called America. Thence to Apse Farm, and crossing Apse Heath, to Queen Bower (so called, it is said, because one of our queens from this pleasant ascent was wont to view the chase; a traditional allusion to Isabella de Fortibus, Lady of the Island), and homeward, *via* Newchurch, Knighton, and Ashey. *g.* As above, to Shanklin, and crossing Shanklin Down to Wroxhall Down; thence, by Span Farm to Stenbury (notice ancient house and moat), southward, to Whitwell (notice ruins of old church), and into the main road at St. Lawrence village (notice small church, Well, *St. Lawrence Cottage*, Mrs. Dudley Pelham; and *Marine Villa*, (Countess of Yarborough). By *Steephill* (Mrs. Hambrough), to Ventnor, 14 miles, and by coach to Ryde; or, if not fatigued, *via* Bonchurch, keeping the cliff-road, to Luccombe Chine, and through Shanklin and Sandown into Ryde, 12 miles. *h.* The usual and prescribed carriage-routes to Ventnor and Bonchurch (*via* Shanklin); to Blackgang and Niton (*via* Godshill); to Newport and Carisbrooke (*via* Arreton); to East Cowes (*via* Wootton); or to Brighstone (*via* Newport and Shorwell), do not require particular indication. And the routes we have already marked out may be diversified at the pleasure of the tourist. For instance, there is a pleasant walk to be found in this direction: —Ryde to Springvale; by road to the right, passing Pondwell, to Barnsley; crossing the Brading road, through Whitefield Wood, to Ashey. Or, Ryde to Springvale; by road to the right, passing Barnsley to Westridge; crossing the Brading road, near St. John's; then take the footpath over the fields to the suburb of Ryde, known as Canada, and enter Ryde by way of *Monk's Meads* (so called, it is said, because an abbot of Quarr bestowed on the owner or holder of the farm at Ninham, where he had been a constant and welcome visitor, the right of taking the first crop of hay, in alternate years, from these very meadows, so long as a certain stone image was there preserved. The tenure is still maintained).

ENVIRONS OF RYDE.

I. BINSTEAD (*Inn:* The Fleming Arms) is a parish and village, one mile from Ryde, separated from the parish of Newchurch by a small stream running into the Solent, at the base of the hill crowned by Binstead Church. It contains 1475 acres. Population in 1861, 486 (224 males + 262 females). Inhabited houses, 105; uninhabited, 9; building, 4. The ground here is broken into deep hollows and grassy rifts,— marking the position of the once famous Binstead quarries, which supplied much of the stone ("composed of comminuted shells, held together by a sparry calcareous cement"—*Mantell*) employed by William of Wykeham in building Winchester Cathedral. The scenery is very pleasant, with water and woodland delightfully intermingled.

In the neighbourhood of Denmark House, and on the Newport Road, some good villas have recently been built.

The most noticeable thing in this pretty parish, and the chief ecclesiastical antiquity of the island, is—

QUARR ABBEY. The scanty ruins of this once wealthy and splendid abbey— the favoured of knights, and princes, and devout "ladies of high degree"—lie in a sequestered valley, which opens out upon the Solent, watered by a pleasant rivulet, and sheltered by leafy groves. The monks of the olden time had a keen eye for the beautiful, and generally cast their lot in pleasant places. And when the woods spread, as once they did, for miles around, and the rivulet was full of light and sparkle, and a stately abbey, rich in slender columns and elaborate arches, towered among the luxuriant leafiness, a fairer spot than this "deep-bowered" valley it would have been difficult to discover!

The Abbey of Quarr, or Quarrera, was founded in 1132-4, by Baldwin de Red-vers, Lord of the Isle of Wight, who peopled it with some Benedictine monks from Savigni,* in Normandy,—whence it was sometimes called "The Daughter of Savigni,"—and endowed it with the manor of Arreton. From the quarries in its neighbourhood, which supplied the materials of his new building, it derived its name—*De Quarrera*, or *De Quar-rariis*. And it was dedicated to St. Mary, the Virgin, by devout De Redvers, who upon his decease was buried in its chapel; and by his side were successively laid his wife Adeliza, and Henry, his youngest son.

Other lords of the island, and many of its knights and gentlemen, at different times bestowed upon it rich endowments, until a considerable portion of the fairest lands of the Wight belonged to the wealthy abbey. Thus it held manors and lands at Luccombe, Shalfleet, Compton, Shorwell, and Chale; at Haseley, Combley, and Niton ; at Whitfield, Wellow, and Binstead. Its abbots were often joined in commission with the captains or wardens of the island to regulate its military defences, and furnished four men-at-arms towards its militia. In 1340 the abbey was strongly fortified, and its grounds enclosed by strong walls, with suitable loopholes, and portcullises at its gates.

William de Vernon was buried here,

and a splendid monument—for which he bequeathed £300, nearly £4500 at the present value of money—was erected to his memory. In August 1507, Lady Cicely, one of the daughters of Edward IV., was interred within its precincts.

In the time of Cardinal Beaufort (A.D. 1404) a taxation was made of the abbey lands, and a result obtained of £96, 13s. 4d.,—or, in the money of to-day, about £1500. Its yearly income had augmented, when Henry VIII. stretched forth his powerful hand and smote to the dust the proud abbeys and rich priories of England, according to Speed, to £184, 1s. 10d. ; according to Dugdale, to £134, 3s. 11d.—that is to say, upwards of £2000 per annum.

The monks of Quarr did not bear, we fancy, a high repute for sanctity. Isa-bella de Fortibus, and afterwards Edward III., came into collision with them; and Lambard, in the early part of the 16th century, spoke of them somewhat . sarcastically. "Although," he says, "Paulus Jovius wrote that the inhabitants of this island be wont to boast merely that they neyther had amongst them monks, lawyers, wolves, nor foxes, yet I find them all, save one (the lawyers), in one monastery, called Quarr, valued at 134 pounds of yearly revenue, and founded in the year 1132, after the order of Savigniac in France."

The abbots of Quarr are stated to have followed each other in the following order: —Gervase ; William ; Peter de York, 1205 ; Henry, 1218 ; Philip, elected, 1234 ; Augustine ; Andrew, 1256; Adam de Arundel, 1279-1301 ; Walter, 1323 ; John Winchester, elected, 1378 ; Thomas Snell, elected, 1396 ; Richard Bartholomew, elected, 1399 ; John Morton, elected, 1466 ; Thomas of London ; Richard Tottenham, 1508 ; William Ripen, 1521.

A curious description of the abbey at the time of its dissolution is given in a *Paper Survey*, preserved in the "Aug-

---

* A few years later (1148), Savigni was united to the Cistercian order, and consequently Quarr became a Cistercian house, the second established in England.

mentation Office." It states the yearly revenue from all sources at £181, 15s. 2d., and the expenditure in fees and certain annual payments at £54, 3s. 11d., leaving a balance of £133, 7s. 3d. at the disposal of the abbot. It then proceeds :—

"The name of the abbot is William Ripen, who hath no certain portion allowed unto him, but is charged with the whole maintenance and governance of the monastery, like as faithful administrator, to minister, provide, and ordain everything vigilantly and honestly, according to the religion, and the rest to keep after his discretion to the use of that monastery.

"The president or superior's name is Dan. Richard Curlewe, who hath nothing appointed unto him but as the convent hath, but only, for his tender obedience, his abbot's reward.

"The second president's name is Dan. Richard Woodhill, and he doth serve the poor church of Binstead, and he hath by the year four marks.

"The monk of the bakehouse's name is Dan. Robert Smythe, who hath nothing but as others of the convent have, save, for his diligence and obedience, his abbot's reward.

"And every other religious man there being present, by the year, in ready money, £1, 6s. 8d."

The common seal of the abbey was round, and small in size, representing the Virgin seated, with the child Jesus in her lap. In the impressions still extant only the commencement of the legend—MARIA VIRGO—can be traced.

At the dissolution, Quarr was purchased by a rich Southampton merchant, George Mills, who dismantled it of its splendours. His son's widow, Mrs. Dowsabell Mills, became the mistress of Sir Edward Horsey. On her death, the estate was purchased by Chief Justice Sir Thomas Fleming, who completed the task of spoliation ; so that little of the ancient building can now be traced. The refectory is said to have

been converted into a barn, which may still be examined. Some portions of the wall, and a sea-gate—an arched window and a broken column—are all else that remain of the magnificent pile which once included thirty acres of land within its precincts.

Several stone coffins have, at different times, been excavated at Quarr ; a few coins and some other relics have also been discovered, but not of a nature or in such abundance as to satisfy the antiquary, or throw any vivid light upon the history of the abbey. In 1857 a curious discovery was made by some labourers engaged in the construction of a new road through the old abbey grounds, of "three small stone boxes or chests, each chest being about two feet in length and one foot wide. They were placed side by side,—two of them nearly close together, and the third a foot or two to the south. Upon removing the heavy stones of which the lids were composed, three human skeletons in a good state of preservation were found. The leg and arm bones were on either side, the ribs and small bones in the centre, and the skulls at the western end, the latter being in all three cases turned upside down. It was evident these remains had been removed at some time or other from the place of their original burial; and that they were of persons of distinction was beyond doubt, or such care would not have been bestowed upon them."— *Isle of Wight Observer.* One of the skeletons was pronounced to be that of an aged man, another that of an aged female, and the third that of "a tall fine man about 40 years of age." It has been suggested, and there is an air of probability about the suggestion, that they were the remains of Count Baldwin, his wife, and his son Henry. They are now in the Museum at Ryde.

This is just the spot where "the violet of a legend" might be expected to blossom, and there are traditions connected with the abbey of a singularly fantastic character. One tells of a deep subterraneous passage, closed by a golden gate, and is evidently the offspring of the awe and wonder created in the minds of the vulgar by monastic wealth and power. Another is wildly fabulous:—"At a short distance south of the ruins of the abbey is a wood, formerly thickly timbered, but now only consisting of a few decayed oaks and brushwood ; it is called Eleanor's Grove, from a tradition that Eleanor of Guienne, queen of Henry II., was imprisoned at Quarr, and frequented this secluded spot, where, after death, it is related, she was interred in a golden coffin, which is supposed still to be protected from sacrilegious cupidity by magical spells."

II. WOOTTON, OR WOOD-TOWN (*Inn:* The Sloop) is about equi-distant between Ryde and Newport. The parish is bounded east by Binstead, south by Arreton, west by Whippingham, and north by the Solent. Population in 1861, 79 (33 males + 46 females); acreage, 1360; inhabited houses, 13. Certainly this parish is scarcely more populous than a recent "clearing" in the backwoods of America,—one house to every 150 acres, and one inhabitant to every 17. The church is a plain building, Near it stood the old manor-house, where Henry VII. passed a night in 1499. A farm-house now occupies its site.

Wootton Creek is formed by the junction of Wootton river—which rises near Mersley Down, and becomes tidal about two miles from its source—with the Solent. It is sometimes called Fishhouse Creek, from the small village of Fishhouse, on the easternmost of the two headlands between which it enters the Solent. There was formerly a good ship-building yard at Fishhouse, where yachts of 250 tons were laid down and launched. It is now only a small boat-builder's settlement. The causeway which carries the Newport road across the creek is 905 feet in length.

Wootton was originally the lordship of a branch of the De Lisle family, the most famous of whom were *Sir John Lisle*, the regicide, a stanch follower of Cromwell, assassinated at Lausanne, after the Restoration, by three Irish bravos ; and his wife, *Dame Alice Lisle*, who, having generously and unwittingly sheltered two of Monmouth's unfortunate partisans after the fatal fight at Sedgmoor, was tried for high treason, foully treated by Judge Jeffreys, and cruelly beheaded, though an aged, grey-haired woman. The tragic tale is told by Lord Macaulay with wonderful power and pathos.

William Lisle, a gallant Cavalier, who faithfully followed Charles II. in his exile, is buried in Wootton Church. The family is now represented in the female line by F. White Popham, Esq., lord of the manor.

III. NEWCHURCH is the largest parish but one (Brading) in the island, and is the most thickly peopled. It crosses the whole island from north to south-east, and includes the two most fashionable towns, Ryde and Ventnor. On the east, it touches the parishes of St. Helen's, Brading, Shanklin, and Bonchurch ; on the west, Binstead, Arreton, Godshill, and St. Lawrence. It presents, therefore, the most surprising varieties of soil and scenery. Acreage, 9200. Population in 1861, including Ryde and Ventnor, 14,008 (6131 males + 7877 females) ; inhabited houses, 2564 (now nearly 3000); uninhabited houses, 84; building, 22. The parochial boundaries formerly included the following churches and chapels of ease :—

Newchurch, vicarage ; Rev. H. Oliver ; £460. In the gift of the Bishop of Gloucester.

St. Thomas's Ryde; now a parish church ; Rev. W. H. Girdlestone, vicar.

Holy Trinity, Ryde; district church ; Rev. A. J. Wade, Rev. J. S. Barrow.

St. James's, Ryde; perpetual curacy ; Rev. W. H. Redknap.

St. Peter's, Haven Street ; perpetual curacy ; Rev. Dr. Knollis.

St. Catherine's, Ventnor ; vicarage ; Rev. J. Marland, Rev. N. A. Macgachen ; in the gift of Mrs. Hambrough.

Newchurch includes the manor of

Ashey, formerly belonging to a rich religious house, a branch of the Abbey of Whorwell. The convent stood on the site of the present farm-house, and has been described as possessing ample revenues, and a goodly estate, with a stately hall, elegant chambers, a refectory, fish-ponds, and other adjuncts of luxurious ease. But it has passed away with a startling completeness—not a stone records its original splendour. The farm-house is worth examining.

Here, as late as the reign of Elizabeth, a widow named Agnes Porter was burnt at the stake for witchcraft.

Ashey Down (424 feet above the sea), raises its rounded and glittering crest just above the farm-house, and is easily recognised at any distance by its seamark, or beacon, a truncated pillar of hewn stone, erected in 1735. From this spot the tourist may enjoy one of the finest—nay, *the* finest view in the Isle of Wight. " Southward it is terminated by a long range of hills (Shanklin, Wroxall, and St. Catherine's) at about 6 miles distant. They meet to the westward another chain of hills, of which the one whereon he sits forms a link; and the whole together nearly encompass a rich and fruitful valley, filled with corn-fields and pastures. Through this vale winds a small stream for many miles; here and there lesser eminences arise in the valley, some covered with wood, others with corn or grass, and a few with heath or fern. One of these hills is distinguished by a church (Newchurch) at the top, presenting a striking feature in the landscape. Villages, churches, country-seats, farm-houses, and cottages, are scattered over part of the southern valley. In this direction also appears an ancient mansion (Knighton), embellished with woods, groves, and gardens. South-eastward is a broad expanse of ocean, bounded only by the horizon. More to the east, in continuation of the chain of hills (Ashey) on which he is sitting, rise two downs (Brading and Bembridge),

one beyond the other; both are covered with sheep, and the sea is just visible over the further hill, as a terminating boundary. In this point are seen ships, some of which are sailing, and others lying at anchor. On the north, the sea (the Solent) appears like a noble river, varying from 3 to 7 miles in breadth, between the banks of the opposite coast and those of the island. Immediately underneath him is a fine woody district, diversified by many pleasing objects. Westward, the hills follow each other, forming several intermediate and partial valleys, in undulations like the waves of the sea, and bending to the south, complete the boundary of the larger valley we have described, to the southward of the hill on which the tourist sits. One hill alone (St. Catherine's), the highest in elevation, and about 10 miles to the south-westward, is enveloped in a cloud, which just permits a dim and hazy sight of a signal-post, a light-house, and an ancient chantry on the summit."—*Legh Richmond.*

Descending the down, southward—in a leafy gorge of singular calm and beauty—lie the scanty relics of a mansion, once the most considerable in the island; the ancient manor-house of *Knighton Gorges*, built in the reign of James I., on the site of a yet older building, the residence of the De Gorges, and afterwards of Mr. Fitzmaurice, who assembled here the Georgian wits, Wilkes, David Garrick, Mrs. Garrick, and others.

" Like many other mansions, Knighton House," we are told, " was reported to be haunted; but the exact nature of the unearthly visitant is not stated, though it was said to intimate its whereabout by a noise resembling the clanking of heavy chains. In later times, however, this noise was confined to one room, which was never opened; and above its entrance was inscribed a Latin legend of such potency as to prevent the troubled spirit's egress. There is a strange story current respecting the death of the last male the Dillington family, who for many years possessed the manor and house of Knighton. The party alluded to, Sir Tristram Dillington, lost his wife and all his children in rapid succession, and finally fell himself by his own hand through despair—leaving two sisters, who afterwards died single. To prevent the forfeiture of the estate by the *felo de se* of his master, the steward, directly he became aware of the tragedy, took the horse his master usually rode, and having reserved the saddle, drove it into the mill-pond close to the house. This countenanced a report which he immediately spread, that Sir Tristram, returning home late at night, inadvertently rode into the pond; and through the slackness of the saddlegirth, fell from his horse, and was drowned before assistance could be rendered. This occurred at least a century ago. It was easy to avoid an inquest, and the stratagem succeeded."—*Walks Round Ryde.*

The village of Newchurch (*Inn: The Pointers*) is a long dull street of insignificant houses, 6 miles from Ryde. The church, a plain cruciform building, is finely situated on the bluff of an abrupt sandstone rock.

IV. BRADING (*Inn: The Bugle*) is the largest parish in the island, and lies between the parish of St. Helen's and Brading Harbour, on the east; the parish of Shanklin, south; Newchurch, west; and the Solent, north. Contains 10,107 acres, mostly of excellent arable and pasture land; and had, in 1861, a population of 3709 (1808 males + 1901 females) against 2701 in 1841, and 3046 in 1851. It includes the corporate town of Brading, the villages or hamlets of Bembridge and Sandown, and the hamlet of Alverstone. In 1861 there were 796 inhabited, 48 uninhabited, and 7 houses building, within its limits—an increase of 183 inhabited houses in 10 years, owing to the rise of Sandown as a fashionable watering place.

The living of Brading is a vicarage (Rev. J. Glover, 1846) in the gift of Trinity College, Cambridge, and valued at £250. Dependent upon it is *Sandown* (perpetual curate, Rev. W. M. Lee), presented to by the Church Patronage Society; and *Bembridge* (perpetual curate, Rev. J. Le Meseurier), valued at £100.

1. *The Kyngs Towne of Brading* (named from its early Saxon settlers, the *Bradingas*) is an old corporate town, controlled by a senior and junior bailiff, a recorder, and thirteen jurats, under various charters of incorporation. The oldest in existence is that of Edward VI., dated 1548, but it expressly alludes to former charters. The common seal is *argent*, a rose *gules*, barbed and seeded proper, and bearing the inscription,—*The Kyngs Towne of Brading*. Near the church-yard there is an old Town Hall over an old Market House, both disused; and an old pair of stocks, disused also. Some of the old houses—and they are very old, with quaint diamonded casements, and timber joists—retain the rings used on festival days to support the tapestry decorations. Half way down the street of Brading—it is a long, dull street, running down one hill and up another—is a small open space to the right, where the cruel sport of bull-baiting was enjoyed of yore, as the iron ring in the ground still evidences. In a lane, also to the right, at the bottom of the hill, stands the rustic dwelling of Legh Richmond's "Young Cottager," whose modest grave is at the south-east angle of the old church-yard.

2. The church is a famous structure, ancient, spacious, and stately. Its interior has recently been restored with great care. Tradition asserts that a church was founded here by Wilfrid, Bishop of Selsey, in 704, and that here he baptized the first Christian convert made in the island after its conquest by Ceadwalla. The present edifice is principally of Transition-Norman date.

3. The village lies at the base of green

and lofty Brading Down, surrounded by the woods of Nunwell, and stretching down the slope to the head of *Brading Haven*, a pleasant sea-water lake, with an area of about 840 acres, which opens into the Solent between the headlands of Bembridge and St. Helen's. At low water it is mostly an expanse of mud, with a narrow channel, through which the Yar meanders to the sea. Many attempts have been made to reclaim this considerable tract. A part was taken in by Sir William Russel, of Yaverland, *temp.* Edward I., and Yar Bridge erected. In 1562, the North Marsh, and adjacent lands, were recovered; and Mill Marsh, and other meadows, in 1594. The chief attempt, however, was made by Sir Hugh Middleton (the projector of the New River), in connection with Sir Bevis Thelwall, who gave one Henry Gibbs £2000 for the grant he had obtained from James I. The embankment across the mouth was commenced, Dec. 10, 1620, and occupied two years. For eight years longer the enclosure answered the expectations of the ingenious adventurers, and then, on the 8th March, 1630, the sea again burst over it, sweeping away houses, barns, and mills. A singular discovery was made, during the progress of the works, of a well, cased with stone, near the middle of the haven,—sufficiently demonstrating that it had once been dry land, and that the sea had overflowed it within the historical period.

At high tide Brading Haven is really a very beautiful object. "From the mouth of the harbour you see a really noble lake embayed between hills of moderate elevation, which are covered pretty thickly with trees, in many places down to the very edge of the water. Along the banks and on the sides of the hills are scattered many neat houses and a church or two; and the head of the lake is surrounded by a lofty range of downs, whilst the surface itself, of a deep azure hue, glitters with numerous glanc-

ing sails, and is alive with hundreds of silver-winged sea-gulls. To one who has not seen, or can forget, a lake among the mountains, this will, if seen under favourable aspects, appear of almost unsurpassable beauty; to every one it must appear very beautiful. An hour or two should be devoted to a sail upon it. The views from the surface are very varied; those looking northward derive much beauty from the way in which the sea, with its ships, and the distant shore, mingle with the lake. The view from the head of the harbour is, especially at sun-set, eminently picturesque and striking." The Ryde and Ventnor Railway now crosses the head of it, and the traveller, as he is swept along, obtains a fine view of its placid basin, which, at high-water, has a noble aspect.

V. BEMBRIDGE (*Inn:* Beach Hotel) lies at the extremity of the ledge, a peninsula which joins the southern boundary of Brading Haven—its white houses close down by the water, and its neat church rising from the woods above. It is 2½ miles from Brading, and 6½ from Ryde by the high road, or 4½ miles from the latter to the pedestrian who makes his way along the sands, and crosses the haven by the ferry. From every point the views are very beautiful, and were it more accessible from Ryde, Bembridge would probably rise very rapidly into favour with the fashionable public.

It is said to derive its name from the bridge or causeway thrown across a portion of the haven by Sir William Russel. Thus, *Within Bridge. Binbridge, Bembridge.—Sir J. Oglander, MSS.* Population in 1861, 783.

Bembridge Down (355 feet) is crowned by an obelisk, raised in 1847, by the Royal Yacht Club, in memory of their commodore, the Earl of Yarborough, and recently removed to its present position. The views from the summit of this down are of extraordinary splendour. " Looking back over Brading Haven, and ir land, they are as diversified as they are extensive; forward, the unbroken view over the sea extends to an amazing distance; eastward, the Sussex coast lies like a faint cloud on the distant horizon; while westward, Sandown Bay, with its reddish clay banks circling the light green waves, and softly swelling hills above, may be looked on from day to day with ever new pleasure."

On the seaward side the Down ends in a steep chalk cliff, 259 feet, known as the *Culver Cliff* — from *culfre* (Saxon), a pigeon—"from the abundance of those birds which made it their haunt." It was also famous for a valuable breed of hawks, whereon Queen Elizabeth set such store, that in 1564 she issued her warrant to the captain of the island, to make diligent search after some that had been stolen, and also "for the persons faultie of this stealth and presumptuous attempt."

There is a cavern in the side of the cliff, about 30 feet beneath the brink, known as *The Hermit's Hole*, from which a very fine effect of sea-prospect is obtained. A large fort has recently been erected on the summit of the Down. It is surrounded by a deep fosse, and armed with 600-pounders. Yaverland Fort, lower down, mounts eight heavy guns; and Redcliff Fort, near the cliff-edge, four 110-pounders. Taken in connection with the new works at Sandown, these defences seem of great strength, and completely command the approach to Spithead.

The Culver cliffs form the southern extremity of *Whitecliff Bay*—the northern being named Bembridge Foreland. This is the point of junction of the fresh-water and marine series of the Isle of Wight eocene deposits, which abound with organic remains and fossils. Originally, the strata were horizontal; but by some amazing movement of elevation they have been raised to a nearly vertical position—lying, in fact, at an angle of 70°. So enormous has been the pressure, that the flints have been actually shivered, without, however, in the least altering their outward appearance; so that what seems a perfect flint splits into fragments when ever so slightly disturbed.

North of Bembridge Down, in a richly-wooded valley, lies Woolverton, anciently (so tradition declares) a considerable town, but now simply a sequestered farm. The parish of "Wulfere's Town" once included three manors, and each had its private chapel, which is mentioned as late as the 46th of Edward III.; but of their foundation scarcely a vestige is now extant. It is possible that during one of the many descents made by the French upon this part of the island they were destroyed. *Centurion's Copse* was the site of a chapel dedicated to St. Urian.

VI. YAVERLAND (or the Upper or Over Land) has an old Norman church, an old Jacobean manor-house, and a dozen small cottages, on the brink of a steep escarpment of chalk, with an abundance of leafiness all about, and some good prospects inland and over the sea. The parish does but contain 11 inhabited houses and 3 uninhabited; and in 1861 its population only numbered 69 souls (32 males + 37 females). Acreage, 1834. The living is a rectory (Rev. R. Sherson), in the patronage of Admiral Sir Andrew Hamond, and valued at £230 per annum.

"The church is pleasantly situated on a rising bank at the foot of a bold chalk hill, and being surrounded by trees, has a rural and retired appearance. In every direction the roads that lead to this sacred edifice possess distinct but interesting features. One of them ascends between several rural cottages from the sea-shore, which adjoins the lower part of the village street; another winds round the side of the adjacent hill; and a third leads to the church by a gently rising approach between high banks covered with young trees, bushes, ivy, hedge-plants, and wild flowers."—*Legh Richmond.*

VII. ST. HELEN'S.—The parish occupies an area of 3676 acres. In 1861 it contained 523 houses inhabited, 47 uninhabited, and 18 building. Its population was then 2586 (1175 males + 1411 females). It includes the hamlets of Sea View, Nettlestone, Spring Vale, and Oakfield, and lies between the parishes of Brading and Newchurch, with the Solent for its northern boundary. The village occupies the extreme northern bank of Brading Haven, lying upon the slope, and terminating in a pit of sand at its mouth; and is built, rather picturesquely, round an ample village-green, being the only village so laid out in the Isle of Wight.

There was here anciently, on the site of the present *Priory* (the seat of H. Smith, Esq.), a foundation of Cluniac monks, established before 1150, but by whom is unknown. During the wars of Edward II. and III., as an alien priory it was seized by the Crown, and its revenues sequestrated; but Henry IV. restored it to the abbey of Cluny. When the alien priories were finally suppressed, Henry VI. bestowed its rental on Eton College, and Edward IV. gave the priory itself to that foundation. The present mansion and estate are still held from Eton College.

The old *Church of St. Helen's* stood on St. Helen's Point, about 150 yards from the sea; but the ever-encroaching waves gradually overtoppled the sacred building, and in 1719 it was found necessary to raise a new structure in a securer position. The new church stands about half way between St. Helen's and Sea View. A new chancel, of good design, has recently been erected, and the traveller will hope that the remainder of the mean edifice may, ere long, be replaced by something better.

St. John's, Oakfield, is an elegant little church, situated upon St. John's Hill, at the angle formed by the junction of the road from Brading with that from Nettlestone to Ryde. It is a perpetual curacy, valued at £100 yearly, in the appointment of the incumbent of St. Helen's.

Sea View (3 miles from Ryde) is a cluster of lodging-houses on the slope of a steep hill, with a neat new church.[*] *Spring Vale* (2 miles) is a line of good houses on the shore, fronting the finest sands in this part of the island. A new battery has been erected here, in connection with the iron-clad forts which are intended to occupy No-man and Horse-shoe Spits, and Bembridge Sand.

SEATS OF THE GENTRY.

In our confined space we can only glance at the *principal* seats in this favoured district of the island, where Fashion has especially chosen to take up her residence. There are few houses, however, of any pretensions but have a certain picturesqueness of aspect, which attracts the traveller's curious gaze.

Westfield, the seat of Admiral Sir Augustus Clifford, stands in the Spencer Road, a short distance from the Club House, and, through the beauty of its grounds and the elegance of its appurtenances, is emphatically one of "the lions" of Ryde. The rooms are decorated with great taste and effect; and there is a choice collection of paintings by good masters, marbles, and other articles of *vertu*. In the drawing-room there is a head of Lady William Bentinck, by Sir T. Lawrence; the Duke and Duchess of Devonshire, by Romney; and Domenichino's Sibyl. In the music-room: a Madonna, by Guido; specimens of Angelica Kaufmann; and marbles by Canova, Tadolini, and Burgoni. In the dining-room are portraits by Phillips, and specimens of Herring and Cook. The picture gallery is an elegant room, arranged with a nice attention to harmony of colouring. The gardens are in the

---

[*] The headland here, called *Old Fort*, is probably the site of the small fortress destroyed by the French in 1545. See *ante*, p. 37.

Italian fashion, with terraces leading down to the sea-shore, from which a marvellous panorama of Spithead and the whole reach of the Solent is unfolded. Sir Augustus Clifford is a K.C.B., Usher of the Black Rod, and an Admiral. He entered the navy in 1800; served at the reduction of St. Lucia and Tobago; and, in 1807, in the expedition to Egypt. Distinguished himself at the capture of a convoy in the Bay of Rosas, 1809, and served on the coast of Italy in 1811. Was appointed Usher of the Black Rod in July, 1832.

Ryde House, a large white mansion seated in its own extensive grounds, between Ryde and Binstead, is the seat of the Player family, founded in the Isle of Wight by Henry Player, Esq., who purchased the manors of Ryde and Ashey from the last of the Dillingtons. The present representatives are three sisters and co-heiresses: Miss Player, Mrs. Brigstocke, and Mrs. Du Thon.

Binstead House is a pretty semi-villa, semi-mansion, combining the pleasantest characteristics of both, and seated in grounds of the most delightful order, sloping, with many a change of knoll, coppice, and lawn, to the very marge of the Solent. The estate has been long enjoyed by the Fleming family, and was devised by the late J. Willis Fleming, Esq., to his widow for her life. Mrs. Fleming was married again, 6th August 1846, to the late General Lord Downes, K.C.B., a distinguished Peninsular hero.

Quarr House, on an elevated ground, sheltered by Quarr Wood, and commanding a fine sweep of inland and marine scenery, is the seat of Admiral Sir Thomas Cochrane, a gallant officer, who served in the expeditions against Belle Isle, Ferrol, Cadiz, and in Egypt, during the great revolutionary war; was Governor of Newfoundland from 1825 to 1834, and Commander-in-Chief on the East India Station, 1842–46.

Beachlands, at the bottom of Dover Street, Ryde, is a handsome mansion,

the residence of Mrs. Sullivan, and of Sir John and Lady Lees.

Appley, the seat of Mrs. Tredwell, stands upon a gentle ascent overlooking the town of Ryde, skirted by a leafy wood, and contiguous to the sea. There are few spots in the Wight richer in a soft and tranquil beauty. The estate formerly belonged to a Dr. Walker, and then passed to the Hutt family; the last proprietor of that name was Governor of West Australia; and the Captain James Hutt who commanded the *Queen* in Lord Howe's victory of the 1st June, and was slain in action, belonged to the same stock. Mr. Bennet was the next proprietor, and on his death, in 1839, it was purchased by the present owner, Mr. Hyde. The house was built by David Bryce, a notorious smuggler, a relation of Rich the actor, who used to conceal his stores in its cellars, and in the caves of the adjoining cliff. His nefarious trade was at length discovered, and he died in extreme distress in 1740.

Appley Tower, an elegant and picturesque Elizabethan mansion, in grounds contiguous to those just described, is the seat of George Young, Esq. The gardens are laid out with great effect, and the mansion is most elegantly decorated. Not the least of its attractions was Mr. Young's exquisite collection of the *chefs-d'œuvres* of English artists—now, unfortunately, dispersed by auction—which included Turner's " Plagues of Egypt; " " A Group of Bacchanals," by Sir David Wilkie; " A Landscape," by Nasmyth ; " A Sea-piece," by Sir Augustus Callcott; two companion pictures, " A Calm Sea," and " An Agitated Sea," by Stanfield; " A Landscape," by Creswick; one of Webster's characteristic sketches; and a Sea-piece, " At Ventnor." painted expressly for Mr. Young by W. Collins.*

---

* Collins resided at Ventnor in 1844, and visited Bembridge, August 1845, sketching the

St. Clare (Colonel F. V. Harcourt, a younger son of the late Archbishop of York, and formerly M.P. for the island) was originally built about 1823, by the late E. V. Utterson, Esq., but purchased by Lord Vernon in 1826, and greatly modified from the original design. It is a castellated mansion in the Tudor style of Gothic. Her Majesty and the late Prince Consort repeatedly honoured St. Clare with their presence; and the orphan princess Garumne Coorg frequently resides here under the guardianship of the Lady Catherine Harcourt.

St. John's, a neat, plain mansion, on the hill above Ryde, eastward, was originally built for General Lord Amherst, who named it in commemoration of his victory at St. John's, New Brunswick, A.D. 1758. The grounds were laid out by Repton, the eminent landscape gardener.

The Priory (Henley Smith, Esq.), in the parish of St. Helen's, about 3 miles from Ryde, "stands at the head of a spacious lawn that gently declines from the house to the brink of a high ridge, the steep bank of which is covered with wood down to the water's edge: through this wood various pleasant walks have been cut, of irregular breadths, according to the steepness of the declivity. In the southern part of the wood are the remains of an ancient watch-tower, supposed to have belong to the Priory. The whole of the demesne is formed of a narrow strip of ground, about a mile in length, extending along the shore." Was formerly the residence of Sir Nash Grose, Justice of the Queen's Bench, of whom Erskine said pleasantly—

"Grose Justice, with his lantern jaws,
Throws light upon the English laws."

Nunwell,[*] anciently Nounwell, has

been the residence of the Oglander family for many centuries. At the base of a lofty down, embowered in venerable woods, and with a noble breadth of groves, hills, meadows, and seas spread out before it, certainly its position befits the mansion of the only one of the knightly families of the island under William Fitz-Osbert which has survived "the lapses of time." The house is a plain brick building, seated "on a rising-ground at the end of a park-like lawn, and backed by a solemn grove of lofty ashes and limes." The park is about two miles in circumference, and contains some oaks of extraordinary size. The Oglander family have held lands in the island since the Conquest, when Roger de Okelandre accompanied William Fitz-Osbert. They came from the chateau d'Oglandres, in the Cotentin, which was afterwards held by Prince Henry (Henry I.) against his brothers, Duke Robert and Prince William. In the reign of James I., John Oglander, lieutenant of the island, was knighted. Died 1665. His son, Sir William, was created a baronet, 1665. Then followed Sir John, died 1685; Sir William, died, 1734; Sir John, died 1767; Sir William, died 1806; Sir William, died 1850; and Sir Henry Oglander, of Nunwell, and Parham, Dorset, the present representative.

Fairy Hill (W. A. Glynn, Esq.) on the uplands, above Sea View, well deserves its poetical appellation.

Puckpool, a charming spot, near Spring Vale; *Westridge* (J. Young, Esq.), on the road to Nettlestone; *Westbrook* (P. Mahon, Esq.); *St. John's Lodge* (Major-General Sir G. Peter Wymer, K.C.B.), in St. John's Road, Ryde: all are mansions of a superior order, and agreeably situated.

PLACES TO BE VISITED BY THE PEDESTRIAN.

Queen's Bower, 7 miles from Ryde, a lovely spot, whither Isabella de Fortibus, the Lady of the Island, was wont to resort

---

romantic beauties of that coast with great fervour and enthusiasm.— *Life of W. Collins,* by Wilkie Collins.

[*] So named, we are told, because the nuns of Ashey were wont to resort for water to the spring still rising in its grounds.

for the pleasures of the chase, the forest being then well stocked with "red and fallow deer;"—Bordwood, as it is still called, was bestowed by Henry V. on Philippa, Duchess of York, A.D. 1417. *Alverstone Mill*, 6 miles from Ryde, a quiet nook, rich in spoils for the botanist; *Bloodstone Well*, in a wooded valley, north-east of Ashey Down, where the pebbles in the stream are covered with the crimson vegetable incrustation of the *byssus purpureus*; *Aldermoor Mill*. 1 mile south of Ryde, an elevation from which a very fine view of Ryde and the outlying country may be obtained; Kerne, at the foot of Ashey Down, anciently *Lacherne*, a manor of the Knights Templars; and *Ninham*, 2 miles south-west of Ryde, where there is a curious stone image in the wall of the old farm-house (see *ante*, p. 113).

DISTRICT V.—SOUTH-EAST.—VENTNOR AND ITS ENVIRONS.

VENTNOR is a town on the south-eastern coast of the Isle of Wight—the capital, so to speak, of the Undercliff—at a distance of 12 miles from Ryde, and 10 miles from Newport, with a population of 3208 in 1861, but now of nearly 3900. It was formerly included in New-church, but it was a distinct parish.* Its name may, perhaps, be derived from the Celtic *Gwent* and *nor*—referring to its position on a *chalky* and *exposed shore*. For centuries the name had been applied to a mere cluster of fishermen's huts on the beach of Ventnor Cove, and no whisper of it was heard throughout the busy history of the island, until it sprang into prosperity some thirty years ago. At Bonchurch to the west, and at St. Lawrence to the south, had churches been founded, and villas gradually erected, but Ventnor made no movement. It was reserved for medical science to raise into a singular celebrity, and with startling suddenness, the region of the Undercliff. "Forty years ago," says a lively writer, "it contained about half a dozen humble cottages; and until the publication of Sir James Clark's work, its few inhabitants were nearly all fishermen. It was the most picturesque spot along the coast. The platform was broken into several uneven terraces. The huge hills towered far up aloft. Down to the broad smooth beach the ground ran in rough slopes, mingled with abrupt banks of rock, along which a brawling rivulet careered gaily towards the sea; and the few fishermen's huts gave a piquant rustic liveliness to all besides. The climate seemed most favourable, and the neighbourhood most agreeable to the invalid. In the open gardens of the cottagers myrtle and other tender plants flourished abundantly, and without need of protection even in winter; snow hardly ever lay on the ground; sunny and sheltered walks abounded; and the beach was excellent for bathing. Ventnor at once caught the attention of the crowd of visitors; and it was one of the first places to provide them suitable accommodation. In the tiny fishing hamlet soon sprang up hotels, and boarding-houses, and shops, and a church. Invalids came here for a winter retreat, as well as a summer visit. Speculation was stimulated. And now, as Fuller has it, 'the plague of building lighted upon it,' and it spread until every possible spot was planted with some staring building, or row of buildings."—*Land we Live In.*

Sir James Clark, when comparing the sanitary condition of the principal towns on the south coast, asserted, with all the authority of a scientific physician, "that

* Until 1866 the town was controlled by a Board of Commissioners, elected by the rate-payers, under the provisions of a local Act obtained in 1844. It is now under the Local Government Act.

it was a matter of surprise to him, after having fully examined that favoured spot, that the advantages it possessed in so eminent a degree, in point of shelter and position, should have been so long overlooked in a country like this, whose inhabitants during the last century have been traversing half the globe in search of climate. The physical structure of this singular district has been carefully investigated and described by the geologist, and the beauties of its scenery have been often dwelt upon by the tourist; but its far more important qualities as a winter residence for the delicate invalid seem scarcely to have attracted attention, even from the medical philosopher. Nothing," he continues, "along the south coast will bear a comparison with it, and Torquay is the only place on the south-west coast which will do so. With a temperature nearly the samê, the climate of Torquay will be found softer, more humid, and relaxing; while that of the Undercliff will prove drier, somewhat sharper, and more bracing."—*Sir James Clark.*

So eulogistic a statement from so eminent an authority set the whole world of invalids in motion, and Ventnor soon acquired a celebrity which it well deserves, and probably will long retain.*

As we have said, the town has no history. In 1793, all that a traveller—and an observant one—could find to say about it was this:—" The little cove of Ventnor is very well known for its romantic scenery and for a considerable cascade of fine water, which, after turning a cornmill, falls upon the beach, as well as for its crab and lobster fishery, all of which are destined for the London markets."—*Wyndham.* We may, therefore, plunge at once *in medias res*, and briefly note down what may now be seen in Ventnor.

* It is the healthiest spot in the United Kingdom, the death-rate being only 15·4 in the 1000.

1. The town is controlled by a Board of Commissioners, elected by the ratepayers under the provisions of a local act obtained in 1844. To their exertions some important improvements must be attributed. A sea-wall was erected in 1848, converting a considerable portion of the beach into a pleasant *Esplanade*, now lined by a row of villas of remarkable architectural characteristics. We may observe, *en passant*, that in no town in England have builders indulged such monstrous vagaries as in this. There is scarcely a villa of modest or unpretending aspect in the whole town; and to pass through its streets is enough to affect a sensitive architect with a hideous nightmare!

2. Ventnor, next to Sir James Clark, has been most indebted to the late Mr. Hambrough, of Steephill Castle, its principal land-owner, for its prosperity. To his liberality it owes its elegant church, dedicated to St. Catherine, and the adjacent parsonage, both erected in 1836–7. The National Schools, Albert Street, were also rebuilt at his expense.

There is an *Independent Chapel* in High Street; two *Wesleyan* in High Street; and a *Roman Catholic* in Trinity Road. An excellent *Literary and Scientific Institution* in the High Street is supplied during the winter session with a succession of lecturers of repute. A very graceful church, dedicated to the Holy Trinity, was built in 1861–62, at the east end of the town. The style is Early Decorated, and the design was furnished by Mr. Giles of Taunton. The spire is 160 feet high.

[3. *Principal Hotels*—the Royal Hotel, Marine, Esplanade and Commercial. There are several respectable *Inns*—the Crab and Lobster, Prince of Wales, Globe, and Freemasons. Lodgings are numerous, and, except at "the height of the season," very moderate. A pier and harbour have recently been constructed; but the speculation, we believe, has not answered the expectations of its promoters. The harbour was seriously damaged by a storm in the spring of 1866. Inhabited houses at Ventnor in 1861, 514; uninhabited, 19; building, 2.]

THE UNDERCLIFF.

The Undercliff is a region of such singular beauty and interest, that we may even admit it deserves all the praise which has been lavished upon it. Its interchange of rock and dell, of lawny slopes and leafy bowers, of rugged masses of cliff, of bare, precipitous ramparts of glittering chalk, of rippling brooks and sleepy pools, of lanes winding in and about thick clusters of blossomy copses—with everywhere " the murmurous noise of waves "—renders it an enchanted land, whose beauties are continually unfolding themselves before our admiring eyes.

> " A murmur from the violet vales !
> A glory in the goblin dell ;
> There Beauty all her breast unveils,
> And Music pours out all her shell."
> *Owen Meredith.*

" It is a region so well known as hardly to require description. Consisting of a platform varying from half a mile to a quarter of a mile in width—bounded on the south by the undulating bays and promontories of the Channel, and on the north by a perpendicular wall of grey rocks, which form the buttress to a range of downs of almost mountainous elevation, it is easy to perceive that it unites two of the principal constituents of a beautiful landscape. But when, besides its guardian hills and ever-varying ocean, we remember the richness of its vegetation, the clearness of its air, and the wild seclusion of its innumerable dells, the glowing expressions of enthusiastic tourists would seem not much, if at all, beyond the truth. . . . . But in addition to its beauty, the district has acquired within a few years another and a better claim to admiration. The peculiarity of its position, guarded from the east and north by its barrier of rock,

the mildness of its air, and the extraordinary dryness of its soil, have made it a chosen spot for the invalid, and a refuge from the attacks of the English destroyer, or, at least, a soother of the English disease—consumption."—*Rev. James White.* Equally warm in his eulogy was Lord Jeffrey, *the* " Edinburgh Reviewer." " The chief beauty of the island," he says, " lies on the south, where it opens to the wide ocean, and meets a warmer sun than shines upon any other spot of our kingdom. On this side it is, for the most part, bounded by lofty chalk cliffs, which rise, in the most dazzling whiteness, out of the blue sea into the blue sky, and make a composition something like Wedgwood's enamel. The cliffs are in some places enormously high—from 600 to 700 feet. The beautiful places are either where they sink deep into bays and valleys, opening like a theatre to the sun and the sea, or where there has been a terrace of low land formed at their feet, which stretches under the shelter of that enormous wall, like a rich garden plot, all roughened over with masses of rock, fallen in distant ages, and overshadowed with thickets of myrtle, and roses, and geraniums, which all grow wild here in great luxuriance and profusion. These spots are occupied, for the most part, by beautiful ornamented cottages, designed and executed, for the most part, in the most correct taste. Indeed, it could not be easy to make anything ugly in a climate so delicious, where all sorts of flowers, and shrubs, and foliage multiply and maintain themselves with such vigour and rapidity. The myrtles fill all the hedges, and grapes grow in festoons from tree to tree, without the assistance of a wall."—*Lord Cockburn's Life of Lord Jeffrey.* Mrs. Radcliffe, the once famous authoress of " The

---

* This was written by Lord Jeffrey during his stay at Ventnor in 1806, at the outset of his brilliant career.

Mysteries of Udolpho," describes this beautiful district in graphic language:—" The Undercliff is a tract of shore formed by the fallen cliffs, and closely barricaded by a wall of rock of vast height. We entered upon it about a mile from Niton, and found ourselves in such a Druid scene of wildness and ruin as we never saw before. The road is, for the most part, close to the wall of rock, which seems to threaten the traveller with destruction, as he passes frequently beneath enormous masses that lean forward. On the other side of the road is an extremely rugged descent of about half a mile to the sea, where sometimes are amphitheatres of rocks, their theatres filled with ruins, and frequently covered with verdure and underwood thåt stretch up the hill-side with the wildest pomp, sheltering here a cottage and there a villa among the rocky hillocks. We afterwards ascended by a steep, rugged road to the summit of the down, from which the views are astonishing and grand in a high degree; we seemed perched on an extreme point of the world, looking down on hills and cliffs of various height and form, tumbled into confusion as if by an earthquake, and stretching into the sea, which spreads its vast circumference beyond. The look down on the shores is indeed tremendous."—*Mrs. Radcliffe.*

The Undercliff extends from Luccombe to Blackgang Chine, forming a tract of wild and wonderful scenery, about seven miles in length, and varying in breadth from a quarter of a mile to nearly a mile. It may be plainly described as an irregular table-land,—or rather, a succession of terraces, backed by a chalk wall of unequal height, and raised 50, 60, and even 100 feet above the sea level. Certain internal agencies—land springs and hidden waters—at work since the dawn of life and light upon the world, have resulted in the separation of this strip of land from the hills of which it was formerly a part, and removing it bodily to a considerable way below them—between *them*, in fact, and the sea. To understand the cause of this subsidence, it is necessary to be acquainted with the geological nature of the rocks, and the influences to which they have been subjected, when the explanation becomes very simple. "The strata, reckoning from the bottom, are first red ferruginous sand, then blue marl, next green sandstone, and at top chalk and chalk marl. The stratum of blue marl is soft and easily acted upon by land springs, when it becomes mud, and oozes out; and the sandstone and chalk being deprived of their support, must of necessity sink down. The subsidence, if thus brought about, might be gradual and scarcely perceptible, except in its ultimate results; but the sea was at the same time beating with violence against the lower strata, and washing out the sand and marl, which were already loosened by the springs. This double process would go on till the superincumbent mass became unable to sustain itself by mere adhesion to the parent rock, when it must necessarily break away and fall forward. That this was the way in which the Undercliff was produced, is evident from an examination of the phenomena it presents, and what may be observed still going on, though on a lesser scale. The great change in the level must have occurred at a very distant period; churches and houses of ancient date, which stand in different parts of the Undercliff, show that no very considerable alteration can have taken place for centuries."—*Thorne.* A landslip, indeed, at East End, destroyed in 1810, 30 acres of ground; a second in 1818, upwards of 50; and a large mass of rock fell in 1847. But the most considerable of these convulsions occurred in February 1799, near Niton, when a farm named Pitlands, and 100 acres of land were hurled in wild confusion towards the shore. These, however, are local changes; and "no great further movement at all is to be dreaded within this district."

Here, in this most delightful land of bowers, the heliotrope, the myrtle, the fuchsia, the petunia, and the verbena, bloom in the open air throughout the winter. "I have counted," says Dr. Martin, "nearly fifty species of garden flowers blooming in the borders in December; and sweet peas blossom on Christmas-day! The bee is on the wing when, in less favoured districts of the island, a bitter frost parches all the meadows. The mean annual temperature is placed by observers at no less than 51° 72'; and as the result of eight years' calculations, Dr. Martin shows that the warmer and more genial winds blow here for the greater portion of the year. Thus: S.W., 96.97 days; E., 60.34 days; N.E., 54.61; W., 52.54; N.W., 30.95; S., 26,72; N., 24.46, and S.E., 18.85. "It would be difficult to find in any northern country a district of equal extent and variety of surface, and, it may be added, of equal beauty in point of scenery, so completely screened from the cutting north-east winds of the spring on the one hand, and from the boisterous southerly gales of the autumn and winter on the other."—*Sir James Clark.*

We have now said enough, and quoted enough, we fancy, to make the reader thoroughly acquainted with the peculiarities of this peculiar region. We shall shortly take him through it, from Luccombe to Blackgang; but first invite him to a consideration of the principal places included by us in the south-west district of the island.

I. SANDOWN.

(*Hotels*: Sandown; Star and Garter; King's Head.

SANDOWN is a hamlet and ecclesiastical district in the parish of Brading, skirting the bay of the same name, and lying in the lowlands between the heights of Bembridge and the lofty masses of Shanklin Down. It is 6 miles from Ryde, and 10 miles from Newport, and contained in 1861 a population of 1743, which since that date, in all probability, has greatly increased. Its growth in the last few years has been very rapid, owing to the exertions of two or three spirited residents, as well as its eminent advantages of position; and it bids fair to become one of the most popular, as it is one of the fairest, of the towns on the south coast of the island. Its bay is eminently beautiful; the chalky heights of *Culver Cliffs* form the northern, and the red sands of *Dunnose* the southern extremity—"the lower chalk, firestone, galt, and greensand appearing in succession, like sloping bands of yellowish white, green, blue, and deep red; the latter denoting the ferruginous sands of the lower group. Sandown Fort marks the low trace consisting of the Weald clay. The church and little town of Sandown are seen on the brow of the sand cliffs which form the western side of the bay, and extend toward Shanklin Cliffs of a dark red ferruginous colour. The eastern termination of the southern range of chalk, forming the lofty downs above Shanklin, next appears, and seaward, the high but subordinate cliff of greensand at Dunnose Point."—*Mantell.*

Sandown, which was anciently named *Sandham* (the *home*, or *settlement* on the *sands*), can boast of a pretty church, superior national schools, numerous elegant little villas, a handsome Early English chapel (Wesleyan), an immense breadth of firm red sands, delicious nooks and angles all leafy and smiling, and the principal fortress in the Isle of Wight. The church was built in 1847, and the schools were completed in 1856. *Sandown Fort* was one of Henry VIII.'s new defences, erected at the epoch of that great French armament intended to humiliate the haughty "Defender of the Faith" (1540), and had for those days a considerable military establishment. The fort lately taken down only dated

SHANKLIN CHINE.

from the reign of Charles I., when the former stronghold was demolished, the sea having encroached upon its very foundations. It was of a quadrangular plan, with strong bastions at each angle, surrounded by a wet moat. A new and stronger fort, faced with granite, and armed with ten heavy guns, has been recently erected, nearer to the Culver Cliff. Other defences are projected, and a lighthouse is to be raised on the heights above the bay. There are large barracks at the extremity of the town, where the road turns off to Shanklin, and generally 600 men are stationed there.

Collins the artist made many of his best sketches in Sandown, Shanklin, and their neighbourhood.

Here the once famous John Wilkes had a cottage, or, as he loved to call it in his *Correspondence*, " a villakin,"— now represented by a drapery establishment in the principal street. He obtained a fourteen years' lease of it from Colonel, afterwards General James Barker, of Stickworth, in May 1788, and immediately fitted it up after his own somewhat *bizarre* ideas. From a floor-cloth manufactory at Knightsbridge, he brought various strange "pavilions," which he placed in prominent positions in his garden, and converted into aviaries and dove-cots. Of birds he was very fond, and daily amused himself watching their habits, while ready to purchase all that the *gamins* in the neighbourhood could catch. Here he raised semi-classical tombs and columns, and wrote inscriptions upon them in a stilted style. A Doric column in the shrubbery was branded,— " *Carolo Churchill, Divino Poetæ, Amico Jucundo, Civi Optimè de Patria merito*" (To Charles Churchill, the divine poet, the pleasant friend, the citizen who has deserved well of his country); on a tablet in a " Tuscan " room was the legend,— " *Fortunæ Reduci et Civitati Londinensi, P. Johannes Wilkes, Quæstor,* 1789;" and in his sitting-room,— " *To Filial Piety and Mary*

Wilkes. Erected by John Wilkes, 1789."

He spent his latter years in this pleasant country-side, with occasional visits to the London world ; writing his own " Memoirs," and entertaining with witty gossip and old wine his numerous visitors. With his powdered *queue* duly tied in a bag, his suit of scarlet and gold, his abundant laces and ruffles, and his long boots above his knees, he stalked about the neighbourhood of Sandown and Shanklin, "the observed of all observers," and the *Deus Major* of the village folk.

Wilkes died at his residence in Grosvenor Square, December 28, 1797, at the ripe old age of 70.

II. SHANKLIN.

(Hotels: The Upper, and Lower; and Crab Inn.)

SHANKLIN, one of the leafiest of leafy villages, whose " romantic glades" attracted the attention of Tom Ingoldsby; whose *chine* is, as it were, reverently " trotted out" at a shilling per head to curious visitors ; whose dells are prodigal of blossoms ; whose hills look out upon " the sounding sea"—is about 2 miles from Sandown, 4 from Ventnor, 8½ from Ryde, and occupies a table-land 300 feet above the sea, at the base of the eastern extremity of the great chalk range of downs which forms " the back-bone" of the island. The entrance into Shanklin from Ventnor is one of the fairest scenes in this fair country-side. The beach here is very fine, and the views seaward are endless in variety and interest, so that the tourist will do well to spend a day or two in the neighbourhood, and examine its chief attractions.

" Shanklin," says Keats, " is a most beautiful place ; sloping wood and meadow ground reach round the chine, which is a cleft between the cliffs of the depth of nearly 300 feet at least. This cleft is filled with trees and bushes in the narrow part, and as it widens becomes bare, if it were not for primroses on one side, which spread to the very verge of the sea, and some fishermen's huts on the other, perched midway in the balustrade of beautiful green hedges along the steps down to the sand."—*Life and Letters.* Here is a picture from another hand, equally graphic :—" This village is very small and scattery, all mixed up with trees, and lying among sweet airy falls and swells of ground, which finally rise up behind to breezy downs 800 feet high, and sink down in front to the edge of the varying cliffs, which overhang a pretty beach of fine sand, and are approachable by a very striking wooded ravine which they call the *Chine.*"— *Lord Jeffrey, Life by Cockburn.* We close our eulogistic quotations with a more detailed description of this famous chine (which, by the way, has always seemed to us much overrated) :—" The cliff, where the stream which forms the chine enters the sea, is about 100 feet in height, and the chasm is perhaps 150 wide at the top, and at the bottom not much wider than the channel of the stream. The sides * are very steep, and in most places are clothed with rich underwood, overhanging the naked sides. At a small distance within their mouth, on a terrace just large enough to afford a walk to their doors, stand two small cottages of different elevations. Rude flights of steps descend to them from the top, and an excavation from the sandy rock forms a skittle-ground to one of them, overshadowed by the spray of young oaks. After proceeding about 100 yards in a direct line from the shore, the chasm makes a sudden bend to the left, and grows much narrower. Its sides are nearly perpendicular, and but little shrubbery breaks their naked surface. The chasm continues widening and de-

* The cliff is 230 feet high, the chasm 300 feet wide at the top, and the chasm extends 450 feet inland from the shore.

creasing in breadth, till it terminates in an extremely narrow fissure, down which the rill, which has formed the whole, falls about 30 feet. The quantity of water is in general so small that the cascade is scarcely worth viewing ; but after great rains it must be very pretty. The sides of the gloomy hollow in which it falls are of the blackish indurated clay, of which the greater part of the soil hereabouts is composed, and the damp of the waters has covered most part of it with shining green lichens and mosses of various shades. The brushwood which grows on the brow on each side overhangs so as nearly to meet ; and the whole scene, though it cannot be considered as magnificent, is certainly striking and grotesque. Above the fall the stream continues to run into a deep and shady channel quite to the foot of the hills in which it takes its rise."—*Sir H. Englefield.* With one or two slight alterations, this graphic account is singularly correct.

The antique *Parsonage* at Shanklin, with its girdle of huge myrtles, is a picturesque object. The *Church* is an interesting little fane.

The sands here, from Sandown away to Dunnose, are firm, broad, and the finest in the island. There is a pleasant walk at low-water to *Luccombe Chine,* a deep ravine in the cliffs, with bare precipitous sides of sand and clay, quite as well worth visiting, to our fancy, as "the lion" of Shanklin. The tourist may continue his walk to *East End,* the commencement of the Undercliff, and the scene of the great landslip of 1818. The rocks displaced by the tremendous convulsion have fallen upon the shore in the wildest and even most grotesque confusion ; masses of dark ferruginous earth, or hot white chalk, partly overgrown with luxuriant vegetation, lying piled upon each other as if they had been the playthings of the Titans, and flung away in scorn.

A stroll *by the road* to Bonchurch and

the Undercliff is also full of interest and variety. The road winds through open groves and green pastures up the flank of the hill of Dunnose, affording at every point the most delightful views. The village, with its leafy gardens, occupies the foreground; then, in succession, the eye surveys the fine sweep of Sandown Bay terminated by the white walls of the Culver, the low marsh-land stretching away to Brading, and even, across the Solent, the shipping in the noble anchorage at Spithead. From the top of the ascent may be observed the chalky heights of Yaverland and the blue seas beyond, the distant hills of Hampshire and Sussex running from west to east in a long clean line, until they melt into the horizon, and the glittering cliffs from Brighton to Beachy Head are sometimes plainly visible.

The parish of Shanklin is bounded north by that of Brading, south by Bonchurch, west by Newchurch, and east by the Channel. It includes 950 acres, and in 1861 its population was 479 (200 males + 279 females); houses inhabited, 96; uninhabited, 7. Near the village are *Fernbank*, the residence of Miss Harriet Parr ("Holme Lee"); and *West Hill*, seat of Major-General Napier.

In the early part of 1819 Keats was staying at Shanklin with his friend Brown, and wrote here the play of "Otho the Great," the plot of which Brown invented, and the fine poem of "Lamia." Lord Jeffrey was here in 1846, the year before his death, seeking to revive his waning energies. "We enjoyed," he says, "three weeks' very sweet, tranquil, and innocent seclusion, which we left with much affection and some regret." —*Life, by Cockburn.*

III. BONCHURCH.
(*Hotel:* Ribbands'.)

BONCHURCH, anciently *Bonecerce*, is one of the oldest villages in the Wight, and is truly "hallowed ground," if the popular tradition that it was the scene of the early labours of St. Boniface—*bonum facere,* to do good—has aught of truth in it. There is a little cove among its rocks which still bears the name of *Monk's Bay,* and is reputed to have been the landing-place of the adventurous priests of the Abbey of Lire, who brought the good tidings of Christianity to the untaught islanders. This, it is said, took place in A.D. 755, when they raised here a village church.

But the *present* old church of Bonchurch cannot claim so remote an antiquity. Most probably it was founded by one of the De Lisles not earlier than the commencement of the 14th century. The new church, a graceful structure, was built in 1847. In the graveyard a plain cross marks the last resting-place of the Rev. James White, author of "The Eighteen Christian Centuries."

The parish of Bonchurch * contains 618 acres, and in 1861 had a population of 564 (216 males + 348 females), 80 inhabited houses, and 5 uninhabited. Its boundaries are—north, Shanklin; south, St. Lawrence; Godshill, west; and east, the Channel. Within its limits are scenes of greater beauty than perhaps exist anywhere else in so confined a space. The sea-shore is continually presenting new features of interest; new surprises occur at every point. Inland there is an unequalled combination of the sublime and the picturesque; of towering walls of glittering chalk; of dells odorous with flowers; of gardens rich in the rarest plants and most exquisite blossoms. The entrance to the village is eminently lovely. The road is bordered by a calm, sweet pool, on whose bosom sleep the broad leaves of the water-lily, and, running under a perfect arch of foliage, it winds in and out of jutting masses of rock covered with prodigal vegetation. The wall of the Undercliff towers above the traveller to the height

* Bonchurch was the birth-place of the gallant old seaman, Admiral Hopson (see *post*).

of 400 or 500 feet, and from its sides leap out little runnels in mimic cascades, filling the air with their musical chime and pleasant freshness.

It is difficult, in our narrow limits, to note down *all* that the tourist ought to see in this agreeable neighbourhood. But he will ascend, of course, the steep sides of *St. Boniface Down* (783 feet above the sea), to enjoy the surpassingly beautiful panorama which spreads beneath and around it. He will visit the Well— *St. Bonny's Well*,*—a perennial spring, bubbling out of the chalky depths of the Down. It was first discovered, says the legend, by a certain bishop who, riding across the hill on a misty night, lost his way, and found his steed, to his horror, slowly sliding down the precipitous side, until at length he suddenly drew up with his hoofs fixed in the hollow of this well. The bishop thereupon vowed to St. Boniface, that if he reached the bottom securely he would dedicate to his honour an acre of land. The saint closed with the bargain ; the bishop got home without further let or mishap ; and the land, known as *The Bishop's Acre*, still belongs to the glebe of Bonchurch. It lies at the foot of the hill, and is marked out by a ridge of turf.

In the old times, on the feast day of St. Boniface, the village maidens were wont to ascend the down and place garlands of flowers about the well, in honour of the patron-saint. There was, also, a superstition attaching to it, that a wish breathed inwardly by the stranger who, for the first time, drank of its water, would assuredly be fulfilled,—a pleasant enough superstition, which the lads and lasses of Bonchurch doubtlessly, in their

* It is supplied by a stream which rises at the foot of the down, and after forming the pool, runs underground and divides into two branches, one of which bubbles up in the gardens of Mountfield, and falls into Horseshoe Bay ; the other, at the side of the church-yard, and falls into the sea at the cliffs below East Dene.

love-making days, turned to good account.

Standing on the brink of this magnificent precipice, we must admit that the picture beneath us is perfect. "The cliff is exquisitely chiselled into horizontal blocks, richly mossed and ivied, and there the chough resorts and the jackdaw builds, and here and there a dove will wing its way, like a snow-flake among the grey and sable daws."— *Dendy*. And spreading afar, like a sheet of molten silver, ever flashes and gleams the apparently motionless sea.

A flight of steps near the pond conducts the tourist to the *Pulpit Rock* (400 feet above the sea), a bold and rugged mass of cliff, now surmounted with a wooden cross in a wooden enclosure,— from which it derives its name,—but formerly bearing a flagstaff, and christened "Shakspeare Rock." In the beautiful grounds of *Undermount* (Sir J. Pringle), rises another and similar mass of crag, called the *Flagstaff Rock*.

There are numerous pretty villas in pretty garden grounds, — almost too many, in fact,—scattered about this singular district. Most noticeable are, *East Dene* (J. S. Henry, Esq.), designed by Mr. Beazley (the architect of the Lyceum Theatre), with a picturesque Elizabethan interior, and an organ which, it is said, has been touched by Queen Bess's fingers ; *Wood Lynch*, the seat of the late Rev. J. White, dramatist and historian, whose "King of the Commons" was the last character created by Macready, and whose popular condensations of English. French, and Greek History, are nearly as well known even as they ought to be ; *Winterbourne*, the residence of the late Rev. William Adams, the author of many exquisite sacred allegories, to which we shall more particularly allude hereafter ; *Westfield, Mountfield, Orchard Leigh, Combe Wood*, and, best to be noticed in this connection, *Hillside*, Ventnor, where John Sterling— Carlyle's John Sterling—spent the last

few months of his life, and died September 18, 1844.

Near Monk's Bay are still remaining a few traces of a Roman encampment, and in the vicinity have been exhumed, at different times, urns, calcined bones, ashes, and other significant relics of the Roman occupants of the Undercliff.

Such is a brief, cold outline of the attractions of this fairy land, which includes within its enchanted limits a thousand varieties—a thousand charms —of scenery. "Take barren rocks," exclaims an enthusiastic writer, " prolific soils, broken masses, elevated cliffs, and precipitous descents, an expanded sea, a winding rivulet, and tranquil lake, the wild flower dell and the rich pasture, the peasant's hut, the farmer's yard, and the admired villa ; employ the colours of the bow of heaven ; let the motions of animated nature be within observation; cover the whole with an expanded arch ; light it with a summer's sun, and call it —Bonchurch."

IV. ST. LAWRENCE.

The parish of St. Lawrence lies between the parishes of Newchurch, east ; Godshill, north ; and Whitwell, west, with the channel for its southern boundary. It contains 332 acres, and in 1861 had a population of 85 (40 males + 45 females), 18 inhabited houses, 0 uninhabited, and 1 building. The *church*, which is the smallest—or one of the smallest—in England ; the *Well*, famous for its refreshing waters; and the beautiful *marine villa* of the Earls of Yarborough, are the principal noteworthy objects in this miniature parish, which is but a narrow strip of land between the wall of the Undercliff and the sea, 1¼ mile in length. The living is a rectory (Rev. C. Malden), valued at £106, in the gift of the Earl of Yarborough.

V. WHITWELL

Lies next to St. Lawrence, with an ocean boundary to the south, the parishes of

Chale and Niton on the west, and Godshill on the north. Acreage, 1963 ; population in 1861, 570 (286 males + 284 females) ; inhabited houses, 123 ; uninhabited, 4 ; building, 0. The living is a perpetual curacy, held by the rector of Niton (who is also vicar of Godshill); but, though in that sense a chapelry, has its own parochial rights.

In this parish was once included the manor of Woolverton (*Wulfere's town*). There were three Woolvertons in the island —the one now referred to, a second near Shorwell, and a third below Yaverland, built by Sir Ralph de Woolverton in 1370. In a shadowy *combe*, or hollow, to the left of the road from St. Lawrence to Niton, lie the ruins of the ancient manor-house of Woolverton, a gabled two-storied building, with lancet windows, ivy-shrouded, gray, and mossy. It was probably erected by John de Woolverton, *temp.* Edward I. A new town is springing up in this beautiful country-side.

On the cliff-road to Mirables is the picturesquely situated hamlet of *Wrongs*, —well worth a visit.

VI. NITON.

The parish of Niton is bounded on the north and east by that of Whitwell, west by Chale, and south by the waters of the Channel. In its limits are included the wildest and rudest portion of the Undercliff, the dangerous coast from Old Park to Rocken End, Niton Down, and many a footprint of the Celt and the ancient Roman. Acreage, 1397: population in 1801, 288 ; in 1811, 370; in 1821, 443; in 1831, 573; in 1841, 613; and in 1851, 684 ; inhabited houses, 133; uninhabited, 8; building, 3 : and in 1861, 700; inhabited houses, 135; uninhabited, 7. The living is a rectory, held in conjunction with the vicarage of Godshill (vicar, Rev. G. Hayton ; curate, Rev. — Hawthorne), valued at £600 *per annum*, and presented to by Queen's College, Oxford, on which foundation the patronage was bestowed by Charles I.

NITON (*Inn*, the White Lion) is a considerable hamlet, lying at the foot of Niton Down, and in the shadow of St. Catherine's Hill (which may be ascended by a pathway from the village near the church), about 5 miles from Ventnor and 8½ from Newport. The church is a large and picturesque edifice of great antiquity, and was one of the six bestowed by Fitz-Osbert upon his favourite Abbey of Lire. There is a Literary Institute in the village, and the National Schools are well conducted. Several new houses have recently been erected here, and tourists will find it a convenient spot from which to direct their explorations of the Undercliff. There is a well-to-do air about the village, which may result from the number of "seats" in its vicinity, and the constant employment thus provided for its inhabitants.

Dr. Thomas Pittis, an eminent divine (see *post*), was a native, and for many years a rector of Niton.

There is a curious camp, or perhaps tin-mart, in a field on the *Beauchamp Farm*, near the church, whose regularity of plan and massiveness of construction may well be examined by the antiquary. Through this parish, by a road still traceable, was conducted the tin traffic of the island, and probably the metal was shipped on board the vessels of the Phœnician merchants at Puckaster Cove. Near the northern boundary of the parish at a place still called Bury (*byrig*, a walled or fortified settlement), may be observed an artificial mound of earth, now reduced to very small dimensions, but which once occupied a base of 30 yards diameter. Near the village there is another mound of similar character, called *Old Castle*, and both are undoubtedly relics of the Celtic earthworks.

Niton is so pleasantly situated, and there is so much of interest in its neighbourhood,—the cottages *ornées* of the Undercliff,—*Mirables, Beauchamp, Knowles, Old Park, Mount Cleeves*, and *Mount Ida*; the Royal Sandrock Hotel, with its cliff gardens; Puckaster Cove, where the Roman fleet used to ride securely, and Charles II. was once driven ashore by stress of weather; St. Catharine's Point, and its brilliant lighthouse; St. Catherine's Hill, and its panoramic prospects,—that it ought to be more generally frequented by those who travel with open eyes and ears to hear. It is sometimes called Crab Niton, to distinguish it from Knighton, near Ashey, and in reference to the crustacea so abundant on the adjacent coast.

VII. GODSHILL,
(*Inn*: The Griffin),

Is a delightfully picturesque hamlet, clustered round a steep knoll, or hill, on which is built its stately and antique church. Like all the island villages, it consists of one long street of shops, cottages, and the better sort of houses strangely intermixed. It is distant from Newport about 5½ miles, from Ventnor 5, and from Ryde 11, and lies in a fertile country, divided into excellent farms, of which Wroxall, Rew, Span, Week, Park, Apleford, Moor, and Stenbury are the principal. The parish includes 6535 acres, chiefly of good arable land, and had, in 1861, a population of 1215 (619 males + 596 females); 237 inhabited houses, and 11 uninhabited. The *tithings* of Stenbury, Roud, Sandford, and Rookley, with Week, as well as the manor of Appuldurcombe, are in this parish. The living is a vicarage, held, as already stated, with the Rectory of Niton. There was once a good *grammar school* in the village (founded in 1595 by one Richard Andrews), whither resorted the sons of the leading gentry of the island, and where Sir Thomas Fleming was educated, but it is now of no account.

The *church* is one of the handsomest in the Wight. Erected upon a steep and lofty knoll, and having a stately tower, it is conspicuously visible from every part of the wide and extensive vale. The interior is divided by a long range of rich early English arches, and contains some superb memorials to the Worsley family.

About 2 miles south-east of the village lies *Appuldurcombe Park* (the property of Mr. R. W. Williams), the ancient seat of the Worsleys, and once the great glory of the island. Even now, in its denuded condition, it claims the tourist's admiration, from the beauty of its extensive grounds and the stateliness of the large Corinthian pile, with its projecting wings, which crowns the head of the green and ample lawny slope. "The park is very famous, and it deserves its celebrity. It is very extensive for the island; the ground is considerably diversified, and there are noble views over the wide glades. Oak, elm, and beech-trees of stately size abound, and the plantations are well arranged. The park and the house are, in short, on a corresponding style of grandeur."—*Knight.* The mansion occupies the site of an Elizabethan building—the remains of the ancient Priory of Appuldurcombe—pulled down by Sir Robert Worsley about 1710; was commenced by him immediately afterwards, and completed by his successor, Sir Richard Worsley, who made it the receptacle of a fine collection of ancient marbles, figured in his *Museum Worsleanum,* and an excellent gallery of pictures. "It is situated at some distance from the road, within the park, and, being built from the quarries of Portland, and unincumbered with adjoining offices, offers a magnificent object to the high road and to the hills above it, particularly when the rays of the sun are reflected from its beautiful stone."—*Wyndham.*

Appuldurcombe is usually derived from the British *Y pul dur y cwm*—"the lake in the hollow"—but the correct etymology is evidently *Apuldre-combe,* the valley of apple-trees.

On the highest point of this down are the remains of an obelisk of Cornish granite, erected in 1744, to the memory of Sir Robert Worsley, Bart., as "an emblem of the conspicuous character he maintained during a long and exemplary life." It was shattered by lightning in 1831. From this point, 685 feet above the sea, the prospect is eminently beautiful, and embraces almost the whole extent of the "Fair Island." On the eastern brink, bowered amidst trees, is an artificial ruin, called "Cook's Castle."

The house and estate, as well as the furniture and a large portion of the rich collection made by Sir Richard Worsley, were disposed of by auction in 1855, by order of the present Earl of Yarborough. The best pictures, however, were removed to his lordship's mansion in London.

A brief account of the Worsley family, so long the principal one in the Isle of Wight, may be of interest to the reader.

1. *Sir James Worsley,* a scion of the Lancashire Worsleys, and a favourite page of Henry the Seventh's, was appointed captain of the island in 1517. By his marriage with the heiress of Sir John Leigh he obtained considerable estates in the island, to which his son succeeded in 1538.

2. *Richard Worsley* was also captain of the island, and lord of Appuldurcombe, where he entertained Henry VIII. in 1539. Died 1565. His two sons were killed "in the lodge or gate-house at Appuldurcombe" by an accidental explosion of gunpowder.

3. *John Worsley,* brother of Richard, married into the Meux family, and further increased the wealth and weight of the Worsleys. Died in 1581.

4. *Thomas Worsley* succeeded: "a brave scholar, a plain but worthy gentleman, and a most plentiful housekeeper." Died about 1604-5, leaving two sons, Richard and John.

5. *Sir Richard Worsley* was knighted at Whitehall, Feb. 8, 1611, by James I., and created a baronet, June the 29th, in the same year. He was probably well esteemed by the retentive Stuart, for when Prince Henry and the king were entertained at Oxford in 1601, and splen-

did gifts were offered by the students to the accomplished prince, the young Worsley presented him with "a book of verses, in foreign languages, beautifully written."—*State Papers, Domestic Series.* He lived in the island in great repute, and is spoken of by his contemporary and friend in most eulogistic language :—"The man of learning, patron of virtue, friend of good fellows, and credit both of his house and island,"—"whose good fame and virtue shall outlive all tombs," "both for natural and artificial gifts, he had not his fellow in the county."—*Sir J. Oglander.* He married Frances, a fair daughter of Sir Henry Neville, whose beauty was much applauded, even in those days of beautiful women ; was Sheriff of Hampshire in 1616, and died of small-pox in 1631-3.

6. *Sir Henry Worsley* married Bridget, a daughter of Sir Henry Wallop, afterwards Lord Lymington, and had two sons, Robert and James. The latter was knighted by Charles II. Sir Henry died in 1666.

7. *Sir Robert Worsley* began the splendid mansion of Appuldurcombe in 1710 ; married Mary, a granddaughter of the Earl of Pembroke; and had two children, Robert and Henry, neither of whom left surviving issue.

8. *Sir James Worsley,* younger son of Sir Henry, succeeded to the estates. He had several children, of whom only one, Thomas, survived him.

9. *Sir Thomas Worsley* married the eldest daughter of the Earl of Cork, by whom he had two children, Richard and Henrietta Frances. Died in 1768.

10. *Sir Richard Worsley* completed the house at Appuldurcombe, begun by Sir Robert in 1710. Having travelled through Italy, Greece, Turkey, and Egypt, he had amassed a fine collection of specimens of ancient art, of which he published an illustrated description, entitled *Musæum Worsleanum.* He also wrote and compiled a "History of the Island," from deeds and MSS. partly collected by his grandfather, Sir James. Was comptroller of the king's household, a privy councillor, sheriff of Hampshire, and governor of the Isle of Wight from 1780 to 1782. Married, in 1775, Miss Seymour Fleming, daughter of a Sir John Fleming, and had one son, Robert Edwin, who died before him. Sir Richard died in 1805, leaving his large estates to his sister, Henrietta Frances, who had married the Hon. John Bridgman Simpson. Their daughter and heiress, Anne Maria Charlotte, married—

11. *Charles Anderson Pelham,* created *Earl of Yarborough* in 1837. This liberal-minded nobleman kept up a splendid hospitality at Appuldurcombe, and interested himself zealously in all that appertained to the weal of the island. He founded the Royal Yacht Club, of which he was commodore for many years, and which he ardently supported by his example and influence. Died somewhat suddenly on board his yacht *Kestril,* off Vigo, 5th September 1846, aged 55.

12. *Charles Anderson,* second Earl of Yarborough, died 1862.

The *Priory of Appuldurcombe* was bestowed by Isabella de Fortibus, towards the close of Henry III.'s reign, on the abbey of St. Mary of Montesbourg. According to Speed, one Nicholas Spencer and Margaret his wife were the founders ; but there is no mention made of them in any document until the reign of Henry IV., when one of the priors granted them a lease. The Norman Abbey maintained here a prior and two monks, who had supervision of all its demesnes at Sandford and Week. During the wars with France, it was seized by the crown as an alien priory, and in the 2d of Henry V. was dissolved. Then it was granted—20 Henry VI.—to the nuns in "the minories without Aldgate," who leased it to the family of Fry. Agnes Fry, an heiress, married Sir John Leigh, of the Isle of Wight, and their daughter Joan conveyed the manor of Appuldurcombe to Sir James Worsley, with her hand.

FROM EAST END TO ST. CATHERINE'S POINT.

Having described with some detail the parishes included in our south-eastern district, we proceed, for the convenience of the tourist, to note down briefly the objects of interest which crowd the Undercliff, from its commencement at East End, to its termination at the headland of St. Catherine.

The tourist had best make his way through the magnificent desolation of *East End* by the foot-path which winds in and out of murmurous copses and lichen-covered masses of cliff. Reaching *Bonchurch*, he will descend the famous *Shute*—all steep hills by the islanders are called shutes—and pause half-way down to observe the new and elegant church of Bonchurch, standing on a sheltered spot of level ground. Lower down the cliff, towards the sea, is seated the ancient church, now disused, but a building of some interest, with two or three curious memorials of olden times. In its sequestered grave-yard sleep John Sterling, and the Rev. William Adams.

Passing through the village by the picturesque *Pool*, the wayfarer next enters *Ventnor*, and will turn aside to the *Esplanade*, a pleasant walk by the sea, or to *Ventnor Cove*, a nook of unrivalled beauty. *The Mill*, once so famous, was burnt down in 1848. Again returning to the high road, he reaches *Steep Hill*,* the seat of Mrs. Hambrough, whose Gothic tower is the great landmark of the country round about Ventnor and St. Lawrence. Steep Hill is a splendid castellated mansion in modern Gothic ; not in the most correct taste, perhaps, but still effective and

---

* Erected on the site of a marine cottage belonging to the late Earl of Dysart, and built by Hans Stanley while governor of the island.

picturesque. It was designed by Sanderson, the architect who "restored Henry VII.'s chapel in Westminster Abbey, and the entrance hall is considered "a happy effort." The great charm of Steep Hill, however, lies in the variety and loveliness of its extensive grounds, which were laid out by Page, of Southampton, and afford the most delightful diversities of landscape scenery. Here are fig-trees of gigantic size ; an orangery containing trees which once belonged to the Prince de Condé ; tender exotic plants blooming vigorously in the open air ; lawns, bowers, fountains, and luxuriant foliage. " I have visited," said Sir Joseph Paxton, "nearly every place of note from Stockholm to Constantinople, but never have I seen anything more beautiful than this."

Descending St. Lawrence Shute, and passing the farm of Bank End, we see to our left the pretty Gothic cottage of Mrs. Dudley Pelham, widow of Captain Dudley Pelham (second son of the late Earl of Yarborough) ; and next, the *Marine Villa* of the Earls of Yarborough, erected by Sir Richard Worsley, who tried here, but without success, the experiment of a vineyard. On the road, to the right, in a recess under a Gothic arch, and overshadowed by some fine trees, bubbles and gushes most refreshingly an abundant spring, long celebrated as *St. Lawrence's Well*. The quaint little edifice which encloses it was built by the late Earl of Yarborough.

We now reach *St. Lawrence's Church*, on the left, which it is a pity the late earl spoiled by lengthening, and whose roof the tourist may easily touch. It is close to the cliff, which all along this shore is broken up into little caves and hollows, once affording admirable shelter to the free-traders of the sea. The population of St. Lawrence was, not long ago, entirely absorbed in smuggling enterprises. "It is related that, one Sunday morning, a congregation could not be assembled at the church, in consequence of all the villagers being employed in relieving a Dutch dogger, then lying off the shore, of her illegal cargo."—*Dr. G. A. Martin.*

To the right of the road, in a sequestered glen, lies *Woolverton Farm,* and adjacent are the venerable ruins, all ivy and moss. of the ancient manorial mansion of *Woolverton.* What remains is in the Early English style. (See p. 133.)

Passing a bye-road to Whitwell, we may descry below us, deeply hidden in foliage, *Old Park* (Sir J. Cheape), with its pretty gardens; and at a short distance from it, *Mirables* (J. Coape, Esq.), which really deserves its name, even if that *be* derived, as we are told, from *mirabel,* —a beautiful prospect. "The broken foreground on the right, covered with its velvet herbage, its bold masses of rock, and miniature dells and brakes, backed by the towering cliffs, renders it a scene replete with beauty; whilst on the left, the bright foliage of its wooded glens, extending to the very strand, with a deep blue sea beyond them, form a prospect of surpassing loveliness."— *Martin.*

On the right is the foot-track which leads to *Cripple Path,* "a way cut by steps in the side of the cliff, and affording seats about half-way down, composed of projecting ledges of the rock, which, though of Nature's forming, are almost artificial in their aspect." We now gain *Orchard Cottage* (Lady Willoughby Gordon), a semi-brick, semi-stone villa, irregular, but picturesque, with terraced gardens of great beauty; and nearly opposite stands *Beauchamp,* originally named from the Beauchamps of Ancaster. Near this spot, in the summer of 1831, was blown from the cliff a young girl, named "Kerenhappuch Newnham," but afterwards popularly called "Happie Ninham." She fell upon the shore below without receiving any injury save the momentary alarm.

The road now narrows considerably, and about a mile from *the Orchard* divides into two branches,—one to the left leads to *Puckaster Cottage* (Lieut.-General Tucker), and then to Niton and the range of villas at *St. Catherine's Terrace.* The main road to the right descends a slight hill, from whose summit *West Cliff* (Captain Kerr), forms a picturesque object, and passes in succession the *Well House,* at the foot of the descent, left, and *La Rosière,* with its Italian campanile) on the right.

The main road again branches off to right and left. The right branch leads to Niton village, and thence to Godshill; the left conducts us to the *Royal Sandrock Hotel,* an elegant and commodious villa, placed in the loveliest of gardens, facing *St. Catherine's Point,* the extensive southern headland of the island. Taking the road to the *Sandrock Spring,* a rather powerful chalybeate, discovered by Mr. Waterworth, a Newport surgeon, in 1808, but now disused, we pass *Mount Cleeves* (J. Mortimer, Esq.), and find ourselves in the *locale* of the great landslip of 1799, which involved in its destructive effects upwards of 100 acres. Then we pass *Buddle Farm,* the ancient farm of *Knowles,* and make our way to *St. Catherine's Point,* the site of a really elegant *lighthouse,* whose white and graceful column forms an attractive object in the landscape.

This lighthouse was erected by the Trinity Corporation, on ground granted by G. P. Holford, Esq., in 1838, and completed in 1840. On the 25th March in that year it was lighted for the first time. Its dimensions are: From the water-mark to level of terrace, 81 feet. From the terrace to the top of the stonework, 100 feet. Lantern and pedestal, 1 foot 6 inches. Extension of glass frame, 10 feet. Roof, ball, vane, and lightning conductor, 11 feet 6 inches. *Total height,* 204 feet. The diameter of the interior is 14 feet; and the staircase to the lantern-room numbers 152 steps. The lighting apparatus consists of one lamp $3\frac{1}{2}$ inches diameter, with four concentrated wicks, reflected through a lens surmounted by 250 mirrors.

From this point the tourist, keeping along the beach, which is firm and sandy, with occasional masses of broken cliff, as at *Rocken End*, where the dangerous reef extends far into the sea, soon gains the *Royal Victoria Hotel*, a pretty lodging-house on the shore of Reeth Bay, with hills and cliffs at the back, and a wide expanse of sea before it; and turning an abrupt headland, finds himself in the sunny, sequestered hollow, called *Puckaster Cove.* Here Charles II. landed, July 1, 1675, after experiencing a terrible storm at sea. The tourist may now, by a pleasant path, regain the road on the summit of the cliff, and return *viâ* St. Lawrence and Steep Hill to Ventnor.

DISTRICT VI.—NORTH-WEST.—YARMOUTH.

YARMOUTH is seated, as its name implies, at the mouth of the western Ere, or Yar, on a low sandy shore opposite the Lymington coast, 104 miles from London, 4 from Lymington, 10½ from Newport, and 12½ from Cowes. There is a weekly market here, on Friday, and on the 25th July an annual fair. Its trade has increased since the opening of communication with London *viâ* Lymington. The living is a rectory (Rev. J. Blackburn, M.A.), in the gift of the Lord Chancellor. The parish includes 143 acres, contains 142 inhabited houses and 8 uninhabited, and a population (in 1861) of 726 (341 males + 385 females), showing a considerable increase upon the returns in 1851 (572), which had exhibited a decrease on the returns in 1831 (586).

In its ancient charters (the first was granted by Baldwin de Redvers, 1135) it is styled *Eremuth*, and its present name does not occur until the charter conferred by James I., wherein it is alluded to as "*Eremue alias* Yarmouth." The provisions of this charter were not disturbed by the Municipal Reform Act, and the town still annually elects its mayor and eleven chief burgesses. Up to the great reform of 1832, it was a close borough returning two representatives to parliament, this privilege being virtually vested in the hands of the two principal landowners, who each elected his member.

The town was originally of considerable extent, and the port was much frequented by coasting vessels. King John landed here in April 1206, and again in February 1214. The town was burnt by the French in 1277, and again in 1524, and has never recovered these serious disasters, especially since Cowes has risen into so important a position. After its losses in 1524, Henry VIII. erected at the eastern extremity of the harbour one of his favourite round forts, and called it *Yarmouth Castle.* A little to the west Sir James Worsley raised a fort, and named it *Worsley's Tower;* and a third in the reign of Elizabeth was erected still nearer to Yarmouth, at *Sconce Point*, by Sir George Carey.

When Sir Robert Holmes became governor of the island, he fixed his residence at Yarmouth, and built a large and stately mansion, now the *George Inn*, where, in 1661 and 1675, he splendidly entertained Charles II. He embanked the marshes, which previously the sea had overflowed so as nearly to surround the town (A.D. 1664), and enlarged and improved its fortification. At the eastern entrance the approach was secured by a drawbridge. Near Thorley Wood a redoubt for small arms was thrown up, three pieces of cannon placed on the common facing the sea, long afterwards called the *Bulwarks;* and some guns were also stationed at the landing-place near the castle.

The present defences are the *Castle*, with a platform of four guns, thoroughly repaired and strengthened in 1855; and on the west bank of the river two small forts, the *Victoria* and *Albert*, garrisoned by the Isle of Wight Artillery, consisting of two captains, two lieutenants, two ensigns, one adjutant, one sergeant-major, five sergeants, five corporals, two drummers, and eighty-one privates. The castle has of late years been put in thorough repair, has a small garrison, and mounts eight heavy guns. Between Yarmouth and Alum Bay are two large forts;—the *Albert*, 44 guns; and the *Victoria*, 52 guns. On the opposite coast is *Hurst Castle*, recently strengthened and enlarged, so that the passage of the Needles is now a rather formidable one for a hostile fleet.

The ancient church occupied the site of the castle. It was destroyed by the French in 1524, and it is said that three of its bells were long reserved at Cherbourg, bearing the inscription—EREMUE, I. of W.

Then a church was erected at the eastern extremity of the town, but this was pulled down at the request of the mayor, burgesses, and minister, by a faculty granted by the Bishop of Winchester, January 11, 1635, because it had fallen to decay, and was unfitted for public worship ("ruinosam, nullo que usui divino accommodatam"). The faculty is issued to James Gray, mayor; John Burley, soldier; and Richard Faulkner, vicar. The present building was then erected in the High Street, opposite the Town Hall.

The *Town Hall*, by the way, is the only public building in Yarmouth—a plain, neat brick house, with this inscription over the entrance, " A.D., 1764. In the fourth year of the reign of his present Majesty, King George III., this hall was rebuilt by Thomas, Lord Holmes, governor of the Isle of Wight. Benjamin Lee, Esq., mayor." The *National Schools* occupy an elegant Elizabethan building, erected in 1856.

There has long existed in the town a New Year custom of the children patrolling the streets singing the following carol :—

> " Wassail, wassail to our town !
> The cup is white and the ale is brown;
> The cup is made of the ashen tree,
> And so is the ale of good barley.
> Little maid, little maid, turn the pin,
> Open the door, and let me come in.
> Joy be there and joy be here,
> We wish you all a happy New Year !"

Communication with Lymington is made during the season by steam-boat, and there is now a branch of the London and South-Western connecting Lymington with London. The boatmen of Yarmouth are skilful, and their charges moderate. Lodgings at Yarmouth, if not numerous, are reasonable. The *George Inn* is a commodious building, and at the *Bugle* the accommodation is also excellent. The latter boasts of a good collection of the birds of the island, made by the landlord, Mr. Butler, well known as a skilful taxidermist.

From Yarmouth, the western district of the island may be visited with the greatest facility. The *main routes* are— 1. Through Shalfleet to Calbourne, and thence through Brook to Freshwater Gate; and 2. Through Freshwater village to Alum Bay, the Needles, and the adjacent coast. We proceed to indicate a few of the more attractive *sub-routes*.

SUB-ROUTES.

a. From Yarmouth, eastward, *via* Thorley, 1 mile (notice its curious barn-like church), through Welmingham 1 mile, leaving Afton House to the right, and crossing the Yar at Blackbridge, *via* Easton, to Freshwater Gate, 2 miles (notice arched rock, caves, new fort, and other objects specified hereafter in our " coast route"). Ascend the High Down from the beacon, and examine the Needles' light-house, 3 miles; return and take the footpath, left, to Alum Bay Hotel, and descend by the chine into Alum Bay, 1½ mile (notice the Warren and its population of rabbits. There is a fine view of the Hampshire coast, Yarmouth, and the west of the island, from the topmost ridge of the Warren, near the coastguard station). Back to Yarmouth, about 4½ miles, through Middleton Green (notice *Faringford House*, Tennyson's residence), Freshwater village, keeping the northern road, past Freshwater House to the hamlet of Norton (notice *Norton Lodge*, Admiral Sir Andrew Hamond's seat). Cross the river by the ferry. *b.* Cross the river, and by the banks through to Freshwater, 2½ miles, to Freshwater Gate, one mile. Ascend Afton Down (notice obelisk on the brink of the cliff to the memory of a little girl who fell over and was killed), and keep along the hills—a beautiful route—to Shalcomb and Chessel, 4 miles (notice the numerous *tumuli*, or burrows, on these heights). The road from Chessel passes some small farms to Ningwood, 2 miles, and by road to the right reaches Shalfleet, 1 mile (notice Norman tower of Shalfleet church. Newtown lies to the northeast about 1½ mile). Return by the main road, *via* Ningwood Green, Ningwood Common, and Bouldner, into Yarmouth, 4 miles. *c.* From Yarmouth, *via* Thorley, to Wellow (supposed to be the *Wealtham* mentioned in the Saxon Chronicle as destroyed by the Danes, A.D. 1001), and through Stonewell to Calbourne, 5½ miles (notice church, and Westover, the seat of the Earl of Heytesbury. Then, *via Swainstone*, the seat of Sir John Simeon, Bart., passing the slopes of Apes Down to Park Cross, and *via* Carisbrooke to Newport, 6 miles. Return *via* Parkhurst Forest to Vittle Field, and through Watchingwell into Shalflet, 6 miles; *via* Ningwood and Bouldner to Yarmouth, 4 miles. *d.* To Freshwater, 2½ miles, *via* Freshwater Gate, 1 mile, along the shore to Brook, 3 miles. By the road, and through Brook Green to Mottistone, 1½ mile (notice church and Longstone), and onward

to Brighstone. The tourist may then adopt any suitable Sub-route laid down in District III. From Brighstone he should, however, return across the downs to Afton, regaining Yarmouth *via* Welmingham and Thorley. He will enjoy such bursts of scenery, sublime, picturesque, or simply rural, as cannot fail to arouse his admiration.

ENVIRONS OF YARMOUTH.

I. THORLEY (perhaps *Tor*, the beacon, and *ley*, a pasture) is a village, pleasantly surrounded with trees, about one mile south-east of Yarmouth. There is nothing here to notice but a curious church, without spire or tower, a considerable farm, and a pretty vicarage. The manor is noticeable as having successively passed through the hands of the Montacutes, Edward, Duke of York, and " George of Clarence."

Thorley parish contains 1574 acres, chiefly arable land and pasture. There are but 25 inhabited houses within its limits, and its population in 1861 only numbered 143 (83 males + 60 females), against a population in 1801 of 128, and 1811 of 138. The living is a vicarage, in the gift of C. R. Colvile, Esq., valued at £100 per annum. The parish has Yarmouth on the north, Shalfleet east, the Yar on the west, and Brook to the south.

II. SHALFLEET is about 4 miles east of Yarmouth, and contains the manors of Shalfleet, Ningwood, and Wellow. Chessel, Hulverston, East and West Hampstead, and Watchingwell also lie within its boundaries. *Shalfleet* was probably derived from *shaw*, a woody glen, and *fleet*, a running stream. The village lies in a well-wooded and well-watered hollow. The church is ancient, with traces of early Norman architecture. Tradition ascribes its origin to William Fitz-Osbert. *Watchingwell*, or *Watchingwood*, claims to have possessed the first royal park formed in England. About 60 acres were enclosed by William the Conqueror. It lies close to the manor of Swainstone. Within the manor is a farm, named Warlands, corrupted from Walleran, the name of its original Norman proprietor—Walleran Trenchard. *Ningwood* is a leafy little hamlet, with a good manor-house, the residence of the Vicar of Shalfleet.

The parish of Shalfleet is bounded east by that of Carisbrooke; west by Yarmouth; south by Calbourne; and north by the Solent. Its acreage is 6623, and its population in 1861 numbered 1196 (612 males + 584 females), occupying 250 houses; 14 were uninhabited. The living is a vicarage (Rev. T. Hockley), value £210 per annum, in the patronage of the Lord Chancellor.

III. CALBOURNE was anciently a Hundred in itself, and was sometimes called *Sweyneston*, or *Swainstone*. It was one of the demesnes of the Bishop and Convent of Winchester, and included Brighstone within its limits. "Calbourne" signifies the *cald* or cold *bourne*, or stream; and "Swainstone" has been fancifully derived from *suanes*, or foreigners,—supposing it to be a settlement of the Danes, after destroying Newtown in 1001. It is obviously, however, from *swain*, a shepherd. The manor was surrendered to the Crown by John de Pontissera, Bishop of Winchester, in the 12th of Edward I.; passed through the hands of the Montacutes, Earls of Salisbury, the Earl of Warwick, the Duke of Clarence, the Countess of Salisbury beheaded by Henry VIII., and her grand-daughter, who bestowed it, with her hand, upon Sir Thomas Barrington. It afterwards came by marriage into the Simeon family.

The church is an interesting building, in the early English style of architecture, with a recently-erected porch, and north transept, used as a mausoleum for the Simeon family.

Calbourne parish contains (including the hamlet and chapelry of Newtown) 6897 acres, 145 inhabited houses, and a population of 728 (358 males + 370 females). *Newtown* has 71 inhabited houses, and 340 inhabitants. The living is a rectory (Rev. A. M. Hoare; curate, Rev. G. Hodges), valued at £464 per annum, in the patronage of the Bishop of Winchester.

Newtown (5 miles west of Newport, and 5 miles east of Yarmouth) is a small village,—a score of houses and a tolerable inn,—seated on the bank of a wide estuary, or haven, of depth sufficient to accommodate vessels of 500 tons. This harbour is in fact an inlet of the Solent, swelled by two or three small streams which rise in the Downs of Afton, Shalcombe, and Chessel, and water the intermediate plains. Newtown anciently bore the name of *Francheville* (or the free town), and had a charter granted to it by Aymer, Bishop of Winchester. It was then and afterwards a considerable corporate town,—with its mayor, and burgesses, and common seal,—and consisted of two long streets (High Street and Gold Street) running from east to west, and connected by numerous shorter streets, running from north to south. Until the Reform Bill it returned two representatives to parliament, the most distinguished of whom have been John Churchill, Duke of Marlborough (1678), and George Canning (1793). It held a weekly market, under a charter granted by Edward II., and an annual fair on the feast of St. Mary Magdalene.

It was destroyed, it is supposed, by the Danes in 1001, and by the French in 1377. The name of *Newtown* usurped the place of *Francheville* after the latter event.

The *Town Hall* is still in existence, and stands upon an eminence overlooking the Harbour. It contains some curious Elizabethan chairs. The upper room is now occupied by a day-school.

The *Chapel* has recently been rebuilt from the designs of Mr. Livesay. There are several salterns in its neighbourhood, but they are not very productive.

Near Calbourne are *Swainstone* (Sir J. Simeon), and *Westover* (Earl of Heytesbury) which we shall describe hereafter.

IV. FRESHWATER parish includes the tythings of Easton, Middleton, Norton, and Weston. It is in effect a peninsula, joined to the body of the island by a narrow neck of land at Freshwater Gate, where the Yar rises, and, flowing northward into the Solent, forms throughout its whole course the eastern boundary of the parish. The source of this pleasant stream is "within a few yards of the sea, which in stormy weather has been seen to break over the narrow ridge of separation, and mingle its salt waves with the fresh waters of the river-head." —*Thorne.* The river is tidal as high as Freshwater Mills, 2 miles from its mouth.

Within this narrow compass—5242 acres—is contained a wonderful variety of natural beauties : lofty ramparts of chalk, white, bare, and precipitous; green slopes of undulating downs ; broad meadows, fenced in with hawthorn hedges, and dotted with clumps of venerable elms ; meandering rills, wandering through depths of shadow ; quiet farmsteads, hidden away in the recesses of silent hills ; yawning caverns in the cliffs, where the wild sea ever beats with a restless anger ; garden-bowers, odorous with blossoms ! The river and the ocean fence in this magical land—

> " A narrow compass, and yet there
> Dwells all that's good, and all that's fair ! "
> *Waller.*

The *village* of Freshwater lies about a mile from the southern shore, on the River Yar, where it begins to widen into an ample stream. A few cottages of the better sort, the usual miscellaneous shops, an excellent inn (the *Red Lion*), and some tolerable houses on its outskirts—*voilà tout !* The church is old, and a noticeable pile, with two or three curious monuments. . Near it a bridge crosses the river, and a good-sized mill is worked by the stream.

Freshwater Gate derives its name from its position at the only *gate*, gap, or entrance in the barrier of downs which stretches from Brighstone to the Needles. There are here two good hotels—*Plumbly's* and the *Albion* ; a few small houses; some bathing-machines ; and a royal museum. On the headland to the west has been constructed a formidable battery, —formidable, that is, if it does not, when discharged, shatter the chalky cliffs about the ears of its gallant defenders. It is usually garrisoned by 60 or 70 men, with one commandant and three officers, and mounts 8 guns, all 68-pounders,—six fixed and two mounted upon pivots.

There stood in this neighbourhood, about 60 years ago, the favourite resort of bold smugglers and hardy fishermen, a small inn named *The Cabin*, which, in 1799, was frequented by no less a celebrity than George Morland, the artist. He much enjoyed its rough, rude company, and introduced them into many of his best sketches. His picture of *The Taproom*, is a faithful representation of the interior of this hostelry. From its romantic neighbourhood he derived the subjects of his " View near the Isle of Wight," "View of the Needles," "Fishermen," " The Smugglers," " View over the Common," " The Castle," " Sea-view from the Isle of Wight," " A Storm-piece," and " Freshwater Cave at moonlight, with a group of Smugglers." [On one occasion while sketching at Yarmouth with two friends, they were arrested as spies, and a report of their capture forwarded to General Don, then commandant of the military forces of the island. By his direction they were removed, well-guarded, to Newport, where, after undergoing an examination before the magistrates, they were duly released. —*Hassell's Life ; Collins's Memoirs of a Picture.* Morland often recounted his island adventures with the most boisterous glee.]

The
this lo
We de
our "(
The
are ve
agreeal
Hill, *
ton, B
most in
At
(*The N*
are co
lodging
The
inhabit
buildin
males
rectory
£710 p
St. Jok
At I
philoso
Hooke,
benefic

(*Fr
The
boat an
FRESH'
mence
a suita
1. He
side of
curvatu
a huge
but no
of some
not on
have b
shape
Anoth
water c
Pond
lo
u
r

n no longer ac-
n. In the lower | and the cliff, and another curious mass called *Old Pepper Rock*. These cliffs are

the habitat, during the summer months, of a world of birds. Fire a pistol, or sound a bugle, and they rise suddenly from a thousand ledges and hollows, and make the air dark with wings. "Their eggs and feathers are the plunder of the country people, who resort to a well-known but daring feat of enterprise in order to obtain them. First driving a strong stake, or iron bar, into the top of the cliff near its edge, the adventurer secures one end of a rope to it, and the other to a piece of wood placed cross-wise so as to resemble a rude seat. By means of this simple apparatus he descends the front of the precipice."—*Barber*. The birds found here are—choughs, pullins, willocks, razor-bills, cormorants, gulls, guillemots, daws, and eider-ducks.

5. Rounding *Sun Corner*, the voyager finds himself in *Scratchell's Bay*, a deep hollow curve of extreme magnificence, terminated northward by the high masses of glittering rock so widely celebrated as *The Needles*. "In the face of the cliff, from the destruction of the lower beds of the bent strata, a magnificent arch 300 feet high has been produced, and forms an alcove that overhangs the beach 150 feet."—*Mantell*. If there is not a heavy ground-swell, the tourist should land on the adjacent strip of shingle; if he does, he should go forward to the extremity of the great arch, looking out from which he will be astonished at the sublime aspect of the bay; the surrounding rocks and the vast overhanging arch assume almost a terrible majesty, especially if a stormy sky is gathering its forces over the distant horizon. There is also, near the Needles, the *Needles Cave*, penetrating 300 feet into the cliff.

6. Upon Needles Point, the western-most extremity of the island, at an elevation of 474 feet, stands *The Lighthouse*. Notwithstanding its height, it is said that its windows are sometimes shattered by stones flung up by the sea. It has ten argand lamps, and the same number of plated reflectors; and its light is visible at a distance of eleven leagues. "Seven hundred gallons of oil are yearly consumed; and in dark and stormy nights the lights attract hundreds of little birds, which dash themselves against the glass reflectors and are killed."—*Moody*. In hazy and foggy weather the elevation of this lighthouse renders it of doubtful service. The Trinity House, therefore, in 1858, caused a new one to be erected on the outer part of the westernmost of the Needles, which was previously cut down close to the water's edge. It is about 100 feet high from the base to the top of the ball, and has only one light with three concentrated wicks, but whose brilliancy is so great that it can be seen ten miles at sea. The shades are alternately white and red. A fog bell during unseasonable weather rings by mechanical agency; its sounds may be heard at a distance of five miles. The base of the building is 38 feet in diameter.

7. The *Needle Rocks* (ingeniously derived by one authority from the German *nieder fels*, or *under cliff*) are five in number, but only three are conspicuously visible. Originally, they formed a portion of the western point of the island, and their present isolated condition is owing to the decomposition and wearing away of the rock in the direction of the joints or fissures with which the strata are traversed. "Their angular or wedge-shaped form has resulted from the highly inclined northward dip of the beds of which they are composed." There was formerly another rock—*Lot's Wife*, the sailors called it—which stood out alone, rising from the waves, like a spire, to the height of 120 feet. It is said to have given its name to the group; it fell in 1764.

"Nothing can be more interesting," says a good authority, "particularly to those who take pleasure in aquatic excursions, than to sail between and round the Needles. The wonderfully coloured cliffs of Alum Bay; the lofty and tower-ing chalk precipices of Scratchell's Bay, of the most dazzling whiteness and the most elegant forms; the magnitude and singularity of the spiry, insulated masses which seem at every instant to be shifting their situations, and give a mazy perplexity to the place; the screaming noise of the aquatic birds, the agitation of the sea, and the rapidity of the tide, occasioning not unfrequently a slight degree of danger;—all these circumstances combine to raise in the mind unusual emotions, and to give to the scene a character highly singular, and even romantic."—*Sir H. Englefield.*

The dangers of the Needles' passage have long been felt by mariners; but that it is the grandest and most fitting approach to England foreigners unanimously acknowledge. Mr. Rush, the American ambassador, writes of it enthusiastically:—" In due time we approached the Needles. The spectacle was grand. Our officers gazed in admiration. The very men who swarmed upon the deck made a pause to look upon the giddy height. The most exact steerage seemed necessary to save the ship from the sharp rocks that compress the waters into the narrow straits below. But she passed easily through. There is something imposing in entering England by this access. I afterwards entered at Dover in a packet from Calais, my eye fixed upon the sentinels as they slowly paced the heights. But these cliffs, bold as they are, and immortalized by Shakspeare, did not equal the passage through the Needles."—*Journal of a Residence, &c.*

There is an association connected with Scratchell's Bay which somewhat savours of the ludicrous. One John Baldwin, of Lymington, having heard his wife threaten " to dance over his grave," gave directions in his will that he should be buried out at sea, and accordingly his body was submerged in Scratchell's Bay, *sans cérémonie.*

8. The voyager, having passed the Needles, finds himself suddenly thrown, as it were, into a world of enchantment, especially if the rays of the setting sun are just falling upon his path, and the cliffs are resplendent with their *purpureum lumen.* This is *Alum Bay;* one side of it a wall of glowing chalk, the other a barrier of rainbows! The contrast is very wonderful; the stillness of the chalky cliffs with these masses of many-coloured earth piled up in picturesque confusion. " The scenery of this bay is, indeed, very superior in magnificence to that of any other part of the island. The chalk forms an unbroken face everywhere nearly perpendicular, and in some parts formidably projecting, and the tenderest stains of ochreous yellow and greenish moist vegetation vary without breaking its sublime uniformity. This vast wall extends nearly a quarter of a mile, and is more than 400 feet in height; it terminates by a thin projection of a bold, broken outline, and the wedge-shaped Needle rocks, rising out of the blue waters, continue the cliff in idea beyond its present boundary, and give an awful impression of the stormy ages which have gradually devoured its enormous mass. The pearly hue of the chalk under certain conditions of the atmosphere and light is beyond description by words, and probably out of the power even of the pencil to portray. The magical repose of this side of the bay is wonderfully contrasted by the torn forms and vivid colouring of the clay cliffs on the opposite side. These do not, as at Whitecliff, present rounded headlands clothed with turf and shrubs, but offer a series of points of a scalloped form, and which are often sharp and pinnacled. Deep, rugged chasms divide the strata in many places, and not a trace of vegetation appears in any part. All is wild ruin! The tints of the cliffs are so bright and so varied, that they have not the aspect of anything natural. Deep purplish red, dusky blue, bright ochreous yellow, grey nearly approaching to white, and absolute

black, succeed each other as sharply defined as the stripes in silk ; and after rains, the sun, which, from about noon till his setting, in summer illuminates them more and more, gives a brilliancy to some of these nearly as resplendent as the bright lights on real silk. Small vessels often lie in this bay for the purpose of loading chalk and sand ;* and they serve admirably to show the majestic size of the cliffs under whose shade they lie diminished almost to nothing." —*Sir H. Englefield.*

9. The northern extremity of the bay is *Headon Hill*, 400 feet in height. The geologist will observe that its geological character is precisely similar to that of Whitecliff Bay, at the eastern end of the island. The chalk joins the London clay and freshwater deposits at both places, though the dislocated strata of Headon Hill give the landscape so different an aspect. At both places the lacustrine and fluviatile deposits are the uppermost series ; the London clay, occupying a vertical position, forms the middle ; and is followed by the Bognor strata, and the mottled clays ; and these abut against a bed of sandy loam, with pebbles and slightly rolled flints, that is in immediate contact with the chalk. The thickness of the eocene strata, from the chalk to the uppermost bed in Headon Hill, is stated by Mr. Prestwick to be 1660 feet, which is 300 feet less than the series at Whitecliff.

"The variegated and deeply tinted sands, marls, and clays, which impart so remarkable and brilliant an aspect to the cliff, are the next in order, and form a total thickness of between 700 and 800 feet. The alternations and variety of the vertical seams or layers are almost innumerable." These strata belong to the London clay series, and are followed by a layer of pure white sand, which is exported for the glass manufactories of London and Bristol, at the rate of 3000 tons yearly.

From the summit of Headon Hill a fine view may be obtained of the various windings of this wonderful coast, of the inland island scenery, of the green trees and misty hills of Hampshire. Yarmouth and the groves of Freshwater lie beneath, and the chalk downs rise up against the distant horizon.

10. The tourist now reaches *Totland*, or *Tollard's Bay*, where the cliffs entirely change their character, and exhibit alternations of marine and freshwater strata. They gradually decrease in height as the boat passes *Colwell Bay*, where, in *Bramble Chine*, "a thick bed of oyster shells is exposed, apparently in its original state, the valves being in contact with each other as when living." Many beautiful fossil shells may be collected in this locality.

11. The extremity of Colwell Bay is called *Cliff End*, where the *Victoria Fort* has recently been erected. This is the nearest point of contact with the mainland—the passage to Hurst Point not exceeding three quarters of a mile. Next comes *Sconce Point*, crowned by the heavy mass of the *Albert Fort*, and then the voyager finds himself abreast of Yarmouth. Viewed from the sea, the island here assumes a very interesting appearance. The gradual rise of the northern side above the sea, the coloured strata of Alum Bay, those singular masses of rock—the Needles, with the majestic chalk cliffs behind them of the most dazzling whiteness, and the precipitous face of the southern side of the downs above Freshwater, compose altogether a picture of the most romantic character.

SEATS OF THE GENTRY.

Swainstone, about 1½ mile east from Calbourne, is the seat of the Simeon

---

* Mr. Wedgwood tried to use the fine white sand in his porcelain manufacture, but the experiment was unsuccessful. Glasses, bottles, paper-weights, &c., filled with these sands in various designs, are sold all over the island.

family. It is a large and handsome mansion of stone, in the Italian style, occupying the site of an ancient palace of the Bishops of Winchester—once visited by Edward II.—of the chapel of which some Early Decorated remains are still extant. The grounds are very beautiful—agreeably alternated with hill and dale, and rejoicing in the most luxuriant foliage. The views, in every direction, are full of interest. Sir John Simeon, M.P., is the eldest son of the late Sir R. Godin Simeon, by the eldest daughter and heiress of the late Sir Fitzwilliam Barrington, who brought the Calbourne estate into the Simeon family. Sir John was born at St. John's, near Ryde, in 1815; educated at Christchurch, Oxon, and graduated M.A. in 1840; married, in the same year, the only daughter of Sir F. F. Baker, of Loventer, in Devonshire; represented the island in parliament from 1847 to 1851 in the Liberal interest, resigning on becoming a convert to the Roman Catholic religion; and succeeded to the baronetcy (created in 1815), on the death of Sir Richard, in 1854.

Westover lies south of Calbourne, in an agreeable situation. The house is commodious, though not of spacious dimensions; its south front ornamented with a Doric colonnade in the centre, verandahs above, and upon each side of it. To the east and north well-sheltered by thick masses of ancient trees. The manor, formerly a possession of the Dillingtons, was sold by one of the Urry family to Lord Holmes, and so descended to Sir Leonard Worsley Holmes, whose daughter and heiress married, in 1833, the Hon. William Ashe A'Court, eldest son of the Earl of Heytesbury, and the present proprietor of Westover. This gentleman thereupon assumed the name and arms of Holmes. He was born in London in 1809; educated at St. John's College, Cambridge, where he graduated as M.A. in 1831; married in 1833; represented the Isle of Wight from 1837 to 1847 on Conservative principles; and succeeded to the Earldom of Heytesbury on his father's death, 1859.

Afton Manor, the seat of B. Cotton, Esq., is a large mansion in a noble and well-wooded park, on the east bank of the Yar, about 2 miles from Yarmouth. Mr. Cotton was for some years the master of the Isle of Wight hounds.

Norton Lodge (the seat of Adm. Sir A. S. Hamond), on the northern shore of the island, and the extreme western bank of the Yar, is a picturesque villa in very pleasant and agreeably diversified grounds. It commands a fine view of Yarmouth and the course of the river,—of the Hampshire coast, and the singular promontory terminated by Hurst Castle. The late Admiral Sir Graham Hamond, Bart., G.C.B., was born in 1779; served as midshipman on board the *Queen Charlotte* in Lord Howe's action—"the glorious First of June;" distinguished himself at the blockade of Malta, and siege of Valetta; in the sanguinary action off Copenhagen, 1801; and at Flushing, in 1809. Promoted to Admiral of the White, 1849. Admiral Sir Andrew Snape Hamond succeeded to the estate and baronetcy on his father's death.

Faringford, 1 mile west of Freshwater Gate, a fine villa almost hidden amidst leafy trees, is the residence of Alfred Tennyson, Esq. In his " Maud, and other Poems," the poet-laureate pleasantly alludes to his island home when addressing his friend, the Rev. F. D. Maurice:—

" Where, far from smoke and noise of town,
I watch the twilight falling brown
    All round a careless ordered garden,
Close to the ridge of a noble down.

You'll have no scandal while you dine,
But honest talk and wholesome wine,
    And only hear the magpie gossip
Garrulous under a roof of pine.

For groves of pine on either hand,
To break the blast of winter, stand;
    And further on, the hoary Channel
Tumbles a breaker on chalk and sand."

It is to be regretted that the intrusive curiosity of ill-bred visitors will probably drive the poet from his island retreat.

PLACES TO BE VISITED BY THE
PEDESTRIAN.

Easton, 1 mile south of Freshwater;
Compton, nestling in a hollow of the
downs, near Brook, and 3 miles south-
east from Freshwater; the Needles Lighthouse, and examine Alum Bay, De Warren, Colwell Bay, and other places by a
route along the cliff; Middleton, a small
hamlet, near Freshwater; Cliff End, and
Sconce Point; Hempstead, and its farm-
house, designed by Nash the architect,
2 miles north-west of Shalfleet, and 3½
west of Yarmouth; Elmsworth, and its
salterns, half a mile north of Newtown.

[Here we complete our *Description of
the Island*, believing that we have not
omitted, in our cursory sketches, any
place of interest to the tourist, either
from its historical associations, or its
attractiveness of scenery; and trusting
that our pictures, however wanting in
art, may, at least, deserve a word of commendation for their accuracy of detail].

PART III.

THE CHURCHES OF THE ISLAND,

WITH

BIOGRAPHICAL NOTICES OF ITS WORTHIES.

ARRETON,—one of the churches given by William Fitz-Osbert to his Abbey of Lire; valued in Cardinal Beaufort's roll at 50 marks, and the tithes of the vicarage at 8; value of superfluous plate and fittings sold by Edward VI.'s Commissioners, £34, 3s. 4d.; consists of an early English double-gabled chancel, with south aisle, and dwarfed Perpendicular tower. The oak ceiling in the chancel, and the stone pulpit, are recent additions.

Brasses.—In the south aisle there is a *brass*, date 1430, with the effigy of a man in plate-armour, his feet upon a lion. Inscription,—

" Here is y . buried under this grave
Harry Hawles . his soule God save.
Long tyme steward . of the Yle of Wyght,
Have m'cy on hym . God ful of myght."

On a brass plate on one of the pillars are graven the following quaintest of quaint rhymes :—

" Loe here under this tomb incoutcht
Is William Serle by name,
Who, for his deed·s of charetie
Deserveth worthy fame.

A man within this Parish borne,
And in the house called Stone,
A glass for to behold a work
Hath left to every one.

For that unto the people poor
Of Arreton, he gave
An hundred pownds in redie coyne,
He will'd that they should have.

To be ymployed in fittest sorte,
As man coulde best invent,
For yearely relief to the Poore,
That was his good intent.

Thus did this man, a Batcheler
Of years full fifty nyne;
And doeing good to many a one,
Soe did he spend his tyme.

Untill the day he did decease,
The first of Februarey,
And in the year of One Thousand
Five hundred neyatie five."

The bequest here described " was laid out in the purchase of a farm called *Garots*, on St. George's Down, from the profits of which a supply of bread is given to the poor of the parish in the winter season."—*Walks round Ryde.*

On the exterior wall is another brass :—

" THE REWARDE OF SINNE IS DEATH. EVERLAS
TINGE LIFE IS THE GIFTE OF GOD THROUGH OUR
LORD AND SAVIOUR JESUS CHRISTE. WHEREFOR
ALL YE THAT LOVE THE LORD DOE THIS· HATE
ALL THINGS THAT ARE EVELL FOR HE DOTHE
KEPE THE SOVLES OF HIS FROM SUCH AS
WOVLD THEM SPILL." *George Serle.*

Another metal plate records the death of *William Colnett*, 1594; and a *brass* in north aisle, *David Wavil*, 1629.

Monuments. — To *Richard Fleming Worsley*, drowned in the river Hamble, (ætat 22), sculptured by Westmacott. To *Sir Leonard Worsley Holmes, Bart.* (ætat 38, in 1825), executed by a native artist, named Haskoll.

The Bells.—There are five bells, but only four can be used. On one, in raised letters, is graven—" WILLIAM . GRIF . FIN . VICOR . GEO . OGLANDER . HENRY

BVLL . CHVRCHWARDENS . CLEMANT . TOSIEAR CAST . MEE . IN . THE . YEAR . OF . 1699." On another, "GOD IS MY HOPE . 1691." On the smallest,— ℑꜧus : nickolaus : seerle : t : alitia : urr : ejus : bebit : me. *Jesus! Nicholas Serle and his wife Alicia gave me.*

Epitaphs.—In the church-yard are numerous singular epitaphs.

On *James Urry of Combley*, ætat. 33, 1815:—

" Death is most certain you may see
For suddenly it came to me,
In perfect Health to me 'twas sent,
By Accident most violent."

On *James Barton*, ætat. 66, 1768:—

" My Sickness was Great I under Went
God gave me Time for to Repent;
My Change I Hope is for the best,
To dwell with Christ and be at rest."

On *Daniel Barton*, ætat. 32, 1778:—

" My parents Dear Grieve not for Me,
I hope in heaven you Both to See;
It was God's will he thought it best,
To take me to A place of rest.".

On *John Barton*, ætat. 40, 1781:—

" In love I lived, in peace I died,
My Life Desir'd but God deny'd;
Now on my Children pity take,
And love them for there fathers Sake."

On *Elizabeth*, wife of the above, ætat. 64, 1804:—

" Calm was her Death, pious was her life,
A careful mother, and a virtuous wife:
Dutiful to her Children and a friend,
Possessing those bright duties to her End."

On *Hannah* and *William Rayner*:—

" Skill'd in the mystery of the pleasing Peal,
Which few can know, and fewer still reveal;
Whether with little Bell- or Bell sublime,
To split a Moment to the truth of Time;
Time so oft truly beat, at length o'ercame,
Yet shall this Tribute long preserve his Name."

On *Elizabeth Wallbridge*, the heroine of Legh Richmond's popular narrative, " The Dairyman's Daughter:"—

Stranger! if e'er by chance or feeling led,
Upon this hallow'd turf thy footsteps tread,
Turn from the contemplation of the sod,
And think on her whose spirit rests with God.
Lowly her lot on earth,—but He who bore
Tidings of grace and blessing to the poor,
Gave her his truth and faithfulness to prove,
The choicest treasures of his boundless love,—
(Faith, that dispell'd Affliction's darkest gloom;
Hope, that could cheer the passage to the tomb;
Peace, that not hell's dark legions could destroy;
And Love that fill'd the soul with heavenly joy).
Death of its sting disarm'd, she knew no fear,
But tasted heaven e'en while she linger'd here.
Oh, happy Saint! may we like thee be blest;
In life be faithful, and in death find rest!"

Arreton is a vicarage in the patronage of J. Fleming, Esq.; valued at £220 *per annum.*

BEMBRIDGE, first erected in 1826, at a cost of £1300, and endowed with £5 annually by the late Edward Wise, Esq. Consecrated in 1827. The foundations proving unsafe, it became necessary in 1845 to erect a new edifice, which is small, but commodious, and Early English in character. Was formerly dependent on the parish of Brading, but is now a perpetual curacy (Rev. J. Le Mesurier), valued at £100 *per annum.*

BINSTEAD, an elegant reproduction (architect, T. Hellyer, Esq., of Ryde) of the ancient early English edifice, which was probably erected and supplied by the monks of Quarr, and on account of its poverty was not included in Cardinal Beaufort's roll, 1404. Over the outer gate notice a curious ancient key-stone, or corbel, representing a human semifigure which terminates in a ram's head. This is popularly called *the Idol.* Some singular emblems in stone of Eternity, Sin, the Holy Dove, &c., from the old church, are preserved in the walls of the new. The church consists of a nave and chancel, divided by early English arch. The octagonal font is noticeable for its workmanship, representing Eve's Temptation, the Expulsion from Eden, the Doom of Labour, Death, Christ's Baptism, Crucifixion, Ascension, and the Last Judgment. The reading desk is supported by a figure of Moses, with arms upheld by Aaron and Hur (Exod. xvii. 8–13).

Epitaphs.—In the grave-yard are some | of which he was elected fellow and tutor.

old
ing.
Goo
and
and
shot
cers
mou
year

B
chur
Old
bish
Cen
chur
tect
with
and
circu
body
prob
site,
N
mur
Jud
Ven
on t
Nor
T
surr
ing
the t
ston
plac
a co
book
Insc

𝔅
of S
of 𝔣
𝔍an
ent
in p

Epitaph.—In the grave-yard are some | of which he was elected fellow and tutor.

old t
ing.
Good
and
and
shot
cers
mout
years

Bo
churc
Old v
bisho
Cent
chur
tectu
with
and
circu
body
prob:
site,
N
mur
Judg
Vent
on th
Nor

To
surr
ing
the t
ston
place
a co
book
Insc

of S

OLD CHURCH—BONCHURCH.

Brading.—A spacious, ancient structure chiefly Trans. Norman in style; consists of a body and chancel, separated by Norman arch; tower; north and south aisles separated from the body by early English arches, and each with a small chapel at the end. The picturesque interior, recently restored with great care, and the Oglander chapel, claim the visitor's admiration. The advowson was bestowed by Charles I. on Trinity College, Cambridge.

Brasses, &c.—Within the altar-rails (notice altar-table of the date of Queen Elizabeth) is a curious and elaborately engraved slab, with effigy of knight in armour, his feet supported by two dogs, and delicate ornamental work, representing a recess, and, apparently, the twelve apostles in side-niches—a very fine specimen, originally inlaid with silver. Inscribed—

Hic jacet nobilis vir Johannes Cherowin armiger, dum vivebat, Connestabularius Castri de Porrestre, qui obiit . anno domini millesimo quadringes^mo^ quadrag^o^ . primo die ultima mense Octobris . anima ejus requiescat in pace. Amen.

(Here lies the renowned John Cherowin, knight, while he lived Constable of the Castle of Porchester, who died A.D. 1441, on the last day of the month of October. May his soul rest in peace! Amen.)

At extreme end of north aisle are two altar-tombs, decorated with a rose *gules*. On one—**Jhu habe mercie on Wylyam Howlys sowl. Amen. mcccccxx.** And on the other—**Helizabeth hys wyf.**

In the beautiful Oglander chapel, south aisle, are the altar-tombs of *Sir William Oglander*, and his son, *Sir John Oglander*, lieutenant of the Wight and lieutenant-governor of Portsmouth, died, ætat 70, in 1655. The effigies are of wood, and represent the knights in complete armour, extended at full length. Also a memorial of *George Oglander, Esq.*, eldest son of Sir John, a loyal cavalier, who died "at Cawne (Caen) in Normandy, July 11th 1652; of his adge 23d." On a monument near the altar—**Master Olyver . Oglawnder —here ye 30th daye of December . ye yer of our lord God m^o^ccccxxx . and for ye wyf of . . . Sir . . . Oglawnder.**

Epitaphs.—The church-yard is peculiarly rich in noticeable inscriptions, some of them of more than average excellence.

On Mrs. Anne Berry (adapted with a very slight alteration from Mrs. Steele's "Lines on the death of the Rev. James Harvey—see her "Poems by Eudoxia," 1760, vol. ii., p. 50—though generally ascribed to the Rev. W. Gill, a former curate of Newchurch. These verses were arranged by Dr. Calcott to a beautiful and well-known glee, composed by him "at St. John's, near Ryde, in the Isle of Wight, Thursday, September 24th, 1794")—

"Forgive, blest shade, the tributary tear
 That mourns thy exit from a world like this;
Forgive the wish that would have kept thee here,
 And stayed thy progress to the seats of bliss.
No more confined to grov'ling scenes of night,
 No more a tenant pent in mortal clay,—
We rather now should hail thy glorious flight,
 And trace thy journey to the realms of day."

On an adjoining stone is this inscription—

"It must be so—our father Adam's fall
 And disobedience brought this lot on all.
All die in him; but hopeless should we be,
 Blest revelation! were it not for thee.

Hail, glorious gospel, heavenly light! whereby
 We live with comfort, and with comfort die;
And view beyond this gloomy scene, the tomb,
 A life of endless happiness to come."

On Jane, the subject of Legh Richmond's tract, "Little Cottager"—

"Ye who the power of God delight to trace,
 And mark with joy each monument of grace
Tread lightly o'er this grave as ye explore,
 The short and simple annals of the poor.

A child reposes underneath this sod,
 A child to memory dear, and dear to God;
Rejoice, but shed the sympathetic tear—
 Jane, the Young Cottager, lies buried here."

Here is an absurd, and, therefore, inappropriate, verse on a person whose name it is not necessary to record :—

> " When she afflicted was full sore,
> Still with pattence it she bore,
> And oft to the Lord did say,
> The Lord have mercy on me, I pray ;
> And when her glass was fully run,
> She closed her eyes without a groan."

There is an inscription near the entrance porch to one *Robert Stacie*, 20th September 1649 ; and another near the chancel wall to *Peter Bryers*, butler, and *Mr. Tobye Kemp*, clerk, to Sir John Oglander of Nunwell, knight, 1637.

Bells.—There are four bells of excellent tone, with inscriptions resembling those of Arreton. On one—" †† BENJAMIN SALTER †RICHARD DAW † CHVRCHWARDENS †† CLEMENT † TOSIEAR † CAST †† MEE IN THE YEAR † 1709†" And on the second—" GOD BE OVR GVYD. 1694."

The *parish registers* date from the year 1547. Here is a curious entry :— "*Burials*, Novemb. yᵉ 20th, 1677. Jowler (alias) John Knight, of Merton, whoe, rather than he would be charitable to himselfe (when he was capacitated), liv'd like a miserable wretch on yᵉ publick charity. He liv'd in a p'petuall slavery through feare and suspicion, and punish'd both his back and belly to fill yᵉ purse. He soe excessively idolized his poore heap of dung yᵗ it was death to him to think of p'ting. He was allwaies soe afraid of want, or yᵗ he should dy as he had allwaies liv'd, a beggar, yᵗ he dar'd not use wh't he had for his oune wellbeing, but liv'd and died with his beloved bagg in his nearest embraces ; and at length, yᵗ he might pay his utmost homage both by life and death to his greate god Mammon, he voluntarily sacrificed himself, and even dyed to save charges. *Left (which was found)* £06, 17s."

The living is a vicarage (Rev. J. Glover, M.A. ; curate, Rev H. P. Marriott), valued at £250, in the gift of Trinity College, Cambridge.

BRIGHSTONE (or *Brixton*) was anciently included in the parish of Calbourne, but was separated *ante* 1305. The church may have been built by one of the bishops of Winchester, to whose see it has always belonged. Value of plate sold by Edward IV.'s commissioners, £5, 9s. 6d.

The church was carefully restored in 1852 by the late rector, and is now a fine specimen of the old village church. It consists of an Early English chancel, Norman north aisle, Perp. side chapel, and low tower. Notice the Dec. arches which separate the south aisle. "Against the westward pier is a shelf for a book, surmounted by a small canopy ; this marks out the original position of the font." The tower is low, with a square turret, terminating in a rather singular conical roof, which may at one time have been surmounted by a stone cross. In the progress of the restorations the arcade of Norman columns and arches on the left was found immured in the wall, showing that there had formerly existed a north aisle, now therefore rebuilt. It was also discovered that the floor line of the church had been raised about 2 feet above its original level. "The chancel floor is laid out in panels formed by the ancient tombstones and encaustic tiles. The tiles within the rails are the gift of Winchester College, in commemoration of Bishop Kew having formerly been rector of this place. The windows are all restored, and filled with stained glass. That in the tower is the gift of the present Bishop of Oxford, in remembrance of his ten years' connection with the parish as its rector."—*Rev. E. M'All*.

The church is dedicated to St. Mary. The registers date from 1566. In 1568 occurs a notice of a *Sance Bell*, or Saint's

Bell, rung in the belfry when the priest intoned the Sanctus. In 1570 there is an entry for "The Paraphrase of Erasmus upon the whole New Testament, divided into two volumes." In October 1692, three shillings are paid to the ringers for ringing on "the Thanksgiving Day for the reducing of Ireland."

Incumbents.—Among those who have held this pleasant cure have been Hopton Sydenham, D.D., ejected for his lack of puritanical principles in 1653; Robert Dingley, who died just before the Restoration, 1659; Thomas Ken, afterwards Bishop of Bath and Wells, well known as a devotional poet, 1667–69; Noel Digby, who was rector for fifty years, 1780–1830; and Samuel Wilberforce, now Bishop of Oxford, 1830–40.

Tombs, &c.—Neither in the churchyard, nor in the church itself, is there any memorial of interest, except a grave-slab, set into the pavement in front of the altar,—" Here lyeth yᵉ body of Mr. Robert Dingley, Minister of this place, 2nd son of Sir John Dingley, Kt., who dyed in yᵉ 40th year of his age, on yᵉ 12th of January 1659."

The living is a rectory (Rev. J. Moberly, D.D., for many years head-master of Winchester College), valued at £505.

BROOK, on rising ground near the shore, is dedicated to St. Mary. The old church was destroyed by fire in 1863, and the present one erected in 1864. It retains the ancient tower; consists of nave and chancel; and has stained glass windows, and fine marble pulpit. One of the Bowermans probably founded the old church, *ante* 1305, when it is named by the Dean of the Island "a chapel." "When it obtained parochial privileges is uncertain; but within the last hundred years the patronage was claimed by St. John's College, Cambridge, on the ground that it was a chapelry belonging to Freshwater. The dispute, however, termi-

nated in favour of the lord of the manor." There was nothing of interest in the interior of the ancient building. A plain marble tablet recorded the deaths of the *Rev. T. Bowerman*, his *wife*, and *daughter;* and a handsome tablet, with scutcheon, &c., those of *W. Bowerman*, 1745; his *wife*, 1749; and *daughter Margaret*, 1734.

The living is a rectory (Rev. J. Pellew Gaze), valued at £250, and, according to the *Clergy List*, in the patronage of the Miss Bowermans.

CALBOURNE, dedicated to All Saints. There was a church here at the time of the Domesday survey, for it is spoken of as "held by Malger," a Saxon, of the Bishop and Convent of Winchester; but the present building does not date further than the middle of the 13th century. In style it is chiefly early English, but much modernised in many parts. The transept and porch were erected, and the arrangement of the arches of the nave altered, by Sir R. Simeon, in 1836. The lancet windows of the chancel are good, and copied from the east window in the south aisle. The tower is low (built about 1752), with a wooden spire.

The north transept, rebuilt by Sir R. Simeon, is used as the mortuary chapel of the Simeon family. Architect, Mr. A. F. Livesay.

Tombs, &c.—A *brass* of a knight in armour, with folded hands, and feet resting on a dog, lies in the floor of the south aisle. It was once inlaid in a slab of marble, and formed part of a stately tomb, with columns of Purbeck marble, which ornamented the north aisle. The columns are now inserted in the windows of the Simeon chapel. The effigy is supposed to be that of one of the Montacutes, Earls of Salisbury, to whom the manor belonged, and the date to be about 1360–80.

On a brass plate, set in the wall of the chancel north, is the following inscription:—

" Blest is the just man's memory
Both here and to eternity.
Being dead he yet speaketh."—Heb. xxii. 2.

IN MEMORY
OF THE
REVERED, RELIGIOUS, AND LEARNED
PREACHER, DANIEL EVANCE,
Who was born at London, March 2, 1613,
And died at Calbourne, December 27, 1652.
This monument was erected by Hannah his
mournful relict.

Who is sufficient for this things,
Wisely to harpe on every stringe,
Rightly divide the word of truth
To babes and men, to age and youth.
One of a thousand where he's found
So learned, pious, and profound—
Earth has but few—there is in heaven
One who answers, ' I can deal even.'

Daniel Evance. (Anagram), *I can deal even.*

Incumbents, &c.—The parish registers
date from 1599, and open with a memo-
randum by " Christopher Hamton, Doctor of Divinitie." Since 1616, the date
of his decease, there have been 16 rectors
of Calbourne. The living (Rev. Arthur
M. Hoare, M.A.; curate, Rev. G. Hodges)
is valued at £464, and is in the gift of
the Bishop of Winchester.

CARISBROOKE, dedicated to St. Mary,
one of the oldest, and certainly the handsomest, of the island churches, consists
of a nave, south aisle, porch, and western tower. The Norman chapel and
transept, "both in a state of decay,"
were pulled down by Sir Francis Walsingham, when lord of the manor, *temp.*
Elizabeth, and 100 marks were given
to the inhabitants by way of compensation. "The tower, of very bold and
good Perpendicular, is built in stages,
embattled with an octagonal turret." A
doorway, early English, is plainly discernible in the north wall. The east
windows of the church were inserted
during the last century.

" The church of the manor" (then
called Beaucombe, or Bowcombe) is mentioned in Domesday Book, and the present structure *may* have been commenced
by William Fitz-Osbert. It formerly
belonged to the Cistercian priory which
he founded in its immediate neighbourhood, and underwent the same mutations
of propietorship. Its plate was returned
by Edward VI.'s commissioners as worth
£55, nearly £600 according to the present
value of money. Its "two bells" are
mentioned as weighing xvi. cwt. By
Charles I. Carisbrooke was granted to
Queen's College, Oxon.

Northwood, Kingston, Newport, and
Chale, were formerly included in its
parochial jurisdiction. Northwood rectory is still presented to by the vicar of
Carisbrooke, and Newport has only just
attained independence. Kingston and
Chale were long ago severed from it.

Monuments and Epitaphs.—Most of
the noticeable tombs and inscriptions in
Carisbrooke Church are recorded in a
MS. in the British Museum, written in
1719 by one William Pavey, and entitled "Church Notes in Hampshire and
the Isle of Wight" (Addit. MSS., 1410).
The portion relating to Carisbrooke runs
as follows:—

"It has a fine old steeple, octagonal
and embattled, with two round turrets
on the front. The body of the church is
divided like two ridged houses closed—
a cross on the west end. Nothing more
remarkable on the outside, but, on a
buttress at the west end, this date (A.D.
1710). On the steeple, cast on the old lead,
this date—1064. The sacristan told me
there had been an old bell in the steeple,
with a Saxon inscription, and every letter crowned.

" What is remarkable in the church
is as follows:—

" Against the pillar in the middle
aisle is a board, on the top of which is
painted a ship, with this inscription—
on the anchor *Spes* (Hope); the card
was a book open with this inscription—
Verbum Dei (God's word); death sitting
on the bowsprit blowing a trumpet,
and behind him a banner flying, with
post mortem (after death); in the main-
top, χ. P. S.; on the foremast, *Fides*
(Faith); on the mizenmast, *Fama loqua-*

tur (Fame speaks). This is the epitaph:—

"'Here lyeth the body of the right worthy William Keeling, Esq., groom of the chamber to our Sovereign Lord King James, General for the Hon. East India Adventurers, where he was thrice by them employed; and dying in this Isle, at the age of 42, Anno 1619, Sept. 12, hath this remembrance here fixed by his loving and sorrowful wife, Ann Keeling.

"' Fortie and two years in this vessel frail,
    On the rough seas of life did Keeling saile ;
    A merchant fortunate, a captaine bould,
    A courtier gracious, yet alas ! not old.
    Such wealth, experience, honour, and high praise,
    Few winne in twice so many yeares or daies.
    But what the world admired, he deemed but dross,
    For Christ : without Christ, all his gains but losse ;
    For him, and his dear love, with verrie cheere,
    To the holy land his last course he did steere :
    Faith served for sails, the sacred word for card,
    Hope was his anchor, glorie his reward ;
    And thus with gales of grace, by happy venter,
    Through straits of death, heaven's harbour he did
        enter.'

"Under the door that goes to the communion table lies the one half of the effigies down to the waist of a monk or prior of the Convent of Black Monks, called St. Mary of Carisbrooke (made a cell first to Lyra in Normandy, and afterwards to the abbey of Montgrace in Yorkshire, and last of all to the Cistercians of Sheen), in his habit, and with a pastoral staff in his hand. By the largeness of the stroke on the stone, I guess it had been inlaid with brass. The lower half lies before the priory door, which is now a farm house on the north side of the church. It had about six windows in front, low, and a large porch. Near at hand were their barns and brewhouse. [The two portions have recently been joined.]

"Within a niche in the north wall kneels (as the sacristan told me) the Lady Wadham, a small figure,—whether very beautifully cut cannot be discovered, for it is white-washed over ; and on each side of her three poor cripples, as a remembrancer of her—she having founded an hospital for poor old impotent people.

[She was the wife of Sir Nicholas Wadham, governor of the island, *temp.* Henry VIII.]

"Over the niche is a cherub holding a book open, with these letters raised—*far.*

"On the south side of the church is a handsome mural monument, the chief part whereof is grey, but where the inscription is it is black marble, on which is engraven this epitaph:"—[To the memory of Sir W. Stephens, Kt., some years Lieut.-Gov. of the Island, d. Oct. 26, 1697—also his wife, his brother Henry, and four children.]

In addition to "the remarkable things" recorded by Mr. Pavey, the traveller will notice tablets to the memory of *Mary*, daughter of *Sir Richard Newdegate;* to *Caroline Kilderbee*, a descendant of Sir William de Horsey, warden of the island, *temp.* Henry II. (a lapidary's fiction?); and *Lieutenant-Colonel W. H. Dennie, C.B.*, who served at Ghuznee and Bamecan, and fell at Jellalabad.

In the church-yard notice the punning epitaph on *Charles Dixon*, a farrier and blacksmith. (It also occurs in Felpham Church, Sussex ; at Bothwell, in Lanarkshire ; and is said to be the composition of the poet Hayley):—

"My sledge and hammer lie reclined,
    My bellows too have lost their wind.
    My fire's extinct, my forge decayed,
    My vice all in the dust is laid ;
    My coal is spent, my iron gone,
    My last nail's driven, my work is done."

Incumbents, Registers, &c.—The parish registers date from 1578. Some of the entries are curious. We quote three: "King James landed at y⁰ Cows, and saw a muster at Hony Hill, and dined at the Castle, and saw in the afternoon most of the Iland, with prince Charles his sonne, and the West Medeane, and hunted in the park, killed a bocke, and so departed again to Bowly [Beaulieu], the 2 of August, Ann. Dom. 1609, being Wednesday."—"Prince Charles landed at the Cows, and came into the forest, and saw a skirmish there, and went from thence to Alvington Down, and looked over the Iland, and came to the castle, and so thence to Newport, where he dined at Mr. James' house, and so his grace departed to Cows, and tooke ship, and went to Portsmouth, in the year 1618, the 27th of August, being Thursday."—" The 6 day of September, King Charles went from the Castell to treat, and the least day of November he went from Newport to Hurste Castell to prison, carried away by to [two] troopes of horse."

Alexander Ross was vicar of Carisbrooke from 1634 to 1650. He was a native of Aberdeen, a doctor of divinity, chaplain in ordinary to Charles I. prior to the commencement of the civil war, and afterwards master of the Free School at Southampton.—*Wood, Athenæ. Oxon.* He wrote *Pansebeia*, a continuation of Sir Walter Raleigh's " History of the World ;" *Virgilius Evangelizans ;* and other devotional works. Butler, in his *Hudibras*, alludes to him sarcastically—

" There was an ancient sage philosopher
Who had read Alexander Ross over."

He died ætat 64, in 1654.

The living is a vicarage (Rev. Edward James, M.A.), valued at £1123.

CHALE, dedicated to St. Andrew, was built by Hugh de Vernun, in the reign of Henry I. It consists of a body, chancel, and south aisle, divided by four Trans. Norman arches, with a chapel at the east end. The tower is a good specimen of Perpendicular, resembling in many respects that of Carisbrooke, and apparently designed by the same builder.

Monuments, Epitaphs, &c.—In the west wall of the chancel is a tablet with the following inscription:—" Patri suo charissimo et matri dilectissimæ *Gulielmo et Annæ Legg* de Atherfield in hac insula parentibus optimis possimis meritissimis qui obdormiverunt in Domino : ille Anno Dom. 1688, illa Anno Dom. 1681. Guli-

elmus Legg filius natu maximus rector de Gretham propè Petersfield in comitatu Southton mærens posuit : Anno Dom. 1704.

" Pro magnis meritis, et dulci munere vitæ:
Vobis cum lacrymis sola sepulcra loco."

(To his very dear father and beloved mother, William and Anne Legg, of Atherfield, in this island, his most excellent parents, who have long slept in the Lord ; he in 1688; she in 1681. William Legg, their eldest son, rector of Gretham, near Petersfield, in the county of Southampton, lamenting, placed this stone, A.D. 1704. For your great deserts and sweet gift of life, to ye with tears I place these solitary tombs.)

There is also a memorial to *Richard Burleigh*, rector of Chale, 1734, and his wife Lydia, 1717 ; another, a handsome and massive monument in marble, surmounted with an escutcheon supported by two soldiers, to *Major-General Sir Henry Worsley, G.C.B.*, of the Bengal army, ætat 73, 17th January 1841.

The church-yard is bare, bleak, and melancholy, with many sad witnesses to the fatal power of the sea which it lies so near. The unfortunate men, women, and children, who perished in the wreck of the *Clarendon*, in the neighbouring bay, are, most of them, here interred. One tomb-stone preserves the names of *Walter Maynard Pemberton*, ætat 48, and his daughter Anne, ætat 11, " who perished together in the wreck of the ship *Clarendon*, in Chale Bay, on 11th October 1836." Another is sacred to the memory of *Captain Samuel Walker*, ætat 34, wrecked on the same occasion, " with twelve of the crew, and all the passengers, eleven in number ;" and a third, *Edmund Cosens*, ætat 17. There are other memorials of deaths at sea.

A fragment of an old stone coffin, and some remains of a mural painting over the vestry door, with the words, " And Jacob awaked out of his sleep," are all else that is noticeable at Chale.

The parish registers date from 1588. The living is a rectory (Rev. A. W. Gother, M.A., 1855), in the gift of J. Theobald, Esq., valued at £334.

COWES, WEST. — The town of West Cowes has two churches, or chapelries, dependent upon Northwood. *West Cowes Chapel* was built in 1653, and, in accordance with the spirit of the times, was not dedicated to any saint. Consecrated in 1662 by Bishop George of Winchester. In 1671 it was endowed by Richard Stephens with £5 yearly, and in 1679 Bishop Morley endowed it with £20 per annum, provided the inhabitants paid their minister £40. The right of presentation was originally vested in the townsmen, but a lapse into the hands of the rector of Northwood having been twice permitted, they have altogether lost the patronage. In 1811 the church was enlarged and improved by the late George Ward, Esq., of Northwood Park, at an outlay of £3000. The west tower, used as the mortuary chapel of the wards, was then erected, from the designs of Nash, the well-known architect. A new church will soon take the place of the present building.

The Church of the *Holy Trinity* was built in 1831-2, and consecrated June 21st in the latter year. Mrs. Goodwin of West Cowes defrayed the cost, provided the site, and endowed it with £1000 in the 3½ per cent consols. The white brick exterior, with stone mullions and window-cases, the long pointed windows, and general early English character, render it an attractive edifice. The architect was Mr. Bramble of Portsmouth. A new chancel has recently been erected.

West Cowes Chapel is a perpetual curacy (Rev. J. B. Atkinson), valued at £256, in the gift of the Vicar of Carisbrooke. Population, including the district of *Holy Trinity* (Rev. E. Silva, M.A.), 1013. The latter, valued at £85, is in the gift of the Goodwin family.

FRESHWATER Church, dedicated to All Saints, consists of a nave, chancel, north and south aisles (each with chapels), and square embattled tower. In the latter there is a lofty pointed arch, with a window which lights the west end of the church. The general character of the architecture is Trans. Norman.

The Church of Freshwater was one of the six bestowed on the Abbey of Lire by William Fitz-Osbert. Its patronage in due course fell to the crown, and James I. bestowed it upon William, Bishop of Lincoln, his keeper of the Great Seal. The bishop, in 1623, presented the advowson to "the master, fellows, and scholars of St. John's College, Cambridge."

Monuments and Epitaphs.—A richly-decorated Norman arch in the north chapel enshrines a slab on which there *has been* a brass effigy. "This is supposed to have been the tomb of the founder of the church. There is a tradition that towards the end of the last century, upon opening this tomb, the skull of the person buried was found placed between his legs, from whence it is inferred that he had been beheaded; and it is also said that the brass, which is now missing, described the person to have been one of the lords of the manor of Afton."—*Tomkins.*

There is a rood-screen, but of poor design; the only one in the island.

In the chancel, north side, close to the altar, there is a curious memorial :—

"MEMORIÆ SACRUM.

"The most vertuous Mrs. Anne Toppe, Daughter of Mr. Thomas Cardell, sometime of the Privy Chamber to Queen Elizabeth, and Wife to Mr. John Toppe of Wiltshire. In her widdowhood by a memorable providence preserved out of the flames of the Irish rebellion. On the 11th of September 1648, and 71st year of her age, expired under the roof of her nearest kinsman, then Rector of this place, to his unspeakable loss and grief.

". . . . repente
Sublatam ex oculis, prosequitur lacrimis
Nepos mœstissimus, CARDELLUS GOODMAN.

If Beauty, Grace, or Vertue's Store
Might have discharged Nature's Score;
If Wit and Language, finely spent,
Or Musick, could the Fates have bent,
Her soul and body had been one
Until the Resurrection,
And then to Heaven (if any might)
Without a Change have taken flight.
The Prophet 'twixt his wheel of fire
Might faster mount, but not got higher
Than she was wont, who, righteous soule,
In Flames of Zeal did upwards rowle.
As Enoch then in Sacred Story
Made but a Step from Earth to Glory,
She needed only a remove
Whose conversation was above.

Scribendi certus, Dolendi via terminus."

On the south side of the chancel there is a tablet to the *Rev. Benjamin Holmes, B.D.*, and another to *Robert Hicks* of Afton. There is a record also of *William Michell, Esq.*, of Norton, and his two daughters.

The living, a rectory (Rev. J. F. Isaacson), is one of the richest in the island, valued at £710 per annum ; in the patronage of St. John's College, Cambridge.

GATCOMBE, dedicated to St. Olave, consists of a body and chancel, separated by an early English arch, and a square embattled tower in the Perpendicular style. A new chancel was added in 1865. It may have been founded by one of the De Lisles, lords of the manor. There is nothing noticeable in it but a recess in the west wall of the chancel, containing an effigy in oak of a knight clothed in chain mail, his feet resting on a heraldic animal, a cherub with outstretched wings at his head. The villagers were wont to call it "the saint," but it commemorates one of the De Lisles, perhaps the founder.

A small annual pension, in lieu of personal service, is paid by the rector of Gatcombe to the vicar of Godshill, in support of the chapelry of St. Radigund at Whitwell, formerly a chapelry in connection with the manor of Gatcombe,— *Cantuaria Manerii de Gatcombe.*

The living is a rectory (Rev. Dr. Barrow), valued at £646.

GODSHILL, dedicated to All Saints, "a spacious cruciform edifice, with a singular bell-turret on the south gable," consists of a chancel, nave, cross aisles, and tower. From its architecture it is obviously of ancient foundation, and a portion of the present edifice may have stood upon the sacred hill when Fitz-Osbert gave it to the Abbey of Lire. Most of the building, however, is Trans. Norman. Its wealth was very great, from the extent of the adjacent demesnes, and in 1404 it was assessed at 100 marks yearly. When Edward VI.'s commissioners sold the superfluous plate, it realized not less than £54, 2s. 7d. The advowson was presented, in 1623, to Queen's College, Oxon, by Charles I.

Monuments.—The picturesque interior of this fine church is adorned by several stately memorials of the dead. Most noticeable is the altar-tomb, beneath an elaborately decorated arch-canopy of the latest Gothic, of *Sir John Leigh*, and his wife *Mary*, who died *temp.* Henry VIII. The tomb bears no inscription, but is richly adorned with rosettes and scutcheons. Observe, also, the monument of *Sir James Worsley* and his wife *Joan*, daughter of the said Sir John Leigh, legendless, but bearing the shields of the families of Worsley, Leigh, Hacket, and Standish. Note, too, the fine monument to their son, *Richard Worsley, Esq.*, with the following laboured inscription in Latin :—

"Richardo Worsley armigero nuper Insulæ Vectis præfecto, unico fratri suo, filio primogenito Jacobi Worsley de Worsley Hall in provincia Lancastriæ oriundi, equitis aurati, ejusdem item insulæ olim præfecti, ex Anna filia Johannis Ley, equitis aurati, apud Appledercombe in eadem insula nata, Johannis Worsley armiger posuit.

" En pia Worselei lapis hic tegit ossa Richardi,
Vectis præfectum quem gemit ora suum.

Et patriæ charus dum vixit, et utilis idem,
Mortuus in patria nunc tumulatur humo.
Quem pater adversa materq. aspectat in urna,
Matris et in medio spectat uterq. parens.
Ad latus hic nati pueri duo, sorte peremptâ
Præpropera, infesti pulveris igne jacent.
Felices omnes, vel quos sors dira coegit,
Tristia funestes claudere fata rogis.
Appledercombus genuit rapuitq. sepulcrum
Ossa habet : Hinc animas vexit ad astra Deus.

"Obiit idem Richardus 12 die Maii A. Dm. 1565. Johannes et Georgius filii dicti Richardi, obierunt 6 die Septembris A. Dm. 1567.

Englished :—

"This sacred stone covers the dust of Richard Worsley, whom Captain of the Wight his shores lament. While he lived, both beloved by and useful to his country ; now in death he is interred in her bosom. His father and his mother regard him from confronting urns, and between them look forth both parents of his mother. Here at his side lie his two children, snatched away by an untimely fate, by the fire of the fatal dust. But happy all, though a dread destiny has constrained them to shut up the gloomy lots in the mournful funeral urns ! Appuldurcombe begat them, and bore them away,—the tomb holds their ashes. God has carried from hence their souls to the stars.

"The said Richard died 12th May 1565. John and George, his sons, 6th Sept. 1567.

"To Richard Worsley, gentleman, formerly Captain of the Isle of Wight, his only brother, eldest son of James Worsley, of Worsley Hall, in the county of Lancashire, knight, also formerly Captain of this island, by Anne, daughter of John Leigh, knight, born at Appuldurcombe in the same island, John Worsley, gentleman, has raised this stone."

There is also a handsome monument erected in 1822 to the memory of *Sir Richard Worsley :—*

"The Right Hon. Sir Richard Worsley, Bart., who was comptroller of the household, a privy councillor, and governor of the Isle of Wight, and who had been for some time the minister plenipotentiary at Venice, died August 8, 1805, aged 54, without issue, leaving his niece, Henrietta Anna Maria Charlotte, daughter of the Hon. Jonathan Bridgeman Simpson, of Babeworthy, in the county of Nottingham, his heiress. He had travelled a good deal abroad, particularly in the Levant ; and the Museum Worsleianum, as well as his collection of paintings and sculptures at Appuldurcombe Park, affords a striking proof of his taste for the fine arts. The above-named Henrietta, his niece, married the Hon. Charles Anderson Pelham, of Brocklesby, in the county of Lincoln, who considered it as a duty to erect this monument to his memory."

Numerous other brasses, tablets, and tombs arrest the attention of the stranger in this famous church. The figures and inscriptions, in most instances, have been ruthlessly stripped off or effaced ; but the following detailed account, from *Sir John Oglander's MSS.* (A.D. 1635), affords some clue to their identity :—

"In the south aisle, next below the chancel, are two fair stones, under whom are buried the bodies of the Frys ; in the stones are pictures of brass, but the inscriptions are stolen away.

"In the south chancel, on a fair stone, is this inscription :—'Hic jacet Johes Frye, filius Ric. Frye et Margaritæ uxoris suæ, qui obiit 11 die January, Anno Dom. 1512, cujus animæ propitietur Deus. Amen.'

"Those Frys were an ancient family, and farmers of Appledercombe, after it was taken away from the abbey of Montes Burgy in France.

"In the south cross is buried one of the Hacketts, with this inscription :—'Pray for the soul of William Hackett, Esq., on whose soul Jesus have mercy. Amen.'

"In this aisle the owners of Appledercombe were buried, as being partly founded by the priors thereof. Where one prior is buried, his portraiture on brass is on a stone.

"Between the two chancels there is a very fair tomb, in which is buried Sir John Leigh and Mary his wife, the daughter and heir of John Hackett, Esq. It is the fairest tomb in our island; in which tomb the said Mary, wife of Sir John Leigh, lieth in her coat of armour, embellished with Hackett's arms, her father, and Leigh's, her husband.

"In the north chancel, in the north side of the wall, is the tomb of Sir James Worsley, without any inscription, only he is there pictured kneeling; erected by his wife.

"Under a fair stone a little below in the same aisle, lieth buried the Lady Worsley, the widow of Sir James, who died a very old woman. There were her arms and an inscription in brass on her tomb, but now defaced.

"In the south wall of the south chancel is the tomb of Richard Worsley, son and heir of Sir James. .

"In the north chancel are many fair stones that heretofore have had both portraitures and inscriptions on them in brass; under whom are interred the bodies of the De Hegnoes, who were Lords of Stenbury and Whitwell, an ancient family; many of them were knights of good account: for all Whitwell buried in Godshill Church till Queen Elizabeth's reign, at what time they had liberty to bury there.

"Also in this church lieth buried many of the De Awlas, or Halls, men of good rank and quality, many of them knights; but of them, and many more that have been buried, there now appeareth no mark of antiquity.

"In the south chancel, about the midst, lieth the body of John Worsley, coffined in lead, who died in London; next to him lieth the body of his son, Mr. Thomas Worsley, a brave scholar, and a plain but worthy gentleman, and a most plentiful housekeeper.

"Next to him in the same chancel lieth the body of his son and heir, Sir Richard Worsley, knight and baronet, a man of worth, learning, and judgment. He died of the small-pox in the 82d year of his age, 1620, or thereabouts.

"Next to him, just by the side of Sir John Leigh's tomb, lieth the body of Ann Worsley, daughter of Sir Richard Worsley, and wife to one Sir John Leigh. She was one of the handsomest women that ever the island bred.

"Nearer to Mr. Richard Worsley's tomb lieth the body of Mr. Thomas Worsley's wife, who was married to one Sir Richard White, a soldier and follower of Henry, Earl of Southampton. She was Mr. St. John's daughter, of Ffarley in Hampshire.

"In the church porch there is on one side a half-obliterated tablet with a Latin inscription, which is translated upon a tablet fixed to the opposite wall:—

" Ecce cumbat Gardi corpus mortale Richardi
Hoc tumulo, verum spiritus astra tenet.
Cujus dona scholis largita et munera egenis
Annua, perpetuo non paritura manent.
Inclyta si pareret multos hæc insula tales,
Qualem jam tandem protulit nuncce virum
Tunc bene pauperibus, meliusq. scholaribus esset,
Sub pede quos pressos quisq. jacere sinit.

"Dictus Richardus Gard, sepultus fuit 5 die Februarii 1617.

Translation:—

" Here lies the mortal part of Richard Gard,
While his freed spirit meets with heaven's reward;
His gifts endowed the schools, the needy raised,
And by the latest memory will be praised.
And may our isle be filled with such a name,
And be like him whom virtue clothed with fame;
Blest with the poor, the scholar too were blest,
Through such a donor that is gone to rest."

The parish registers date from 1558. Dr. Cole, Dean of St. Paul's, was born at Godshill. (See *post*.)

The living is a vicarage, held in conjunction with the rectory of Niton and perpetual curacy of Whitwell (Rev. G. Hayton, M.A.; curate, Rev. T. Ratcliff), valued at £600 per annum, and in the gift of Queen's College, Oxon.

HELEN'S, ST., dedicated to the saint

whose name it bears, is comparatively a new church, having first been built in 1718-19, and consecrated by Sir Jonathan Trelawney on the 27th of June 1719, the same day that St. Thomas's, Ryde, was consecrated; and *rebuilt*, all but the chancel, in 1830.

The old church of St. Helen's stood upon a point of land, the northern extremity of Brading Haven, until the encroachments of the sea compelled its removal. The tower, however, having been found useful as a sea-mark, was faced with brick, repaired, and strengthened, and still occupies its original position. The monks of the neighbouring priory built the ancient church, and supplied its pulpit, until the canon law compelled vicars to be resident. But even then, so small and poor was the parish, the bishop permitted mass to be celebrated and the sacraments administered by the Prior of St. Helen's. At the dissolution of religious houses the advowson of the vicarage, as well as the priory, was bestowed upon Eton College.

The new church is a small, uninteresting building, with chancel, transept, and low tower. There are sittings for 297 persons, 129 of which are free. " Over the altar is a well-executed painting of a cross surrounded by a glory." —*Barber*. The transept-windows are rather handsome.

Monuments. — The only noticeable things in the interior are the memorials to the Grose family; one to *Sir Nash Grose, Knt.*, a Judge of the Court of Queen's Bench, of whom Lord Campbell says, he always showed his wisdom by being right when everybody else was in the wrong; died, 1814; and another to his son, *Captain Edward Grose*, of the Guards, killed at Waterloo, 1815.

Incumbents, Registers, &c.—The registers date from 1658. There are several entries relative to the burials of seamen " washed on shore," arising from the fact, that during the French convulsions of 1798-1815, when Spithead was crowded with men-of-war, those who died on board were sown up in their hammocks, and incontinently committed to the deep. We quote one or two passages :—" *Mem.* The bishop of this diocese, Sir Jonathan Trelawney, came over from Gosport early on y⁰ 27th of June 1719, and the same morning consecrated the church of St. Helen's (which was built on new ground, the church as it stood before was too much expos'd to y⁰ wash of the sea); and presently after it, on y⁰ same day, he consecrated alsoe y⁰ chappel of Ride in this parish, built by Mr. Player, at whose house in Ride he din'd, and went over again the same day." " The remains of a person, found on the shore in a hammock, were deposited in y⁰ old churchyard, Feb. 17, 1810." " Ten persons were unfortunately drowned in going from Portsmouth to *H.M.S. Leviathan.* Feb. 18, 1804."

The living is a perpetual curacy (Rev. W. H. Dearsley), in the gift of Eton College, valued at £100. The district of St. John's, near Ryde, is included in this parish.

KINGSTON, dedicated to ...., is a small and totally uninteresting edifice, consisting of a body and chancel, early English. It was probably founded by one of the De Kingstons, lords of the manor, and is now presented to by the Ward family. Observe, on the south wall, inserted in a stone slab, a brass, date 1436 :—" Mr. Rychard Mewys, whych deceasd the iii. day of March, in the yere of o⁻ Lord God, mᶜᵉᶜᶜᶜᵒ. and xxxb." The effigies represent a knight armed, three children, and a shield.

The living is a rectory (Rev. J. B. Atkinson), valued at £204, in the gift of G. H. Ward, Esq.

LAWRENCE, ST., dedicated to the saint of that name, one of the smallest of our English churches—25 feet 4¾ inches long, 11 feet ¼ inch broad, and 11 feet 4¼ inches in height. The grave-yard is 90 long by 42 feet wide. It was probably founded by one of the De Aulas, lords of the manor, about the reign of Henry I.; and appears to have been called, "The Church of the Wath" (or Cliff). From the De Aulas, the manor and the advowson of the rectory passed to the Russells; then the Hackets; next the Leighs; and finally into the Worsley family, whose descendant, the Earl of Yarborough, is the present proprietor. The church was originally only 20 feet long, 11 wide, and 6 in height, but was repaired and enlarged by the late Earl of Yarborough, who added the chancel. Observe the windows, Norman in style, and the transparency in the interior, representing Christ's resurrection.

The living is a rectory (Rev. C. Malden), valued at £106 per annum.

MOTTISTONE, dedicated to St. Peter and St. Paul, is a quaint little church, of the Decorated period, consisting of a body, tower, chancel, and aisle. "The two former appear the oldest portions, and were probably erected before the reign of Edward IV., in whose time the aisle was perhaps built as a chancel. This supposition is derived from the form of the pointed window at the east end of that aisle, as well as from the carved rose that decorates one of the terminations of its label. The *present* chancel seems to have been added about the time of Henry VIII.; the window at its east end being square-headed, as are all the other windows in the building, with the exception of one which is very obtusely pointed. The arches in the body are tolerably high-pointed, and supported by polygonal columns; those between the chancel and aisle are obtuse, the columns clustered and fluted, and were probably substituted, at the erection of this part of the structure, for the original south wall of the aisle, or first chancel."—*Barber.*

Observe in the interior a very massive old altar-tomb, the name and date entirely obliterated, but probably for one of the Chyke, or Cheke family, formerly lords of the manor. There are also tablets to *Sir Richard Bassett, James White Bassett,* and *Richard Bassett,* his son.

Close to the north gate is a time-defaced and weather-beaten pair of stocks —obsolete long years ago.

The church was restored in 1864, at the expense of Mr. Seely of Brook House. The chancel roof is of cedar-wood.

NEWCHURCH, dedicated to All Saints, one of the plainest churches in the Isle of Wight, consists of nave, chancel, north and south aisles, and tower—erected about the beginning of the 13th century, on the site of an older building, granted to the Abbey of Lire by William Fitz-Osbert. It afterwards came into the possession of the Abbey of Beaulieu, and on the dissolution of that religious house, was bestowed by Henry VIII. on the Bishop of Bristol (now Gloucester and Bristol).

Monuments, &c.—There is a good tablet to *Lieut.-Gen. Maurice Bocland,* twice M.P. for Yarmouth, died 1765; a memorial to *W. Thatcher,* died 1776; another to *W. Bowles,* died 1748; and in the chapel in the north aisle, eight inscriptions for different members of the *Dillington* family (1674–1749).

Registers and Incumbents.—The registers date from 1582. We quote a few entries: "*May* 29, 1687.—Received of Sir Rob*t* Dillington, Bartt., the sume of fifty shillings, being one moyety of five pounds for Sir Robert his father, not buryd in woollen,—the other 50s. p*d* to Mr. David Urry, informer."—"Paid William Callaway for ringing beer, when King George came to England, and when he was crowned, Sept. and Oct. 1714."—"At 20 m. before 3, on the morning of the 30th day of November 1811, was felt at Portsmouth, in Ryde, and other parts of the Isle of Wight, and in many other places on the Hampshire and Sussex coast, a very smart shock of an earthquake."

" When these my records I reflecting read,
  I find what numerous ills these births succeed,
  What powerful griefs the nuptial ties attend,
  With what regrets these painful journeys end ;
  When from the cradle to the grave I look,
  This I conceive to be a melancholy book."

From 1680 to 1862 there have been nine incumbents of Newchurch.

Newchurch formerly included the chapelries of Ryde and Ventnor, and the district churches of Holy Trinity and St. James, Ryde, and St. Peter's Haven Street. The living is a vicarage, valued at £460, in the gift of the Bishop of Gloucester. St. Thomas's, Ryde, has been formed into an independent vicarage.

NEWPORT.—The ancient church of *St. Thomas à Becket* was founded about 1180 (between 1173 and 1184) by Richard de Redvers, who covenanted with the priory of Carisbrooke that two monks should officiate there daily on payment to the priory of two marks per annum, and with the proviso that on high festivals the townsmen should continue to worship in the mother-church of Carisbrooke. The men of Newport laboured zealously on the sacred edifice, each *guild,* or trade, contributing according to its handicraft ; and their distinguishing signs were accordingly wrought in stone upon the walls. It remained a chapelry of Carisbrooke until the late vicar consented to its separation. The townsmen, however, claimed the right of appointing their own minister, who, at first, was supported by voluntary contributions, and, at a later period, by a town-rate. During the latter part of Charles I.'s reign, and the Commonwealth, they were engaged in constant endeavours to render the church parochial, and the *Journals of the Houses of Parliament,* from 1640 to 1660, contain numerous proofs of their energetic exertions. Their proceedings are also detailed with curious minuteness in the books of the corporation, which record the frequent presentation of petitions, couched in puritanic phrase, to the House of Commons. We must content ourselves with a single illustration (February 1, 1640) :—

" *The humble petition of the Maior and Burgesses, and other the chiefe inhabitants of the Burrough of Newport, in the Isle of Wight.*

" Sheweth,

" 1. That the said Burrough is a Corporation, a port Towne, and auntient Markett Towne, wch serveth the whole Isle of Wight. Seated in the hart of the Island, consisting of about three thousand soules there in habitant, adourned wth a very convenient Church lately enlarged, and well-fitted, and bewtified by the greate expense of the Inhabitants.

" 2. That the said Church being called St. Thomas Chappell is but a Chappell of Ease unto the p'ish of Carisbrooke, wch is a greater p'ish, the viccarage thereof, wth the other profitts thereto belonging, being reputed to be worth twoe hundred pounds at the least, and the obventions, oblations, and proffitts due to the Vicar, out of Newport, xx^{li} pound, or thereabouts, whereof Mr. Alexander Rosse, the nowe Incumbent (liveing out of the Island), alloweth but ten pounds p^r annum to the nowe curate, namely, Mr. William Harby, Master of Arts, an able and laborious preacher, and a man of honest conversation, whoe for the time of his abode in Newport, being about twelve yeares, hath not omitted preaching there on any Saboth day (unless by sickness or other necessity he hath been p'vented).

" 3. That the cure of soules in Newport hath been but meanly served in times past, and like enough would be soe nowe, did not the Inhabitants, by a voluntary benevolence to the said Mr. Harby make an addition to his meanes to keepe him wth them. And it is greatly feared that in time to come the Inhabitants may suffer much want of spirituall foode for their soules—if their preachers needes be not augmented.

" Y^r Pet^{rs} therefore most humbly pray

that the p'misses may be taken into y^r ho^{ble} and pious consideration. And that y^t may be enacted and settled by Parliam^t, if that high and ho^{ble} house think it convenient, that the said Burrough of Newport may be a distinct p'ish of ytself. And that y^{or} Pet^{rs} and their successors may have the p'sentation of the parson thereof for ever, w^{ch}, if it may be obteyned, y^r Pet^{rs} (albeit the Towne is very poore, and they have ben at extraordinarie charge already unto the Church), yet for the advancem^t of preaching the word of God in the said Burrough, they are very willing that it be also enacted that twelve pence of every pound of the yearly rents of the houses and lands wthin the said Burrough (wch it is considered will amount to a competency) shall be raysed for an addition of means to the parson of the said Burrough for perpetuity, wch y^{or} Pet^{rs} conceive will be a greate worke of piety, and must tend to the glory of Almighty God, the greate comfort of the soules of his people in the said Burrough inhabiting and thither resorting, ffor wch y^{or} Pet^{rs} shall ever be bound to thankfulness."

The legislature duly considered these petitions, appointed committees, introduced bills to accomplish the wishes of the inhabitants; and finally, on the 30th March 1657, we meet with the following record: " A bill for raising maintenance for the minister of Newport, in the Isle of Wight, was this day read the third time, and, upon the question, passed. *Ordered*, that the Lord Protector's consent be desired to this bill."

The Lord Protector's consent was given June 9, 1657, but Newport nevertheless remained dependent upon Carisbrooke for two centuries later.

The church, it is said, when Newport was burnt by the French in 1377, suffered considerably. When pulled down in 1854, signs of fire were visible on many stones. The plague broke out in Newport in 1580 with such severity, that the grave-yard at Carisbrooke was unable to contain the dead. License, therefore, was granted to the townsmen to form a cemetery in connection with their own church.

A new and singularly carved pulpit was bestowed on the church by Stephen March, a wealthy burgess of Newport, in 1631. It was the work of an artist named *Caper* (whose symbol, a goat, is upon it), and now adorns the *new* church.

A graphic description of the ancient edifice is given in a MS. in the British Musuem, from which we have already quoted—" Church Notes in Hampshire and the Isle of Wight," by one William Pavey, March 1718-9 (see *Carisbrooke*). As it fully records the monuments it contained, and most of which are now to be examined in the *new* church, the reader may not be displeased to have it placed before him *in extenso* :—

" The church is like, at first view, three ridged houses joined, embattled on the top. On the upper part are five windows between six leaden spouts, and underneath four large windows, with a large porch, which is the grand entrance, in the middle of the south side. The tower is pretty lofty, and embattled with four pinnacles.

" Within the church is one of the most curious carved *pulpits* that I ever saw, the work of one Thomas Caper (who now lies buried in Salisbury), An^o. Dm. 1630, in which year the seats likewise were erected. It was a donation of one (Stephen) March, whose crest is against the back of the pulpit.* As for the carving, round the sounding-board of it is this inscription in neat, wrought, and gilded letters : ' *Cry aloud and spare not ; lift up thy voice like a trumpet.*' The pulpit is divided into two rows of bas-relief carved images. On the uppermost row are curiously described the four Cardinal Virtues and the three Graces, with their types ; and on the lower rank the seven liberal

---

* This is an error. The *goat* is evidently a symbol of the artist's name (*Caper*).

sciences—namely, Grammatica, Dialectica, Rhetorica, Musica, Arithmetica, Geometria, and Astronomia, with the several symbols and characteristics of each science. 'Tis a true church militant, for. there is a cannon placed to defend the church now it is in danger.* Nothing more remarkable in it, but a neat, light grey marble font. [This is now in the new building, and bears an inscription—*The giver of Anne Keith, Widow*, 1637.]

"Underneath the step that goes up to the altar is the vault wherein is interred the *Lady Elizabeth*, daughter to King Charles I.; and this is the inscription, as Mr. John Gilbert, jun., told me :—

"'THE LADY ELIZABETH, DAUGHTER TO KING CHARLES THE 1ᵉᵗ, SEPT. 8, MDCL.'

"Against the south wall is the famed tomb of Sir Edward Horsey, Knt., who was often sent thither in Henry VIII.'s time, to defend it from any sudden invasion from France. It is a curious marble monument, on which lies his effigies at length, armed at all points complete, with his hands held up, and joined in a praying manner, and on an oval piece of black marble this epitaph:—

"' Edvardus qvi miles erat fortissimvs Horsey.
Vectis erat praeses, constans terraq. mariq.
Magnanimvs placidis svb pacis nomine fortis
Jvstitiae Cvltor quam fidvs amicvs amico
Favtor Evangelii delectvs Principe vixit
Mvnificvs Popvlo mvltvm delectvs ab omni
Vixit et vt sancte sic stamina sancte peregit.'

"' Qvi ob. 23 die Marcii,
Anno Domini 1582."

[Edward Horsey, who was a most gallant knight, was governor of the Wight,—firm and magnanimous both at sea and on land,—and brave, though with the appearance of great gentleness; a lover of justice, and a faithful friend. A confessor of the gospel, he lived beloved by his prince; and, liberal-handed, was much affected by the people. Died, 23d March 1582.]

---

* Every parish in the island was originally bound to provide and maintain a small cannon.

"This is all that is worth notice in the church.

"In the church-yard, which is about a quarter of a mile west of the church, neatly walled in, are the following remarkable inscriptions :—

"' Here lyeth the body of Mastʳ George Shergold, late minister of Newport, who, during sixteen years in discharge of his office, strictly observed the true discipline of the Church of England, disliking that dead bodies should be buried in God's house, appointed to be interred in this place. He dyed universally lamented and esteemed, January 28, 1707.'"

[This tablet was afterwards removed, and on its reverse was engraved a simple inscription* relative to the burial-place of the Princess Elizabeth (Oct. 1793). It was then placed on the stone which covered her vault. See *ante*, p. 66–7.]

"On a head-stone on the south side of the church-yard, this :—

"' Here lyeth yᵉ body of John Smith, who departed this life yᵉ 12th day of August, in yᵉ year of our Lord 1712, in yᵉ 24th year of his age.'

"' Stay, gentle reader, spend a tear
Upon ye dust yt sleepeth here;
And whilst thou read'st ye state of me,
Think on ye glass yt runs for thee.' "

"On a brass plate on a fine raised tomb near yᵉ middle of yᵉ churchyard :—

"' Here is laid yᵉ body of Mr. John Stanner, who departed this life yᵉ 26th of March 1713, in yᵉ 65th year of his age: a man exemplary for piety, and forward. in works of charity, especially worthy of a good and lasting (*sic*) for an act of gratitude more than common, as in return for a seasonable (tho' noe great) benefaction, he bequeathed yᵉ greatest share of his estate (gotten by an honest industry) to come to yᵉ great-grand-children of that his benefactor.'

---

* "Underneath, in a lead coffin, rest yᵉ remains of Elizabeth, second daughter of King Charles yᵉ First. Obiit Sept. 8, 1650, aetat. 14.'

" ' See by this how yᵉ bread that a man may have cast upon yᵉ waves, cometh to be again found after many days.' "

"On another stone in the north part of the church-yard, exactly transcribed :—

" ' Johes Gilbert, de Pan, Gefi. : repentina morte, xxx. Julii, M.D.C.XC.VI. ΕΥΠΟΤΜΟΤΕΡΟΣ ΔΙΑ ΤΟΥΤΟ ΚΑΙ ΚΑΚΟΝ ΑΠΕΙΓΑΤΟΣ ΕΤΕΛΕΥΤΗΕΕΝ.

" ' Subita morte modo non improvisa, Felicius transitur ad portum.' "

[By a sudden death, not unprepared for, he is borne more happily to the haven.]

" This is all I could gather during my short stay here."—*Addit. MSS.*, 14,296.

While on the subject of epitaphs and monuments, we may add that in the old church-yard there is a tomb-stone to the memory of Lieutenant Shore and his children, drowned in the wreck of the *Clarendon*, in Chale Bay. There are some other noticeable grave-stones.

The complete decay of the old church rendering necessary its demolition, or thorough repair, it was resolved, in 1853-4, to erect on its site a new and more elegant edifice, which should be worthy of the metropolis of the island, and a graceful specimen of modern ecclesiastical architecture. Funds were readily provided by the townsmen, by the gentry of the island, largely assisted by the Queen and the Prince-Consort, and the new building was commenced under the most cheering auspices. Mr. Daukes was selected as the architect ; the builders were Messrs. Dashwood, of Ryde ; and the carvings were intrusted to Mr. Baker, of Kennington.

The foundation stone was laid by Prince Albert, August 24, 1854; the new building was opened for divine worship, December 1856. The total cost was little under £10,000.

St. Thomas' New Church consists of a nave with clerestory, side aisles, north and south porches and chapels, chancel, sacristy, grand west entrance arch and tower, in the architectural style known as decorated early English. It is, emphatically, a beautiful building, and reflects no little honour on the architect, who has displayed considerable fertility of invention, as well as skill in adaptation. The west entrance, a richly-decorated, and elaborately-wrought arch of more than ordinary height, claims hearty admiration.

The interior is light and elegant, with timbered roof, corbels beautifully moulded, richly ornamented windows, and columned aisles of fine proportion.

The tower, to the top of the turret, is 132 feet high ; the height of the roof of the nave, 65 feet ; of that of the chancel, 56 ; of the side aisles, 48 ; of the chapels, 38 feet.

Observe, in the interior, the monuments from the old building grouped together at the west entrance. Notice also the *font*, already described ; the *pulpit ; Sir Edward Horsey's monument ;* and that of the *Princess Elizabeth.*

The latter was erected at the sole expense of the Queen, who has also contributed the stained glass of two of the windows. It represents the princess reclining at full length on her side, her cheek resting on an open Bible,—the position in which, it is said, she died. The likeness is from a portrait in her Majesty's possession. The figure is of pure marble, and reposes in a gracefully ornamented niche or shrine. Altogether, this beautiful monument must be regarded as one of Baron Marochetti's happiest efforts, and lends an additional attraction to a most attractive building. The inscription on the *facia* runs as follows : " To the memory of the Princess Elizabeth, daughter of Charles I., who died at Carisbrooke Castle on Sunday, Sept. 8th, 1650, and is interred beneath the chancel of this church, this monument is erected—a token of respect for her virtues, and of sympathy for her misfortunes—by Victoria R., 1856.

The living (Rev. G. H. Connor) is in the appointment of the vicar of Carisbrooke. Population, 3994. The income is derivable from pew rents and other sources.

NEWPORT.—*St. John's* is a district church of no architectural pretensions, belonging to the Rev. R. Hollings, who is also the incumbent. It will accommodate about 800 persons,—one-third free sittings. It contains absolutely nothing to attract the tourist's attention. Population of the district, 2951.

NEWPORT.—*St. Paul's*, or *St. Paul's, Barton*, is a district church, supplying a populous suburb of Newport, though ecclesiastically included in *the parish of Whippingham*. It is a pretty edifice, Norman in style, consisting of a nave, north and south aisles, apse, and tower, and spire at the west end of the south aisle. Was erected from the designs of Mr. J. W. Wild; the cost defrayed by voluntary subscriptions, and a grant from the Church Aid Society. The present perpetual curate is the Rev. W. L. Sharpe. The living is valued at £100. Accommodation provided for 800 (200 free seats).

NITON,* dedicated to St. John the Baptist, consists of a nave and chancel, separated by an arch, Norman, a south aisle separated by four obtuse arches, south porch and west tower. In the north wall are some remains of early Norman arches, showing that the church once possessed a north aisle. "In the chancel is a square opening, formerly the entrance into the rood-loft. The south porch is rather remarkable, being barrel-roofed, with stone ribs. The tower is low and battlemented, but surmounted by a small spire. On the north side of the tower is a building, formerly a charnel-house. In front of the south entrance is the square base of a large cross, somewhat peculiarly placed,—the angles, and not the sides, being opposite the cardinal points."—*Davis.*

---

* At Niton was born D: Thomas Pittis (*see post*).

The church was one of the six with which William Fitz-Osbert endowed his Abbey of Lire. Afterwards passing into the possession of the crown, Charles I., at the intercession of Queen Henrietta, supported by Lords Coventry, Carlisle, and others, gave it, with Godshill, Carisbrooke, Newport, and Northwood, to Queen's College, Oxon, November 12, 1626.—*MS. Ashmol. Museum*, F 28, fol. 95.

The registers date from 1560. The following entry is of historical value :—
"July the 1st, Anno Domini 1675, Charles II., King of Great Britain, France, and Ireland, &c., came safely ashore at Puckaster, after he had endured a great and dangerous storm at sea.

Ut regnet diu et feliciter
Vovit et exoptat Thomas Collinson,
Rector de Nighton."

(That he may reign long and happily Thomas Collinson prays and ardently desires.)

The living is a rectory, held together with the vicarage of Godshill and perpetual curacy of Whitwell (Rev. G. Hayton, M.A.; curate, Rev. T. Ratcliff), valued at £600, and in the gift of Queen's College, Oxon.

NORTHWOOD, dedicated to St. John the Baptist, is built of stone, and in some parts plastered; consists of a nave, north and south aisles, chancel, porch, and singular wooden turret. Was a chapelry to Carisbrooke until, *temp.* Henry VIII. (A.D. 1545), parochial privileges were granted to it; and is still held included in the presentation to the vicarage of Carisbrooke. The two livings are in the patronage of Queen's College, Oxon, and are together valued at £1123 per annum. Present incumbent, Rev. E. B. James, M.A.

The burying-place was consecrated in 1486. Previously the inhabitants of Northwood were compelled to bury their dead at Carisbrooke.

Observe in the interior a singular monument to *Rev. Thomas Smith*, formerly minister of Northwood; died, 1681. It is formed of one piece of chalk, 3 feet long and 4 feet wide, curiously carved with hieroglyphic characters.

RYDE—*St. Thomas'*.—The inhabitants of Ryde, in consequence of the insignificance of the village, originally worshipped at the *parish church*, six miles distant—Newchurch; but, in 1719, Henry Player, Esq., lord of the manor, built, and endowed with a yearly stipend of £10, "the chapel of St. Thomas," a plain and inelegant structure. In 1827 this was pulled down, and on its site George Player, Esq., erected a more graceful building, early English in character, with nave, chancel, west and south aisles, and a west tower with spire,—the whole of Binstead stone, with coigns of white brick. The interior is graceful and unpretending. At the east end are three large lancet windows of stained glass. Against the wall, under the west gallery, is a marble tablet, inscribed: "THOMAS PLAYER, Armiger, Domus Dei magis quam suæ, elegantiâ et nitoris studiosus hoc sacellum, tam advenis quàm incolis, diù multumq. desideratum condidit (anno 1719). Æmulationis Opus non Invidiæ."—(Thomas Player, gentleman, more solicitous for the splendour and elegance of God's house than his own, built in 1719 this sanctuary, by visitors as well as residents long and eagerly desired. A work for imitation, not for envy).

Epitaphs, &c.—In the south aisle is a memorial to *Mrs. Margaret Collier*, died 1791, ætat 77; referred to by Fielding, in his "Journal of a Voyage to Lisbon," for her liberal hospitality. In the cemetery sleeps the *Rev. Edward Cannon*, the "Godfrey Moss" of Theodore Hook's "*Maxwell*," and the friend of the Rev. R. C. Barham (*Thomas Ingoldsby*). The Rev. E. Cannon was one of the king's chaplains, and always a welcome guest at Carlton House; but, his ambitious hopes receiving no fulfilment, he became a soured and disappointed man, and in his conduct grew so disdainful of social courtesies that he was at length dismissed from the chapel royal. He then retired to Ryde, where, after some years' painful seclusion and comparative poverty, he died "almost forgotten and alone." In the " Life of Barham," prefixed to the complete edition of the " Ingoldsby Legends," are recorded many amusing anecdotes of this eccentric but talented man.

The living of St. Thomas' is held by the Rev. W. H. Girdlestone, M.A., and is now an independent vicarage.

RYDE—*St. James* is a district and proprietary church, erected in 1827, by W. Hughes Hughes, Esq., an alderman of the city of London, and immediately licensed by the Bishop of Winchester. The exterior is stuccoed, and its style of architecture *builders' Gothic*. The interior, however, is handsome and commodious.

From Mr. Hughes the proprietary was purchased by the Rev. Waldo Sibthorpe, who, after a few years' ministry, seceded to the Church of Rome, when it passed into the hands of the Rev. Augustus Hewitt. From him it was purchased, in 1849, by the Rev. W. Tilson Marsh (now of Cheltenham), who held it until compelled by ill health, in 1856, to retire. He appointed as his successor the Rev. H. Ewbank, who was followed by the Rev. W. H. Redknap, M.A.

The church will accommodate about 800 persons; 360 in free sittings.

RYDE—*Holy Trinity*, a district and proprietary church, of remarkably elegant appearance, designed by Mr. T. Hellyer of Ryde; style, early English; consists of a nave, north and south aisles, divided by an arcade into seven bays, and a west tower and spire, 146 feet in height. This graceful edifice was erected in 1845-6,—the cost being defrayed by voluntary contribution. The site and endowment were provided by Mrs. Lind of Westmont. Accommodates 1000 persons,—500 in free seats. The living is a perpetual curacy (Rev. A. J. Wade; curate, Rev. J. S. Barrow); income not returned in the *Clergy List*.

RYDE—*St. John's, Oakfield*, is a district church, supplying a suburb of Ryde, though, for ecclesiastical purposes, included in the parish of St. Helen's. It is a picturesque early English edifice, consisting of a nave, north and south transept, north and south porches, and at the west end a double bell-gable. It was built in 1843, on ground presented by Sir R. Simeon, Bart. Accommodates 300 persons,—150 in free sittings. (Architect, Mr. T. Hellyer of Ryde).

The living is a perpetual curacy (Rev. C. J. Garrard), in the patronage of the incumbent of St. Helen's.

RYDE—*Haven Street*, dedicated to St. Peter, is included in the parish of Arreton, but more conveniently reached from Ryde. The church, an elegant edifice, and regarded as *a district church to Newchurch*, is Early English in style, was designed by Mr. Hellyer of Ryde, and consists of a nave and chancel, south porch, and bell-gable at west end. Both interior and exterior have architectural features which deserve examination. Observe also the parsonage, Tudor in style, by the same architect.

RYDE — *Swanmore*, a graceful new church, dedicated to St. Michael and All Angels, was built in 1862.

SANDOWN (Christ Church), district church to Brading; style, Early Decorated English, from the designs of Mr. J. Woodman; was built in 1845–6, and consists of a nave, chancel, aisle, and tower with spire. Is an elegant building, with an interior commodious and well-arranged. The adjacent school-house and parsonage are worth notice. The site was presented by Sir W. Oglander, Bart., and the expenses (£2600)

made up by voluntary contributions and £400 from the Church Aid Society.

The perpetual curacy (Rev. W. M. Lee, 1846) is in the gift of the Church Patronage Society.

SEA VIEW.—A small district church, Early English, was built here in 1859. Architect, T. Hellyer, Esq.

SHALFLEET is a peculiar, and, in many respects, an interesting structure; the tower and north doorway Norman, the rest of the building early English. "The windows of the south aisle are singularly beautiful, the heads being pierced with ovals, inclining towards the apex, surmounted by a circular aperture. The nave is divided from the aisle by early English arches upon very beautiful Purbeck columns, now unfortunately covered with whitewash. The chancel arch is remarkable for a peculiarity of treatment at the impost, the increased width of the arch being terminated by a partial foliation. The church is lit, north and south, with lancet-windows of good style. The entrance to the church, from the north, is by a Norman door-way, in the tympanum of which is the representation of David with the lion and bear (?) rather rudely and grotesquely carved on one stone. With the exception of this work, the door-way is nearly plain. The tower is Norman, with shallow buttresses; but the original windows have been foliated at a later period. It is now surmounted by a wooden spire erected with money raised by the sale of the bells and the gun belonging to the church; but from the very large area of the tower and the extreme thickness of the walls, the spire or tower has probably been of considerably greater elevation."—*Davis*.

This ancient and note-worthy edifice, according to tradition, was erected by William Fitz-Osbert. Whether it can claim so illustrious a parentage is doubtful, but that it was erected shortly after his decease is very probable.

Monuments.—In the chancel observe a stone to the memory of *Robert Harvey*, died 1730; two shields enclosed in a stone moulding, date 1630, in the south aisle; and a curious monumental slab, broken in two, with a shield and spear, crosswise, upon it, supposed to be of the date of the 11th, or early in the 12th century, was dug up some years ago in the church-yard, where it probably marked the resting-place of one of the knightly Trenchards.

Remark the fragments of stained glass, on the north side of the church, blazoned with the arms of Montacute, Earl of Salisbury, and (on the south) of Isabella de Fortibus.

The living is a vicarage (Rev. T. Cottle, 1849) valued at £210, and in the patronage of the Lord Chancellor.

SHANKLIN, dedicated to St. John the Baptist, consists of a nave, chancel, transept, and shingled spire, retaining no vestige of antiquity. According to some authorities it was founded by Henry de Blois, Bishop of Winchester, *temp.* Stephen; by others it is ascribed (and more probably) to one of the De Lisle family, who certainly endowed it with 50 acres of land.

Observe, in the interior, a good *piscina;* memorials of the White and Popham families; and an ancient oaken chest, elaborately wrought with the initials T. S., and round the lid, in full, *Dominus Thomas Silksted, Prior*, An. Dm. 1512. Silksted was the last prior of Winchester.

The living is a perpetual curacy (Rev. G. W. Southouse). A new church, close to the cliff, is to be erected on ground given by Mr. Young.

SHORWELL, dedicated to St. Peter, consists of a nave, side aisles, tower, and south porch. "It is almost entirely of the Perpendicular style, with the exception of a few earlier fragments, and the decorated base of the tower, which is crowned by a low stone spire, divided into two stages by a small band." —*Davis.*

Observe, in the interior, a stone pulpit (with the iron frame which used to contain the hour-glass), entered by a flight of steps through a segmental arch, piercing what would otherwise be a very massive pier, in a central position of the north aisle.

The church was carefully restored in 1847 by the Rev. E. Robertson, and is one of the most interesting edifices in the island. Over the north doorway, inside, are the remains of some very characteristic *mural paintings*, descriptive of the legend of "St. Christopher bearing the infant Jesus upon his shoulders." The fresco measures 11 feet wide by 6½ high, and is very distinct and graphic. The saint is depicted leaving his wicked companions (upper corner to the left), and grasping the tree with which he is to ford the stream before him. A stone cross is by his side, surmounted with figure of Jesus crucified. On the bank is a person fishing, and hauling ashore a monster fish. Next, we see the saint, considerably increased in size, fording the stream, with the infant Jesus on his shoulder; a ship and a boat are shown upon the waters. From a hermitage in the distance comes forth a monk, holding a lamp to guide the wayfarers. Finally, we see the saint bound to a tree, and undergoing martyrdom. He is already filled with arrows, but two archers are incontinently shooting at him. The king who condemned him to death is at hand, with the executioner by his side, and an arrow in his right eye,—a just punishment for his cruelty, as the well-known legend enforces.

Over the south door are the scanty remains of a mural painting of "the Last Judgment."

Monuments and Epitaphs.—There is a *brass*, near the altar-steps, with a curious effigy of a priest with his hands folded, and the inscription,—

" Of yoʳ charitie pray for the soule of

S⟨r⟩ Richarde Bethell, late vicar of this churche of Sherwell, y⟨e⟩ which deceased the xxiii day of Marche, the yer of of Lord MDXLIII, on whose soule Jhu have m'cy."

The north aisle is thronged with interesting records of the knightly family of Leigh. One is very singular,—

"To the remembrance of y⟨e⟩ two most worthie and religious gentlewomen, His late deare and loyall wives, Mrs. Elizabeth Bampfield who died the viith March 1615, Having bin y⟨e⟩ mother of 15 hopeful children. And Mrs. Gartrude Parsevall who died childles, the xxii of Decemb⟨r⟩ 1619, was this monument consecrated by their loving and sorrowful husband, Barnabas Leigh, Esq.

"Since neither penne nor pencill can set forth
Of these two matchles wives the matchles worth,
W⟨e⟩ are forc't to cover in this silent tombe
The prayses of a chast and fruitful wombe,
And with Death's sable vaile in darknes hide
The ritch rare vertues of a barren brida.
Sweet saint-like paire of Soules in whom did shine
Such modells of perfection feminine,
Such pietie, love, zeale, that though we sinners
Their lives have lost, yet still themselves are winners;
For they secure heaven's happines inherit
Whilst we lament their losse, admire their merit."

This is accompanied with an illustration of *the two wives*, one with her children, and the legends, *Sicut vitis frugifera*, and *Sicut plantulæ olivarum* (Like to the fruitful vine, and Like unto the olive branches),—the other, with the legend, *An non ego melior tibi quam decem filia?* (Am I not better to thee than ten sons?) The *third* wife of the composer of this cheerful allegory is symbolled by a hand (with inscription, *Væ Soli*—Woe to the lone one), holding a ring, which encloses a heart.

There is also a monument, with two childish figures, to "the religious and vertuous *Elizabeth Leigh*, daught. of John Dingley, Esq⟨r⟩., late wife of Sir John Leigh, Knt. Died y⟨e⟩ 27 day of Oct⟨r⟩. Ano. Dm. 1619. And lieth here interred.

"Sixteene a maid, and fiftie yeares a wife,
Make ye sume totall of my passed life.

Long thred, so finelie spunne, so fairlie ended,
That few shall match this patterne, fewer mend it;
What wealth I lately had, what parentage,
What friends, what children, what blest marriage,
Dead I forgette; living I light esteemed;
For thy deare love (O Christ), yt has redeemed
My soull from Hell, and shortly shall upraise
This mortall dust, in Heaven to singe thy praise."

There is, moreover, a stone altar-tomb raised on three steps, with the effigy of a knight kneeling and praying before a desk, whereon an open book is laid. Behind him kneels a child, also in the attitude of prayer. In the compartments underneath are inscriptions to the memory of *Sir John Leigh* of Northcombe, died January 18, 1629, ætat 83; and of *Barnabas Leigh*, his great-grandson, died January 25, 1629, ætat nine months, and "was laide in the tomb of his great-grandfather, who saw his heir of the fourth generation." Then follows—

"Inmate in greive, he tooke his grandchilde heire,
Whose soul did haste to make to him repaire,
And so to heaven along as little page
With him did poast to wait upon his age."

A beautifully decorated marble records the death of *John Leigh* of Northcombe, Feb. 22, 1688, ætat 38; and *Anna*, his son's wife, died Sept. 25, 1715, ætat 32. Her daughter *Judith* is also commemorated. She died, 1722.

Then a stone shield, with initials E. L., and date 1569, bears the following:—

"Elizabeth Leigh, Davghter of Francis Helton of Portsmouth, Gent. Having bin 10 years y⟨e⟩ most loving and vertvovs wife of Edward Leigh of Shorwell, Gent., departed this life y⟨e⟩ first of July 1621, and together with her two sonnes, John and Tho. Leigh, lyeth here interred.

"In Christ's faith and fears to live and die
Directlie leads to immortalitie,
Glads saints and angells, grieves or foes infernall,
Conquers the worlde, and wins a crown eternall.
Thy late experience (deare Elizabeth)—
When, dying, thou didst triumph over death—
And with sole faith and innocencie armed,
Nimblie escape his bloodie hands unharmed,
Proves this most true,—now liv'st thou with the just,
And leav'st nought here imprisoned but thy dust."

Finally, we may note that there are

eight tablets to different members of the *Bennet* family, and one in the north aisle to *General Sir James Willoughby Gordon*, Bt., died January 4, 1851, ætat 79, father of the present owner of North-court and the manor of Shorwell.

The communion table (1661), the chalice (1569), and a curiously wrought patine, are worth inspection.

The living is a rectory, held with that of Mottistone.

THORLEY, dedicated to St. Swithin, consists of a nave, chancel, and south porch, without any tower. Its erection is attributed to Amicia de Clare, Countess of Devon, who bestowed it upon the priory of Christchurch. One of its vicars was the Rev. William Petty, uncle of the celebrated Sir W. Petty, and employed by the Earl of Arundel in the collection of the *Arundelian Marbles*.

VENTNOR, dedicated to St. Catherine, a district and proprietary church in the parish of Newchurch, designed by Mr. Robert Ebbels; consists of a nave, short chancel, aisles, and tower, with spire 110 feet high. It was erected in 1837, at the sole expense (£3400) of J. Hambrough, Esq. of Steep-hill Castle, who also provided an endowment of £1000; built a parsonage, at an outlay of £2500; and rebuilt the National Schools.

Length of church, 59 ft.; width, 36 ft. 6 in. Site presented by Major P. Hill.

VENTNOR—*Holy Trinity Church*, near Bonchurch, a handsome new building, in the Early Decorated style, was erected in 1861-2, at the cost of an unknown benefactor, on condition a daily service was performed. It consists of a nave, aisles, chancel, transept, and recessed entrance. The tower, with open belfry windows, is crowned by a tall and shapely spire. Architect, Mr. Giles of Taunton.

WHIPPINGHAM.—The old church was of small pretensions; it consisted of nave, chancel, transept, two small aisles, low

tower, and spire. Nothing of it deserved a word of commendation but the chancel and aisles, added at the Queen's expense in 1855. The Queen and her attendants occupied the aisles at the east end. The royal pews were very plainly furnished.

It was one of William Fitz-Osbert's gifts to Lire Abbey, and, at the demolition of religious houses, fell to the crown.

The living is a rectory (Rev. G. Prothero), valued at £757, in the gift of the Lord Chancellor.

WHIPPINGHAM: *East Cowes*, dedicated to St. James, is a chapelry in the parish of Whippingham. The designs were furnished and the site presented by the architect Nash, and the foundation-stone laid by the Queen (then Princess Victoria) and the Duchess of Kent, 6th September 1831. It was consecrated in 1833. The cost, £3000, was defrayed by voluntary contributions, liberally assisted by the Queen and the Duchess.

WHITWELL, formerly a chapelry to Niton, but with parochial privileges, consists of two distinct chapels in one building,—that of "Our Lady of Whitwell," and that of "St. Radigund." The latter is now the chancel, which has recently been well restored (1866) at a cost of £200, and belonged to Gatcombe, whose rector is bound to pay an annual sum for its support. The former has always been supplied by the rector of Niton. The building is Norman and Early English, and most of it would seem to have been erected about the time of Henry III. The pulpit and reading-desk cost 51s. in 1623-4. De Estur, Lord of Gatcombe, founded "the chantry of Our Lady."

The living has recently been separated from Niton, and Whitwell now forms an independent parish. The present rector is the Rev. R. B. Oliva.

WOOTTON, dedicated to St. Edmund, consists only of a nave and chancel, and is a small but ancient building, with little of interest in its architectural features. The doorway has a fine Norman arch.

Wootton was rendered independent of Whippingham by Walter de Insula, in the reign of Henry III., who then built a small chapel in connection with his manor-house, and endowed it with certain glebe, arable, and pasture lands. This edifice was destroyed by fire, and rebuilt, *temp.* Edward IV.

The patronage remained with the De Lisle (or De Insula) family for centuries, but, upon the extinction of the male line, passed into other hands, and finally into the Popham family.

The living is a rectory (Rev. R. E. Scott), valued at £240, and in the patronage of F. Popham, White, Esq.

YARMOUTH, dedicated to St. James. In our notice of the town of Yarmouth, we have sketched the fortunes of its church, which was built, as we have there pointed out, in the reign of Charles I., and not, as is usually stated, in 1543. The edifice *then* erected stood at the east end of the town, and was pulled down on account of its ruinous condition.

The present building, consisting of a nave, chancel, aisles, and small chapel near the chancel, was thoroughly repaired in 1831, chiefly at the expense of the late D. Alexander, Esq., who also raised the tower (30 feet) to its present height. The gallery was built by the corporation.

Monuments, &c.—In the chapel there is a very fine marble statue of *Sir Robert Holmes*, in complete armour, placed in an arched recess, and supported by a massive pedestal. A long Latin inscription (written by Dr. Freind) records the deeds of this gallant admiral, once governor and captain of the Wight, but no translation or repetition of it is necessary, as they are set forth in full in the early pages of this volume. The monument was erected by his son, Henry Holmes, lieutenant - governor of the island.

There is also a monumental tablet to *Henry*, the son of Thomas Lord Holmes, died June 11, 1751, ætat 5; and to *Thomas*, Lord Holmes, himself, died July 7, 1764, ætat 65.

A tablet with urn, sculptured by Nollekens, purports to have been erected by Vice-Admiral Biggs, in 1802, to a *Captain John Urry*; and in the pavement are various slabs to the memory of *William Hide*, alderman of the town, died May 21, 1648; his wife, *Mary Hide*, died 12th April, 1660; and his son *William*, died 8th March, 1679. Also, to *Peter Pryavlx*, alderman of Southampton, died 11th June, 1644. There is nothing else of any interest to the stranger.

The living is a rectory (Rev. S. Blackburn), valued at only £100 per annum, in the gift of the Lord Chancellor.

YAVERLAND, a picturesque edifice, is supposed to have been built of Sir William Russell, lord of the manor, in the reign of Edward I. In the first of Queen Mary, this manor was purchased by German Richards, Esq., in whose family it continued for two centuries. It was then bequeathed to a Rev. Mr. Wright, and continued with his successors, until the death of J. A. Wright, Esq., of Crowsley Park, Oxford, in 1822. The manor and advowson of the church were subsequently purchased by Admiral Sir Graham Eden Hamond, Bart., of Norton Lodge, near Freshwater.

All that is noticeable in this pleasant little church is the fine Norman doorway, and equally fine Norman arch which separates the nave from the chancel. Most of the ancient casements have been blocked up, and hideous modern windows inserted by those demons of misrule, the churchwardens of the last generation.

The living is a rectory (Rev. R. Sherson), valued at £230 per annum, and in the gift of Admiral Sir Andrew Hamond, Bart.

THE WORTHIES OF THE ISLAND.

DR. THOMAS PITTIS—ADMIRAL HOPSON—DR. ROBERT HOOKE—DR. THOMAS JAMES—MR. RICHARD JAMES—SIR THOMAS FLEMING—DR. THOMAS ARNOLD.

WE propose to conclude our Handbook to the Isle of Wight with brief biographical sketches of those of its worthies whose careers have not been detailed in the preceding pages.

DR. THOMAS PITTIS.

Dr. Thomas Pittis, the son of Captain Thomas Pittis, was born at Niton, about 1635. Where he was educated his biographers have not recorded, but in 1652 we find him entered as a commoner at Trinity College, Cambridge. After graduating as B.A., he removed to Lincoln College, where "he was esteemed by his contemporaries a tolerable disputant." But the monarchical principles which he introduced into all his speeches, were then held in disfavour by the university authorities, and, in 1658, he was expelled from his college.

After the restoration he was amply compensated for his losses by being appointed to the rectory of Gatcombe. In 1665 he obtained the degree of B.D., and in 1670, D.D., and chaplain in ordinary to the king. Bishop Morley gave him the good living of Holyrood, Southampton, and the king bestowed the rectory of Lutterworth, in Leicestershire, which he exchanged for that of St. Botolph, Bishopsgate. The latter he held in conjunction with Holyrood and Gatcombe, and the lectureship of Christ Church, Newgate Street, until his death, December 28th, 1687. He was buried at Gatcombe, or, according to some authorities, at Niton.

His works consist of Occasional Sermons, a Private Conference on the Obligation of Oaths, a Discourse on Prayer, and a Discourse concerning the trial of the Spirit.—*Wood's Athenæ. Oxon.*, and *Chalmers' Biographical Dictionary.*

ADMIRAL SIR THOMAS HOPSON.

This gallant seaman was born at Lingfield, about 1648, of reputable parents, from whom, it is said, at an early age, he ran away to sea. A curious story is told of his early adventures : he was apprenticed to a tailor at Niton, and one day, while sitting on his shopboard, observing a squadron of men-of-war off the coast, he suddenly ran down to the shore, sprung into a boat, and rowed to the admiral's ship, where he was received as a volunteer. His boat, which he cast adrift, was afterwards picked up ; and his hat being found upon the shore, his friends naturally concluded he was drowned. Meanwhile, the squadron fell in with a French fleet, and an engagement took place. Hobson, or Hopson, grew impatient at its duration, and inquired of a comrade for what object the two fleets contended. " Being told that the action must last till the white *rag* at the enemy's masthead was struck, he exclaimed, 'Oh, if that's all, I'll see what *I* can do.' At this moment the ships of the two admirals were engaged yard-arm and yard-arm, and both obscured in smoke." Hopson, observing this circumstance, ascended the rigging, and, unperceived, gained the main-yard of the French vessel. Mounting with the utmost celerity to the main-top-gallant-mast-head, he seized the flag, and returned with it in triumph. " The disappearance of the flag was soon noticed;" the British shouted "Victory;" the French were dismayed, and the battle was won. Whereupon Hopson was immediately promoted.

Notwithstanding the circumstantiality of this wonderful story, we are bound to pronounce it a fiction. All that is really known of Hopson's early career is, that he left his birth-place while a boy, and entered the navy. (He did not, by the way, return to his friends until he was an admiral, when he suddenly surprised them with a visit.) But victories are not won by such accidents as that which the compilers of the Isle of Wight guide-books have loved, for many years, to repeat.

Hopson served in the Dutch war in 1672, and, by a steady discharge of his duties, gradually obtained promotion. James II. in 1688, gave him the command of the *Bonadventure*, but did not succeed in binding him to his cause. Hopson cordially acceded to the revolution which placed William III. on the English throne, and was rewarded with an appointment to the command of a 60-gun ship, the *York*, which he handled skilfully in the battle off Beachy Head, leading the rear division of the red squadron under Sir George Rooke.

In 1693 he was promoted to Rear-Admiral of the Blue, and, in due time, became Vice-Admiral of that division. He blockaded Dunkirk, August 1694, and gradually grew in public estimation as a trustworthy and gallant seaman.

Having been promoted in March 1702 to Vice-Admiral of the Red, he went as second in command to Sir George Rooke in the expedition against Cadiz, and gallantly led the van in the hot fight off Vigo. For his services he was knighted (November 29, 1702), and the Queen settled upon him a pension of £500 per annum, with a reversion of £300 to his wife.

He represented Newtown in his native island in 1705, and after a long career of honour and service, died on the 12th October 1717, aged about 69. — *Charnock's Biographia Navalis; Campbell's Admirals.*

ROBERT HOOKE.

Robert Hooke was born at Freshwater, where his father was rector, on the 26th July 1635. As a child he was of a very weakly frame, but his temper was sprightly and his mind active, and so ready was his intellect, that his father determined to bring him up to the Church. His natural appetite, however, was for mechanics. He invented curious toys; made a wooden clock which marked the time; and built a ship, a yard long, which fired guns by machinery.

After his father's death, which happened in 1648, he was placed with Sir Peter Lely, but the smell of the oils brought on intense neuralgic pains, and incapacitated him for work. Dr. Busby, of Westminster School, therefore, took charge of him, and supported him while he attended on that foundation. His mental powers here made a rapid development, and we are told that he taught himself the organ, and invented thirty different modes of flying!

He removed in 1653 to Christ Church College, Oxon, and speedily attracted the attention of the scientific notabilities of that learned university. He made the acquaintance of the Hon. Robert Boyle, and Dr. Seth Ward, the Savilian Professor, and applying himself to the improvement of the pendulum, invented in 1658 the pendulum watch. He also completed the air-pump, and perfected several astronomical instruments.

Such was his scientific reputation, that on the establishment of the Royal Society in 1662, he was appointed the Curator of their experiments. In the following year he graduated at Oxford as M.A., and, in 1664, the Royal Society elected him Professor of Mechanics.

His *Micrographia*, a description of the results of experiments made by magnifying glasses, appeared in 1665; his *Lampas*, on improvements in lamps, in 1667; and his *Philosophical Collections* in 1681.

In the beginning of 1687 he lost his niece, Mrs. Grace Hooke, who had lived with him for many years, and his temper, always irritable, now became insupportably harsh and cynical. He had already quarrelled with Helvetius and Sir Isaac Newton, and for the remainder of his life was continually on the alert to attack a foe's error or a friend's weakness.

Robert Hooke died at his lodgings in Gresham's College, March 3, 1702, and was buried at St Helen's Bishopgate.— *Waller's Life of Hooke; Birch's Royal Society;* and *Ward's Lives of the Gresham Professors.*

DR. THOMAS JAMES.

Dr. Thomas James was born in Newport, about 1570, of a reputable family, which had been settled in the borough for many years. He was the fifth son of John James and Jane Annemon, of Newport.

He received his education at Winchester, and afterwards removed to New College, Oxon,*—his fellow-student at both places being the famous Dr. Cole. At Oxford he laboured with such zeal and assiduity as speedily to distinguish himself among the learned, and gained the degree of M.A. in 1599.

Sir Thomas Bodley was at that time completing the valuable library which has worthily immortalized his name, and Mr. James, to prove his fitness for the post of librarian, collated the MSS. of the *Philobiblion* of Richard of Durham, and published a corrected text. In the following year (1600) he produced his *Ecloga Oxonio-Cantabrigiensis.†* These works, and his just repute for high scholastic attainments, procured him the

position he coveted, and in 1602 he was appointed the First Keeper of the Bodleian Library, whereupon he left his college. So extensive was his erudition, that he received the flattering appellation of "the Living Library," and it gained from quaint old Fuller the following eulogium: "On serious consideration, one will conclude the library made for him, and he for it; like tallies, they so fitted one another. Some men live like moths in libraries, not being better for the books, but the books the worse for them, which they only soil with their fingers. Not so Dr. James, who made use of books for his own and the public good. He knew the age of a manuscript by looking upon the face thereof, and by the form of the character would conclude the time wherein it was written."

In 1614 he was honoured with the diploma of D.D., and shortly afterwards received, unsolicited, the rectory of Mungeham in Kent, and the subdeanery of Wells. In 1620 he was appointed a Justice of the Peace, and resigned his post as librarian, after having held it for eighteen years, with ever-increasing repute. In a letter to a friend, in 1624, he speaks of the studies which now engrossed him: "I have of late given myself to the reading only of MSS., and in them I find so many and so pregnant testimonies, either fully for our religion, or against the Papists, that it is to be wondered at." He writes also to Archbishop Usher, with whom he often corresponded, to acquaint him of his success in removing Papistical corruptions from the MSS. of the Fathers, and states that in thirty quires of paper he had restored no less than three hundred citations.

He felt so deeply the benefits that Protestantism would derive from a thorough purgation of the manuscripts of the early Christian writers, that in the Convocation held with the Parliament of Oxford, in 1625, he moved that a commission might be appointed for the purpose of

---

* He removed to New College in 1593. The entry in the register runs as follows:— "A.D. 1593. Thos. James, de Insulâ Vectâ in com. South. Theologiæ Primus Bodleianæ Librariæ præpositus, et in eccle. Wellen. Sub-Decanus, &c. Sepult. in choro Coll. Nov."

† This was a catalogue of the college libraries at Oxford and Cambridge. Wood says that while employed in drawing it up, James, if he found any colleges careless about their MSS., borrowed and took away what he pleased, and placed them in the public library.

examining the manuscript Fathers in all public and private English libraries, that the perversions of Papistical commentators might be detected and removed. To this design, it is supposed, the great Camden alludes: "Thomas James Oxoniensis, vir eruditus et verè φιλόβιβλος, qui se totum literis et libris involvit, et jam publici boni studio in Angliæ Bibliothecis excutiendis (Deus opus secundet!) id molitur, quod Reipublicæ literariæ imprimis erit usui."—[Thomas James, of Oxford, an erudite man and an ardent lover of books, who gives himself up wholly to letters; and is now searching the libraries of England from a desire to benefit the public, designs (may God prosper his labours!) that which will be of notable assistance to the republic of letters.]—He pointed out to the members of Convocation, as he had previously done to Archbishop Usher, the small expense at which his plan might be carried out, but he failed to secure their co-operation. *

This learned and enthusiastic Protestant, who well deserved the character given him by Anthony Wood, of being "the most industrious and indefatigable writer against Popery that had been educated at Oxford since the Reformation," died at Oxford in 1629, and was buried towards the upper end of New College Chapel, Oxon.

His principal works are—an edition of the *Philobiblion*, published in 1599; *Ecloga Oxonio-Cantabrigiensis*, 1600; *Cyprianus Redivivus*, and *Spicilegium divi Augustini*, published with the Ecloga; *Catalogus Librorum in Bibliothecâ Bodleianâ*, 1608, which Joseph

* In a letter to Usher, January 28, 1623, he says that he has secured the help of "the flower of the English divines," and needs only twelve more assistants, at £40 to £50 yearly,—four to transcribe orthodox writers; four to compare old reprints with new; and four ' to compare the Greek translations by the Papists." At his own cost he attempted something, but his useful labours were cut short by death.

Scaliger praised; *Apology for John Wickliffe*, 1608; *Treatise on the Corruption of Scriptures, Councils, and Fathers*, 1611; *Jesuits' Downfall threatened*, 1612; *Vindiciæ Gregorianæ*, 1625; *Specimen Corruptelarum Pontificiorum in Cypriano, Ambrosio, Gregorio Magno*, &c., 1626. — *Berry's Genealogies*; *Wood's Athenæ Oxonienses*; *Usher's Life and Letters*; *Fuller's Worthies*; *Biog. Britannica, Suppl. to*, &c.

MR. RICHARD JAMES.

Mr. Richard James was the third son of Andrew James, third son of John James and Jane Annemon, of Newport, and Dorothy, daughter of Philip Poore, of Derington, in the county of Wilts. His father was an elder brother of the Dr. Thomas James whose virtues we have already noted.

He was born in Newport about 1592; was probably educated at Winchester; was certainly admitted a scholar of Corpus Christi College on the 23d September 1608. His progress was rapid, for in February 1611,—when he was scarcely 19 years old,—he obtained his degree as Bachelor of Arts. In January 1615 he won the higher honour of M.A.; and, after no long interval, the greatest university distinction which he ever obtained, a Bachelorship of Divinity. At this time he was in the habit of preaching frequently.

He travelled much, though at whose cost we find it impossible to discover. He visited Wales, Scotland, Shetland, and even Greenland; and certainly extended his peregrinations to Russia (1618-19). According to one authority, he went to Newfoundland as "a minister."

On his return he resumed his pulpit duties, and, we are told, preached three sermons concerning the observation of Lent—one of them without a text, a second against the observance, a third "beside it."—*Wood's Athen. Oxon.*, ii. His fame for scholarship rapidly extended, and soon secured him the patronage and friendship of Sir Robert Cotton. Even the erudite Selden is constrained to speak of him as " vir multijugi studiique indefatigabilis;" and his greatest detractor, Sir Symond d'Ewes, while accusing him of being "atheistical and profane," admits he was "witty and moderately learned." Wood affirms that, had he obtained a sinecure or a prebend, "the labours of Hercules would have seemed to him a trifle." "He was," Wood adds, "a very good Grecian, poet, an excellent critic, antiquary, divine, and admirably well skilled in the Saxon and Gothic Languages."

He arranged and classified Sir Robert Cotton's valuable library, but is accused by Sir Symond d'Ewes of lending out Sir Robert's most precious MSS. for money, and of neglecting many important works in his zeal for perusing the priceless tomes that passed through his hands.

In 1629 he incurred the displeasure of the Privy Council, and involved in his troubles the Earls of Bedford, Somerset, and Clare, his benefactor Sir R. Cotton, James St. John, Burrell, and the erudite Selden. It is said that he lent a rare MS.—purporting to show "how a prince might make himself an absolute tyrant" —to young St. John, who, surprised at its contents, placed it in the hands of his friends.* At last it reached Sir Robert Cotton himself, who, we are told, was ignorant that the manuscript had ever had a place in his library, and employed a young man resident in his house to transcribe it. This "untrusty fellow" made several copies, and disposed of them for his own advantage. One got into the hands of Wentworth, afterwards Earl of Strafford, who brought it to the notice of the Privy Council. Sir Robert Cotton's library was thereupon sealed up; the offenders committed to the Tower; and the terrors of the Star Chamber brought to bear upon them. After a brief interval they were released; but Sir Robert's anxiety brought on a fatal disease, and he died on the 6th of May 1631.

The chief literary work in which James was engaged, but to the successful prosecution of which his poverty proved an insuperable obstacle, was a new " Life of Thomas à Becket," and his uncle—in a letter to Archbishop Usher—thus eulogises both the work and its author. After stating that his nephew's design was to paint Becket as " an arch-rebel," not "an arch-saint," he adds,—"he is of strength, and well both able and learned to effectuate somewhat in this kind, critically seen both in Hebrew, Greek, and Latin, knowing well the languages both French, Spanish, and Italian, immense and beyond all other men in reading of the MSS., of an extraordinary style in penning . . . . such a one as I could wish your lordship had about you ; but *paupertas inimica bonis est moribus*, and both fatherless and motherless, and almost (but for myself) I may say (the more is pity) friendless."

He died of a quartan ague, induced by intense and unremitting study and great privations, at the house of Sir Thomas Cotton,* Westminster, in 1638, bequeathing to posterity a considerable number of valuable MSS., and a few published tractates, which display unusual erudition.

His principal works are,—*Poemata quædam in mortem clarissimi viri Roberti Cottoni, et Thomæ Allen*, published in 1633 ; several Sermons in Latin and English ; and a translation of " *Minutius Felix*" and " *Octavius*," published in 1636. His more important MSS. (of which he left no less than forty-five), are,—*Decanonizatio Thomæ Cantuari-*

---

* Letters of Mead to Sir Martin Stuteville, given in "*Court and Times of Charles I.*," vol. ii.

* A satisfactory proof that James was considered by the Cotton family innocent in the unfortunate transaction whose worse result was Sir Robert's death.

ensis et suorum, in 760 pages, being the work alluded to by Dr. James; *Commentaria in Evangelium Sancti Johannis*, in two parts; *Notæ in aliquot locas Bibliæ; Epistolæ ad amicos suos doctos; Epigrams* in Latin and English; *Reasons concerning the attempts on the Lives of Great Personages; Two Sermons; Iter Lancastrense*, in verse, published by the Camden Society; *Glossarium Saxonicum Anglicum; Russian Dictionary; Observations made in his Travels* through some parts of Wales, Scotland, Shetland, Greeenland, &c.; and *Observations on Russland*,—forming twenty-four volumes quarto, and seven folio. The "*Antiquitates Insulæ Vectæ*," hitherto unpublished, is preserved among his MSS. in the Bodleian, and though evidently the preliminary to a large and elaborate work, may be regarded as a favourable specimen of his Latinity.—*Wood's Athenæ Oxonienses; Usher's Life and Letters; Nicholson's Historical Library; Sir Symond d'Ewes' Diary; Court and Times of Charles I.; Gentlemen's Magazine*, vol. xxxvii.; &c.

SIR THOMAS FLEMING, L.C.J.

Thomas Fleming, Knight, and Lord Chief Justice of the King's Bench, was born at Newport. His father was a mercer and general trader, occupying "a house on the east side of the entrance to the Corn Market from the High Street, on the site where the house now occupied by Mr. Avery stands." The family was of respectable extraction, and had long been connected with the Isle of Wight. One "John Fleming and Hawise his wife" were suitors against "Thomas Blake, for lands in Horingford," in the 52d of Henry III. (1268). They had a son named Hugh. In 1497 (12 Henry VII.), a John Fleming is recorded as bailiff of Newport—an office he again filled twenty-three years later (1520). In the *Hampshire Visitation* made by the heralds in this reign, his name oc-

curs—a proof of the excellence of his position. He died in 1531, leaving a son, by his wife Isabell, also named John, who married Dorothy Harris in 1543, and had a son Thomas, born in April in the following year.

He received his education in the school at Godshill, then the principal resort of the sons of the opulent, and afterwards proceeded to Oxford. In 1570 (Feb. 13) he was married at St. Thomas's, Newport, to Mary James,[*] his cousin, the daughter of Dr. Mark James, physician-in-ordinary to Queen Elizabeth. He next entered upon the study of the law; and his rise in his profession was so rapid that, in 1594, he was called to the degree of serjeant; shortly afterwards made Recorder of London; and on the promotion of Sir Edward Coke to the Attorney-Generalship, was preferred by Lord Treasurer Burleigh to the dignity of Solicitor-General (1595). It has been conjectured that his rapid preferment was partly owing to the influence of the queen's cousin, Sir George Carey (afterwards Lord Hunsdon), then captain of the island, and resident at the castle, while Mr. Fleming resided at the Priory of Carisbrooke. The lease of the Priory he had purchased from Sir Francis Walsingham, the Secretary of State. "That some powerful influence," it has been said,[†] "was exercised [at this time] in favour of Newport interests, may be inferred from the fact that, at the same time that Fleming held the office of Solicitor-General, his two cousins, Drs. Edes [‡] and James, were also attached to the queen's household—the former, the son of a clothier who dwelt at the corner

[*] "Thomas Fleming & Marie James married y⁰ 13 of Febrvary 1570."—From the Registers.

[†] *Vide* a paper by J. Hearn, Esq., in the *Isle of Wight Mercury*, 1857.

[‡] Laurence Edes married Alice, eldest daughter of Thomas James and Elizabeth Collins. Dr. Mark James was a son of Thomas James by his second wife, Alice Porter.

house in the Cattle Market, being chaplain-in-ordinary in addition to his preferments of Rector of Freshwater and Dean of Worcester ; and the other, Dr. James, whose father, Mark James, was a merchant, and lived in the house in which Sir Thomas Fleming was born, was physician-in-ordinary, and daily read to the queen." It is worth noting that the immortal Bacon was a rival candidate for the Solicitor-Generalship.

In 1601 he was returned to the House of Commons as the representative of a Cornish borough. He broke down completely in his maiden speech (November 20th), and was so dismayed by his failure that he never again addressed the house. Nevertheless, he was returned to several parliaments as member for Southampton. On the accession of James I. he was reappointed Solicitor-General ; and in the following year (1604) was knighted, and elevated to the bench as Chief Baron of the Exchequer. In this capacity he tried, in conjunction with the other judges, the notorious Guy Fawkes and his fellow-plotters ; but " he followed," says Lord Campbell sneeringly, " the useful advice for subordinate judges on such an occasion—' to look wise, and say nothing.'"

As a lawyer, however great his talents, he was not free from the prevailing vice of the great men of the age—a leaning towards the exaltation of the crown ; and his decision in the great " Case of Impositions" was an injustice to the subject. The particulars of the case are briefly these : Shortly after the accession of King James, parliament had imposed an import duty upon currants of 2s. 6d. per cwt. The king, of his own will, raised the duty to 10s. There is always to be found in similar conjunctures a man determined enough to assert the rights of the people. On this occasion, one Bates, a Levant merchant, refused to pay the monarch's additional 7s. 6d., and accordingly was prosecuted by the law officers of the crown in the Court of Exchequer.

The point at issue necessarily was—Could the sovereign, of his own volition, raise a revenue by the imposition either of taxes or import duties ? Fleming decided in favour of the crown—a decision legally correct, but opposed to the spirit of the English constitution, and calculated to annihilate English freedom.

In 1607, on the death of Sir John Popham, this able lawyer was elevated to the post of Lord Chief Justice of England. He enjoyed his high dignity, however, but six years, dying suddenly on the 7th of August 1613. On his return from the Northern Circuit, he had given to his servants and farm-labourers what is called in Hampshire a " hearing day." After joining in the blithesome revels, he went to bed, apparently in sound health, but was taken suddenly ill, and died before morning. He was buried in the parish church of North Stoneham, where a stately monument records the numerous successes of his career. It is ornamented with recumbent whole-length figures of the Chief Justice in his robes, with his official insignia ; and his wife, with ruff and hood, and the singular waist favoured by ladies of the Tudor era. Underneath is the following inscription, as truthful, perhaps, as most monumental legends :—

" In most Assvred Hope of A Blessed Resvrection,
Here Lyeth Interred 'ye Bodie of Sir Thomas Flemyng, Knight, Lord Chief Jvstice of England ; Great Was His Learning, Many Were His Virtves. He Always Feared God & God Still Blessed Him & ye Love & Favour Both of God & Man Was
Daylie Upon Him. He Was In Especiall Grace & Favour With 2 Most Worthie & Virtvoos Princes Q. Elizabeth & King James. Many Offices and Dygnities Were Conferred Upon Him. He Was First Sargeant At Law, Then Recorder Of London ; Then Solicitor Generall to Both ye Said Princes. Then Lo ; Chief Baron of ye Exchequer & after Lo: Chief Justice of England. All Which Places He Did Execvte With So Great Integrity, Justice & Discretion that Hys Lyfe Was Of All Good Men Desired, His Death Of All Lamented. He Was Borne at Newporte In ye Ille Of Wight,

Brough Up In Learning & ye Studie Of ye Lawe. In ye 26 Yeare Of His Age He Was coopled in ye Blessed State of Matrimony To His Virtvovs Wife, ye La: Mary Fleming, With whom He Lived & Continewed In that Blessed Estate By ye Space Of 43 Yeares. Having By Her In that Tyme 15 Children, 8 Sonnes and 7 Davghters, Of Whom 2 Sonnes & 5 Davghters Died In His Life Time. And Afterwards In Ripeness of Age and Fulness Of Happie Yeares yt Is to Saie ye 7th Day of Avgvst 1613 in ye 69 Yeare of His Age, He Left This Life For a Better, Leaving Also Behind Him Livinge Together With His Virtvovs Wife

6 Soones & 2 Davghters." *

In 1608 Sir Thomas obtained from James I. a Charter of Incorporation for his birth-town, which provided for the election of a mayor instead of the ancient bailiff. Just before his death he had assisted in the establishment of a free grammar school; but the completion of this project was reserved for his son, Sir Thomas.

It may be added, that his liberality to his kin kept pace with the growth of his fortunes. Thus, in 1573, while living at the " Priorie of Carisbrooke," he transferred to his wife's father his corner tenement, with " the shoppes and loftes thereto belonging," which he held of the bailiff and burgesses of Newport, " in the south side of the High Streate at the west end of the Flesh Shambles," being the house formerly occupied by his father.

Sir Thomas amassed considerable wealth, and purchased various estates— the principal being Hyde Abbey, the Stoneham estate, and the Priory of Carisbrooke, of the Earl of Southampton; and the Quarr lands of two Southampton merchants, named John and George Mills.—*Hearn's paper in Isle of Wight*

* His children were—Sir Thomas; Philip, Steward of the Isle of Wight; Walter; John; James; Sir Francis, master of the horse to Oliver Cromwell; and William; and Elizabeth, Mary, Jane, Eleanor, Dowsabell, Mary, and another.— *Berry's Genealogies, Burke's Commoners*, &c.

Mercury, Lord Campbell's Lives of the Chief Justices, Burke's Landed Gentry, Eng. Histories, Life of James I., Berry's Genealogies, &c.

DR. THOMAS ARNOLD.

It would be out of place here to attempt any exposition of the great educational services rendered by Dr. Arnold, or to consider his merits as an historian. We must simply confine ourselves to a succinct statement of the principal facts of his too brief career.

He was born at East Cowes, in the Isle of Wight, on the 13th of June 1795, and named after Thomas, Lord Bolton, then governor of the island. His father, of an old Suffolk family, was collector of customs for the port of Cowes. After being educated at Warminster and Winchester, he entered the University of Oxford in 1811. He took a first class at the degree examination in 1814; and in the following year was elected Fellow of Oriel College. While at Oxford he became acquainted with many men who, in after life, exercised a considerable influence on English thought; with the present Sir John Coleridge, the lamented Keble, Copleston, late Bishop of Llandaff, and Archbishop Whately. He was noted at college for the freedom and boldness of his political opinions, his erudition, his passionate love of poetry, and his scarcely less passionate love of country walks and bathing.

He remained at Oxford, studying hard, and taking pupils, till 1819, when he settled at Laleham, near Staines, in Middlesex; took unto himself a wife, Mary, daughter of the Rev. John Penrose, a Nottinghamshire rector; and commenced receiving pupils to prepare for the universities. He had been ordained deacon in the Church of England prior to his marriage, but delayed taking priest's orders until 1828, owing to the conscientious scruples he entertained in reference to some portions of the Thirty-Nine Articles, and the Athanasian Creed.

He remained at Laleham for nine years, and there his six eldest children were born. He was slowly acquiring a reputation as an able tutor and an educational reformer of large and liberal views; and his friend Dr. Whately, appreciating the resources of his intellect, and anxious to see them employed in a broader field, prevailed upon him, in 1828, to offer himself as a candidate for the head-mastership of Rugby Grammar School. His influential testimonials and bright Christian character decided the trustees to appoint him to the vacancy. He entered upon his duties in August 1828; and, until his death in 1842, continued in active superintendence of the school, which he completely re-organized, and raised from a failing and insignificant position to one of brilliant influence. But he not only reformed Rugby; he reformed, by his example and teaching, the public-school system of England; while, by his happy faculty of securing the love and confidence of his pupils, his clear insight into their character, and the force of his own personal purity and high-mindedness, he accomplished an amount of good in individual cases which it is impossible to over-estimate. His *modus operandi*, and his singular power over the minds and hearts of those with whom he came in contact, are very vividly illustrated in Mr. Hughes' popular work of " Tom Brown's School-Days."

In 1841 Dr. Arnold was appointed, by Lord Melbourne, to the Professorship of Modern History at Oxford. He delivered an inaugural course of lectures in the following year, which attracted a large and enthusiastic audience of students.

His contributions to historical literature were of an important character. They include a valuable edition of " Thucydides," and a " History of Rome," to the end of the Second Punic War, which is remarkable for close reasoning, sagacious observations on men and events, and judicious and always dispassionate criticism. Among his miscellaneous works may be mentioned his " Sermons," his " Commentary on the New Testament" (unfinished), and the inaugural lectures on "Modern History." But it was as a man rather than as a writer that Dr. Arnold was great; and he must be judged, not so much by his works as by his influence for good on his generation.

He died very suddenly—of *angina pectoris*—on the 12th of June 1842, in the maturity of his powers, but only at the threshold, as it appeared, of a long career of literary usefulness. His life has been eloquently and powerfully written by Dean Stanley; and no one can read its interesting pages without appreciating his good and manly character, his noble truthfulness, his chivalrous generosity, and his earnest, unaffected piety.

THE TOURIST'S COMPANION.

PART IV.

THE TOURIST'S COMPANION.

VOYAGE ROUND THE ISLAND.

[*Steamers* leave SOUTHAMPTON and RYDE for this excursion two or three times a-week during the season; but the tourist will best enjoy it if he hires a stout *wherry*, and makes the voyage at his leisure. If he sails from RYDE, eastward, he may stop for the night at *Niton* or *Blackgang*, landing at *Puckaster Cove;* if he sails westward, his best landing-place will be at *Freshwater Gate.* If he sails westward from VENTNOR, he may stop at *Yarmouth;* if eastward, at *Freshwater Gate.* If he starts from COWES, his resting-places should be *Sandown,* or *Puckaster Cove.* But much must, of course, depend upon "wind and tide."]

To describe the various places which the voyager round the Isle of Wight will successively observe, would be to repeat, to a considerable extent, the information already given. We shall, therefore, content ourselves with enumerating the objects of interest on the island-coast in the order in which they present themselves, referring the tourist for details to our preceding pages.

Starting from RYDE, westward, we pass—
Buckingham Villa; Westfield, Sir Augustus Clifford's seat (p. 121); *Ryde House,* lying back from the shore in the centre of deep, glossy foliage (p. 122); *Binstead* (p. 118), where bright and blooming garden-grounds descend to the very margin of the sea (p. 122); *Quarr Abbey,* whose wild ruins are clearly discernible (pp. 113-116); *Wootton Creek,* running inland through a wooded country (p. 126); *King's Quay,* the small inlet associated by tradition with the memory of King John (p. 78); *Barton,* and *Osborne Woods* (p. 77); *Osborne,* with its exquisite terraces and lawn (pp. 77, 78); *Norris Castle* (p. 79); *East Cowes* (p. 75); conspicuous on the bluff of the hill, *East Cowes Castle* (p. 79); and the broad estuary of the Medina, with *West Cowes* on its further bank,—Messrs. White's dock-yard and the Royal Yacht Club House (West Cowes Castle) principally attracting the attention (pp. 72-74.)

From WEST COWES we pass on to—
Egypt, a picturesquely situated mansion; *Gurnard Bay* (p. 76), and its low, uninteresting shore; *Rew Street,* the point where the old Romano-Celtic road across the island terminated (p. 74). The cliffs here are composed of "alternating beds of clay and limestone, the latter abounding in fresh-water shells and *gyrongonites.* In *Thorney Bay* [which we next reach], similar strata are exposed, with layers of blue clay and sand, containing marine shells." *Newtown River* (p. 142), and *Hampstead Lodge,* consisting of calcareous marls, where fluviatile shells are abundantly found, are next gained, and sweeping along a low, wooded coast, we soon arrive at *Yarmouth,* and the mouth of the river Yar (pp. 139, 140).

From YARMOUTH we proceed to—
The headland formerly crowned by *Worsley's Tower* (p. 38) and *Carey's Sconce* (p. 40), observing the new defences, which, in conjunction with Hurst Castle on the mainland, command the passage of the Needles. Next we enter *Colwell Bay* (p. 147), where marine and freshwater strata are alternated; and "in the fissure called *Bramble Chine* a thick bed of oyster-shells is exposed, apparently in its original state, the valves being in contact with each other as when living." Fossil shells are here abundant, and the *Cytherea incrassata* and *Neretina concava* are sometimes found. Doubling *How Ledge,* we enter *Totland Bay,* characterized by the same geological peculiarities (p. 147); round *Hatherwood Point* we pass into *Alum Bay* (p. 146), whose brilliantly coloured vertical strata seem the phenomenon of a fairy world, and land to examine its wonders at our leisure. The height which overhangs its sandy shore is *Headon Hill* (p. 147), where the visitor may obtain an abundant supply of fossil shells. Dr. Mantell particularly enumerates the following:—" Potomomya gregaria, Potamides concavus, P. plicatus, P. ventricosus, Planorbis euomphalus, Linnæus fusiformis, L. longiscatus, Paludina angulosa, Melanopsis fusi-

formis, M. brevis, Psammobia solida, and Cytherea incrassata." Round the Needles into *Scratchell's Bay* (p. 145), and doubling Sun Corner, we sail in the shadow of the mighty cliffs known as *Main Reach* and the *Nodes* (p. 144), until we reach *Freshwater Bay.* The points of interest along this line of coast are fully described at pp. 144–146. At *Freshwater Gate* (p. 143), or at the village 2 miles inland (p. 143), we pass the night, and resume our voyage the next morning.

From FRESHWATER GATE we proceed to—

Compton Bay (p. 101), looking across the water to the lofty, undulating chalk range of Afton, Chessel, and Shalcombe Downs; at *Brook Point* we land (if the tide serve) to examine its petrified forest (p. 101). Next we pass *Brook Chine*, leading up to the village, and voyage along an interesting coast to *Chilton Chine, Grange Chine, Ship Ledge, Barnes Chine,* and *Cowleaze Chine,* reaching the southeast boundary of *Brixton Bay* and *Atherfield Point* (see pp. 102, 103). Entering *Chale Bay* (p. 103), we recognise its swarthy, barren cliffs, so terribly ominous to the mariner, and notice *Whale, Walpan,* and *Blackgang Chines* (p. 104); over the latter towers the lofty hill of St. Catherine's (p. 104), crowned by its pharos and ruined cell. Passing *Rocken End,* we observe St. Catherine's Lighthouse (p. 138), and the commencement of the wonderful region of the *Undercliff* (pp. 137–139); at *Puckaster Cove* (p. 139), where King Charles II. landed in 1675, we moor our boat, and land for a few minutes' stroll. [The tourist will do well to walk from this point along the cliff to *Steep Hill Cove,* where he may again embark to continue his homeward voyage.]

From VENTNOR we sail by the cliffs of *Bonchurch* (pp. 131–133), with Boniface Down rising grandly against the sky; *Chine Head; Luccombe Chine* (p. 130); the cliff of greensand at Dunnose Point; *Shanklin Chine* (p. 130); the bold curve of *Sandown Bay,* with the village, church, and fort of Sandown (pp. 128, 129); the magnificent chalk cliffs of the *Culvers,* which form the eastern termination of *Bembridge Down* (p. 120), easily distinguishable by its obelisk; *Whitecliff Bay,* and "its highly inclined chalk strata;" the dangerous ledge of the Foreland; *Bembridge Point* and village (p. 119); the mouth of *Brading Haven* (p. 119); the old church tower of St. Helen's (p. 121), now used as a sea-mark, on its north-west bank; *Watch House Point;* the well-wooded shores and pleasant sands of *Priory Bay* (p. 121), "a low bank or cliff of the freshwater eocene marls and limestones, being the only indication of its geological structure;" the village of *Sea View* (p. 121), on a declivity which descends sharply to the seamarge; the low *Salterns,* bounded inland by a range of well-wooded hills; the little hamlet of *Spring Vale; St. Clare* (p. 123), Colonel Vernon Harcourt's agreeable seat; *Appley Wood* (p. 122); the long level of the *Esplanade;* and *Ryde Pier* (p. 108).

GEOLOGICAL TOUR.

1st Day.—From Ryde or Ventnor to Newport. Examine the chalk-pits of Mountjoy. Thence to Calbourne, and visit the quarries of freshwater limestone. Onward to the hotels at Freshwater Gate or Alum Bay, and pass the night.

2d Day.—Examine the strata of Headon Hill and Alum Bay; a good locality for fossils. Cross the Downs to Freshwater Gate, and thence to Brook Point, where the fossil forest should be closely investigated. Proceed by Brixton, through Atherfield, to Blackgang Chine. Stop at Blackgang or Niton.

3d Day.—Walk along the Undercliff *via* St. Lawrence, Ventnor, Bonchurch, and Luccombe, to Shanklin Chine. Numerous fossils may be gathered in this vicinity, and along the shore to Dunnose Point. Stop at Shanklin.

4th Day.—Walk along the shore to Sandown Bay; visit the Culvers and White Cliff Bay. Continue as far as Ryde, and examine the quarries at Binstead.

[See Dr. Mantell's "Geological Excursions round the Isle of Wight.]

ANTIQUARIAN TOUR.

1st Day.—From Ryde to Ninham and Quarr Abbey, and thence to Carisbrooke Castle, Carisbrooke Church, and Roman villa; Calbourne Church, and remains of ancient palace at Swainstone; Shalfleet Church; Yarmouth.

2d Day.—Through Freshwater across the Downs; observe the numerous *tumuli*; to Mottistone Church and the Longstone. Thence to Brighstone. Cross to Rowborough, Gallibury, and Newbarns (Celtic relics) and visit Shorwell Church. On to Newport.

3d Day.—From Newport to Arreton

Church. Thence to Kingston Church, Chale Church, and Ecclesiastical Relics in Chale Abbey Farm. Traces of Celtico-Roman road and encampment at Niton. Visit Kingston, and pass through Godshill (Church) and Appuldurcombe to Ventnor.

4th Day. — Visit St. Lawrence Church. Return to Ventnor, and then, through Bonchurch (Old Church), to Shanklin (Church) and Brading (Church). Cross to Ashey and Knighton. Back to Ryde.

POINTS OF VIEW.

NEAR RYDE. — Appley Wood. The road near Brading, looking down upon Brading Haven. Brading Down. Ashey Down, for view of Ryde, the Solent, and surrounding country. Newchurch. The hill near Binstead Church. The road above Wootton Bridge. From Bembridge Down. From Yaverland.

NEAR WEST COWES.—The hill above the town. A point near Northwood Church. The road to Osborne. The ascent above King's Quay. A point near Whippence Farm, commanding views of Hampshire, as well as of the island-scenery.

NEAR NEWPORT.—Carisbrooke Castle. The Keep. Bowcombe Down. The road near Gatcombe. Arreton Down. Stapler's Heath. Mountjoy. The road near North Court. Shorwell. On the road to Brighstone, where,

having ascended the hill, a fine prospect of the Channel and the south coast of the island is suddenly presented.

NEAR BRIGHSTONE. — Brighstone Down. Mottistone Down. On the brink of the hill over Calbourne. From St. Catherine's Down. The ridge above Niton. Looking out from Blackgang Chine.

NEAR FRESHWATER. — From almost any point on the long and lofty chalk-range known as Chessel, Shalcombe, and Afton Downs. The Needles' Lighthouse. From the Warren, looking down upon Yarmouth. Norton, at the mouth of the Yar river.

NEAR VENTNOR.—Godshill Church. Appuldurcombe Down. At any point along the Undercliff. Boniface Down. From Bonchurch Old Church. The hill overlooking Luccombe. Shanklin Down. The road near Sandown.

TRAVELLER'S ROUTES.

A Week's Excursion through the Island.

1st Day. — Start from Ryde: To Binstead (Church) 1 mile; Quarr Abbey, ruins of, 2 m.; Fish-house Creek, 1 m.; through the coppice into the high road, and by Wootton, 1 m.; to Arreton (Church) 3 m.; cross St. George's Down, and across Shide Bridge, to Carisbrooke (Castle and Church), 4 m.; to Newport (St. Thomas's Church), 1 m.

2d Day.—From Newport to Osborne, passing Whippingham Church, right, 4 m.; East Cowes (East Cowes Castle and Norris Castle), 1 m.; cross by ferry to West Cowes, and passing Northwood, right, to Parkhurst (Barracks and Reformatory), 3 m.; through Parkhurst Forest to Newton (new Church and ancient Townhall), 3½ m.; Shalfleet (Old Church) 1 m.; and by Thorley (Church) to Yarmouth (Church, Fort, and pleasant "seats"), 4 m.

3d Day.—From Yarmouth to Freshwater (Church), 2 m.; and across the Downs to Alum Bay (and the Needles), 2 m.; to Freshwater Gate (caverns, rocks, &c.), 1 m.; over Afton Down to Brook (Church, and petrified forest), 2¼ m.; to Mottistone (Church and ancient cairn), 1 m.; across Brixton Down to Calbourne and Westover (two ancient "seats"), 2 m.; cross Bowcombe Down, and by the Celtic

remains at Rowborough, to Shorwell (Church, and Northcourt House), 4 m.; to Brighstone, 2 m.

4th Day.—From Brighstone, along the cliffs, noticing the chines, to Chale (Church and Blackgang Chine, and St. Catherine's Hill), 5 m.; to Niton, 1 m.; back to Blackgang, and by the cliffs, to Puckaster Cove, 2 m.; to St. Lawrence (Church), 1 m.; to Ventnor (Boniface Down), 1 m.; and Bonchurch (Church, Cliffs, Downs, &c.), 1 m.

5th Day.—Ventnor to Appuldurcombe (House), 3 m.; to Godshill (Church), 2 m.; Newchurch (Church and fine views), 3½ m.; to Apse (old farm), 3 m.; by Wroxall to Ventnor, 5 m.

6th Day.—Through Luccombe (Chine) to Shanklin (Chine, Church, Sands, &c.), 4 m.; to Sandown (Bay, Fort, Church), 2 m. · Bembridge Down, 1 m.; Yaverland (Church and old Manor House), 1 m.; Brading (Church, Down, and Nunwell House), 2 m.; St. Helen's (Church and Village), 2 m.; Sea View, 1 m.; Spring Vale, 1 m.; Ryde, 2 m.

Four Days' Excursion from Ryde.

1st Day.—From Ryde to Brading, 4 m.; St. Helen's, 2 m.; cross, by ferry, to Bembridge, and over the Downs to Yaverland, 3 m.; Sandown, 2 m.; Lake, 1 m.; Shanklin, 2 m.;

Luccombe, 1½ m.; Bonchurch, 1½ m.; Ventnor, 1 m.

2d Day.—Ventnor to Steephill, 1 m.; St. Lawrence, 1 m.; Sandrock, 2 m.; Niton, 1 m.; Blackgang, 2 m.; Kingston, 2 m.; Shorwell, 2 m.; Brixton, 2 m.; Mottistone, 2 m.; Brooke, 2 m.; Freshwater Gate, 3 m.

3d Day.—Alum Bay, 2 m.; Freshwater, 2 m.; Yarmouth (by coach-road), 4 m.; or, crossing by ferry, 2 m.; Shalfleet, 4 m.; Newtown, 1 m.; Parkhurst, 4 m.; Carisbrooke, 1 m.; Newport, 1 m.; West Cowes, 4 m.

4th Day.—To East Cowes, by ferry, ½ m.; or by coach-road, through Newport and Whippingham, to Osborne, 7 m.; East Cowes, for pedestrians, through Barton to Wootton, 4 m.; and thence to Arreton, 3 m.; or, by coach-road, to Newport (Shide Bridge), 6 m.; Arreton, 2 m.; Godshill, 4 m.; Appuldurcombe, 1 m.; New Church, 4 m., Ashey Down, 2 m.; Ryde, 4 m.

Four Days' Excursion from Cowes.

1st Day.—Cowes, to East Cowes and Osborne, 1 m.; to Whippingham, 2 m.; Newport, 2 m.; Parkhurst, 1 m.; Carisbrooke, 2 m.; Arreton, 3 m.; Godshill, 4 m.; Appuldurcombe, 1 m.; Ventnor, 3½ m.

2d Day.—Ventnor to Steephill, 1 m.; St. Lawrence, 1 m.; Sandrock, 2 m.; Niton, 1 m.; Blackgang, 2 m.; Chale, 1 m.; Brighstone, 3

m.; Mottistone, 2 m.; Brooke, 2 m.; Freshwater Gate, 3 m.; Alum Bay, 2 m.

3d Day.—Alum Bay to Yarmouth (by ferry from Norton) 3 m.; Thorley, 1 m.; Shalfleet, 3 m.; Newtown, 1 m.; Parkhurst, 4 m.; Carisbrooke, 1 m.; Arreton, 3 m.; Ryde, 4 m.

4th Day.—Ryde to Brading, 4 m.; Yaverland, 2 m.; Sandown, 2 m.; Shanklin, 1 m.; Luccombe, 1½ m.; Bonchurch, 1½ m.; Ventnor, 1 m.; Newchurch, 4 m.; Ashey Down, 1 m.; Newport, 4 m.; by coach to Cowes, 4 m.

Three Days' Excursion from Ryde.

1st Day.—Ryde to St. Helen's, 4 m.; Bembridge, by ferry, 1 m.; Yaverland (Church and Manor-House), 3½ m.; Sandown, 2 m.; Shanklin, 3 m.; Luccombe, 1½ m.; Bonchurch, 1½ m.; Ventnor, 1 m.; Steephill, 1 m.; St. Lawrence, 1 m.; Niton, 3 m.

2d Day.—Sandrock, 1 m.; Blackgang, ½ m.; Chale, ½ m.; Kingston, 2½ m.; Northcourt, 2 m.; Brighstone, 2 m.; Mottistone, 2 m.; Brooke, 2 m.; Freshwater Gate, 4 m.; Needles Point, 3 m.; Alum Bay, 1 m.

3d Day.—Alum Bay, by Freshwater and Norton, to Yarmouth, 4 m.; Calbourne, 6 m.; Carisbrooke, 4½ m.; Newport, 1 m.; West Cowes, 4 m.; East Cowes and Osborne, 1 m.; Whippingham, 1½ m.; Wootton, 3 m.; Quarr Abbey, 1½ m.; Ryde, 2 m.

DISTANCE TABLES.

	Ryde.	Newport.	Cowes W.	Ventnor.	Sandown.	Shanklin.	Brighstone.	Bonchurch.	Yarmouth.
	Miles.	Miles.	Miles.	Miles.	Miles.	Miles.	Miles.	Miles.	Miles.
Afton	20½	13½	17	21	23	24	6	21	4
Alum Bay	24	13	21	23	22	24	10	25	6
Arreton	8	4	8	7	6	6	12	8	13
Bembridge {	5	12	12½	11	4	6	18	10	23
	7								
Bonchurch	11	11	16	1	5	3	12	...	21
Brading	4	8	11½	8	2	4	17	7	22
Brighstone	13	7	10	11	12	15	...	12	10
Brooke	17	10	14	15	16	19	5	16	5
Calbourne	13	5½	10½	16½	16½	18½	4	17½	5
Carisbrooke	8½	1	6	9	10	18	5	10	11
Chale	16	10	14½	6	12	10	4	7	14
Cowes, East	8	5	½	14	13	19	11	15	11
Cowes, West {	7½	5	...	15	13½	18	10	16	10
	11								
Freshwater Gate	18	11	18	18	20	21	8	19	3
Godshill	11	6	12	5	6	6	7	6	18
Lake	7	9	14	5	1	1	12	5	19
Luccombe	10	12	17½	2½	4	2	10	1½	21½

	Ryde.	Newport.	Cowes W.	Ventnor.	Sandown.	Shanklin.	Brighstone.	Bonchurch.	Yarmouth.
	Miles.	Miles.	Miles.	Miles.	Miles.	Miles.	Miles.	Miles.	Miles.
Mottistone	15	9	12	13	16	16	2	14	8
Newtown	13	6	5	16	15	16	8	17	6
Newport	7	...	5	10	10	10	6	11	10
Needles Point	21	14	18	21	23	25	10	22	6
Niton	16	8½	12¼	5¼	11½	9½	7	6¼	17
Osborne	7	4½	1	13½	18½	13½	10½	14½	11
Puckaster Cove	17	10½	14½	5	11	9	7	6	17
Quarr Abbey	3	4	4	15	9	11	14	14	14
Ryde	...	7	7½	12	6	8	13	11	17
Sandown	6	10	15	6	...	2	14	5	20
Shanklin	8	10	15	4	2	...	13	3	22
Saint Lawrence	14	11	16	2	7	5	10	2	21
Saint Helen's	4	11	11	13	5	7	19	12	21
Thorley	16	9	9	19	15	17	9	20	1
Ventnor	13	10	15	...	6	4	11	1	20
Whippingham	5	3	2	12	13	13	9	14	12½
Yarmouth	17	10	10	20	20	22	10	21	...

Distances of Places from Ryde.

	Miles		Miles		Miles
Appley	¾	Cowes, E.	7½	Shanklin	8
Barnsley	1½	Fairy Hill	4	Ventnor	12
Bembridge (by ferry)	5	Quarr Abbey	3	Whippingham	7
Binstead	1	Sandown	6	Wootton	4
Brading	4	Sea View	3	Yaverland	6
Cowes, W.	8				

Distances of Places from Newport.

	Miles		Miles		Miles
Albany Barracks, Parkhurst	½	Carisbrooke	1	Ryde	7
Arreton	4	Cowes, E.	5	Shorwell	5
Calbourne	5½	Cowes, W.	5	Westover	6
		Osborne	4½	Wootton	3

Distances of Places from Ventnor.

	Miles		Miles		Miles
Appuldurcombe	2	Brading	8	Ryde	12
Arreton	7	Godshill	5	Sandown	6
Blackgang	7	St. Lawrence	2	Shanklin	4
Bonchurch	1	Niton	5½	Yarmouth	20

Distances of Places from Freshwater Gate.

	Miles		Miles		Miles
Afton Down	2	Needles Cove	3	Wilmington	1
Alum Bay	3	Newport	11	Yarmouth (by bridge)	4
Lighthouse	2¾	Ryde	18		

WALKS AND DRIVES FOR TOURISTS.

FROM RYDE.

1. From Ryde, by Spencer road, and across the fields to Binstead (Church). Visit ruins of Quarr Abbey. Strike through the copse to Wootton Bridge, and return by the road. For carriages or equestrians this route is not available = 17 miles.

2. From Ryde, by route 1, or by turnpike road to Wootton. Ascend the hill, and at the Old Rectory turn off to the right. Visit Wootton Church. Keep across the fields to Palmer's Farm, and thence through Brock's Coppice and Whippingham Street, to Barton and Osborne. Descend through East Cowes Park (East Cowes Castle on the right) to the ferry, and cross to West Cowes. Return to East Cowes. Homeward by Whippingham Church, into the Newport road, and return by Wootton = 17 miles. Available for equestrians.

3 From Ryde, along the shore to Spring Vale, Sea View, and Brading Haven. Visit Bembridge. Return by ferry, and ascend the hill to St. Helen's village. A turning on the left leads to St. Helen's Church. Thence by a by-road to the Priory, and passing Nettlestone Green and Fairy Hill, cross the fields to Spring Vale. Turn to the right, and return to Ryde by way of Puckpool, St. Clare, and St. John's. Available for pedestrians only = 8 miles.

4. By road to Brading, visit the church, Bullring, Nunwell, &c. Ascend the hill, turn to the left, and crossing Yarbridge, proceed to Yaverland. Thence by the foot of Bembridge Down to Bembridge. Here the pedestrian may cross by the ferry, and return by route 3. Carriages must return by the road they came = 11 miles.

5. A favourite day's journey (for carriages) is through Sandown, Shanklin, and Bonchurch, to Ventnor. The route homeward should be by Wroxall, Appuldurcombe, Godshill, and Arreton, or by Wroxall, Appuldurcombe, Whiteley Bank, Apse Heath, NewChurch, and Ashey Down.

6. Another day's journey may be through Newport and Shorwell to Brighstone, returning by way of Gatcombe and Arreton.

7. Another day's journey should be to Blackgang Chine, through Arreton, Godshill, and Chale, returning through Niton, Whitwell, Godshill, Sandown (where stop to bait), and Brading.

8. Through Newport to Carisbrooke. After visiting the Castle, &c., proceed through Long Lane to Arreton. Thence, by Knighton, to Ashey Down, and back to Ryde by Aldermoor and Smallbrooke = 19 miles.

9. From Ryde by Play Street and Copt Hall, into Haven Street. Return by Crook's Heath, pass the Aldermoor Mill and Smallbrook, cross the Brading road, and keep down the hill, by Westridge and Westbrook, to Sea View. Return by the shore, or, for carriages, by the road, passing Puckpool, St. Clare, and Appley.= 10 miles.

10. Leave Ryde by St. John's, and keep along the Brading road to Whitfield Wood. Turn to the right, through the wood, and ascend Ashey Down. Return by the high road = 10. For pedestrians.

[For other routes, see pages 112, 113.]

FROM EAST AND WEST COWES.

[These routes, by means of the floating bridge, may be made available from both places.]

11. From West Cowes to Egypt. Turn to the right, and proceed by Debourn to Cockleton. Then, by way of Tinker's Lane, to Great Thorness. Turn to the left, and skirt Parkhurst Forest as far as Vittlefield Farm. Turn to the right, and keep along the wood to Parkhurst barracks. Return by way of Northwood = 14 miles.

12. The pedestrian may keep along the shore to Gurnard Bay and Thorness. Ascend by Whippence Farm into the road, and return by Tinker's Lane and Cockleton = 5 miles.

13. From East Cowes to Whippingham, cross by Whippingham Street, through Brock's Coppice, and by Palmer's Farm to Wootton Church. Thence into the high road, and keep (south-east) to Newport. Visit Carisbrooke, and return by Parkhurst and Northwood = 13 miles. For equestrians and pedestrians.

14. From East Cowes to Newport. Return by the passage boat.

15. From East Cowes to Whippingham. Descend to the river side at the Folly Inn, and cross by boat to Werror Farm. Thence to Northwood Church, and home by the high road = 7 miles. For pedestrians only.

16. By Tinker's Lane, Thorness, and Porchfield, to Shalfleet. Thence, by way of Ningwood to Yarmouth. Return by Thorley and Shalfleet. For carriages and equestrians = 25 miles.

17. From East Cowes, by Wootton Bridge and Quarr Abbey, through Binstead, to Ryde. Return the same way. For carriages = 16 miles.

18. By route 11, to Vittlefield Farm. Turn to the right through Watching Well, and by Swainstone to Calbourne. Thence, by Stony Cross and Elm Copse, to Shalfleet. Return by Porchfield, Thorness, and Tinker's Lane. For carriages = 18 miles.

[For other routes see pp. 74, 75. The routes from Newport may also be adopted,—the tourist, in that case, riding to and from Newport, to save time and prevent fatigue.]

FROM NEWPORT.

19. To Carisbrooke, along the Mall, or, leaving Newport by Node Hill, cross Mountjoy, descend by the New Cemetery, and climb the hill to the Castle. A whole day should be devoted to the Castle, Church, and Roman Villa.

20. From Newport to Nodgen. Climb Bowcombe Down. Keep in the track of the ancient Romano-British road (the traject of the tin trade) to Rowborough Down. Examine the site of British village. Descend into the high road by Rowborough Farm. Keep towards Newport for about a mile, to Watergate. Turn to the right, and proceed by Ganson's Barn across the hill to Whitcombe. Cross Mountjoy to Node Hill, and so into Newport = 11 miles. For pedestrians only.

21. From Newport, through Long Lane, to Arreton. Cross Arreton and Beuly Down to Knighton. Thence, by Ashey and Brading Downs, to Brading. By the high road to Ryde. Return by Binstead, Quarr, Wootton, and Stapler's Heath. A day's journey for equestrians and carriages.

22. From Newport, through Parkhurst and Northwood, to West Cowes. Cross by Ferry, and return through Whippingham = 10 miles.

23. From Newport to Carisbrooke. Turn to the right, and proceed by way of Park Cross and Swainstone (on the left) to Calbourne. Carriages return by the same route. Pedestrians may proceed south to Calbourne Bottom. Cross Brighstone Down into Brighstone, and return through Shorwell = 17 miles.

24. From Shide to Rookley. Turn to the left, and proceed by Sheat Farm into Gatcombe. Through Snowdrop Lane, and by Ganson's Barn, into the Shorwell road. Return through Carisbrooke = 13 miles.

25. Carriage drive; Across Stapler's Heath, and by Wootton Bridge into Ryde. Return through Haven Street to Arreton, and by Long Lane into Newport.

26. Carriage drive: Through Shorwell to Brighstone. Thence to Chale and Blackgang. Return through Kingston and Gatcombe.

27. Carriage drive: Through Rookley, Godshill, and Appuldurcombe into Ventnor. Return through Shanklin to Lake, and home by way of Apse Heath, Stickworth, and Arreton

28. Carriage drive: Through Shalfleet to Yarmouth. Return by way of Thorley and Calbourne.

29. Through Calbourne, and across the downs, to Freshwater Gate. Return across the downs to Brook. Through Mottistone, Brighstone, and Shorwell, into Newport.

[For additional routes see pp. 86, 87.]

FROM BONCHURCH OR VENTNOR.

30. To St. Lawrence, and along the Undercliff to Puckaster Cove. Cross, by Westcliff, to Niton and Whitwell. Thence, by Dean, into the high road at St. Lawrence = 11 miles.

31. Cross St. Boniface Down, and by Steven's Bush, Rew Farm, and Span, reach Appuldurcombe Down. Descend into Stenbury, and thence, through Whitwell, to Niton. Return by route 30 = 13 miles.

32. Along the Undercliff to Blackgang. Cross St. Catherine's Down into Niton, and thence, by Whitwell, to Godshill. Return by Whiteley Bank into Shanklin, and back by the high road = 20 miles.

33. Through St. Lawrence to Sandrock Hotel. Return by Niton and Whitwell to Stenbury. Ascend the down, and return by Rew Farm and Steven's Bush = 13 miles.

34. From Ventnor, through Shanklin, Sandown, and Brading, into Ryde, and back by the same route. A carriage drive.

35. From Ventnor, through Wroxall, to Whiteley Bank. Thence, through Godshill, Rookley, and Gatcombe, into Newport. Visit Carisbrooke, and pass the night at Newport. A carriage drive.

36. From Newport, through Shorwell, to Brighstone. Thence to Chale, and back into Newport by the Undercliff. Available for equestrians and carriages.

FROM SHANKLIN OR SANDOWN.

37. From Sandown to Yaverland. Cross Bembridge Down, and through "the Peninsula" to Bembridge. By ferry to St. Helen's. Keep through the village into the Brading road. Thence into Brading, and by Yarbridge to Sandown (or Shanklin) = 11 miles (Sandown). For pedestrians.

38. Through Sandown and Brading to Ryde. Thence, by way of Ashey Down, to Newchurch. Return by Queen Bower, Lower Northwood, and Cheverton, to Lake. Thence to Sandown (16 miles) or Shanklin (18½ miles).

39. Through Shanklin, Luccombe, and Bonchurch, to Ventnor. Return by Wroxall to Whiteley Bank, and thence into Shanklin. About 14 miles (Shanklin).

40. From Sandown to Lake and Cheverton. Thence to Apse Heath, and, turning to the left, keep south to Apse Farm. Cross through the woodlands of America into Shanklin, and return by the shore = 9½ miles.

41. From Sandown, along the shore, to Luccombe Chine. Ascend the cliffs, and proceed by the footpath through the landslip to Bonchurch. Return by the road = 11 miles.

42. From Shanklin to Languard (manorhouse). Keep northward to Merry Gardens, and north-east to Northwood, Queen Bower, and Newchurch. Return by Wacklands and (south-east) Pidford to Apse Heath. Then by Apse Farm and America, or by Apse Farm and Cliff, into Shanklin. About 10 miles.

43. From Shanklin, by Whiteley Bank, to Godshill, and thence, by Lashmere Pond, Northground, and Stroud Green, into Chale. Visit Blackgang, and return by the Undercliff. For carriages = 24 miles.

44. From Shanklin, through the fields, to Cook's Castle. Cross Shanklin and Boniface Downs into Bonchurch. Return through the Landslip to Luccombe Chine, and thence, by the shore, or from Monk's Bay by the shore = 9 miles.

FROM BLACKGANG CHINE HOTEL.

45. Through Chale and Chale Street, and across Kingston Down, to Kingston. Then through a picturesque hollow lane to Shorwell. From Shorwell to Brighstone, and return along the cliffs to Blackgang = 13 miles.

46. Along the cliffs to Atherfield Point, and home by the shore if the tide permits = 7 miles.

47. Along the Undercliff to Ventnor, returning by Whitwell and Niton. For carriages = 15 miles.

48. To St. Catherine's Down. Descend into Niton, and return by Westcliff and Sandrock to Puckaster Cove. Then along the cliffs to Blackgang. For pedestrians = 9 miles.

49. Through Chale, Chale Street, and Stroud Green, to Godshill. Return by Appuldurcombe and Wroxall into Ventnor. Home, along the Undercliff. For carriages = 15 miles.

50. Through Kingston, via Billingham, Ramsdown, and Chillerton, into Gatcombe, and thence to Newport. Return by Carisbrooke, Shorwell, and Kingston. For carriages = 21 miles.

FROM FRESHWATER GATE.

51. Along the Downs to the Needles Point. Descend into Alum Bay. Ascend Headon Hill, and cross by Weston, Colwell, and Hill Farm, to Niton. Cross to Yarmouth, and return by Thorley, Wilmingham, and Afton. = 13 miles.

52. Ascend Afton Down and Shalcombe Down. Descend through the valley to Brook. From Brook to Mottistone. Cross the Down to Calbourne Bottom, and return over Cheasel Down to Shalcombe Farm. Return by road to Afton, Easton, and Freshwater = 15 miles.

53. By boat to Yarmouth. Cross the bridges to Norton, and return by More Green to Freshwater village. Thence into Middleton, and back by way of Farringford to Freshwater Gate = 9 miles.

54. To Middleton Green. Turn to the right, and keep towards the cliff. Then along the cliff to Colwell and Bramble Chines, Albert Fort, and Norton. Returning by way of More Green and Freshwater = 9 miles.

55. There is a carriage-road to Alum Bay. Then proceed through Freshwater to Norton. Cross the bridge, visit Yarmouth, and return by way of Thorley, Wilmingham, and Afton.

[For routes from BRIGHSTONE, see pp. 97, 98; and from YARMOUTH, pp. 140, 141. The routes set forth above, and those contained in the body of the book, are nearly 100 in number, and comprehend a thorough exploration of every part of the Isle of Wight.]

PRINCIPAL SEATS.

Afton House, B. Cotton, Esq.; Appley, J. Hyde, Esq.; Appuldurcombe (at present unoccupied); Binstead (unoccupied); Brooke House, C. Seely, Esq.; St. Clare, Colonel V. Harcourt; East Cowes Castle, Lady Gort; Fern Hill, J. Galt, Esq.; Gatcombe House, ...; St. John's, Sir J. Simeon; Mirables, Captain Coape; Ningwood, Rev. T. Cottle; Norton Lodge, Sir Andrew Hamond, Bart.; Nunwell, Sir H. Oglander, Bart.; Northwood

Park, G. H. Ward, Esq.; Northcourt, Sir H. Gordon; Norris Castle, Robert Bell, Esq.; Osborne House, Her Majesty the Queen; The Orchard, Sir H. Gordon; Puckaster Cottage; The Priory, Henley Smith, Esq.; Quarr House, Sir T. Cochrane; Steephill, Mrs. Hambrough; Swainstone, Sir J. Simeon, Bart.; Westover, ...; Westhill, near Ryde, Sir Aug. W. J. Clifford, Bart.; West Ridge, James Young, Esq.

THINGS WORTH SEEING.

Carisbrooke Castle. [Yaverland.
Sandown Fort, and Forts at Bembridge and Fort Victoria, the Forts and Defences at Freshwater and Yarmouth.
Quarr Abbey, Ruins of.
The Cromlech, Cairn, or Druid Stone, at Mottistone.
The Celtic Pits and Earthworks at Rowborough, Gallibury, and Newbarns.
The Barrows or Tumuli on Afton and Chessel Downs.
The Alexandrian Pillar at Appuldurcombe.
The Lighthouse and Hermitage on St. Catherine's Hill.
The Lighthouse on St. Catherine's Point.
The Lighthouse on Needles Down.
The Lighthouse on the Needles Rock.
The Culver Cliffs and Cavern.
The Chines at Shanklin, Luccombe, Blackgang, Walpan, Cowleaze, and Brook.
The Natural Curiosities from Freshwater Gate to Yarmouth, Alum Bay, Scratchell's Bay, Arched Rock, Caverns, &c.
Churches at Arreton—A brass, and grave of "Dairyman's Daughter."
　„　Bonchurch — Norman building, with mural paintings.

Churches at Brading—Oglander monuments, &c.
　„　Brighstone—Interesting interior.
　„　Brooke—New edifice.
　„　Calbourne—Early English, an old brass, &c.
　„　Carisbrooke—Perp., monuments, &c.
　„　Freshwater.
　„　Godshill—Rich altar-tomb, and handsome monuments.
　„　Mottistone.
　„　St. Thomas', Newport—Princess Elizabeth's and Sir E. Horsey's monuments.
　„　Niton—Good church. [fice.
　„　Swanmore, near Ryde—New edi-
　„　Shalfleet—Norman tower and doorway, rest Early English.
　„　Shorwell—Brass, stone pulpit, and Leigh monuments.
　„　St. Lawrence—Small church.
　„　Yarmouth—Sir Robert Holmes's monument.
　„　Yaverland—Norman arches, the rest Early English.
Parkhurst Barracks and Prison.

ECCLESIASTICAL DIVISIONS, POPULATIONS, PARISHES, &c.

V., Vicarage; *R.*, Rectory; *P. C.*, Perpetual Curacy.

EAST MEDINA.

Parishes.	Acres.	Population in 1861.	Name in Doomsday Book.
1. Arreton, V................	8633	1880	Adrington.
2. Binstead, R................	1140	486	Benestede.
3. Bonchurch, R................	430	564	Bonecerca.
4. Brading, V*................	9564	3709	Berarding.
5. Godshill, V................	6400	1215	Goddeshull.
6. Newchurch †................	8870	14,008	
7. Niton, R................	1170	700	Neeton.
8. St. Helen's, P. C................	1880	2586	
9. St. Lawrence, R................	350	85	——
10. Shanklin, P. C................	950	479	Sencliz.
11. Whippingham, R................	4390	3915	Wipingeham.
12. Whitwell, P. C................	1920	570	——
13. Wootton, R................	530	79	Odetone.
14. Yaverland, R................	670	69	Evereland.

* Sandown, 1330; Bembridge, 855.　　　　† Ryde, 7147; Ventnor, 2560.

WEST MEDINA.

Parishes.	Acres.	Population in 1861.	Name in Doomsday Book.
15. Brixton, R.......................	2700	630	————
16. Brooke, R.......................	750	156	Broc.
17. Calbourne, R.......................	5090	728	Cauborne.
18. Carisbrooke, V *.......................	8627	7502	Bovecoma.
19. Chale, R.......................	1880	584	Cela.
20. Freshwater, R.......................	4760	1678	Frescewatra.
21. Gatcombe, R.......................	1392	201	Gatecoma.
22. Kingston, R.......................	833	68	Chenistone.
23. Mottistone, R.......................	1070	160	{ Messetone and Modrestan.
24. Newport, P. C. *.......................	—	8819	
25. St. Nicholas-in-Castro, C..........	410	265	Sa. Nicolaus.
26. Northwood, C. †.......................	4270	6534	————
27. Shalfleet, V.......................	6260	1196	Seldeflet.
28. Shorwell, V.......................	4060	612	Sorewelle.
29. Thorley, V.......................	1574	143	Torlel.
30. Yarmouth, R.......................	50	726	Ermud.

* Newport, municipality of, 8819; the borough of, 13,560.   † West Cowes, 5492.

DENOMINATIONAL CHAPELS.

RYDE.

Christ Church, Baptist (Rev. T. A. Binns).
Congregational (Rev. G. A. Coltart), George Street.
Free Wesleyan Baptist Chapel (Rev. W. C. Jones), High Street.
Primitive Methodists (Rev. H. G. Button), Star Street.
Wesleyan (Rev. T. Workman), Nelson Street.
St. Mary's Roman Catholic (Rev. H. S. Phillips), High Street.

NEWPORT.

Baptist, Castle Hold.
Bible Christians, Quay Street.
Congregational, St. James's Street.
Congregational, Node Hill.
Irvingites, Holyrood Street.
Plymouth Brethren, Union Street.
Primitive Methodists, Pyle Street.
Quakers, High Street.
Unitarian, High Street.
Wesleyan, Pyle Street.
Roman Catholic (Rev. Mr. Fryer), Pyle Street.

VENTNOR.

Roman Catholic (Rev. F. S. Bowles), Trinity Road.
Bible Christians, St Catherine Street.

Congregationalist, High Street.
Wesleyan, High Street.
Free Wesleyan, High Street.
Plymouth Brethren, Tulse Hill.
Primitive Methodist, Albert Street.

WEST COWES.

Bible Christians, Cross Street.
Independent (Rev. T. Wilkes), Union Road.
Free Wesleyan, St. Mary's Street.
Primitive Methodist, Market Hill.
Wesleyan, Birmingham Road.
Roman Catholic (Rev. S. Bowers), Carvel Lane.

EAST COWES.

Independent.
Wesleyan.

SANDOWN.

Wesleyan (Rev. F. B. Sandback).
Bible Christians (Rev. J. Horwill).
Congregational Chapel.

SHANKLIN.

Bible Christians.
Congregationalist.
Wesleylan Methodist.

HOURS OF DIVINE SERVICE.

Trinity Church, Ryde—11.0 A.M., 3.0 P.M., 6.30 P.M.

St. James's Church, Ryde—11.0 A.M., 6.30 P.M.

St. Thomas's Church, Ryde—11.0 A.M., 3.0 P.M.

St. Michael and All the Angels, Swanmore—11.0 A.M., 7.0 P.M.

St. Thomas's Church, Newport—10.30 A.M., 3.0 P.M., 6.30 P.M.

St. Catherine's Church, Ventnor—11.0 A.M., 6.30 P.M.

Holy Trinity Church, Ventnor—11.0 A.M., 6.30 P.M.

West Cowes Chapel—10.30 A.M., 6.30 P.M.

HOTELS, INNS, &c.

Alum Bay—*The Needles Hotel.

Arreton—Hare and Hounds.

Bembridge—*The Hotel.

Binstead—The Fleming Arms.

Blackgang—*Chine Hotel.

Bonchurch—*Ribband's Hotel.

Brading—Bugle Inn.

Brighstone—*The New Inn, The Five Bells.

Brooke—Rising Sun.

Calbourne—The Sun.

Carisbrooke—*Eight Bells, The Bugle.

Cowes, West—*The Fountain, *Marine Hotel, *Vine, *Globe, and Red Lion Inns.

Cowes, East—*The Medina Hotel.

Freshwater—*Red Lion.

Freshwater Gate—*Freshwater Hotel, *Albion Hotel.

Newchurch—The Pointerd.

Newport—*The Bugle, *The Star, *Green Dragon, *Swan, and *Wheatsheaf.

Niton—*White Lion, *Buddle Inn, *Sandrock Hotel.

Ryde—*The Royal Pier Hotel, *Royal Kent Hotel, *Yelf's Hotel, *Sivier's Hotel, *York Hotel, *Royal Eagle Hotel, *Salter's Belgrave Family Hotel, Kemp's Esplanade Hotel; *Crown (Commercial), Castle Inn, Thatched House, and Green Dragon Inns.

Sandown—*Star and Garter, *Hale's Hotel.

Sea View—*Crown Hotel and *Cuss' Hotel.

Shanklin—*Hollier's, *Daish's, and *The Crab and Lobster.

Shalfleet—Sun Inn.

Shorwell—Five Bells.

Ventnor—*The Royal, *Marine, *Esplanade and Commercial Hotels; *The Crab and Lobster, *Globe, *Prince of Wales, and *Freemason Inns.

Whippingham, near Osborne—The Prince of Wales.

Wootton—The Sloop.

Yarmouth—*The George, *The Bugle.

At the hotels and inns thus (*) indicated, the traveller may obtain beds.

[Breakfast, 1s. to 2s. 6d.; Dinner, 1s. 6d. to 5s.; Tea, 1s. to 3s.; Beds, 1s. to 2s. 6d.]

CONVEYANCES.

Steamboats.

Steamboats run several times daily between Ryde and Portsmouth; Ryde, Cowes, and Southampton; and Yarmouth and Lymington; but as the times of their departure are constantly being altered, the tourist must consult the Monthly Time-Tables, or the advertising columns of the local newspapers, for information.

Railways.

Cowes to Newport.

Ryde to Brading, Sandown, Shanklin, Bonchurch, and Ventnor.

[For times at which trains start to and from these places, see Monthly Time-Tables.]

Coaches.

Ryde to Newport—9.45, 12.0, 2.0, 3.30, 5.15. Sundays—9.45, 2.0, 6.0.

Newport to Ryde—8.15, 9.45, 12.0, 1.30, 3.0, 4.0. Sundays—8.15, 2.15, 3.45, 7.0.

[During the season Omnibuses run from Ventnor to Blackgang, and Newport to Freshwater. Particulars may be obtained at any hotel or inn in Ryde, Ventnor, and Newport.]

Ryde Pier Dues.

Passengers—2d. each, for landing on or embarking from. Luggage—Packages of 14 lbs. weight, carried by the owner, exempt from toll; packages not exceeding 56 lbs., toll 1d.; not exceeding 112 lbs., toll 2d.; over 112 lbs., 3d. each cwt.

RYDE.—HACKNEY CARRIAGES.

Fares for Distance.

	Carriages drawn by one horse or by a mule or mules			Carriages drawn by two horses.		
Pier Street and Dover Street Stand.						
To or from any part of the town, as far east as the boundary of the town; as far west as the west side of West Street; as far south as Lind Street and Melville Street, including the south side of those streets.....................................	£0	1	0	£0	2	6
To or from any other part of the town......................................	0	1	6	0	3	6
Lind Street Stand.						
Southward, to or from any part of the town, as far as and including the Infirmary, eastward, northward, and westward, to the boundary...	0	1	0	0	2	6
To the boundary southward of the Infirmary............................	0	1	6	0	3	6
Upper Dover Street Stand.						
To or from any part of the town, lying to the north of St. John's Road, Green Street, and Newport Lane, as far as West Street; west as far as West Street; east to the boundary of the town; as far south as Monkton Bridge....................................	0	1	0	0	2	6
To all other parts of the town, southward and westward of the above boundaries...	...			...		

Fares for Distance for Hiring beyond the Boundaries of the Town.

For all hiring of one-horse carriages to places beyond the boundary of the town, the fare, to be calculated from the place of hiring, shall be at the rate of 1s. 6d. per mile, for any distance not exceeding two miles; 1s. 3d. per mile for any distance beyond two miles.

An addition of one-third part of the above rates for carriages with two horses. On all hiring for distances beyond the boundary of the town, the driver, if required, to carry the full number of passengers for which the carriage is licensed. Half the above fares to be paid by persons returning by the same carriage.

CARRIAGES—USUAL CHARGES.

RYDE.—One-horse carriage, 1s. 3d. per mile, 3s. per hour, £1, 1s. per day; two horses, 1s. 8d. per mile, 5s. per hour, £1, 10s. per day (including driver's fee).

NEWPORT, WEST COWES, VENTNOR, SANDOWN, SHANKLIN.—One-horse carriage, 1s. per mile, 2s. 6d. per hour, 15s. per day; two horses, 1s. 6d. per mile, 5s. per hour, £1, 5s. per day. Driver's fee—for a single horse, 3s. 6d. or 4s. per day; for two horses, 5s. per day.

POSTAL ARRANGEMENTS.

	Box Closes.		Extra Stamps.		Deliveries.	
	A.M.	P.M.	A.M.	P.M.	A.M.	P.M.
RYDE......................	6.15, 9.15	2.0, 4.30, 8.30	9.10	4.35, 8.50	7.30	2.30
NEWPORT.................	9.0	7.15	9.15	7.30	7.0	4.0
COWES.....................	9.15	7.30	9.30	7.50	7.0	3.30
SANDOWN.................	8.30	8.0	8.35	8.5	7.0	4.0
SHANKLIN.................	8.15	7.30	8.20	7.40	7.0	4.0
VENTNOR.................	7.30	6.30	7.35	6.45	7.0	6.0

MONEY ORDERS AND ELECTRIC TELEGRAPH OFFICES.

Money Orders—Newport, Ryde, Cowes, Niton, Shanklin, Sandown, Ventnor, and Yarmouth.

Electric Telegraph—Newport, Ryde, Cowes, Ventnor, and Yarmouth.

HOUSE AGENTS.

RYDE.—Union Street—Messrs. Wallis, Marvin, Scott, G. Riddett, and J. Hancock. Pier Street—Mr. C. Knight.

NEWPORT.—St. James's Square — Mr. F. Pittis.

WEST COWES.—High Street—Messrs. J. J. May, J. Moore, and J. R. Smith.

VENTNOR.—Post Office—Mr. J. Spary. Alto House—Mr. C. Bull. High Street—Messrs. Knight and Son.

SANDOWN.—Mr. B. Mearman.

SHANKLIN.—Mr. J. Buckell.

BONCHURCH.—Mr. W. Jolliffe.

BATHS—PROPRIETORS.

RYDE.—E. Minter, J. Williams.

VENTNOR.—J. Barton, W. Bull, J. Whittington.

WEST COWES.—A. Barton, J. Hewitt.

SANDOWN.—J. Duff, Boyce.

SHANKLIN.—J. Sampson and Moorman.

SURGEONS.

At Ryde.—Messrs. R. W. Bloxam, D. Beaton, Dr. Cottle, F. Fowke, Ollard, Broome, Pinniger, Jones (Isle of Wight Infirmary), Bryan, Wilmott, and Woodward.

At Ventnor.—Messrs. Gawthorpe, Gooch, Leeson, G. A. Martin, J. B. Martin, and Tuttlett.

At Newport.—Messrs. J. E. Beckingsale, Buckell, Castle, Foster, Dabbs, Lynch, Tuttlett, Waterworth, Wavell, and Wilkins.

At West Cowes.—Messrs. Cass, Davids, Gibbson, Dr. Hoffmeister, and Kernott.

At Yarmouth.—Dr. Hollis.

At Bonchurch.—H. B. Leeson, M.D.

At Niton.—C. Holman, Esq.

At Sandown.—Messrs. Leeson, Martin, Meers, and Smith.

At Shanklin.—H. F. Middleton, Esq.

At Freshwater.—Dr. Meeres.

LITERARY INSTITUTIONS.

Literary and Scientific Institute, Lind Street, Ryde.

Working Men's Club, High Street, Ryde.—President, Rev. W. H. Girdlestone.

Literary and Scientific Institute, Ventnor.

Literary and Scientific Institute, Grange Road, Shanklin.

Literary and Scientific Institute, Newport.

Isle of Wight Museum, Cross Street, Ryde, open daily.—Curator, B. Barrow, Esq., F.G.S.

Isle of Wight Museum, Lugley Street, Newport, open daily.—Curator, E. P. Wilkins, Esq., M.D., F.G.S.

OFFICIALS.

Mayor of Newport—T. B. Mew, Esq.

Town Clerk, Newport — James Eldridge, Esq.

Chairman of Ryde Commissioners—T. Dashwood, Esq.

Town Clerk, Ryde—W. H. Pullen, Esq.

DIRECTORY

To the Seats of the Gentry, Interesting Localities, &c., of the Isle of Wight.

Corrected up to March 1867.

1. ARRETON.

[9 miles from Cowes, 4 miles from Newport, 8 miles from Ryde, 7 miles from Ventnor, 6 miles from Sandown, and 10 miles from Brighstone.]

Church, partly Norman, partly early English; brasses, monuments, &c. (p. 150.)

Arreton Manor House, date James I. (F. Roach, Esq.), near the Church.

Parsonage, near the Church.

Standen, East, near the foot of St. George's Down, 3 miles north-west; Barrows on the Down; "Dairyman's Daughter's" Cottage; Haseley (see p. 89), 3 miles south-east, at the foot of Shepherd's Lane.

II. BEMBRIDGE.

[16 miles from Cowes, 11 miles from Newport, 8 miles from Ryde, 10 miles from Ventnor, 4 miles from Sandown, 24 miles from Brighstone.]

Church, early English (p. 151).

Bembridge Parsonage (Rev. J. Le Mesurier), in Bembridge Street.

Fair Oak (Dr. Urquhart).

East Cliff, on the high road.

Hill Grove, on the high road.

Bembridge Down, White Cliff Bay (fossils), and Woolverton (Wulfere's Town), 3 miles south-west.

III. BINSTEAD.

[11 miles from Cowes, 6 miles from Newport, 1 mile from Ryde, 13 miles from Ventnor, 7 miles from Sandown, 15 miles from Brighstone.]

Church, early English; Norman gateway, and "The Idol" (p. 151).

Binstead Cottage (Sir C. Locock, Bart.)

West View (Col. Hill).

Binstead Rectory (Rev. P. Hewett, M.A.), near the Church.

Kite Hill (D. Hollingworth, Esq.), on the high road, near Wootton.

Quarr House (Admiral Sir T. Cochrane), beyond Quarr Abbey, near Fishhouse.

Quarries for fossils and freshwater shells; ruins of Quarr Abbey, about 1 mile west.

IV. BONCHURCH.

[16 miles from Cowes, 11 miles from Ryde, 11 miles from Newport, 1 mile from Ventnor, 5 miles from Sandown, 14 miles from Brighstone.]

Old Church, Norman; New Church, Norman; graves of Adams and Sterling (p. 152).

East Dene (J. S. Harry, Esq.), on the road to the Old Church.

Hawthorndene (Rev. Edmund Venables).

The Maples (Dr. Leeson), on the Upper Terrace.

Westfield (G. Giles, Esq.), near Bonchurch Pond.

Combe Wood (Mrs. Hulsh).

Sea View (Miss Sewell).

Upper Mount (...........), on the high road.

Under Mount (Sir J. Pringle, Bart.), on the high road.

Underrock (Edmund Peel, Esq.)

Woodlynch (Rt. Hon. Sir Lawrence Peel).

Pulpit Rock, Flagstaff Rock, St. Boniface Down, Monk's Bay, The Cliffs, &c.

V. BRADING.

[17 miles from Cowes, 8 miles from Newport, 4 miles from Ryde, 8 miles from Ventnor, 2 miles from Sandown, 21 miles from Brighstone.]

Old Church, Trans-Norman and early English; monuments, Oglander Chapel, epitaphs, &c. (p. 153).

Brading Vicarage (Rev. J. Glover, M.A.), below the Church.

Hill House (J. Harrison, Esq.)

Nunwell (Sir H. Oglander, Bart.)

Brading Down, and Haven; bull ring, stocks, old cannon (date 1549), and Nunwell Park.

VI. BRIGHSTONE.

[12 miles from Cowes, 7 miles from Newport, 14 miles from Ryde, 13 miles from Ventnor, and 12 miles from Sandown.]

Church, Norman, early English, Dec., and Perp.; stained glass, piscina, encaustic tiles, &c. (p. 154.)

Brighstone Parsonage (Rev. Dr. Moberly), adjoining the Church.

Brighstone Cottage (The Misses Wilson), in the village.

Waitscourt (Miss Arnold), near the Church.

Bull Rock, Chilton Chine, Grange Chine, Barnes' Chine, Shepherd's Chine, Cowleaze (Cow-leas) Chine, on the coast; Brighstone Down, Barnes (Romano-British pottery), and Lemerston, 1½ mile east.

VII. BROOK.

[15 miles from Cowes, 10 miles from Newport, 17 miles from Ryde, 16 miles from Ventnor, 18 miles from Sandown, and 3½ miles from Brighstone.]

Church, late early English (p. 155).

Brook Parsonage (Rev. J. Pellew Gaze, A.M.)

Brook House (C. Seely, Esq., M.P.), on the right of the road into the village.

Shalcombe Down (barrows), 2 miles north-west; Mottistone Down, 1 mile north-east; Cheasel Down (ancient Saxon cemetery), 3 miles north; Brook Point (fossil forest), Brook Chine, Compton Chine, Compton Bay, Afton Down (barrows), 4 miles north-west; Freshwater Bay, about 6 miles north-west of Brook Church.

VIII. CALBOURNE.

[10 miles from Cowes, 5 miles from Newport, 12 miles from Ryde, 15 miles from Ventnor, 14 miles from Sandown, 5 miles from Brighstone.]

Church, Norman, and early English; brasses, &c. (p. 155).

Calbourne Rectory (Rev. A. M. Hoare).

Swainstone (Sir J. Simeon, Bart.), about 2½ miles north-east of the village.

Westover (.....................), south of the village.

Chessel, Mottistone, Brighstone, and Gallibury Downs; remains of Celtic settlement at Rowborough; Calbourne Bottom; Watchingwell, 4 miles north-east of the Church.

IX. CARISBROOKE.

[6 miles from Cowes, 1 mile from Newport, 8 miles from Ryde, 10 miles from Ventnor, 10 miles from Sandown, 6 miles from Brighstone.]

Church, Trans-Norman and Perp.; monuments, &c. (p. 156.)

Carisbrooke Vicarage (Rev. E. B. James, M.A.), south of the village, on the side of the hill.

Carisbrooke House (............).

Castle House (............).

Marvel (............), 1½ mile south of Shide Bridge.

Parkhurst Barracks (............), on the Cowes Road.

Parkhurst Prison (George Hall, Esq.)

The Castle; Roman villa; Bowcombe Down, 2½ miles south-west; Clatterford, 2 miles south-east; Rowborough, 5 miles south-west; Parkhurst Forest.

X. CHALE.

[15 miles from Ryde, 13½ miles from Cowes, 8½ miles from Newport, 6 miles from Ventnor, 12 miles from Sandown.]

Church, Trans-Norman and Perp. (p. 158).

Blackgang Chine, and hotel, 1 mile south; St. Catherine's Hill; St. Catherine's Point, and Lighthouse; Puckaster Cove; the Undercliff, &c.

XI. COWES, EAST.

[5 miles from Newport, 8 miles from Ryde, 15 miles from Ventnor, 14 miles from Sandown, 12 miles from Brighstone.]

Church, pseudo-Gothic (p. 174).

East Cowes Castle (Viscountess Gort), half a mile east of the town.

East Cowes Parsonage (Rev. R. H. Gibson, M.A.)

Fairlee (............), 3 miles south of Whippingham Church, on the road to Newport.

Norris Castle (Robert Bell, Esq.)

Osborne House (Her Majesty the Queen).

Slatwoods (Miss Sheddon), on East Cowes Hill.

Broadlands, Barton (H. Nunn, Esq.), nearly 2 miles from East Cowes.

Whippingham Parsonage (Rev. G. Prothero, B.D.), near the Church.

Osborne; Whippingham Church, 2 miles south; Barton, 1 mile south-east of Osborne, adjoining the royal gardens; King's Quay, 3½ miles south-east.

XII. COWES, WEST.

[5 miles from Newport, 12 miles from Ryde, 15 miles from Ventnor, 14 miles from Sandown, 12 miles from Brighstone.]

Church, recent design (p. 159).

Parsonage (Rev. E. Silva).

Egypt (R. White, Esq.), on the sea shore, north of the town.

Prospect House (............).

Northwood Park (W. G. Ward, Esq.), south of the town, on the hill.

West Hill (Misses Ward).

West Cliff (Capt. Legard).

Northwood Church, Norman and Trans-Norman, 2½ miles south; Gurnard Bay, 1½ mile west; New Street, 2½ miles south-west; Parkhurst, 4 miles south; Medham, on the river bank, 2 miles south; and Dodnor, 4 miles south.

XIII. FRESHWATER.

[14 miles from Cowes, 10 miles from Newport, 17 miles from Ryde, 20 miles from Ventnor, 19 miles from Sandown, 9 miles from Brighstone. Freshwater Gate is nearly 2 miles further; Alum Bay, from 3 to 4 miles.]

Church, Trans-Norman and early English; monuments, &c. (p. 159).

Afton House (B. Cotton, Esq.), 1 mile north of Freshwater Gate.

Faringford (Alfred Tennyson, Esq.), 1 mile north-west of the Gate.

Faringford Hill (............).

Marina (Rear-Admiral Crozier), north of the village.

Middleton (Rev. J. F. Isaacson), nearly 2 miles south-west.

Norton Cottage (Mrs. Mitchell), near Norton Lodge.

Norton Lodge (Rear-Admiral Sir A. S. Hamond, Bart.), opposite Yarmouth.

West Hill (Rear-Admiral Crozier, R.N.)

Alum Bay, 4 miles south-west; The Needles; Freshwater Gate; Yarmouth, 2½ miles, through Norton, and across the new bridge; Afton Down; Brook, 7 miles south-east.

XIV. GATCOMBE.

[8 miles from Cowes, 3 miles from Newport, 10 miles from Ryde, 8 miles from Ventnor, 9 miles from Sandown, 9 miles from Brighstone.]

Church, Norman, late Perp.; effigy; stained glass (p. 160).

Gatcombe House (Mrs. Bidgood), near the Church.

Sheat, manor house, date James I., 1 mile south-east; Chillerton Down, 2 miles south-west; Cridmore Wilderness, 3 miles south; Ramsdown, 2½ miles south-west.

XV. GODSHILL.

[10½ miles from West Cowes, 11 miles from Ryde, 6 miles from Newport, 5 miles from Ventnor, 6 miles from Sandown, 7 miles from Brighstone.]

Church, Dec. and Perp.; effigies and ornaments (p. 160).

Appuldurcombe Park (.........), about 1½ mile south-east, to the right of the road to Ventnor.

Stenbury, manor house, date James I., 1½ mile south; Wroxall Down, 2 miles south-east; Rookley, 2 miles north-west; Whiteley Bank, for scenery, about 2 miles east.

XVI. KINGSTON.

[13 miles from Cowes, 7 miles from Newport, 14 miles from Ryde, 10 miles from Ventnor, 11 miles from Sandown, 7 miles from Brighstone.]

Church, early English; brass; stained glass (p. 163).

Kingston Manor House (.........).

Ivy House, half a mile north-east; Billingham House, half a mile beyond Ivy House; Chale, 3 miles south.

XVII. MOTTISTONE.

[8½ miles from Newport, 13½ miles from Cowes, 15½ miles from Ryde, 14½ miles from Ventnor, 13½ miles from Sandown, and 1½ mile from Brighstone.]

Church, early English (p. 164).

Mottistone Manor House, date 1557 (...........), near the Church.

Pitt Place (S. E. Walmisley, Esq.), on the road to Brighstone.

Mottistone Down and Long Stone; Brook, Chine, and Point, 2 miles west; Calbourne Bottom, 2 miles north-east.

XVIII. NEWCHURCH.

[10½ miles from Cowes, 6 miles from Newport, 6 miles from Ryde, 6 miles from Ventnor, 3½ miles from Sandown, 11 miles from Brighstone.]

Church, early English and Dec. (partly), (p. 164).

Newchurch Parsonage (Rev. R. B. Oliver, M.A.)

Queen's Bower, 1½ mile south-east; Kingston, ruins of manor house, 2 miles north-east; Ashey Down, 2 miles north-west; Apse, ancient manor house, 3 miles south.

XIX. NEWPORT.

[5 miles from Cowes, 7 miles from Ryde, 10 miles from Ventnor, 10 miles from San-

down, 10½ miles from Yarmouth, 13 miles from Alum Bay, 7 miles from Brighstone, 6 miles from Godshill, 10 miles from Shanklin, 5 miles from Shorwell, and 9½ miles from Blackgang.]

Church, early Decorated; tombs, &c. (p. 165).

Bellecroft (............).

Holyrood House (............).

Node Hill (J. Eldridge, Esq.

Poplars, The (............).

Shide House (.........), south of the town.

St. Cross (G. Kirkpatrick, Esq.), north of the town.

Free Grammar School, Lace Manufactory, Town Hall, Museum; Parkhurst; Carisbrooke, Church and Castle, 1 mile south-west; Pan Down, 1 mile south-east; Gatcombe Park, 3 miles south; Stapler's Heath, 1½ mile east; Hunny Hill, 1 mile north; Arreton, 4 miles south-east.

XX. NITON.

[14 miles from Cowes, 8½ miles from Newport, 15½ miles from Ryde, 5½ miles from Ventnor, 10 miles from Sandown, 12 miles from Brighstone.]

Church, early English, and Dec.; piscina, rood loft, monuments (p. 169).

Beauchamp (.........), north of Mirables.

Ida Cottage (............), near Reeth Bay.

Mirables (Captain Coape), on the Undercliff.

Old Park (Sir J. Cheape), 1½ mile from St. Lawrence.

Orchard (Sir H. P. Gordon, Bart.), half a mile west of Mirables.

Puckaster Cottage (Lieut.-Gen. Tucker), above Puckaster Cove.

West Cliff (Captain Kerr), on the Niton road.

St. Catherine's Hill, 1½ mile west; Whitwell, 1½ mile north-east; Puckaster Cove, 1 mile south; Blackgang Chine, Sandrock Hotel, Rocken End, &c.

XXI. RYDE.

[12 miles from West Cowes, 7 miles from Newport, 12 miles from Ventnor, 6 miles from Sandown, 17 miles from Yarmouth, 20 miles from Alum Bay, 14 miles from Brighstone, 13 miles from Godshill, 9 miles from Shanklin, 12 miles from Shorwell, 16 miles from Blackgang.]

For the Churches, see p. 170.

Appley (Mrs. Tredwell), east of the town, above Appley Wood.

Appley Tower (G. Young, Esq.), on the road to Sea View.

Beachlands (Mrs. Sullivan, and Sir J. Lees, Bart.), at the foot of Upper Dover Street.

Beldornie Towers (W. H. Anderson, Esq.), Spencer Road.

Brookfield (Mrs. Franklyn), on the Newport Road.

Buckingham House (J. B. Danbury, Esq.), at the commencement of the Spencer Road.

Bucklands (Mrs. Alleyne Yard), Spencer Road.

Gwydyr House (Rev. W. H. Girdlestone, M.A.), Spencer Road.

St. Clare (Colonel Vernon Harcourt), on the road to Spring Vale.

Fairy Hill (W. A. Glynn, Esq.), on the road from Sea View to St. Helen's.

St. John's (.............), at the top of St. John's Hill.

St. John's Lodge (Major-General Sir G. Wymer), at the foot of St. John's Hill.

Oak Hill (H. Leacock, Esq.), near Fairy Hill.

Priory, The (Henley Smith, Esq.), about half a mile south-east of Nettlestone Green, on the shore.

Puckpool (— Vincent, Esq.), below St. Clare.

Ryde House (Miss Player), at the end of Spencer Road.

Saxonbury Lodge (Hon. J. P. Ward), at the top of West Street.

Sea View House (Thomas Le Marchant, Esq.), facing the sea.

Springfield (— Callender, Esq.), at Spring Vale.

Stonelands (Admiral Loring), north of Ryde.

Stone Pitts (Captain Brigstocke), on the Binstead Road.

Thornbury House (Mrs. Kirkpatrick), in Spencer Road.

Uplands (C. Payne, Esq.), above Spring Vale.

Westbrook (Pakenham Mahon, Esq.), on the road from St. John's to Sea View.

Westridge (J. Young, Esq.), 2 miles from Ryde, on a cross road leading to Sea View.

Westfield (Admiral Sir Aug. W. J. Clifford, Bart.), Spencer Road.

Willow Bank, St. Clare (Miss Johnson).

Vernon Villa, St. Clare (Rev. Barry Cole).

Woodlands (T. Fowke, Esq.), on the road from St. John's to Sea View.

For interesting localities near Ryde, see pp. 113–124.

XXII. SANDOWN.

[15 miles from Cowes, 10 miles from Newport, 6 miles from Ryde, 6 miles from Ventnor, 12 miles from Blackgang, 22 miles from Alum Bay, and 12 miles from Brighstone.]

For Church, see p. 171

Cliff Villa (T. Webster, Esq.), above the Bay.

Culver Lodge (T. Gibson, Esq.)

Guadaloupe (Rev. R. Agassiz).

Royal Heath Villa (Major Smyth), on the main road.

Shanklin Chine and Down, 3 miles north; Brading, 2½ miles north, Yaverland, Bembridge Down, Whitecliff Bay, &c.

XXIII. SHALFLEET.

[11 miles from Cowes, 6 miles from Newport, 13 miles from Ryde, 16 miles from Ventnor, 14 miles from Sandown, 7½ miles from Brighstone.]

Church, Norman and early English; monumental slab, &c. &c. (p. 171.)

Ningwood (Rev. Thomas Cottle, M.A.)

Hampstead Hill, 2 miles north-west; Warlands (or Walleran's), half a mile south-west; Ningwood, nearly 2 miles west; Newtown, 2 miles north-east; Calbourne, 2½ miles south.

XXIV. SHANKLIN.

[15 miles from Cowes, 10 miles from Newport, 9 miles from Ryde, 3½ miles from Ventnor, 2½ miles from Sandown, 16 miles from Brighstone.]

Church, early English (p. 172).

Fernbank (Miss Harriet Parr).

Tower Cottage (Mrs. Cameron).

Rosecliff House (E. M. Frere, Esq.)

West Hill (Major-General Napier).

Swiss Cottage (Mrs. Cameron).

Parsonage (Rev. G. Southouse, A.M.)

Shanklin's Chine and Down; Sandown Bay; Luccombe Chine, 1½ mile; America, woods, 2 miles north-west.

XXV. SHORWELL.

[10 miles from Cowes, 5 miles from Newport, 12 miles from Ryde, 11 miles from Ventnor, 10 miles from Sandown, 2 miles from Brighstone.]

Church, early English; monument, fresco, &c. (p. 172.)

Northcourt (Sir H. P. Gordon, Bart.), at the Newport entrance to the village.

Vicarage (Rev. T. Renwick, M.A.), behind the Church.

.........Misses Worsley.

Atherfield Point, 3 miles south; Gatcombe, 2 miles north-west; Woolverton, manor house, three-quarters of a mile south-west; Westcourt, manor house, half a mile west; Brighstone Down.

XXVI. ST. LAWRENCE.

[16 miles from Cowes, 11 miles from Newport, 14 miles from Ryde, 2 miles from

Ventnor, 3 miles from Sandown, 11 miles from Brighstone.]

Church, Norman (p. 163).

St. Lawrence Cottage (Countess-Dowager of Yarborough).

Cottage (Hon. Mrs. Dudley Pelham).

Woolverton, ruins of chapel (house?), half a mile south; the Undercliff to Blackgang; St. Boniface Down; Ventnor and Luccombe.

XXVII. THORLEY.

[11 miles from Cowes, 16 miles from Ryde, 9 miles from Newport, 19½ miles from Ventnor, 18 miles from Sandown, 8 miles from Brighstone.]

Church, Norman (p. 174.)

Thorley Parsonage (Rev. T. Hockley, M.A.); Yarmouth, about 1½ mile north-east; Afton Down, 4 miles south.

XXVIII. VENTNOR.

[15 miles from Cowes, 10 miles from Newport, 12 miles from Ryde, 3½ miles from Shanklin, 13 miles from Brighstone, 6 miles from Sandown, 2 miles from Appuldurcombe, 6 miles from Blackgang, 23 miles from Alum Bay, and 4½ miles from Sandrock Hotel.]

For churches, see p. 174.

Belgrave House (Dr. G. A. Martin), in Belgrave Road.

Cove Cottage (Sir Raymond Jarvis), near the Royal Hotel.

Elm Grove (J. Haskins, Esq.), above the Church.

Hillside (Captain Newall), on the old Shutes.

Parsonage (Rev. J. Marland, M.A.), near the Church.

Pelham House (Lady Cosway), Undercliff.

Steephill Castle (Mrs. Hambrough), beyond the town.

Ventnor Cottage (Mrs. Hadfield), in the grove.

St. Boniface Down, St. Lawrence, 2½ miles south-west; the Undercliff, Dunnose, Luccombe Chine, Rew, Week, and Wroxall Downs.

XXIX. WHITWELL.

[13 miles from Ryde, 9 miles from Newport,

14 miles from Cowes, 4 miles from Ventnor.]

Church, Norman, and early English (p. 174).

Down Court (T. Hawkins, Esq.), at the foot of the Down, 1½ mile west.

XXX. WOOTTON.

[4 miles from Cowes, 3½ miles from Newport, 3 miles from Ryde, 10 miles from Ventnor, 9 miles from Sandown, 16½ miles from Brighstone.]

Church, Norman and early English (p. 174).

Fern Hill (J. Galt, Esq.), on the road to Arreton.

Kite Hill (D. Hollingworth, Esq.), on the hill above the Creek.

Old Rectory (F. White Popham, Esq.), on the Newport Road.

Arreton Church and Down, about 5½ miles south from Wootton Rectory; Firestone Copse, 1½ mile south-east; Fish-house, 1 mile north-east; Quarr Abbey, 2 miles north-east; Osborne, 3½ miles north-west.

XXXI. YARMOUTH.

[12 miles from Cowes, 10½ miles from Newport, 17 miles from Ryde, 20½ miles from Ventnor, 19½ miles from Sandown, 9 miles from Brighstone.]

Church, date Charles I.; monument, &c. (p. 175).

Parsonage (Rev. J. Blackburn, M.A.), in Bank Street.

For interesting localities in this neighbourhood see pp. 141–149.

XXXII. YAVERLAND.

[14½ miles from Cowes, 9½ miles from Newport, 5½ miles from Ryde, 8 miles from Ventnor, 2 miles from Sandown, 13 miles from Brighstone.]

Church, Norman (p. 175).

Yaverland Rectory (Rev. R. Sherson, M.A.), near the Church.

Yaverland manor house, date James I., adjoining the Church.

Brading, 2 miles south-east; Sandown, 2 miles north-east; Bembridge Down, half a mile north-east; Culver Cliffs, 2½ miles east.

APPENDIX.

ROMAN NEWPORT. (See p. 11.)

WE abridge from some interesting lectures by the Rev. Edmund Kell, M.A. (*Hampshire Independent*, 1852), the following synopsis of the arguments advanced by those who maintain the Roman origin of Newport:—

1. *The regularity of the plan* on which the ancient town was built. Four streets—Crocker Street, Holyrood Street, Corsham Street, and West Lane—form nearly a square, and are crossed by the intermediate streets at right angles. Probably it was built before A.D. 137, as a coin of the Emperor Hadrian's was found enclosed in a stone wall in a house in the Corn Market.

2. Another point deserving of attention in the laying out of the town is, that it exactly fulfils the condition of the Roman towns in being placed *near a position of defence;* also by a river side, and, where practicable, at the confluence of two streams, so that the population might have a copious supply of water—the Medina flowing at the east, and the Lukely stream upon the north, exactly fulfilling these latter conditions. It will also be observed that it has been conveniently situated in relation to the Roman station at Carisbrooke Castle, its main street, Castlehold, pointing directly to it; thus fulfilling the former.

3. Another proof is its *name*, which is deserving of particular attention, as being undeniably Latin, and a term significant in that language of its locality. In all ancient records it is referred to as *Medina*, from the Latin word *medium*, or the middle. Of the ten streets which make up the town, the names of seven are Latin. Thus, Pyle Street, from *pylum* a gate or port, and until the last seventy or eighty years Pyle Street was the way out, the gate, or port, from Newport to Ryde, over the ford at the bottom of Pyle Street. Lugley Street is from *lux*, light, as in Luguvallum (Carlisle), and Lugum (Lowth). Crocker Street reminds us of *Crocolana* (the town of Brough in Nottinghamshire), and seems to be from *crocus*, yellow. Scarrots Lane may be derived from *scarrosus*, rough. Castlehold is from *castellum*, the castle. Corsham is Roman in its first syllable, *cor*, a heart. The rivers Medina and Lukely are both Roman in name; so is Pan Down, and Mount Joy may be a corruption of *Mons Jovis*.

4. Mr. Kell adduces, in further confirmation of his position, the Roman remains discovered at Newport, consisting principally of Greek and Roman coins of various dates, which it is not necessary to particularize, and which would probably have been more numerous but for the desolating attacks to which the town was exposed in its earlier history "In the thirteenth year of Edward III., for instance, the population was greatly alarmed, and took extraordinary means of defence; and it is supposed that 4000 silver pennies lately found in Castlehold were deposited about this period. The attack from the French was repulsed by the brave Theobald Russell, with the loss of his own life and many of his men. Other plunderings took place in the reigns of Henry V. and Henry VIII.; but the principal attack was made by the French in the second year of Richard II.; when, with the exception of Carisbrooke Castle, they seem to have roamed over and to have completely mastered the island, and violence and depredation of the most deplorable kind was committed." The reader will probably be of opinion that these arguments are somewhat insubstantial. At all events, the etymologies are very fanciful, and many of them seem to us without the slightest foundation.

THE ROMAN VILLA AT CARISBROOKE. (See p. 94.)

The remains of an extensive Roman villa were discovered in 1858 by some workmen employed in making certain alterations in the garden attached to Carisbrooke vicarage. Its position is admirable. A considerable hill sheltered it in the rear, while before it glimmered the waters of the Medina, fertilising a fair, rich valley; and beyond, on a lofty mound, rose the Roman towers of Carisbrooke. It evidently belonged to a person of distinction, from its size and general arrangements. Its mosaics are not equal in workmanship to those which have been discovered in other localities; but not the less must the villa be regarded as a most interesting memorial of Roman supremacy in the Isle of Wight.

Instead of a minute elaboration of its ruins, which the tourist will best appreciate from a careful personal inspection, we propose to extract Lord Lytton's graphic, and generally accurate description of the arrangements of a Roman villa, from the pages of the "Last Days of Pompeii," by way of affording the reader an insight into the "domestic economy" of the mighty conquerors of the world:—

"You enter, then, usually by a small entrance-passage (called *vestibulum*) into a hall, sometimes with (but more frequently without) the ornament of columns; around three sides of this hall are doors communicating with several bed-chambers (among which is the porter's), the best of these being usually appropriated to country visitors. At the extremity of the hall, on either side, to the right and left, if the house is large, there are two small recesses, rather than chambers, generally devoted to the ladies of the mansion; and in the centre of the tessellated pavement of the hall is invariably a square, shallow reservoir for rain-water (classically termed *impluvium*), which was admitted by an aperture in the room above, the said aperture being covered at will by an awning. Near this impluvium, which had a peculiar sanctity in the eyes of the ancients, were sometimes placed images of the household gods; while in some corner of the most ostentatious place was deposited a huge wooden chest, ornamented and strengthened by bands of bronze or iron, and secured by strong hooks upon a stone pedestal so firmly as to defy the attempts of any robber to detach it from its position. It is supposed that this chest was the money-box, or coffer, of the master of the house; though, as no money has been found in any of the chests discovered at Pompeii, it is probable that it was sometimes rather designed for ornament than use.

"In this hall (or *atrium*, to speak classically), the clients and visitors of inferior rank were usually received. In the houses of the more 'respectable' an *atriensis*, or slave peculiarly devoted to the service of the hall, was invariably retained, and his rank among his fellow-slaves was high and important. The reservoir in the centre must have been rather a dangerous ornamen' but the centre of a hall was like the grass-plot of a college, and interdicted to the passers to and fro, who found ample space in the margin. Right opposite the entrance, at the other end of the hall, was an apartment (*tablinum*), in which the pavement was usually adorned with rich mosaics, and the walls covered with elaborate paintings. Here were usually kept the records of the family, or those of any public office that had been filled by the owner. On one side of this saloon, if we may so call it, was often a dining-room, or *triclinium;* on the other side, perhaps, what we should now term a cabinet of gems, containing whatever curiosities were deemed most rare and costly; and invariably a small passage for the slaves to cross to the further parts of the house without passing the apartments thus mentioned. These rooms all opened on a square or oblong colonnade, technically termed peristyle. If the house was small, its boundary ceased with this colonnade; and in that case its centre, however diminutive, was ordinarily appropriated to the purpose of a garden, and adorned with vases of flowers placed upon pedestals; while under the colonnade, to the right and left, were doors, admitting to bed-rooms,[*] to a second *triclinium*, or eating-room (for the ancients generally appropriated two rooms at least to that purpose, one for summer, and one for winter, or, perhaps, one for ordinary, the other for festive occasions), and, if the owner affected letters, a cabinet, dignified by the name of library—for a very small room was sufficient to contain the few rolls of papyrus which the ancients deemed a notable collection of books.

"At the end of the peristyle was generally the kitchen. Supposing the house was large, it did not end with the peristyle, and the centre thereof was not, in that case, a garden, but might be, perhaps, adorned with a fountain, or basin for fish; and at its end, exactly opposite to the tablinum, was generally another eating-room, on either side of which were bed-rooms, and perhaps a picture-saloon, or pinacotheca.[†] These apartments communicated again with a square and oblong space, usually adorned on three sides with a colonnade like the peristyle, and very much resembling the peristyle, only usually longer. This was the proper *viridarium*, or garden, being commonly adorned with a fountain or statues, and a profusion of gay flowers; at its extreme end was the gardener's house; on either side, beneath the colonnade, were

---

[*] The Romans had bed-rooms appropriated not only to the sleep of night, but also to the day siesta (*cubicula diurna*).

[†] In the stately palaces of Rome this picture-room generally communicated with the atrium.

sometimes, if the size of the family required it, additional rooms. The apartments themselves were ordinarily of small size; for in those delightful climes they received an extraordinary number of visitors in the peristyle (or portico), the hall, or the garden: and even their banquet-rooms, however elaborately adorned and carefully selected in point of aspect, were of diminutive proportions; for the intellectual ancients, being fond of society, not of crowds, rarely feasted more than nine at a time, so that large dinner-rooms were not so necessary with them as with us. But the suite of rooms, seen at once from the entrance, must have had a very imposing effect; you beheld at once the hall, richly paved and painted; the tablinum, the graceful peristyle, and (if the house extended further) the opposite banquet-room and the garden, which closed the view with some gushing fount or marble statue."

The villa at Carisbrooke seems to have occupied an area of about 120 feet by 50, and to have included among its apartments two large halls, one about 22 feet square, the other about 40 feet by 22 feet. Another apartment, 14 feet square, exhibits a good mosaic pavement. To the south-west is a semi-circular bath.

THE LONG STONE, OR CROMLECH, AT MOTTISTONE. (See p. 98.)

Mr. Wright's remarks upon these cromlechs, or British cemeteries, will interest the reader:—"A cromlech," he says, "is a rude chamber constructed of massive flat stones, three forming usually its three sides, the fourth being open, and a fourth flat stone serving for roof. There can be little doubt that monuments of this description belong to the ancient Britons, because they are certainly not more modern than the Roman period, while they are as certainly not Roman; and they are found in great numbers in Ireland, where a Celtic population was established. Increased knowledge on these subjects has left no room for doubt that the cromlechs are nothing more than sepulchral chambers. The ashes of the dead—for in most of these interments we find that the bodies of the deceased had been burned—were collected into an urn of rude pottery, and placed, with a few other articles, within the chamber, and the whole was then covered with a mound. In opening many such mounds in different parts of the kingdom, the cromlech, with the sepulchral deposit within, have been found perfect; when the cromlech is now found exposed to view [as here, at Mottistone], without a mound, it has been robbed of its covering of earth by accident or design at some remote period "—(*Wanderings of an Antiquary*, p. 173). The reader will perceive that this description tallies exactly with that of the cromlech at Mottistone. The four stones are still extant, and their present positions may be accounted for by a variety of assumptions.

ADDENDA.

RYDE.—A Railway, worked by a locomotive, is to be laid down upon the Pier, so that visitors to Ventnor will have no occasion to change their carriages, but, on leaving the steamboat, will at once enter the Ventnor train.

A new church is to be built in the Newport Road.

CARISBROOKE.—It is intended to form a collection of "Isle of Wight objects of human and natural history" at Carisbrooke Castle, as the Island Memorial to the late Prince Consort. It will be called the Royal Albert Museum. Patron: Her Majesty. The committee charged with the development of the scheme have at their head the Right Hon. Viscount Eversley, and Sir John Simeon, Bart., M.P.

EAST COWES.—A new church, from the designs of Mr. Hellyer of Ryde, is to be erected on the site of the present St. James's Church. It will afford accommodation for 510 adults and 250 children.

YARMOUTH.—A painted window, by Gibbs, of good design, has been placed in the Parish Church by the rector, the Rev. J. Blackburn, M.A., Canon of York, as a memorial to two of his children. It measures 12 feet by 8 feet, and represents our Saviour and the Virgin Mary encircled by little children.

April 1867.

N.B.—After April 22, 1867, the parish of Newchurch will be divided into three independent parishes, Ryde, Newchurch, and Ventnor.

INDEX.

Breinigsville, PA USA
05 July 2010
241147BV00002B/8/P